The School
SUPERINTENDENT

Second Edition

Preface

The current quest for school improvement is not unlike the myriad of educational reform eras that preceded it. For example, public dissatisfaction is again rooted in philosophical dissonance and citizens disagree either over the need for change or over the prudence of proposed changes. At the same time, however, this present pursuit of educational excellence that began circa 1980 is undeniably distinct in two important ways. First, the pursuit has been atypically protracted; second, it has been atypically resilient. After more than 25 years of experience with ideas and strategies that arguably have had only minor success, the fervor and intensity of the change proponents remain high.

Responding to harsh criticisms presented in the highly publicized report, *A Nation at Risk* (National Commission on Excellence in Education, 1983), lobbyists and elected officials in virtually every state initially concluded that lazy and unengaged students were responsible for public education's lack of productivity. Concluding that the system would not engage in self-improvement, they embraced the strategy of forcing educators to make students do more of what they were already doing. Common legislative actions included lengthening the school year, lengthening the school day, and increasing high school graduation requirements. Within just two to three years, however, the would-be reformers grew impatient with the results. Rather than reconsidering the value of their intensification mandates, they extended their problem statement by blaming both lazy students and incompetent educators for the declining performance of public schools. Led by this conviction, they pressured education schools to increase their standards, and passed laws designed to make licensing for teachers and administrators more rigorous. By the early 1990s, it became evident that the process of laying blame had not ended. Still disappointed that their actions had not produced sufficient improvements in student test scores, the reformers finally listened to scholars who had repeatedly advised them that the effectiveness of their top-down, one-size-fits-all initiatives was seriously limited. Recognizing that the governance of local districts and organizational structure of schools were critical variables, the reformers now embraced a strategy in which states set broad educational goals and gave local school boards more autonomy to determine how they would be met.

More than any other single factor, the ongoing pursuit of school improvement, now characterized by strategies such as decentralization and school restructuring, defines the current context of superintendent practice. In the eyes of many experienced and aspiring practitioners, this pursuit has produced seemingly contradictory role expectations. Many school board members, for instance, want a superintendent to be both a visionary leader and a stern manager, both a cunning politician and an ethical role model, and both a demanding boss and a compassionate colleague. When it comes to making important decisions, these board members also expect their chief executive officer to be guided both by professional knowledge and by the community's political will. Despite such mixed messages, the fact remains that the superintendency is public education's most visible and most influential position; in a recent study, only 6% of the nation's superintendents indicated that they experienced no (.3%) or little (5.7%) job satisfaction (Glass, Björk, & Brunner, 2000).

Consider the experiences of a novice superintendent employed in a small but diverse district. In the first three months, he discovered that an employee was a convicted felon, that a teen gang was controlling high school students, and that the district's $7.2 million budget had to be reduced by 8%. Having only limited perspectives about his role, he considered his first weeks in office as a calamity. As he gained experience, though, he realized that his job was not that unique and he learned that support from his family and others was essential to effective practice. Looking back, he believes he was fortunate to have survived that first year. Now recognizing the rewarding dimensions of his practice, he concludes that regardless of whether you are a bus driver, a custodian, a teacher, a principal, or a superintendent, your charge remains the same—to make a difference in the lives of students (Ceglarek, 2004).

The primary audiences for this book are school administration students, practitioners, school board members, and professors. Although the second edition infuses additional research and broadens the discussion of practice, the text's primary intent is unchanged. That objective centers on a balanced discussion of the theory and practice that defines the position's responsibilities. School administration is treated as both a science and a craft, involving an intricate blend of theory and artistry, leadership, and management.

Each chapter concludes with questions designed to encourage reflection, which is followed by a brief case study of practice, with its own set of questions.

The School SUPERINTENDENT

Theory, Practice, and Cases

Second Edition

Theodore J. Kowalski
University of Dayton

SAGE Publications
Thousand Oaks ▪ London ▪ New Delhi

For information:

 Sage Publications, Inc.
2455 Teller Road
Thousand Oaks, California 91320
E-mail: order@sagepub.com

Sage Publications Ltd.
1 Oliver's Yard
55 City Road
London EC1Y 1SP
United Kingdom

Sage Publications India Pvt. Ltd.
B-42, Panchsheel Enclave
Post Box 4109
New Delhi 110 017 India

Printed in the United States of America on acid-free paper

Library of Congress Cataloging-in-Publication Data

Kowalski, Theodore J.
The school superintendent : theory, practice, and cases / Theodore
J. Kowalski.—2nd ed.
        p. cm.
Includes bibliographical references and index.
ISBN 1–4129–0677–6 (cloth)
    1. School superintendents—United States. 2. School management and organization—United States. 3. School superintendents—United States—Case studies. 4. School management and organization—United States—Case studies. I. Title.
LB2831.72.K69 2006
371.2′012—dc22

                                                          2005003606

05   06   07   08   09   10   9   8   7   6   5   4   3   2   1

Acquiring Editor:	Diane McDaniel
Editorial Assistant:	Marta Peimer
Production Editor:	Sanford Robinson
Typesetter:	C&M Digitals (P) Ltd.
Copy Editor:	Richard Adin, Freelance Editorial Services
Cover Designer:	Edgar Abarca

Contents

By integrating chapter content with your professional experiences, you are able to expand your professional knowledge base and gain a better understanding of yourself in conjunction with the position of school superintendent.

Many individuals contributed to this book. I wish to thank five prominent superintendents who served as an editorial panel for the case studies: Michael Benway, Superintendent, Valparaiso, Indiana; Philip McDaniel, Superintendent, Rock Hill, South Carolina; Douglas Otto, Superintendent, Plano, Texas; Wendy Robinson, Superintendent, Fort Wayne, Indiana; and C. Steven Snider, Superintendent, Maine Township High School District 207, Park Ridge, Illinois. Their comments and recommendations were invaluable, and I am truly grateful for their assistance. I also express appreciation to Professor Lars Björk from the University of Kentucky for coauthoring revisions to Chapters 8 and 12, Elizabeth Pearn, my office assistant, who assisted with editing the manuscript, and Nancy Seyfried, my doctoral assistant, who helped with literature reviews. Finally, I thank the reviewers

Albert F. Inserra, Dowling College

James C. Christman, Pittsburg State University

Mike Boone, Texas State University, San Marcos

Joanne P. Newcombe, Anna Maria College

Ralph A. Waltman, Kent State University

John A. Kaufhold, Texas A&M University, Kingsville

Floyd Boschee, The University of South Dakota

who provided insightful ideas for improving the book.

REFERENCES

Ceglarek, N. E. (2004). Lonely at the start: A first-year superintendent. *School Administrator, 61*(2), 13.

Glass, T. E., Björk, L., & Brunner, C. C. (2000). *The study of the American superintendency 2000: A look at the superintendent of education in the new millennium.* Arlington, VA: American Association of School Administrators.

National Commission on Excellence in Education (1983). *A nation at risk: The imperative for educational reform.* Washington, DC: Author.

PART I

School District
Superintendents

CHAPTER 1

Defining Practice

KEY FACETS OF THE CHAPTER

○ Levels of public education governance

○ School district superintendents

○ Requirements for being a superintendent

○ Quality-of-life considerations

The November 1907 cover of the *School Board Journal* featured a cartoon in which a vacancy notice for a superintendent of schools had been posted on the front door of a board of education office. The solicitation noted that the board was seeking an individual who must please everybody, from ultraconservatives to radical progressives. The thought-provoking cover illustrates that even in public education's formative years, superintendents were expected to appease patrons with divergent philosophies. Today's context of democratic pluralism makes the context of public education even more political than it was in 1907; superintendents are drawn continually into conflict-laden situations by elected officials, competing special interest groups, and even school board members (Björk & Keedy, 2001). Having to lead in this context of competing philosophical position and political interests is a primary reason why the position of school district superintendent frequently is portrayed as a difficult assignment. Even so, thousands of practitioners have been highly successful and view this administrative role as being challenging, gratifying, and personally rewarding.

This chapter first examines the governance structure of public education in the United States. This information provides a context for the three levels at which superintendents are found: the state level, the intermediate district level, and the local district level. Next, historical and contemporary perspectives of the school district superintendent are provided. This information is followed by a discussion of the three common requirements for accessing this position: preparation through graduate study, state licensing, and professional experience. Lastly, quality-of-life considerations associated with the position are identified. This chapter provides foundational information about the position of superintendent and the organizational structures in which it functions.

LEVELS OF PUBLIC EDUCATION GOVERNANCE

Control of American public education is nested in legal foundations that flow from federal and state constitutions, statutes, and case law. Constitutions grant legislative bodies authority to enact laws in the public's interest, statutes provide actual laws, and case law establishes interpretations of constitutions and legislative acts (Alexander & Alexander, 1998). Essentially there are four levels to the governance structure: federal, state, intermediate, and local; the last three are all part of state government (Kowalski, 2003a). Superintendents serve as chief executive officers in each of the tiers of the state's system of public education. The following sections describe the four governance levels.

Federal Level

The federal government's role in public education has evolved over the past two centuries. Because the United States Constitution does not mention education, education is deemed a state's right under provisions of the Tenth Amendment (powers not delegated to the federal government by the Constitution, nor prohibited by it to the states, are reserved to the states or to the people). Based largely on this interpretation, each state has had the right to establish a system of public schools and all have done so (Kowalski, 2003a). Despite the acceptance of state authority, all three branches of the federal government have intervened, directly or circuitously, in public elementary and secondary education.

At the legislative level, Congress has enacted laws focused on issues deemed to be in the nation's interest. Examples include promoting vocational education (e.g., Smith-Hughes Act in 1917); promoting stronger curricula in mathematics, science, and foreign language (e.g., National Defense Education Act in 1958); providing supplemental services for disadvantaged students (e.g., Elementary and Secondary Education Act in 1965); mandating special education under civil rights provisions (e.g., Education for All Handicapped Children Act in 1975); and promoting school productivity in relation to enhancing the nation's economic welfare (e.g., No Child Left Behind Act in 2002). A myriad of other federal laws not pertaining specifically to education, such as those detailing wages on public construction projects, also have affected schools.

Federal courts become involved in public education because pertinent federal law displaces inconsistent state law (Valente, 1987). The frequency of federal court intervention has increased incrementally since 1950. Federal courts basically have jurisdiction when one of two conditions is established: (a) the litigation involves a federal constitutional question or federal statute or (b) litigants reside in more than one state (Reutter, 1985). Issues such as parental rights, student rights, the rights and authority of school officials (school boards, administrators, teachers, and other employees), and the rights of racial and ethnic minorities or other protected groups (e.g., racial discrimination, gender or age discrimination) have been addressed by federal courts.

Executive responsibilities (i.e., the administrative aspects of federal interventions) were created by the various laws and court decisions affecting elementary and secondary schools. Four agencies handled these matters during the past century:

- Prior to 1939, the Department of Interior
- 1939 to 1952, the Federal Security Agency
- 1953 to 1978, the Department of Health, Education, and Welfare
- 1979 to present, the United States Department of Education (DOE)

One of the DOE's major responsibilities has been to develop rules and regulations deemed necessary to enforce federal laws. This agency also dispenses federal aid and grants. Since its inception, the DOE has been a controversial agency; opponents argue that it erodes the rights of states to govern public education, whereas proponents argue that it is necessary to preserve federal interests. Support for federal interventions has shifted from issue to issue reflective of the general philosophical division in society (Radin & Hawley, 1988).

The president, subject to congressional approval, appoints the secretary of education and this person serves as the chief executive officer of the DOE and is a member of the president's cabinet. Persons appointed to this influential position have had varied backgrounds, but most have been professional educators.

State Level

After 1787, Virginia, South Carolina, Vermont, and Missouri created state educational boards but it was not until Massachusetts had established an eight-member state board in 1837 that the pattern spread across most states. In large measure, Horace Mann is credited with making the structure politically acceptable. Appointed the first secretary of the Massachusetts state board, his principal duties were to collect and disseminate school information. During the 12 years he held office, he convinced political leaders and the public that state government could and should play a vital role in public elementary and secondary education. By 1880, 24 states established a state presence in public education by enacting legislation establishing state boards of education (Butts & Cremin, 1953).

Once established, state boards of education focused primarily on being the enforcement agency for the common school movement. The movement had three distinct foci: (a) an emphasis on educating all children in a common schoolhouse, (b) the idea of using schools as an instrument of government policy, and (c) the creation of state agencies to control local schools (Spring, 1994). State departments of education and state superintendents became extensions of state boards. The superintendent and state department administrators were deemed the control agents in the state's hierarchical system and their responsibility in relation to the common school movement was to ensure that public schools implemented the prescribed uniform curriculum. Formalizing the role of state government in public elementary and secondary education paralleled a philosophical shift in America toward centralized governance (Butts & Cremin, 1953).

The very first state superintendent was appointed in New York in 1812. In addition to developing a plan for common schools, he was assigned the duties of reporting on the management of public funds and providing school-related information for the state legislature. Between 1830 and 1850, every northern state and some southern states created this office. In doing so, however, several states merely relegated the responsibilities of this new office to a state official who already held another position (Butts & Cremin, 1953).

Today, every state has a chief executive officer for public education, although some are called state commissioners of education instead of state superintendents. Qualifications for this office, selection methods, and duties vary markedly; state superintendents are appointed to office in 35 states and elected to office in the remaining 15 states. Even the specifications for appointment and election vary (see Table 1.1). To this day, policymakers across the states differ with respect to choosing between partisan and professional administration in a state's public school system. This philosophical difference explains why some

Table 1.1   Methods for Selection of State Superintendents

Selection Method (No.)	% of All States	States Using the Method
Appointed by state board (22)	44%	Alabama, Arkansas, Colorado, Connecticut, Hawaii, Illinois, Kansas, Kentucky, Louisiana, Maryland, Massachusetts, Michigan, Mississippi, Missouri, Nebraska, Nevada, New Hampshire, New York, Ohio, Rhode Island, Utah, West Virginia
Appointed by state board with approval from the governor (2)	4%	Alaska, Vermont
Appointed by the governor (10)	20%	Iowa, Maine, Minnesota, New Jersey, New Mexico, Pennsylvania, South Dakota, Tennessee, Texas, Virginia
Appointed by the governor and confirmed by the legislature (1)	2%	Delaware
Total appointed to office (35)	**70%**	
Elected on partisan ballot (9)	18%	Arizona, Florida, Georgia, Indiana, Montana, North Carolina, Oklahoma, South Carolina, Wyoming
Elected on nonpartisan ballot (6)	12%	California, Idaho, North Dakota, Oregon, Washington, Wisconsin
Total elected to office (15)	**30%**	

states do not require their chief school officer to be a professional, licensed educator.

Both the state superintendent and state department of education are part of the executive branch of government. In most states, the state superintendent functions as the chief executive of this department. Consequently, the power of a state superintendent has often been determined by the authority granted to the state department of education. This nexus has been most evident with respect to recent reform strategies. Some departments have remained hierarchical, powerful, and in control of the reform agenda and consequently, the state superintendents have had an opportunity to exercise considerable influence. Other state departments have preferred a decentralized or quasi-decentralized strategy. That is, the task of setting a reform agenda either has been transferred to local school boards entirely or it has been pursued statewide using citizen and educator involvement to reach consensus (Lusi, 1997). In these states, the superintendent has played more of a facilitative and coordinating role.

The organizational structure of the state department, however, does not always reflect the state's reform agenda or the legitimate power of the state superintendent. Kentucky is a case in point. That state's reform act, the Kentucky Education Reform Act (KERA) passed in 1989, required schools to focus on learning outcomes and mandated the creation of a new state department of education that would support (not dictate) locally-driven reforms. Studying KERA's implementation, Lusi (1997) concluded that instead of following the law's dictate, the newly created department remained hierarchical. She attributed this outcome largely to intense pressure from the state legislature to implement mandates and restricted timelines for change. In Wisconsin, the superintendent functions essentially without a state department of education; this division of government was eliminated in the mid-1990s by the governor and legislature, but the superintendent position continued because it is protected by the state constitution. Table 1.2 lists possible functions of state departments of education.

Since the early 1980s, state legislatures have generally taken a more active role in formulating public education policy. These bodies can, and often do, pass laws based entirely or primarily on narrowly focused concerns such as the state's economy or business development. Often these laws are promulgated with little input from educators and produce unfunded or underfunded mandates. The proclivity of state legislatures to force change on public education remains controversial; advocates of state interventions believe that centralized controls are essential to ensure reasonably equal educational opportunities. Critics argue that such coercion directly or circuitously erodes local control. From a legal perspective, however, state legislatures basically have plenary power to determine policy in their respective states (Kimbrough & Nunnery, 1976).

Intermediate District Level

Intermediate school districts exist in most states and are known by various names, including Regional Educational Service Agencies, Regional Service Centers, and Board of Cooperative Educational Services. In essence, these

Table 1.2   Examples of Functions Assumed by State Departments of Education

Area	Primary Responsibility
State and federal law enforcement	Ensuring local district compliance
State and federal law interpretation	Providing briefs, directions, and legal counsel
Technical assistance	Providing services to local school districts
Federal aid	Serving as distribution and accountability agent
Statistical data	Creating, maintaining, and distributing data
Federal reports	Compiling and filing required statewide reports
Staff development	Providing programs and facilitators to local districts
Curriculum	Monitoring compliance and providing materials
Facilities	Developing and enforcing standards
Statute and policy recommendations	Formulating material for the legislature or state board
Needs assessments	Conducting statewide studies
Testing	Administering/evaluating statewide testing programs
State accreditation	Evaluating districts and schools
State funding	Administering the state funding formula

organizations are downward extensions of state authority over public education; that is, an intermediate administrative service agency situated between local districts and the state departments of education. The office of *county superintendent* was the earliest iteration of an intermediate governance level and the primary function of this office was to provide services and management to weak and ineffective school districts (Knezevich, 1975). County superintendents were more prevalent during the first half of the last century than they are now. Then many rural counties had a school district in each township operating under the jurisdiction of elected township trustees. Because these districts had neither a superintendent nor school board, the township trustees relied on the county superintendent to provide necessary services, such as ensuring compliance with state laws and curriculum. The arrangement permitted very small districts to operate rather independently and at relatively low cost.

The concept underlying intermediate districts has remained rather straightforward—they provide services to school districts too small or too poor to offer complete programs (Campbell, Cunningham, Nystrand & Usdan, 1990). Through cooperative purchasing, media libraries, equipment repair, shared staff development programs, and similar functions, the intermediate district can provide cost savings and programmatic improvements.

Intermediate districts are often confused with two other forms of joint ventures. These are education service cooperatives and study councils. Cooperatives exist in some states to provide joint services; that is, several school districts offering programs cooperatively in special education or vocational education. Study councils, however, are not part of the formal state systems of public education. Membership in them is voluntary and they generally conduct collaborative research, staff development, and other functions designed to provide information and services for educators rather than direct programming for students (Kowalski, 2003a). Some school districts simultaneously hold membership in a special education cooperative, a vocational education cooperative, a study council, and an intermediate school district.

Most intermediate school districts also are described as confederations of local districts established to facilitate communication and decision making between local school systems and state government. The word *confederation* connotes that the member districts have substantial control over the scope of activities conducted by the organization (Knezevich, 1984). Funding typically is a mix of state support, member participation fees, and grants (including federal funds).

The history of intermediate districts is not uniform across states (Campbell et al., 1990). Most notably, the degree of control they have over local school systems differs. In Illinois, for instance, regional superintendents have some degree of authority over all public schools in their jurisdiction and they perform certain functions commonly provided by state government, for example, registering teacher and administrator licenses. In neighboring Indiana, membership in regional service centers is voluntary and directors do not perform official functions on behalf of the state board of education, state superintendent, or state department of public instruction. Overall the trend has been to reduce the number of regional service centers in states that previously had one in each county (e.g., Wisconsin and Illinois).

Local District Level

There are approximately 14,500 local school districts in the United States. The governance structure of federal involvement accompanied by states relegating considerable power and authority to local communities is unique to the United States. This configuration is rooted in the cherished principles of liberty and equity. In colonial America, public education was governed through town meetings and subsequently schools were placed under the control of town selectmen. This system of control was carried over into the new American republic (Russo, 1992). Thus long before the creation of state departments of education, communities had been self-determining both the type and scope of education provided.

While local control was perceived by many citizens to be congruent with the prevalent philosophy of an emerging democracy, astute state government officials feared that unfettered local control would produce inadequate and unequal educational opportunities. More precisely, they worried that some local officials would deliver an insufficient amount of education or an inferior level of instruction—deficiencies that would produce learning opportunities less equal to those found in the state's other districts. They concluded that state control was necessary to avert this problem. At the same time, however, they realized state control would be seen by many citizens as an infringement on local control. Thus, they began searching for a way to balance the competing interests of liberty, adequacy, and equity. The preferred solution was to simultaneously establish state control and reaffirm local control. This seemingly contradictory strategy was accomplished by creating state agencies to oversee public education while delegating select policy powers to local school boards. The tactic effectively made local school boards legal extensions of state government. It was within this context that state officials achieved the compromise between seeking adequacy and equity through a state system of public education and the provision of liberty through local boards of education (Butts & Cremin, 1953).

The rural nature of America and a lack of transportation resulted in schools being dispersed so that students had pedestrian access. Consequently, there were literally more than 100,000 relatively small school districts, many consisting of just one school. This condition gradually changed because of population growth, urbanization, and increased transportation; local districts became larger in land mass, in the number of schools operated, and in student enrollment. Following World War II, the large cities spilled into suburbs and the new communities almost always created their own school districts. In rural areas and smaller towns, economic realities and educational goals encouraged states to enact school consolidation laws that led to fewer but larger units of local government. Collectively, these trends reduced the number of school districts in the United States from approximately 119,000 in 1937 to 14,859 in 2001 (*Digest of Education Statistics,* 2002). Even so, there are substantial differences in the size of local districts based on student enrollment. Districts with 25,000 or more students, for example, comprise only about 1.5% of all districts but they enroll nearly one-third of all public elementary and secondary school students. Conversely, districts with fewer than 300 students comprise 22% of all districts but enroll only 1% of the nation's public school students (*Digest of Education Statistics,* 2002).

Powers vested in school boards are specified in state constitutions and statutes. Commonly, these powers include the ability to raise money via taxes, expend public funds, enter into legal contracts, and otherwise function as a legal entity. Overall, boards have three primary responsibilities: (a) assure that state laws, rules, and regulations are followed; (b) establish policy in areas not covered by state laws, rules, and regulations; and (c) employ a superintendent to serve as chief executive officer. The duties and functions of school boards are examined in much greater depth in later chapters.

From an organizational perspective, local school districts have tended to be rather unique institutions. Describing them, Campbell et al. (1990) wrote, "Their diversity illustrates the tenaciousness with which Americans hold to these remnants of localism and grassroots expression of the public will" (p. 107). From their inception, local districts have been political entities (subdivisions of the state that serve to balance centralization and decentralization), legal entities (quasi-municipal corporations), geographic entities (defined by specific boundaries), social institutions (engaged in symbiotic relationships with their communities), and educational entities (agencies with specific responsibilities for transmitting knowledge and skills) (Knezevich, 1984).

Although the specific scope of responsibility and authority granted to local boards varied among the states, these subdivisions of state government generally were given the duties of establishing schools, erecting buildings, employing a superintendent, establishing policy and rules necessary to govern the schools, and raising and expending public funds (Campbell et al., 1990). But despite a common base of authority providing broad discretion, local school boards have often exhibited significant differences with respect to exercising power, especially in the arena of promulgating public policy. These variations are explained by the extent to which members of the local boards of education actually represent the population of the schools, and the actual amount of power wielded by boards of education in relation to the professional staffs of schools (Spring, 1985). Even within a given state, the efficacy of local school boards varies markedly.

SCHOOL DISTRICT SUPERINTENDENTS

Although public schools were established as early as 1640, the superintendency was not created until the mid-1800s (Griffiths, 1966). Between 1837 and 1850, 13 urban districts established the position; by 1890, most major cities had followed this lead. However, this trend was not uniformly supported. For instance, a number of political bosses feared that school superintendents would amass their own power base and then be able to stand apart from the entangled mechanisms of big-city government. Ambivalence regarding the necessity of the position and the potential political threats the position posed were evidenced by the fact that some cities disestablished and then reestablished the post (Knezevich, 1984). Even in these formative years, it was evident that politics and professionalism were on a collision course. Political bosses were suspicious of government officials who sought independence, and they became extremely distrusting of superintendents who attempted to use professionalism as a shield against their political machines (Kowalski, 2004).

Historical Context

In large measure, the evolution of the superintendency paralleled the development of the graded school. One-room schools were operated by one educator who typically was the teacher, the principal, and, at times, even the custodian (Brubacher, 1966). But as the one-room schoolhouse was replaced with graded schools organized into local districts, one of the major responsibilities of the superintendent became the writing of a uniform course of study that could be implemented in all schools in the system. In this vein, Spring (1994) wrote:

> The development of the role of the superintendent was important in the evolution of the hierarchical educational organization. The primary reason for creating the position was to have a person work full-time at supervising classroom instruction and assuring uniformity in the curriculum. (p. 119)

As previously noted, the original need for state and local district superintendents was generated by the common school reform movement. Within local districts and schools, superintendents were expected to communicate elements of the common curriculum and provide supervision to ensure its implementation.

As early as 1820, some school boards retained clerks to assist them with day-to-day operations and the position of district superintendent evolved from this practice. The first official superintendent, assigned to be a "school inspector," was appointed in 1837 in Buffalo, New York (Brunner, Grogan, & Björk, 2002). In summary, early superintendents had little authority and often spent their time doing routine tasks relegated to them. Most commonly, they were to assist school boards in ensuring that state requirements were being met.

During the first decade of the 20th century, many community elites (i.e., school board members, professionals, and businessmen who influenced public policy and opinion) were continuing efforts to restrict the role and status of superintendents by relegating them to menial assignments and detail work. Their actions were attributed to two motives: First, the elites wanted to reinforce their conviction that superintendents should be servants to, rather than leaders of, school boards. Second, the elites had little confidence that superintendents could be effective managers because the teachers appointed to this office had not been prepared academically or experientially to control human and material resources (Knezevich, 1984).

In the early 1900s, reasons underlying the appointment of superintendents varied. Some were selected because they looked like leaders—a quality deemed to have political merit because the public would view the office holder as being competent. Some were selected because they were viewed as effective teachers— a quality deemed important with respect to ensuring compliance with the state curriculum and effective instructional practices. Some were selected because they were connected politically to the individuals who made the appointment. And some were selected simply because they were males, a decision reflecting a contemporary bias about organizational management. Virtually none of the superintendents appointed prior to 1910, however, was selected because of managerial skills (Kowalski, 2003a).

Circa 1910, several circumstances converged to move this pivotal position in a new direction. The Industrial Revolution and related conditions (such as urbanization) had elevated the value placed on organizational management skills (see Table 1.3 for specific factors). At the same time, school districts started getting larger, emphasis on standardized practices was increasing, and the specialization of school administration was being formalized.

Eaton (1990) defined professionalism as a concerted effort, over time, to create a distinct occupational role and then persuading others to accept this role as the standard. According to him, both actual skills and preferred behaviors are involved. He wrote, "In exchange for systematic training and endorsement of a code of ethics, the professional demands autonomy in the process of exercising judgment over practice" (p. 33). There were multiple reasons why superintendents sought this standing. Beyond the obvious desire to gain status, at least three other motivations were evident:

Table 1.3   Examples of Factors That Encouraged a Managerial Role for the
Superintendency Circa 1910–1930

Factor	*Explanation*
Principles of scientific management	Practices deemed successful in industry were applied to schools.
Casting schools as agencies of control	Close supervision was necessary to assure that the goals of the common school effort would be attained.
Separating teaching from administration	Management was deemed to be a male responsibility; teaching was cast as a subordinate role to be performed largely by women.
Establishing bureaucratic-like structures	Efficiency would be achieved if administrators carefully managed material and human resources; teachers and other employees required supervision to assure that they did their work in accordance with policies and rules.
Quest for identity and prestige	School administration most likely would be recognized as a responsibility separate from and superior to teaching if it was viewed by the public as a managerial responsibility.
Demarcation between policy development and policy administration	School boards would be responsible for determining what should be done and administrators would be responsible for determining how things would get done.

1. The economic and social successes of industrial management were viewed positively by the general public, thus the idea of being classified as a professional manager was appealing to many school administrators.

2. Professionalism almost always produced individual powers for those who were so classified.

3. Breaking free of the big-city bureaucracies made it more likely that key decisions could be made on the basis of educational rather than political considerations.

The quest for professionalism also was abetted by those professors who saw an opportunity to establish educational administration as a respected specialization, one equal to management in the private sector. They especially wanted to separate administration from the teaching. Progressively, they succeeded; in the eyes of the public, principals and superintendents became managers and teachers were relegated to a subordinate role (Callahan, 1962).

During the first half of the 20th century, three new role conceptualizations of superintendents emerged. They cast the ideal superintendent first as an effective organizational manager, second as a democratic statesman (or politician), and third as an applied social scientist. These roles, one that preceded them (teacher-scholar) and one that followed them (communicator), are discussed in detail in Chapter 2.

Contemporary Context

Today regardless of school district size, most superintendent job descriptions verify that the position is demanding and complex. Officeholders are expected to have knowledge and skills spanning a number of academic disciplines associated with their leadership and management responsibilities. A national report approved by a joint committee consisting of representatives from the American Association of School Administrators (AASA) and the National School Boards Association (NSBA) identified the following specific responsibilities for superintendents:

- To serve as the school board's chief executive officer and preeminent educational adviser in all efforts of the board to fulfill its school system governance role.
- To serve as the primary educational leader for the school system and chief administrative officer of the entire school district's professional and support staff, including staff members assigned to provide support service to the board.
- To serve as a catalyst for the school system's administrative leadership team in proposing and implementing policy changes.
- To propose and institute a process for long-range and strategic planning that will engage the board and the community in positioning the school district for success in ensuing years.
- To keep all board members informed about school operations and programs.
- To interpret the needs of the school system to the board.

- To present policy options along with specific recommendations to the board when circumstances require the board to adopt new policies or review existing policies.
- To develop and inform the board of administrative procedures needed to implement board policy.
- To develop a sound program of school/community relations in concert with the board.
- To oversee management of the district's day-to-day operations.
- To develop a description for the board of what constitutes effective leadership and management of public schools, taking into account that effective leadership and management are the result of effective governance and effective administration combined.
- To develop and carry out a plan for keeping the total professional and support staff informed about the mission, goals, and strategies of the school system and about the important roles all staff members play in realizing them.
- To ensure that professional development opportunities are available to all school system employees.
- To collaborate with other administrators through national and state professional associations to inform state legislators, members of Congress, and all other appropriate state and federal officials of local concerns and issues.
- To ensure that the school system provides equal opportunity for all students.
- To evaluate personnel performance in harmony with district policy and to keep the board informed about such evaluations.
- To provide all board members with complete background information and a recommendation for school board action on each agenda item well in advance of each board meeting.
- To develop and implement a continuing plan for working with the news media. (American Association of School Administrators, 1994, pp. 11–12)

The nature of a school district usually determines what superintendents do on a daily basis. In large systems, for instance, the officeholder can specialize in one or two areas of administration because other official responsibilities can be delegated to support staff. Recognizing this, large city school boards have at times purposely sought executives reputed to be experts in an area deemed critical to the district, for example, fiscal management or public relations. By contrast, superintendents in small-enrollment districts almost always have to be generalists because they have no supporting administrators other than principals. But despite these differences between large and small systems, school boards across all local districts generally have emphasized curriculum, finance, and public relations (including communication skills) in seeking new superintendents (Chand, 1987).

In the late 1970s, Morris (1979) found that school superintendents and chief executives in business tended to have different orientations to the social dimension of their work. Whereas top managers in business spent considerable time interacting with persons outside the organization, superintendents tended to interact primarily with subordinates. This insulation subsequently was criticized by would-be reformers who believed that schools officials were insensitive to community needs and impervious to changing economic, political, and social conditions. Studying superintendents during the 1980s, Blumberg (1985) wrote:

> . . . what we seem to have is a growing insight that the role of the superintendent involves an ever more sophisticated understanding of the community as an organism, of its political structure, of the need to deal with power centers outside of the superintendent's office, and of the wide variety of both human and technical skills needed to create a viable educational organization. (p. 43)

Expectations that superintendents maintain an ongoing dialogue with the wider community are stronger today than ever before. In large measure, this is because the public increasingly expects superintendents to be builders rather than caretakers. Put another way, they expect superintendents to be leaders first and managers second. Leading involves making decisions about what to do to improve the organization whereas management concentrates on making decisions about now things should be done (Kowalski, 2003a). Although both functions are integral to administration, superintendents historically have focused much more on management. Addressing the growing pressures of school reform, Johnson (1996) wrote: "New superintendents are expected to diagnose local educational needs and recommend strategies for improvement" (p. 276). Today's ideal superintendent is supposed to be a transformational leader, an individual guiding others to rebuild organizational cultures and climates collaboratively. Superintendents are expected to share authority and to engage others in making democratic decisions. Rather than exercising traditional forms of authority, superintendents are now expected to be engaged in

> . . . developing a widely shared, defensible vision; in the short run, directly assisting members of the school community to overcome obstacles they encounter in striving for the vision; and in the long run, increasing the

capacity of the members of the school community to overcome subsequent obstacles more successfully and with greater ease (Leithwood, Begley, & Cousins, 1992, p. 8).

One highly visible example of this transition is found in Kentucky, a state that initiated massive restructuring with the passage of the KERA. Ruling that existing laws, policies, and regulations were invalid, the courts ordered a complete reconstruction of governance, curriculum, and financing in the state's system of public elementary and secondary education. This unprecedented strategy of totally rebuilding a public institution gave local district superintendents little choice but to rethink their roles. After the reform law was enacted, they "saw themselves as managing more by consensus than by command and as facilitating rather than controlling" (Murphy, 1994, p. 27). Generally, KERA has produced at least three emerging themes for the school district superintendency: (a) a redefining of leadership expectations (e.g., a greater emphasis on the facilitating role); (b) an emphasis on the superintendent's role in community development (e.g., rebuilding a symbiotic relationship between the school and its wider environment); and (c) an expectation of providing support and direction to individual schools as they experience substantive change (Murphy, 1994).

Attempts to redefine the superintendency also are evident in scholarly pursuits and the activities of national organizations. For instance, researchers are beginning to examine superintendent behaviors in relation to effective schools and effective student performance in those schools (e.g., Griffin & Chance, 1994; Morgan & Petersen, 2002). In past decades, scholars in educational administration concentrated on social psychological processes in organizations and only assumed that effective practices led to desirable outcomes (Boyd, 1992). Now there are more forceful demands for evidence regarding the effects of superintendent behavior and imposed organizational structure on school effectiveness.

What leadership styles are most effective in redesigned school districts? What mix of centralization and decentralization produces the most favorable outputs? Questions such as these prompted the primary professional organization for school superintendents, the AASA, to develop revised standards for practice. Looking at contemporary conditions, the commission charged with this responsibility declared:

Recent research on the superintendency makes one point amply clear—top-down bureaucratic management is being replaced by bottom-up executive leadership that encourages shared decision making among school staff, community, business, and other stakeholders. (Hoyle, 1993, p. 3)

After obtaining input from practitioners, school board members, professors of educational leadership, and other interested parties in the early 1990s, the AASA embraced eight standards that broadly defined practice. An outline of these standards is presented in Table 1.4. John Hoyle (1994), chairman of the AASA Commission on Standards for the Superintendency, declared that these standards provide benchmarks for improving the selection, preparation, and development of superintendents. He additionally asserted that they reflect an environment in which superintendents are expected to be decentralized enablers rather than centralized controllers. Even so, some believe the standards are not sufficiently comprehensive. Noted scholar Larry Cuban (1994), for example, expressed surprise that none of the standards held superintendents accountable for student academic performance, teaching improvement, and principal performance.

REQUIREMENTS FOR BEING A SUPERINTENDENT

Traditional requirements for becoming a school district superintendent have included professional preparation, licensing, and experience. Recently, several would-be reformers have attacked these traditional requirements, arguing that they prevent competent executives in business, the military, and politics from occupying the position (English, 2003b). The following sections discuss the nature of these requirements and the demands for reforming them.

Professional Preparation

As in all professions, the requirement of academic preparation is established and maintained by state licensing standards. By the 1980s, 82% of the states had promulgated laws or policies that required school administrators to complete a prescribed program of graduate study and subsequently obtain a state-issued license (or certificate) to be employed as a district superintendent. All but three of these states specified courses that had to be completed.

Prior to the mid-1980s, the content and effectiveness of university-based programs and the reasons why they were structured as they were rarely received attention. This indifference is largely explained by two conditions. First, many school administration departments faced only token competition resulting in an ample supply of students—a condition unfavorable to sweeping reforms. Second, reform foci prior to 1990 rarely included district and school governance; consequently, policymakers were not demanding massive changes

Table 1.4   General Professional Standards for the Superintendency Developed by the
American Association of School Administrators, 1993

Standard	Foci
Leadership and district culture	Developing a collective vision; shaping school culture and climate; providing purpose and direction for individuals and groups; demonstrating an understanding of international issues affecting education; formulating strategic plans, goals, and change efforts with staff and community; setting priorities in the context of community, student, and staff needs; serving as an articulate spokesperson for the welfare of all students in a multicultural context
Policy and governance	Developing procedures for working with the board of education that define mutual expectations, working relationships and strategies for formulating district policy for external and internal programs; adjusting local policy to state and federal requirements and constitutional provisions, standards, and regulatory applications; recognizing and applying standards involving civil and criminal liabilities
Communicative/community relations	Articulating district purpose and priorities to the community and mass media; requesting and responding to community feedback; demonstrating consensus building and conflict mediation; identifying, tracking, and dealing with issues; formulating and executing plans for internal and external communications; exhibiting an understanding of school districts as political systems and applying communication skills to strengthen community support; aligning constituencies in support of district priorities; building coalitions to gain financial and programmatic support; formulating democratic strategies for referenda; relating political initiatives to the welfare of children
Organizational management	Exhibiting an understanding of the school district as a system by defining processes of gathering, analyzing, and using data for decision making; managing the data flow; framing and solving problems; developing priorities and formulating solutions; assisting others to form reasoned opinions; reaching logical conclusions and making quality decisions to meet internal and external expectations; planning and scheduling personal and organizational work; establishing procedures to regulate activities and projects; delegating and empowering at appropriate organizational levels; securing and allocating human and material resources; developing and managing the district budget; maintaining accurate fiscal records

Standard	Foci
Curriculum planning/development	Designing curriculum and a strategic plan that enhance teaching and learning in multiple contexts; providing planning and future methods to anticipate occupational trends and their educational implications; identifying taxonomies of instructional objectives and validation procedures for curricular units, using theories of cognitive development; using valid and reliable performance indicators and testing procedures to measure performance outcomes; describing the proper use of computers and other learning and information technologies
Instructional management	Exhibiting knowledge of instructional management by implementing a system that includes research findings on learning and instructional strategies, instructional time, advanced electronic technologies, and resources to maximize student outcomes; describing and applying research and best practice on integrating curriculum and resources for multicultural sensitivity and assessment strategies to help all students achieve high levels
Human resources management	Developing a staff evaluation and development system to improve the performance of all staff members; selecting appropriate models for supervision based on adult motivation research; identifying alternative employee benefit packages; describing and applying the legal requirements for personnel selection, development, retention, and dismissal
Leadership values/ethics	Understanding and modeling appropriate value systems, ethics, and moral leadership; knowing the role of education in a democratic society; exhibiting multicultural and ethnic understanding and related behavior; adapting educational programming to the needs of diverse constituencies; balancing complex community demands in the best interest of the student; scanning and monitoring the environment for opportunities for staff and students; responding in an ethical and skillful way to the electronic and printed news media; coordinating social agencies and human services to help each student grow and develop as a caring, informed citizen

in the curricula of school administration programs. Neither of the conditions remained true during the 1990s. Both declining enrollments in school administration programs, caused by a waning interest in administrative careers, and the establishment of new school administration programs intensified competition. Concurrently, reformers and scholars within the profession began to question the effectiveness of school district governance (Kowalski & Glass, 2002). Two national groups, The National Commission on Excellence in Educational Administration (1987) and the National Policy Board for Educational Administration (1989), produced reports indicating that many programs had become detached from the realities of practice. Subsequently, national standards, developed specifically for superintendents by the AASA and for all administrators by the Interstate School Leadership Licensure Consortium (ISLLC), were adopted (Table 1.5).

Apprehensions about the quality of professional preparation have been framed primarily by school administration professors who were seeking to improve program quality. They have included a preoccupation with management and insufficient attention to leadership (e.g., Sergiovanni, 1991); a lack of curricular relevance (e.g., Achilles, 1998; Hallinger & Murphy, 1991); inadequate funding and staffing for professional education (e.g., Twombly & Ebmeier, 1989); inadequate clinical education (e.g., Gousha & Mannan, 1991); inattention to gender-related issues (e.g., Shakeshaft, 1989; Skrla, 1998); abysmal admission and graduation standards (e.g., Clark, 1989; Keedy & Grandy, 2001); and the absence of a national curriculum (e.g., Kowalski & Glass, 2002). More recently, other critics, most associated with private foundations and special interest groups, have argued that administrator preparation is basically unnecessary; they advocate deregulating licensing—a policy action that makes professional preparation irrelevant. One example of this extreme position is the document, *Better Leaders for America's Schools: A Manifesto,* published by the Broad Foundation and Thomas B. Fordham Institute (2003). Presenting largely opinions and anecdotal descriptions, it refers to university-based preparation programs and state licensing standards as meaningless hoops, hurdles, and regulatory hassles. The composers declared, "For aspiring superintendents, we believe that the states should require only a college education and a careful background check" (p. 31). Some scholars (e.g., English, 2003a) have argued that efforts to remove professional preparation from the university are driven by the profit motives of those who want to provide alternative forms of preparation and are part of a broader agenda designed to dismantle the country's public elementary and secondary education system (English, 2003b).

Criticisms of superintendent preparation have rarely been considered in context. More than 500 colleges and universities offer courses in educational

Table 1.5   Interstate School Leadership Licensure Consortium Standards for All
School Administrators

Standard	Content
1	A school administrator is an educational leader who promotes the success of all students by facilitating the development, articulation, implementation, and stewardship of a vision of learning that is shared and supported by the school community.
2	A school administrator is an educational leader who promotes the success of all students by advocating, nurturing, and sustaining a school culture and instructional program conducive to student learning and staff professional growth.
3	A school administrator is an educational leader who promotes the success of all students by ensuring management of the organization, operations, and resources for a safe, efficient, and effective learning environment.
4	A school administrator is an educational leader who promotes the success of all students by collaborating with families and community members, responding to diverse community interests and needs, and mobilizing community resources.
5	A school administrator is an educational leader who promotes the success of all students by acting with integrity, fairness, and in an ethical manner.
6	A school administrator is an educational leader who promotes the success of all students by understanding, responding to, and influencing the larger political, social, economic, legal, and cultural context.

administration and many of them do not prepare superintendents. Some of these institutions offer only a handful of courses taught exclusively by part-time faculty; others offer multiple graduate degrees, including the doctorate, and employ 10 or more full-time faculty members. Even among those institutions preparing superintendents, there is no national curriculum. Thus, painting all school administration programs with the same brush is both inappropriate and unfair. This is why students aspiring to be superintendents should exercise great care in determining where they will complete their graduate studies.

Although proponents of deregulation contend that conditions of practice have made professional preparation increasingly irrelevant, data obtained from superintendents do not support this assertion. National studies conducted in

1982, 1992, and 2000, years spanning the modern reform movement, found that approximately three of four superintendents rated their preparation as "excellent" or "good"; in 1992, only 4.6% rated their preparation as poor and this percentage actually dropped to 3.6% in 2000 (Glass, Björk, & Brunner, 2000). At the beginning of the current century, nearly half of all superintendents (45.3%) possessed a doctoral degree (Ed.D. or Ph.D.); this compares to only 29.2% in 1971. Those holding a doctoral degree were most likely to be in districts with more than 25,000 students and least likely to be in districts with fewer than 300 students. However, 99.7% of all superintendents had some type of graduate degree (Glass et al., 2000). Several states, e.g., Indiana and Iowa, require an advanced graduate degree (Ed.S., Ed.D., or Ph.D.) to obtain a superintendent license and several other states, for example, Arkansas and Minnesota, require either the completion of an advanced graduate degree or advanced graduate program (typically a minimum of 32 semester hours beyond a master's degree).

Licensing

States license practitioners in various professions (e.g., medicine, law, and education) and occupations (e.g., barbers and plumbers) to protect the public from incompetent or unscrupulous service providers. Although the words "certification" and "licensing" have basically held the same meaning in education, they are distinguishable in all other professions. Licensing is used appropriately to connote a mandatory requirement; for example, one cannot practice medicine without a medical license. A license is supposed to signify that the holder possess a sufficient level of knowledge and skills to practice in a given profession (Tannenbaum, 1999). Certification, by comparison, is used appropriately to connote a level of competence not required for basic practice; for example, a physician may obtain board certification in surgery by meeting the standards set for that specialization after being licensed. Hence, a license informs the public that an individual has been approved to practice a profession; certification informs the public that the licensed practitioner has achieved a high level of competence in a given area of medicine.

Many states have moved or are moving away from issuing certificates to issuing licenses for both teachers and administrators largely for three reasons. First, distinctions between the two terms have become more apparent and education lobby groups have encouraged the transition. Second, professional standards boards, composed primarily or entirely of professional educators, have replaced certification agencies in some states (e.g., Connecticut and Indiana); these boards have shown a proclivity to use the word licensing. Third, some professional groups (e.g., the Association of School Business Officials and National Board of Professional Teaching Standards) now issue certification in specializations indicating competence beyond basic license requirements (Kowalski, 2003a).

Although several states still issue certificates and not licenses, the latter is used generically in the remainder of this chapter. Each state, the District of Columbia, and territories of the United States (e.g., Puerto Rico) control the licensing of educators in their jurisdictions, and licensing criteria among these authorities are less than uniform (Kowalski, 2003a). A professional license issued by a governmental board or agency is not a property right; that is, it is not a contract between the holder (e.g., a school administrator) and the issuer (e.g., the state) (Hessong & Weeks, 1991). Therefore, a state may change conditions of licensure without concern for violating the holder's property rights. State legislatures and licensing boards, however, usually grant exemptions to license holders, commonly called "grandfathering," that protect licenses from being adversely affected by new requirements (Kowalski, 2003a). Additionally many states have reciprocity agreements ensuring that persons licensed in one state are virtually assured of obtaining a license to practice in a cooperating state.

Not only do licensing criteria vary across the United States, the magnitude of the differences has increased as a result of policies promulgated over the past two decades. While all states issue licenses to teachers, not all do so for school superintendents. In 1990, 23 states required superintendents to hold either a superintendent's license and 16 required a superintendent's endorsement on a general administrative license; all but 2 states required superintendents to have at least a master's degree (Ashbaugh & Kasten, 1992). A more recent study (Feistritzer, 2003) reported that while 41 states continue to require preparation and licensing for superintendents, more than half (54%) have provisions allowing waivers or emergency certificates to be issued. In addition, 15 of the 41 states (37%) allow or sanction alternative routes to licensure (i.e., other than university-based study).

Critics who favor deregulating professional preparation usually view licensing as counterproductive. Hess (2003), for example, argues that licensing is no longer necessary because school administrators "work in an extremely visible context, for larger organizations, and can now be monitored on the basis of a wealth of readily available data" (p. 7). Such views, clearly reflecting a bias that principals and superintendents should be treated as political appointees and not as professionals, unfortunately have appealed to dissatisfied policymakers and community elites. Overall, the trend is toward rescinding requirements for this key position as evidenced by radical policy decisions such as in Tennessee where the only remaining requirement for being a superintendent is a bachelor's degree (Kowalski & Glass, 2002). Michigan and South Dakota do not require licensing for either superintendents or principals, and Florida, Hawaii, North Carolina,

Tennessee, and Wyoming issue licenses to principals but not superintendents. States not issuing or not requiring a superintendent license allow local school boards to set their own employment criteria (Feistritzer, 2003).

Several states have moved in the opposite direction, electing to stiffen licensing criteria by requiring written licensing examinations. The Educational Testing Service has developed such an examination based on the ISLLC national standards for school administrators. Known as the *School Leaders Licensure Assessment,* the test consists of 25 constructed response items based on a series of vignettes and case studies (Holloway, 2002). Proponents argue that national standards for practice often become meaningless unless they are directly connected to preparation and licensing; licensure testing essentially requires school administration students and their professors to focus on the standards (Latham & Pearlman, 1999).

Professional Experience

In addition to graduate study, professional experience has been a common requirement for obtaining a superintendent license. In a recent national study, Feistritzer (2003) reported that nearly all states require administrators to have had prior teaching or related experiences. Requirements, though, vary substantially across the states with respect to the quantity and nature of experiences. For example, Indiana requires a minimum of two years of teaching experience but no prior administrative experience. Louisiana, by comparison, requires five years of teaching experience and an additional five years of administrative experience.

Historically, the requirement of teaching experience has been predicated on the ideal role of principal as instructional leader. Because virtually all superintendents had been principals, this criterion either directly or indirectly became an expectation for superintendents. Today, support for requiring teaching experience has been bolstered by state deregulation and district decentralization—strategies that raise expectations for local district leaders to build visions and long-range plans for instructional improvement. Discussing this reform environment, Petersen and Barnett (2003) noted that the actions and conversations of teachers and principals must focus continually on teaching and learning. They then concluded that superintendents had to participate in the discourse and provide resources for the efforts to be sustained. In this vein, Spillane and Louis (2002) wrote, "Without an understanding of the knowledge necessary for teachers to teach well . . . school leaders will be unable to perform essential school improvement functions such as monitoring instruction and supporting teacher development" (p. 97). Deregulation advocates (e.g., Hess, 2003) have countered by arguing that the belief that only former teachers can lead in districts and schools is fundamentally flawed, either because the activity requires generic skills possessed by all managers or because most administrators ignore this responsibility anyway. Such thinking is to be expected from critics who seek to refashion the position of school superintendent as a purely political appointment.

QUALITY-OF-LIFE CONSIDERATIONS

There are many reasons why some educators aspire to be school superintendents. First, the position offers the highest average salary of any employee group in public elementary and secondary education; in many locations, superintendents actually are the highest paid public official in the community. In 2001, the average salary for superintendents in districts with 25,000 or more students was approximately $153,000 (Council of Great City Schools, 2001). Across all districts, the average daily compensation for superintendents during the 2002–2003 school year was $534 per day; this compared to an average of $241 for classroom teachers, $339 for elementary school principals, $356 for middle school principals, $373 for high school principals, and $417 for assistant superintendents (Forsyth, 2003). Superintendent salaries, however, vary considerably among and within states. For instance, superintendents in suburban New York City are paid much higher salaries than are superintendents in rural South Dakota. In addition, demographic variables, such as school district size, academic degrees, and professional experience, almost always influence salaries.

Fringe benefits provided to superintendents also vary considerably. In some districts the chief executive receives the same package provided to all other professional employees, whereas in others the benefits may be much more lucrative. Community affluence and past practices often influence board members in determining these matters. Many superintendents seek to negotiate supplemental benefits rather than to seek higher salaries because the latter is typically highly publicized by the local media. Popular fringe benefits include tax-sheltered annuities, employer payment of personal retirement contributions, an automobile (in some instances with approval for personal as well as business use), professional dues, expense accounts, and insurance policies exceeding those provided to other employees. Several states have specific restrictions on the scope and type of benefits that may be given to any public employee.

Whereas salary and fringe benefits often are positive considerations, job security frequently is seen in a different light. Overall, superintendents remain in office in a single district for about 6 to 7 years (Glass et al., 2000; Cooper,

Fusarelli, & Carella, 2000) and this average is not substantially different than the averages reported in the previous three decades (Glass et al., 2000). Findings reported in some job tenure studies, however, are misleading because they do not truly report the amount of time a superintendent spends in a given position; they report how long the superintendent has been in the job at the time of the study (Yee & Cuban, 1996). Tenure data also need to be considered in light of the fact that many superintendents change positions voluntarily as a means of advancing their careers; that is, they progressively move to more lucrative superintendencies (Kowalski, 2003b). The shortest tenure for superintendents in a single position arguably has been reported in two types of districts: large urban and small rural (Kowalski, 1995).

In addition to salary and job security, a multitude of factors affect the quality of life experienced by a superintendent. One is a loss of privacy. Blumberg (1985) found that many superintendents believed that their communities treated them as public property. He described two facets of this condition:

> The first is the public perception that he (the superintendent) is and ought to be accessible, regardless of time, place, or occasion. The second is that somehow, because of both the publicness of his position and his position as chief among the educators of the community's children, his personal life should be above reproach. (p. 156)

Yet even within this fishbowl, some superintendents are admired, respected, and attain stature in their communities.

Some educators are drawn to the position for reasons not readily recognized. They often pertain to professional freedom and increased responsibility. Compared to teachers and principals, superintendents typically have greater latitude in allocating personal time; they often make major decisions that have a monumental effect on a school district (e.g., building a new school); they have considerable access to community and state leaders; they are in a position to affect the lives of hundreds of educators and thousands of students. These opportunities can make the position intrinsically rewarding.

FOR FURTHER REFLECTION

The governance structure of public education in the United States has four tiers: federal, state, intermediate, and local. Superintendents function in the last three levels. Even so, almost everyone identifies the position with local school systems because the vast majority of administrators holding this title are found at this level. The position of school district superintendent has evolved for more than 150 years, and contemporary practice is probably more demanding and complex than at any time in the past.

While entry into the superintendency in the past has been based on professional preparation, state licensing, and experience, conditions in some states have or are changing. A few states no longer issue a superintendent's license; a few states issue but do not require this license; and approximately one-third of the states issues emergency licenses or permits non-traditional forms of professional preparation. Clearly, school reform interventions over the past 25 years have magnified a long-standing philosophical division between those who believe that superintendents should be professional leaders and those who believe that they should be political appointees.

Although conflict may well be the DNA of the superintendency (Cuban, 1985), many contemporary officeholders continue to find the position to be rewarding (Glass et al., 2000). This is because the position provides the highest level of compensation in elementary and secondary education and opportunities to influence the lives of thousands of educators and students.

As you consider the content of this chapter, answer the following questions:

1. Why has the federal government played a limited role in public elementary and secondary education? Since the late 1970s, how has this role changed?

2. What are intermediate school districts? What is the relationship of intermediate districts to state systems of public education and local public schools?

3. What is the legal relationship between state systems of public education and local school districts?

4. What are the differences between "superintendent as political appointee" and "superintendent as professional leader"? Which concept do you favor?

5. What is the difference between "managing" and "leading"? How does each function relate to administration?

6. What do you consider to be the most and least attractive features of the district superintendent role?

7. Based on your experiences and knowledge of school administration, do you believe that professional preparation should be required for the position of district superintendent? Why or why not?

8. What are purposes of licensing professionals? Are these purposes valid in the case of school administration?

Case Study

Debra Jackson has always considered herself a risk taker. She was the first person in her family to complete college. She was the first African American to be employed as a teacher in one of the state's most affluent suburban school districts; she was the first female high school principal to be elected to the state's athletic association. When she finished a doctoral program in school administration at age 38, she was employed by the state's largest district as the assistant superintendent for secondary education. After just two years in that role, she became a superintendent.

Technically, the Habar School District is located in a suburb but it is clearly not an affluent community. Bordering the state capital, it was developed after World War II to provide housing for employees in the steel and auto industries. Since 1965, however, the school district's enrollment has declined from 13,500 to 4,700. In addition, the demographic and economic composition of the community has changed considerably as these data reveal:

	1975	Now
Total population	82,000	54,000
Minority population	1,300	27,000
Free and reduced lunches	1,100	3,200
Percentage of nonresidential property tax	13%	52%

The school district is governed by a school board consisting of five elected members. They voted unanimously to employ Dr. Jackson, the first female to be appointed to the position in this district. She replaced Dr. Samuel Ivory who retired after serving 28 years in the district and 14 years in the superintendency.

Dr. Jackson had pledged publicly that she would devote much of her energy to improving student academic performance. After assuming her new position, she realigned responsibilities with her three assistant superintendents so that she could spend time working directly with principals and curriculum committees. As she prepared materials for her first school board meeting, Debra discovered that her predecessor rarely provided the school board with recommendations for action items that appeared on the board agenda. At first, she thought that Dr. Ivory may have preferred to communicate his recommendations verbally, but her discussions with staff members revealed that this was not the case. Dr. Ivory simply did not make recommendations on most action items.

One of the items on the July board meeting agenda was the purchase of three new school buses. The business manager had received bids from five vendors and the details were arranged in a written summary. The business manager, however, did not evaluate the bids nor did he recommend one of the bidders. Debra discussed the matter with the business manager and he told her that the board members preferred to decide these matters on their own. She indicated that this type of procedure was unacceptable and she asked the business manager to evaluate the bids and recommend the lowest and best of them. The next day, she received a revised report and decided to endorse it. She included the report and a statement indicating that she supported the business manager's analysis and stated that the buses should be purchased from the recommended vendor.

After the board materials were distributed three days prior to the meeting, Debra received a call from the board president. He indicated that he had already gotten calls from two other board members about the bus bids. He asked, "Dr. Jackson why are you spending time with bus bids? Financial matters, buses, and buildings are usually items handled by the support staff and the board. We have some board members who know quite a bit about these things."

Dr. Jackson explained that as superintendent she had a responsibility to make a recommendation for all action items considered by the board. The board president reacted with surprise. "We hired you to improve test scores and the district's image. We weren't looking for another business manager. Some of the board members prefer to have the staff stay out of financial decisions. After all, we're the ones elected to office; we represent the people; we should decide how tax dollars get spent."

Dr. Jackson respectfully disagreed. She told the board president, "My job is to lead and to manage. I rely on my professional staff, in this case the business manager, to provide guidance. The board should rely on me to provide the same type of guidance to them." The board president did not respond as she had hoped. Rather, he indicated that she needed to schedule an executive session so that she could discuss her role with the entire board.

Case Discussion Questions

1. Do you support the position taken by Dr. Jackson relative to making recommendations on all board action items? Why or why not?

2. What factors might explain why some school board members prefer to not have recommendations on all action items?

3. Dr. Jackson did not discover that her predecessor did not make recommendations until she was preparing for her first board meeting. To what degree is she at fault for not having learned this earlier?

4. The chapter discussed tensions between the conflicting perspectives of the superintendency: professional versus political. Relate the chapter's content on this subject to this case.

5. Dr. Jackson could seek counsel on this matter from the state department of education, the state's superintendent association, and the state's school board association. What might she learn from each of these agencies that would be relevant to issues addressed in the case?

6. If Dr. Jackson were to respond professionally to this conflict what would she do? If she were to respond politically, what would she do?

7. The demands placed on superintendents by board members are often caused by public pressures. What pressures might be associated with a policy position that the superintendent should restrict her recommendations to matters of curriculum and instruction?

8. What lessons can be learned from this case?

REFERENCES

Achilles, C. (1998). How long? *The AASA Professor, 22*(1), 9–11.

Alexander, K., & Alexander, M. D. (1998). *American public school law* (4th ed.). Belmont, CA: Wadsworth.

American Association of School Administrators (1994). *Roles and relationships: School boards and superintendents.* Arlington, VA: Author.

Ashbaugh, C. R., & Kasten, K. L. (1992). *The licensure of school administrators: Policy and practice.* East Lansing, MI: National Center for Research on Teacher Learning. (ERIC Document Reproduction Service No. ED347163)

Björk, L. G., & Keedy, J. (2001). Politics and the superintendency in the U.S.A: Restructuring in-service education. *Journal of In-service Education, 27*(2), 275–302.

Blumberg, A. (1985). *The school superintendent: Living with conflict.* New York: Teachers College Press.

Boyd, W. L. (1992). The power of paradigms: Reconceptualizing policy and management. *Educational Administration Quarterly, 28*(4), 504–528.

Broad Foundation & Thomas B. Fordham Institute (2003). *Better leaders for America's schools: A manifesto.* Los Angeles, CA: Authors.

Brubacher, J. S. (1966). *A history of the problems of education* (2nd ed.). New York: McGraw-Hill.

Brunner, C. C., Grogan, M., & Björk, L. (2002). Shifts in the discourse defining the superintendency: Historical and current foundations of the position. In J. Murphy (Ed.), *The educational leadership challenge: Redefining leadership for the 21st century* (pp. 211–238). Chicago: The University of Chicago Press.

Butts, R. F., & Cremin, L. A. (1953). *A history of education in American culture.* New York: Henry Holt and Company.

Callahan, R. E. (1962). *Education and the cult of efficiency.* Chicago: University of Chicago Press.

Campbell, R. F., Cunningham, L. L., Nystrand, R. O., & Usdan, M. D. (1990). *The organization and control of American schools* (6th ed.). Columbus, OH: Merrill.

Chand, K. (1987). *A handbook for the school boards in America for the selection of the superintendent of schools.* East Lansing, MI: National Center for Research on Teacher Learning. (ERIC Document Reproduction Service No. ED277120)

Clark, D. L. (1989). Time to say enough! *Agenda, 1*(1), 1, 4.

Cooper, B. S., Fusarelli, L., & Carella, V. (2000). *Career crisis in the superintendency?* Arlington, VA: American Association of School Administrators.

Council of Great City Schools (2001). *Urban school superintendents: Characteristics, tenure and salary.* Washington, DC: Author.

Cuban, L. (1985). Conflict and leadership in the superintendency. *Phi Delta Kappan, 67*(1), 28–30.

Cuban, L. (1994). Muddled reasoning will limit standards' impact. *School Administrator, 51*(7), 28.

Digest of Education Statistics (2002). Washington, DC: Government Printing Office.

Eaton, W. E. (1990). The vulnerability of school superintendents: The thesis reconsidered. In W. Eaton (Ed.), *Shaping the superintendency: A reexamination of Callahan and the cult of efficiency* (pp. 11–35). New York: Teachers College Press.

English, F. W. (2003a). Cookie-cutter leaders for cookie-cutter schools: The teleology of standardization and the de-legitimization of the university in educational leadership preparation. *Leadership and Policy in Schools, 2*(1), 27–46.

English, F. W. (2003b, November). *Debating the manifesto.* Paper presented at the annual meeting of the University Council for Educational Administration, Portland, Oregon.

Feistritzer, E. (2003). *Certification of public-school administrators.* Washington, DC: The National Center for Education Information.

Forsyth, J. (2003). Punchback: Answering the critics. *The School Administrator, 11*(60), 6.

Glass, T., Björk, L., & Brunner, C. (2000). *The 2000 study of the American school superintendency.* Arlington, VA: American Association of School Administrators.

Gousha, R. P., & Mannan, G. (1991). *Analysis of selected competencies: Components, acquisition and measurement: Perceptions of three groups of stakeholders in education.* East Lansing, MI: National Center for Research on Teacher Learning. (ERIC Document Reproduction Service No. ED336850)

Griffin, G., & Chance, E. W. (1994). Superintendent behaviors and activities linked to school effectiveness: Perceptions of principals and superintendents. *Journal of School Leadership, 4*(1), 69–86.

Griffiths, D. E. (1966). *The school superintendent.* New York: The Discourse for Applied Research in Education.

Hallinger, P., & Murphy, J. (1991). Developing leaders for tomorrow's schools. *Phi Delta Kappan, 72*(7), 514–520.

Hess, F. M. (2003). *A license to lead? A new leadership agenda for America's schools.* Washington, DC: Progressive Policy Institute.

Hessong, R. F., & Weeks, T. H. (1991). *Introduction to the foundations of education* (2nd ed.). New York: Macmillan.

Holloway, J. H. (2002). A defense of the test for school leaders. *Educational Leadership, 59*(8), 71–75.

Hoyle, J. R. (1993). *Professional standards for the superintendency.* Arlington, VA: American Association of School Administrators.

Hoyle, J. R. (1994). What standards for the superintendency promise. *School Administrator, 51*(7), 22–23, 26.

Johnson, S. M. (1996). *Leading to change: The challenge of the new superintendency.* San Francisco: Jossey-Bass.

Keedy, J. L., & Grandy, J. (2001). Trends in GRE scores for principal candidates in the United States: A call for international debate on the intellectual quality of principal candidates. *International Journal of Educational Reform, 10*(4), 306–325.

Kimbrough, R. B., & Nunnery, M. Y. (1976). *Educational administration: An introduction.* New York: Macmillan.

Knezevich, S. J. (1984). *Administration of public education: A sourcebook for the leadership and management of educational institutions* (4th ed.). New York: Harper & Row.

Kowalski, T. J. (1995). *Keepers of the flame: Contemporary urban superintendents.* Thousand Oaks, CA: Corwin.

Kowalski, T. J. (2001). The future of local school governance: Implications for board members and superintendents. In C. Brunner & L. Björk (Eds.), *The new superintendency* (pp. 183–201). Oxford, UK: JAI, Elsevier Science.

Kowalski, T. J. (2003a). *Contemporary school administration: An introduction* (2nd ed.). Boston: Allyn & Bacon.

Kowalski, T. J. (2003b, April). *The superintendent as communicator.* Paper presented at the annual meeting of the American Educational Research Association, Chicago.

Kowalski, T. J. (2004). The ongoing war for the soul of school administration. In T. J. Lasley (Ed.), *Better leaders for America's schools: Perspectives on the Manifesto* (pp. 92–114). Columbia, MO: University Council for Educational Administration.

Kowalski, T. J., & Glass, T. E. (2002). Preparing superintendents in the 21st century. In B. S. Cooper & L. D. Fusarelli (Eds.), *The promises and perils facing today's school superintendent* (pp. 41–60). Lanham, MD: Scarecrow Education.

Latham, A., & Pearlman, M. (1999). From standards to licensure: Developing an authentic assessment for school principals. *Journal of Personnel Evaluation in Education, 13*(3), 263–282.

Leithwood, K., Begley, P. T., & Cousins, J. B. (1992). *Developing expert leadership for future schools.* London: Falmer.

Lusi, S. F. (1997). *The role of state departments of education in complex school reform.* New York: Teachers College Press.

Morgan, C., & Petersen, G. J. (2002). The superintendent's role in leading academically effective school districts. In B. S. Cooper & L. D. Fusarelli (Eds). *The promise and perils of the modern superintendency* (pp. 175–196). Lanham, MD: Scarecrow Press.

Morris, J. R. (1979). Job(s) of the superintendency. *Educational Research Quarterly, 4*(4), 11–24.

Murphy, J. (1994). The changing role of the superintendent in Kentucky's reforms. *School Administrator, 50*(10), 26–30.

National Commission on Excellence in Educational Administration (1987). *Leaders for America's schools.* Tempe, AZ: University Council for Educational Administration.

National Policy Board for Educational Administration. (1989). *Improving the preparation of school administrators: An agenda for reform.* Charlottesville, VA: Author.

Petersen, G. J., & Barnett, B. G. (2003, April). *The superintendent as instructional leader: History, evolution and future of the role*. Paper presented at the annual meeting of the American Educational Research Association, Chicago.

Radin, B. A., & Hawley, W. D. (1988). *The politics of federal reorganization*. New York: Pergamon Press.

Reutter, E. E. (1985). *The law of public education* (3rd ed.). Mineola, NY: The Foundation Press.

Russo, C. J. (1992). The legal status of school boards in the intergovernmental system. In P. First & H. Walberg (Eds.), *School boards: Changing local control* (pp. 3–20). Berkeley, CA: McCutchan.

Sergiovanni, T. J. (1991). The dark side of professionalism in educational administration. *Phi Delta Kappan, 72*(7), 521–526.

Shakeshaft, C. (1989). *Women in educational administration* (Updated ed.). Newbury Park, CA: Sage.

Skrla, L. (1998, April). *The social construction of gender in the superintendency*. Paper presented at the Annual Meeting of the American Educational Research Association, San Diego.

Spillane, J. P., & Louis, K. S. (2002). School improvement processes and practices: Professional learning for building instructional capacity. In J. Murphy (Ed.), *The educational leadership challenge: Redefining leadership for the 21st Century* (pp. 83–104). Chicago: University of Chicago Press.

Spring, J. H. (1985). *American education: An introduction to social and political aspects* (3rd ed.). New York: Longman.

Spring, J. H. (1994). *The American school, 1642–1993* (3rd ed.). New York: McGraw Hill.

Tannenbaum, R. (1999). Laying the groundwork for licensure assessment. *Journal of Personnel Evaluation in Education, 13*(3), 225–244.

Twombly, S., & Ebmeier, H. (1989). *Educational administration programs: The cash cow of the university?* Notes on Reform, Number 4, The National Policy Board for Educational Administration. Charlottesville: University of Virginia.

Valente, W. D. (1987). *Law in the schools* (2nd ed.). Columbus, OH: Merrill.

Yee, G., & Cuban, L. (1996). When is tenure long enough? A historical analysis of superintendent turnover and tenure in urban school districts. *Educational Administration Quarterly, 32*, 615–641.

CHAPTER 2

Role Characterizations

KEY FACETS OF THE CHAPTER

○ Evolution of role expectations

○ Superintendent as teacher-scholar

○ Superintendent as organizational manager

○ Superintendent as democratic statesman

○ Superintendent as applied social scientist

○ Superintendent as communicator

As far back as the late 1800s, prominent scholars recognized the office of school superintendent had become the most influential position in public education. Noted scholar-physician Joseph Mayer Rice (1892) declared that "the importance of the position cannot be overestimated" (p. 11). Charles Thwing (1898), president of Western Reserve University, wrote that many superintendents in the late 1800s were "rendering a service to the people far greater than that which any other citizen was rendering" (p. 30). Despite such accolades, officeholders subsequently were subjected to myriad political and social forces that refashioned their normative roles and the public's image of school administration. During the 20th century, the superintendency incrementally became more complex, demanding, and controversial.

Unless one understands the history of the superintendency, one is unlikely to comprehend the scope of modern practice. This is because the position as it currently exists has evolved for more than 150 years. Both its origin and the reasons underlying its development remain highly relevant in a political climate in which far too many policymakers remain ambivalent about the professional status of this pivotal administrative office.

This chapter examines five role conceptualizations that have evolved since the mid-1800s. The first four—*teacher-scholar, organizational manager, democratic statesman,* and *applied social scientist*—were chronicled by noted historian Raymond Callahan (1966); the fifth, *communicator,* developed in conjunction with America's transition into an information-based society (Kowalski, 2001; Kowalski, 2003b). As each new conceptualization emerged, existing expectations waxed and waned, but none became irrelevant (Cuban, 1976).

SUPERINTENDENT AS TEACHER-SCHOLAR

Historical Perspectives

As noted in the previous chapter, states developed a common curriculum for public schools intended to assimilate students into American culture by offering them common education experiences. The responsibility for ensuring that teachers would implement the prescribed curriculum was delegated to school superintendents (Spring, 1994). During the last half of the 19th century, conflict between democracy and professionalism became increasingly apparent. Many local school boards hired superintendents reluctantly and resisted yielding power to them over finances and personnel functions such as teacher employment (Carter & Cunningham, 1997). The political behavior of school boards, however, prompted complaints about the misuse of funds, poor facility management, and the employment of unfit teachers. Several prominent educators stepped forward and recommended a realignment of authority. One who stepped forward was Andrew Draper, president of the University of Illinois and later commissioner of education in New York. In 1895, he issued a report bearing his name that urged school boards to delegate to superintendents the power to employ teachers, supervise instruction, and manage finances (Callahan, 1962). The Draper Report was immediately attacked, not on the grounds that allegations of school board abuse were untrue, but rather on the basis that Draper's suggestions were incongruous with the cherished principle of local control. William George Bruce, then editor of the *American School Board Journal,* was one of Draper's harshest critics; using his publication as a political platform, he denounced the report (Callahan, 1966).

After the Civil War, urban school systems developed rather rapidly and their superintendents typically provided standards of best practice for public school administration. These education leaders were uniformly characterized as "master teachers" and their behavior was emulated by superintendents in less-mature districts (Callahan, 1962). In addition to being instructional leaders in their districts, they frequently authored professional journal articles about philosophy, history, and pedagogy (Cuban, 1988) and some subsequently became state superintendents, professors, and college presidents (Petersen & Barnett, 2003). The characterization of superintendent as teacher-scholar was summarized in an 1890 report on urban superintendents:

> It must be made his recognized duty to train teachers and inspire them with high ideals; to revise the course of study when new light shows that improvement is possible; to see that pupils and teachers are supplied with needed appliances for the best possible work; to devise rational methods of promoting pupils. (Cuban, 1976, p. 16)

During the formative years in which school administration was being shaped as a distinctive academic field, the most highly respected scholars were superintendents or former superintendents (Willower & Forsyth, 1999). Consider the following characteristics of these school administrators circa 1890 to 1920:

- They were directly aligned with the teaching profession.
- They were the most influential members of the National Education Association.
- Many were reluctant to broaden their practice beyond instructional leadership, fearing the public would view them as managers or politicians if they did so.
- They often tried to protect themselves from ambitious mayors and city council members who wanted to usurp their authority over curriculum and instruction by claiming professionalism (Callahan, 1966).

Political elites often saw superintendents who self-defined themselves as professional educators as manipulative individuals driven by two motives: amassing power and remaining independent of local politics (Kowalski, Björk, & Otto, 2004).

Although the conceptualization of the district superintendent as teacher-scholar began to wane circa 1910, it did not disappear. Literature pertaining to this subject, however, indicates that the necessity and attainability of this role have been questioned almost continuously and for varying reasons over the past 100 years (Petersen & Barnett, 2003). Such challenges have centered on one critical query: Should superintendents be professionals or domesticated government employees?

Contemporary Perspectives

Persons who promote the idea that school administration is a distinctive profession believe that superintendents require a solid grounding in pedagogy and experience applying that knowledge in the classroom. Conversely, antiprofessionists—individuals who view school administration as a generic management function—argue that such requirements are senseless hurdles created to protect the interests of the education lobby. The authors of documents opposing professionalism in school administration (e.g., Broad Foundation & Fordham Institute, 2003; Hess, 2003) reject the contention that only former teachers can monitor classroom activities, mentor teachers, and support instructional improvement. Antiprofessionists favor deregulating academic preparation and licensing so that school boards would have unrestricted authority to employ administrators. Contrary to such thinking, many contemporary reform strategies require strong instructional leaders who understand teaching and who are able to establish credibility with teachers (Elmore, 1999–2000; Murphy, 1992, 2002; Negroni, 2000). When deregulation is considered in relation to these expectations, such policy seems precarious.

The role of superintendent as instructional leader also has been scrutinized in relation to position instability and school board member expectations. Research findings on the superintendent's influence over educational outcomes have been mixed. For instance, Zigarelli (1996), using data from the National Education Longitude Study for 1988, 1990, and 1992, concluded that the evidence did not support a claim that the relationships between district administrators and schools improved instruction. Studies having a broader perspective of superintendent influence usually paint a different picture. Examining seven of them (Bredeson, 1996; Coleman & LaRocque, 1990; Herman, 1990; Morgan & Petersen, 2002; Murphy & Hallinger, 1986; Petersen, 2002; Peterson, Murphy, & Hallinger, 1987) Petersen and Barnett (2003) concluded that superintendents "can influence the views of school board members and others by articulating and demonstrating involvement, a sincere interest in the technical core of curriculum and instruction and viewing it as their primary responsibility" (p. 15). Björk (1993) noted that superintendents indirectly influence instruction through functions such as staff selection, principal supervision, and budgeting—decisions that often are undervalued with respect to overall effectiveness.

SUPERINTENDENT AS MANAGER

Historical Perspectives

As early as 1890, reservations were being expressed about the ability of traditional superintendents to administer large city districts. These concerns focused primarily on a perceived lack of managerial knowledge and skills. As Cuban (1976) noted, heated debates were waged on this topic and "the lines of argument crystallized over whether the functions of a big-city superintendent should be separated into two distinct jobs, i.e., business manager and superintendent of instruction" (p. 17). Qualms about managerial competencies intensified as America began its transition from an agrarian to industrial society. New factories sparked a demographic chain reaction, first producing urbanization and then large school systems. In this context, school board members focused more directly and intensely on resource management. They and other political elites began demanding that superintendents infuse the tenets of classical theory and scientific management, perceived then to be the successful underpinnings of the Industrial Revolution, into school administration (Callahan, 1962). By 1920, the role transformation had been officially completed; superintendents were expected to be scientific managers, individuals who could improve operations by concentrating on time and efficiency (Tyack & Hansot, 1982).

From approximately 1900 to 1920, leading education scholars, including Ellwood Cubberly, George Strayer, and Franklin Bobbitt, joined political elites in demanding that school administrators learn and apply the principles of scientific management (Cronin, 1973). The mounting pressures for this role transformation prompted officials at several leading universities to offer courses and subsequently graduate degrees in school management. Simultaneously, prominent superintendents were reevaluating the merits of protecting their public image as professional educators. Many decided that relinquishing this persona was necessary if policymakers and the general public were to accept the contention that administrative work had become separate from and more important than teaching (Thomas & Moran, 1992).

Opposition to the refashioning of superintendents into industrial managers came from two groups: many mayors, city council members, and other political bosses who feared that casting superintendents as managers would increase the stature, influence, and power of this position (Callahan, 1962), and some leading education scholars who opposed the management conceptualization because they thought it was counterproductive to the principle of local control. More precisely, the latter group feared that business and government power elites would act in concert with superintendent-managers to seize control of public education, thus diminishing participatory democracy (Glass, 2003).

In his book *Education and the Cult of Efficiency,* historian Raymond Callahan (1962) chronicled how and why the infusion of business values into educational philosophy and the role transformation of superintendents became inextricably intertwined. Referring to this era as a tragedy, he concluded that both social forces and the collusion of leading big-city superintendents were responsible for an anti-intellectual context in which school administrators paid little or no attention to teaching and learning. He was especially harsh in his assessment of superintendents, concluding that they lacked conviction and courage. He called them *dupes,* powerless and vulnerable pawns unwilling to defend their profession and their school districts. His analysis, referred to as the *thesis of vulnerability,* has been widely accepted by many but not all education scholars (Eaton, 1990). Burroughs (1974) and Tyack (1974), for example, disagreed with Callahan; they characterized the same superintendents as cunning, intelligent, political pragmatists who had merely responded to the societal realities imbued in their work context. Thomas and Moran (1992) offered a third point of view; they posited that these administrators were opportunists who had embraced classical theory and scientific management because it expanded their legitimate power base. Overall, however, history has shown that "Callahan was correct about the influence of business on education administration program development in universities and on the operation of public schools" (Lutz, 1996, p. 8).

Although historians disagree about motives, they concur that management became the dominant role expectation for school superintendents in the early 1900s (Kowalski & Brunner, 2005). Budget development and administration, standardization of operation, personnel management, and facility management were the first tasks they assumed (Callahan, 1962). By 1930, however, the still relatively new business manager conceptualization was being subjected to intense criticism. The great stock market crash and subsequent economic depression had tarnished much of the glitter that the captains of industry had acquired during the Industrial Revolution. Some prominent superintendents who previously were praised for emulating industrial managers were now being disparaged. In addition, many local school district patrons were overtly protesting the level of power administrators had acquired; most felt disenfranchised by bureaucratic structure that had been imposed on their local districts (Kowalski, 2003a). In the midst of this dissatisfaction, leading progressive educators, such as George Sylvester Counts, intensified their criticisms, arguing that business values imposed on public education were incongruous with the core political values of a democratic society (Van Til, 1971). To this day, many individuals equate the core values of classical theory with the function of management. Counts (1952), for example, viewed management as essential in all large organizations. His criticisms made circa 1930 did not focus on the fact that superintendents were performing management functions; rather, they pertained to the concentration of power in the hands of superintendents and political elites. He believed that the application of classical theory in public organizations was detrimental because it diminished public participation. Consequently, it is important to distinguish between management as a function and scientific management as a philosophy.

Contemporary Perspectives

Studying the evolution of the managerial role, Thomas Glass (2003) observed that both context and district size have been critical issues. He noted that the work of a superintendent in a small-enrollment rural district was quite dissimilar from the work of a superintendent in a large-enrollment urban district. Consequently, he cautioned that generalizations about managerial responsibilities are typically precarious. Management, especially fiscal management, has been stressed heavily in small districts where superintendents often have little or no support staff. In these settings, a superintendent manages the largest transportation program and food service program in the community.

Even though the degree of emphasis placed on management has fluctuated, the importance of the role is rarely questioned. Experienced practitioners recognize that many of their leadership attributes become insignificant when budgets are not balanced, school facilities are deemed not to be safe, and personnel problems routinely result in litigation. Superintendents in larger-enrollment and more affluent districts often can relegate managerial responsibilities to their staff, but even those able to do so are held accountable for efficient and productive operations (Kowalski, 1995). Commenting about contemporary school administration, John Kotter, Harvard Business School Professor, noted that superintendents must be both effective leaders and effective managers. As all organizations move toward decentralization and democratization, the demands placed on chief executives, including district superintendents, increase. Correspondingly, the minimum levels of knowledge and skills escalate (Bencivenga, 2002). Professor Kotter's observations illuminate the reality that the challenge facing today's superintendent is not choosing between leadership and management, it is establishing equilibrium between these two essential roles.

SUPERINTENDENT AS DEMOCRATIC LEADER

Historical Perspectives

The role of democratic leader is often equated with *statesmanship*. Björk and Gurley (2003) traced the origins of statesmanship from Plato to Alexander

Hamilton. Plato believed that a statesman acted unilaterally and paternalistically to control and direct critical societal functions. Hamilton viewed a statesman as a true politician who juggled the interests of the common people and the interests of the economic elite while remaining an aristocrat. Callahan's (1966) conception of the superintendent as statesman was probably not in total agreement with either of these perspectives; his analysis of the period between 1930 and the mid-1950s centered primarily on political leadership in a democratic context. After studying various perspectives of the superintendent as "statesman," Björk and Gurley concluded that the term "is not and may never have been an appropriate role conceptualization, inasmuch as the role has never been about a stately, patriarch ubiquitously and benevolently guiding school systems single-handedly" (p. 35). Their analysis led them to conclude that superintendents more accurately were expected to be astute political strategists.

The democratic leader characterization is anchored in both philosophy and political realities. In the 1930s, scarce fiscal resources forced school officials to engage more directly in political activity,[1] especially in relation to lobbying state legislatures. Previously, the behavior of highly political superintendents was regarded as unprofessional (Björk & Lindle, 2001; Kowalski, 1995). But such convictions faded when it became apparent that public schools had to compete with other governmental services for limited state funds. At approximately the same time that superintendents were being pushed to be more politically active, a cadre of prominent education professors were attempting to reverse the negative effects of the management role on participatory democracy in local districts. One of the most vocal in this group was Ernest Melby, a former dean of education at Northwestern University and New York University (Callahan, 1966). Melby (1955) believed that the infusion of business values had led superintendents to become less reliant on their greatest resource—the community. He warned administrators about the dangers of insulating themselves from the public and urged superintendents instead to "release the creative capacities of individuals" and "mobilize the educational resources of communities" (p. 250). In essence, democratic leaders were expected to galvanize policymakers, employees, and other taxpayers to support the district's initiatives (Howlett, 1993).

Contemporary Perspectives

By the mid-1950s, the idea of having superintendents engage in democratic administration also met with disfavor. Detractors argued that the concept was overly idealistic and insufficiently attentive to realities of practice. They believed that democratic administration, as it had been characterized, produced difficulties for the superintendents who adopted the style and for the organizations in which they were employed. Detractors of democratic administration argued that the everyday problems of superintendents were largely economic, social, and political and, therefore, knowledge and skills in these disciplines, and not philosophy, were necessary to solve them (Björk & Gurley, 2003).

Although the ideal of democratic administration became less prominent after the 1950s, it never died. It has resurfaced across all types of organizations, including school districts, because of an intricate mix of changing values and economic realities. In the case of public education, scholars (e.g., Hanson, 2003; Wirt & Kirst, 2001) recognize that even the best education policies often prove to be ineffective when they are rejected politically. Consequently, superintendents continuously face the difficult choice of deciding whether a problem should be approached on the basis of expertise, shared decision making, or both. Perhaps more so now than in the past, ideological and moral differences among community factions require facilitation and conflict management (Keedy & Björk, 2002). In a democracy, policy and politics are squarely joined and this reality perpetuates expectations of democratic administration.

SUPERINTENDENT AS APPLIED SOCIAL SCIENTIST

Historical Perspectives

As with earlier role conceptualizations, the view of superintendent as applied social scientist was forged by a mix of societal and professional forces. Callahan (1966) identified the following four forces as the most influential:

1. *Growing dissatisfaction with democratic leadership after World War II*— As previously noted, the concept of democratic leadership had come under attack by those who perceived it to be overly idealistic. These detractors thought that shared authority and decision making exacerbated political, social, and economic problems rather than solving them.

2. *Rapid development of the social sciences in the late 1940s and early 1950s*—The social sciences were being developed rapidly during this era. The seminal book, *Toward a Theory of Action* (Parsons & Shils, 1951), exemplified this fact. Many scholars concluded that the social sciences were at the core of administrative work, including practice in districts and schools.

3. *Support from the Kellogg Foundation*—During the 1950s, the Foundation provided more than $7 million in grants, primarily to eight major universities, to support the research of school administration professors in the area of the social sciences (Kellogg Foundation, 1961).

4. *A resurgence of criticisms of public education in the 1950s*—Changes in role conceptualizations were fueled by public dissatisfaction and the image of superintendent as applied social scientist was no exception. During this era, however, the displeasure related to emerging social and political concerns. The end of school desegregation seemed apparent, families were leaving cities to move to new suburbs, the first wave of post-World War II baby boomers was entering public education, and the escalating cold war with the Soviet Union intensified national defense concerns. Such issues presented unique challenges to public elementary and secondary education, and many policymakers and public opinion shapers concluded that local district superintendents were not prepared to deal with them.

At least two other factors now appear to have been equally influential. First, circa 1955, efforts to make school administration an established academic discipline equal to business management and public administration were intensifying (Culbertson, 1981). Redefining administrators as applied social scientists and infusing the social sciences into the curriculum for preparing school administrators were viewed as positive steps toward that goal (Crowson & McPherson, 1987). Second, prior to the 1950s, the practice of administration had focused largely on internal operations, but gradually systems theory was employed to demonstrate how external legal, political, social, and economic systems affected organizations (Getzels, 1977). School administration professors recognized that such theoretical constructs were equally essential for their students.

The model of superintendent as social scientist encouraged professors and practitioners to emphasize empiricism, predictability, and scientific certainty in their research and practice (Cooper & Boyd, 1987). The intent was to rewrite the normative standards for practice; superintendents in the future were expected to apply scientific inquiry to the problems and decisions that permeated their practice. The study of theory was at the core of this normative transition, as evidenced by the changes in school administration textbooks: Those written prior to 1950 never mentioned theory; virtually none written after 1950 omitted theory (Getzels, 1977). By the 1970s, the behavioral sciences had become thoroughly integrated into school administration literature, including primary textbooks (Johnson & Fusarelli, 2003).

Similarities between the onset of the management role and the onset of the applied social scientist role are striking. In both instances, public dissatisfaction was atypically high, school administration professors were seeking to elevate their profession's status, and administration was described as being distinctively different from and more demanding than teaching (Kowalski, 2003a). Consequently, it is not surprising that both roles were subjected to similar criticisms. Depicting superintendents as experts unavoidably resurrects fundamental questions about the inherent tensions between professionalism and democracy (Kowalski, 2004). How much power should superintendents possess? Can professionalism and democracy coexist in the administration of a public agency? In truth, public administration differs from other forms of administration in that professional knowledge is applied in highly political contexts and subject to political scrutiny (Wirt & Kirst, 2001). Clearly then, vulnerability to public contempt increases when superintendents act unilaterally or devalue public opinion (Kowalski, 1995).

Contemporary Perspectives

Although emphasis on the behavioral sciences lessened after 1980, research and theories from constituent disciplines had already become embedded in school administration's knowledge base. Addressing the role in more recent times, Fusarelli and Fusarelli (2003) identified school reform and the quest for social justice as relevant issues. In the former, superintendents are expected to have the expertise necessary to research deficiencies and to recommend policy to ameliorate them. This includes the ability to reshape institutional cultures that deter positive change. In the latter, superintendents are expected to have expertise necessary to deal with social and institutional ills such as poverty, racism, gender discrimination, crime, and violence. Both expectations require knowledge and skills from various social science disciplines, including psychology, sociology, anthropology, economics, and criminology.

Emphasis on data-driven decision making also has contributed to renewed interests in superintendents functioning as applied social scientists. This includes both the ability to conduct research related to problem solving and the ability to consume and apply existing research to problem solving (e.g., Manheimer & Manning, 1995). Technology has made data accumulation and retrieval much easier for administrators and, consequently, most districts are inundated with facts and figures. Although the technology of data-driven decision making is not unduly complicated, adoption by superintendents is often thwarted by institutional cultures in which politics and emotion take precedence over rationality (Doyle, 2002).

SUPERINTENDENT AS COMMUNICATOR

Historical Perspectives

The ever-prescient Peter Drucker (1999) labeled the new era of organizations the Information Age: What matters in times of unremitting global competition and availability of huge amounts of information are the skills of accessing and processing information and making decisions based on that information. As early as the late 1970s, Lipinski (1978) and other scholars predicted that technology would move society away from a manufacturing base to an information base. *A Nation at Risk* (National Commission on Excellence in Education, 1983) sounded an alarm that public schools were not sufficiently performance-driven with respect to preparing students to be competitive in a global economy. America's public schools have always been expected to be efficient institutions and computers exacerbated that anticipation (Kearsley, 1990). Dyrli and Kinnaman (1994), for instance, argued that technology could increase productivity through increased processing speed, greater memory capacity, miniaturization, decreased cost, and increased ease of use. Media reports on international comparisons, however, suggested that American public schools had become neither more efficient nor more productive (Bracey, 2003).

Historically, communication in school administration has been treated as a skill; that is, something one does well when assuming a role. Consequently, skills tend to be role-specific; the nature of the skill is shaped by the role characterization. As an example, appropriate managerial behavior and appropriate political behavior are often dissimilar. Today, however, basing communication on the nature of administrative role expectations is no longer encouraged. Today, normative communicative behavior is pervasive. That is, administrators are expected to communicate in the same manner regardless of the functions being addressed. The normative standard specifies consistent, two-way, symmetrical interactions.

The view of superintendent as communicator emerged in conjunction with America's transition from a manufacturing society (Kowalski, 2001). Communicative expectations for administrators reflect a confluence of reform initiatives and the social environment in which they are being pursued. Virtually every major school improvement concept and strategy encourages superintendents to work collaboratively with principals, teachers, parents, and other taxpayers to build and pursue collective visions. Yet, many districts and schools retain cultures that sustain work isolation (teachers and administrators working individually and in seclusion) (Gideon, 2002) and closed organizational climates (administrators attempting to avoid community interventions) (Blase & Anderson, 1995).

Unfortunately, the treatment of communication in school administration appears to have been determined by two myopic assumptions: anyone can communicate effectively and administrators should alter their communicative behavior as they transition from one role to another. These convictions have become much more consequential—both for local schools systems and for superintendents—in the context of an information-based and reform-minded society. Studies centered on performance evaluation (e.g., Beverage, 2003; Peterson, 1999) and on administrator dismissals (Davis, 1998), for instance, reveal the penalties administrators incur for inconsistent and incompetent communication. Although communication now receives much more attention and is an integral part of standards documents guiding administrator preparation and licensing, the school administration profession has yet to develop a practice-based definition of communication, curricular guidelines for teaching communication, and specific criteria for assessing communication effectiveness.

Contemporary Perspectives

Since the early 1990s, policy analysts (e.g., Bauman, 1996; Fullan, 1996; Hess, 1998) have concluded that meaningful school reform requires revising institutional climates, including organizational structure and culture. In addition, current reform efforts are largely predicated on the conviction that restructuring complex institutions necessitates a social systems perspective (Chance & Björk, 2004; Murphy, 1991; Schein, 1996). "Systemic thinking requires us to accept that the way social systems are put together has independent effects on the way people behave, what they learn, and how they learn what they learn" (Schlechty, 1997, p. 134). In this vein, the nature of public schools is influenced by human transactions occurring within and outside the formal organization—exchanges often conducted in midst of fundamental philosophical differences (Keedy & Björk, 2002). Restructuring proposals that ignore the ubiquitous nature of political disagreements almost always fail either because key implementers and stakeholders are excluded from visioning and planning or because the values and beliefs expressed in the reforms are incongruous with prevailing institutional culture (Kowalski, 1997; Schlechty, 1997).

Many scholars (e.g., Henkin, 1993; Murphy, 1994) believe that school improvement needs to be pursued locally and that superintendents must be key figures in the process. This assignment, though, is highly intimidating for many superintendents for one or more of the following reasons:

1. Topics that inevitably produce substantial conflict must be discussed openly and candidly with groups inside and outside the organization (Carlson, 1996).

2. Often administrators either have been socialized to believe that conflict is counterproductive or they feel insecure managing it (Kowalski, 2003b).

3. Many educators are dubious about reform, having experienced a myriad of change failures during their careers (Sarason, 1996). Even new teachers and administrators often come to accept things as they are (Streitmatter, 1994).

Despite these obstacles, superintendents must realize that they are unlikely to achieve authentic school restructuring unless they identify and challenge what individuals and groups truly believe and value about education (Trimble, 1996) and how they promote and accept change (Leithwood, Jantzi & Fernandez, 1994). Increasingly, scholars are concluding that communication and culture are inextricably linked. For example, Conrad (1994) wrote, "Cultures are communicative creations. They emerge and are sustained by the communicative acts of all employees, not just the conscious persuasive strategies of upper management. Cultures do not exist separately from people communicating with one another" (p. 27). Although organizational research typically has categorized culture as a causal variable and communication as an intervening variable (Wert-Gray, Center, Brashers, & Meyers, 1991), the relationship between the two is more likely reciprocal (Kowalski, 1998). Axley (1996), for instance, wrote the following about interdependence: "Communication gives rise to culture, which gives rise to communication, which perpetuates culture" (p. 153). In this vein, communication is a process through which organizational members express their collective inclination to coordinate beliefs, behaviors, and attitudes—in schools, communication gives meaning to work and forges perceptions of reality. As such, culture influences communicative behavior and communicative behavior is instrumental to building, maintaining, and changing culture (Kowalski, 1998).

In the case of local school districts, normative communicative behavior is shaped largely by two realities: the need for superintendents to assume leadership in the process of school restructuring (Björk, 2001; Murphy, 1994), and the need for them to change school culture as part of the restructuring process (Heckman, 1993; Kowalski, 2000).

A nexus between effective practice and communication skills is not unique to education; recent studies of business executives revealed that most who found themselves under attack were ineffective communicators (Perina, 2002).

In the case of district superintendents, the role of effective communicator is framed by relatively new expectations that have become apparent since the early 1980s. Examples include engaging others in open political dialogue, facilitating the creation of shared visions, building a positive school district image, gaining community support for change, providing an essential framework for information management, marketing programs, and keeping the public informed about education (Kowalski, 2004). And as communities become increasingly diverse, superintendents also have the responsibility of building more inclusive cultures (Riehl, 2000).

FOR FURTHER REFLECTION

With respect to the superintendency, it is difficult to determine where we are and where we are likely to go if we do not fully grasp where we have been. Consequently, the five role conceptualizations are central to comprehending the complexity of this administrative position and the nature of work performed. Present-day superintendents across all types and sizes of school districts must wear several different hats if they are to be effective. In fact, the ability to function in all five roles is arguably more critical in small districts than in larger districts because superintendents in the former rarely have the support staff found in the latter. Less than 2% of the nation's school systems have 25,000 or more students but 71% enroll fewer than 2,500 students. Even more noteworthy, 48% of all districts enroll fewer than 1,000 students (National Center for Education Statistics, 2004).

As new role conceptualizations emerged, existing ones became less relevant. Even so, they never became totally inconsequential. As social, political, and economic issues changed, the balance among role expectations fluctuated. The most glaring example of this pattern is found in the current resurgence of the superintendent's instructional leadership role. State reform programs, for example, require local school boards to produce meaningful visions and plans—a task that invariably increases their dependency on professional leadership. The current social context in which superintendents are expected to possess expert power in the areas of curriculum and instruction demonstrates that role conceptualization can be resurrected rather quickly.

Often, persons in the superintendency believe that expectations placed on them are listed precisely in their formal job descriptions. Research on practitioners (e.g., Blumberg, 1985; Kowalski, 1995), however, suggests that this often is not the case. Many superintendents eventually discover that they also have invisible job descriptions that contain real rather than espoused expectations.

This is another reason why it is critically important to comprehend the five established role expectations.

As you consider the content of this chapter, answer the following questions:

1. Initially, superintendents were viewed as teachers of teachers. Their work focused largely on implementing a state approved curriculum and on assisting teachers to improve instruction. What factors, circa 1910, prompted these administrators to move toward industrial management?

2. What is democratic administration? Why is the conceptualization of superintendent as democratic administrator controversial?

3. In the current context of school reform, what factors have increased expectations that superintendents possess expert power in curriculum and instruction?

4. Why are the management aspects of the superintendency often viewed negatively?

5. What is an applied social scientist? Why have superintendents been expected to assume this role?

6. What factors contributed to the emergence of the role conceptualization of superintendent as communicator?

7. When a new role conceptualization has emerged for superintendents, what has happened to the existing roles?

Case Study

Willow Springs is located adjacent to a large city in the Pacific northwest. The community developed in the 1940s to provide relatively low-cost housing for factory employees. Since 1980, the demographic profile of the community has changed substantially. The percentage of families living below the poverty line, for example, tripled between 1980 and 2000. During the same period, the school district's enrollment declined by 35% and its dropout rate increased by 20%.

Last year, three of five school board members were replaced. Two were defeated in an election after the state department of public education threatened to take control of the district unless student performance on state tests improved; the third, the board president, moved out of the community and resigned. They were replaced by three individuals committed to improving conditions in the school district. The most influential politically was Reverend Mark Taylor, minister of the largest congregation in Willow Springs and a prominent community leader. He became board president immediately after assuming a position on the board.

One week after the two new board members were elected, and several months before the three new board members took office, the superintendent, William Trace, resigned. He had been superintendent for three years and was closely aligned with the board president who had left the community. Because Superintendent Trace would be leaving on June 30th and the new board members would not take office until July 1, the old board members in concert with the new board members conducted the search collectively. Even so, the new board members dominated the process.

The board appointed Dr. Calvin Brown as superintendent. He formerly was a teacher in Willow Springs but left six years ago to pursue his doctorate. Since completing the degree, he has been an elementary school principal in the large city district adjoining Willow Springs. Recognized as a skilled instructional leader, Dr. Brown was selected as the state's outstanding principal the year prior to becoming superintendent.

During his interview with the school board, Dr. Brown admitted that he was apprehensive about becoming a superintendent because he knew little about school finance—a concern that was made worse by the recent announcement that the business manager also would be leaving the district. Reverend Taylor and his allies were convinced, however, that Dr. Brown was the person they needed. They promised to employ a competent business manager and ensured Dr. Brown that he could devote his attention to improving the district's educational program.

With 3,700 students, Willow Springs was large enough to justify having several support personnel in the central office. The new business manager, Ernesto Rodriguez, had a degree in business administration and sold insurance for the past 18 years. A long-term resident of Willow Springs, he was a personal friend of Reverend Taylor. The curriculum director was Deborah Hastings, a former middle school principal in the district.

In his first three months as superintendent, Dr. Brown worked closely with Ms. Hastings and the district's seven principals. He initiated a community-wide process to build a collective vision and plan that hopefully would alleviate the concerns of the state superintendent. The school board and parents were very supportive and praised their new superintendent at every opportunity.

Shortly after Thanksgiving, Mr. Rodriguez informed Dr. Brown that he had discovered some serious financial concerns. The budget adopted by the previous superintendent and business manager required $2.5 million more than the district's estimated revenues. The business manager urged the superintendent to immediately draft a plan to reduce expenditures. Dr. Brown indicated that he was totally focused on the district's education program and told Mr. Rodriguez to meet with the principals to develop a list of proposed budget cuts. Dr. Brown also asked him to prepare a report to the school board members so they could be apprised of the situation.

Several days before the holiday vacation period, Mr. Rodriguez met with the superintendent and expressed frustration with the principals' unwillingness to recommend budget cuts. He had met with them on three occasions and each time, they refused to recommend reductions. The high school principal, the unofficial spokesperson for the group, bluntly told the business manager, "You and the superintendent need to do this. A lot of people are going to be angry about budget cuts and we're not going to be blamed for a problem we didn't create."

Dr. Brown told Mr. Rodriguez to require the principals to comply with his instructions. Mr. Rodriguez pointed out that he had no official authority over principals. Dr. Brown then said, "If you don't get them to make budget cuts, you're going to have to do this. I'm not a finance expert and the board knows it. This is your responsibility."

Frustrated by the conversation, Mr. Rodriguez went to see Reverend Taylor. He told the board president that he would resign before making unilateral budget cuts. After conferring with several board members, Reverend Taylor met with Dr. Brown and instructed the superintendent to become directly involved in the matter. Dr. Brown reminded Reverend Taylor that he had told the board of his lack of expertise in finance. The board president did not respond positively. "Dr. Brown, we all understood that you would prefer to work in curriculum but that was before any of us knew about the revenue problem. You either have to take a heavy hand with the principals and get them to act or you're going to have to do this yourself. Ernesto is no education expert and making him decide on the cuts doesn't make sense. We don't want to lose him and he says he'll resign before doing so. You may not like it, but the ball is in your court."

Dr. Brown was devastated. He left a good job to come back to Willow Springs and now he felt betrayed. He told the board the truth and he trusted Reverend Taylor and the others. Now, he was being placed in an impossible situation. Working with the principals on this issue would pull him away from his work on educational programs; even worse, forcing them to make budget reductions would likely destroy his rapport with them. Sitting at his desk, he became increasingly depressed. He reached for the file containing the district's budget and after reading for a few moments, he threw it down on his desk. He asked himself, how can I make reductions in a document I don't even understand?

Case Discussion Questions

1. How does this case relate to the content of this chapter?

2. Evaluate the position taken by Mr. Rodriguez. Do you agree or disagree with his behavior? Why or why not?

3. Do you believe that Reverend Taylor and the board members who support him are being unfair with Dr. Brown? Why or why not?

4. Are there any circumstances under which a superintendent would not have to have a basic understanding of school finance? If so, what are they?

5. What alternatives does Dr. Brown have to resolve this matter? If you were in his position, which of them would your pursue?

NOTE

1. Politics is defined here as competition for scarce resources.

REFERENCES

Axley, S. R. (1996). *Communication at work: Management and the communication-intensive organization.* Westport, CT: Quorum Books.

Bauman, P. C. (1996). *Governing education: Public sector reform or privatization.* Boston: Allyn & Bacon.

Bencivenga, J. (2002). John Kotter on leadership, management and change. *School Administrator, 59*(2), 36–40.

Beverage, L. H. (2003). *Inhibiting factors to effectiveness and the adaptability of new superintendents in Virginia.* Unpublished doctoral dissertation, University of Virginia, Charlottesville.

Björk, L. G. (1993). Effective schools—effective superintendents: The emerging instructional leadership role. *Journal of School Leadership, 3*(3), 246–259.

Björk, L. G. (2001). Institutional barriers to educational reform: A superintendent's role in district decentralization. In C. C. Brunner & L. G. Björk (Eds.), *The new superintendency* (pp. 205–228). New York: JAI.

Björk, L., & Gurley, D. K. (2003). *Superintendent as educational statesman.* Paper presented at the annual meeting of the American Educational Research Association, Chicago.

Björk, L., & Lindle, J. C. (2001). Superintendents and interest groups. *Educational Policy, 15*(1), 76–91.

Blase, J., & Anderson, G. (1995). *The micropolitics of educational leadership: From control to empowerment.* New York: Teachers College Press.

Blumberg, A. (1985). *The school superintendent: Living with conflict.* New York: Teachers College Press.

Bracey, G. W. (2003). PIRLS before the press. *Phi Delta Kappan, 84,* 795.

Bredeson, P. V. (1996). Superintendents' roles in curriculum development and instructional leadership: Instructional visionaries, collaborators, supporters, and delegators. *Journal of School Leadership, 6*(3), 243–264.

Broad Foundation & Thomas B. Fordham Institute (2003). *Better leaders for America's schools: A manifesto.* Los Angeles, CA: Authors.

Burroughs, W. A. (1974). *Cities and schools in the gilded age.* Port Washington, NY: Kennikat.

Callahan, R. E. (1962). *Education and the cult of efficiency: A study of the social forces that have shaped the administration of public schools.* Chicago: University of Chicago Press.

Callahan, R. E. (1966). *The superintendent of schools: A historical analysis.* East Lansing, MI: National Center for Research on Teacher Learning. (ERIC Document Reproduction Service No. ED0104410)

Carlson, R. V. (1996). *Reframing and reform: Perspectives on organization, leadership, and school change*. New York: Longman.

Carter, G. R., & Cunningham, W. G. (1997). *The American school superintendent: Leading in an age of pressures*. San Francisco: Jossey-Bass.

Chance, P. L., & Björk, L. G. (2004). The social dimensions of public relations. In T. J. Kowalski (Ed.), *Public relations in schools* (3rd ed., pp. 125–148). Upper Saddle River, NJ: Merrill, Prentice Hall.

Coleman, P., & LaRocque, L. 1990. *Struggling to be good enough: Administrative practices and district ethos*. London: Falmer.

Conrad, C. (1994*). Strategic organizational communication: Toward the twenty-first century* (3rd ed.). Fort Worth, TX: Harcourt Brace College Publishers.

Cooper, B. S., & Boyd, W. L. (1987). The evolution of training for school administrators. In J. Murphy & P. Hallinger (Eds.), *Approaches to administrative training in education* (pp. 3–27). Albany: State University of New York Press.

Counts, G. S. (1952). *Education and American civilization*. New York: Teachers College Press.

Cronin, J. M. (1973). *The control of urban schools: Perspective on the power of educational reformers*. New York: Free Press.

Crowson, R. L., & McPherson, R. B. (1987). The legacy of the theory movement: Learning from the new tradition. In J. Murphy & P. Hallinger (Eds.), *Approaches to administrative training in education* (pp. 45–64). Albany: State University of New York Press.

Cuban, L. (1976). *The urban school superintendent: A century and a half of change*. Bloomington, IN: Phi Delta Kappa Educational Foundation.

Cuban, L. (1988). How schools change reforms: Redefining reform success and failure. *Teachers College Record, 99*(3), 453–477.

Culbertson, J. A. (1981). Antecedents of the theory movement. *Educational Administration Quarterly, 17*(1), 25–47.

Davis, S. H. (1998). Why do principals get fired? *Principal, 28*(2), 34–39.

Doyle, D. P. (2002). Knowledge-based Decision making. *School Administrator, 59*(11), 30–34.

Drucker, P. F. (1999). *Management challenges for the 21st century*. New York: HarperCollins.

Dyrli, O. E., & Kinnaman, D. E. (1994). Preparing for the integration of emerging technologies. *Technology and Learning, 14*(9), 92, 94, 96, 98, 100.

Eaton, W. E. (1990). The vulnerability of school superintendents: The thesis reconsidered. In W. E. Eaton (Ed.). *Shaping the superintendency: A reexamination of Callahan and the cult of efficiency* (pp. 11–35). New York: Teachers College Press.

Elmore, R. F. (1999–2000). Building a new structure for school leadership. *American Educator, 23*(4), 6–13.

Fullan, M. G. (1996). Turning systemic thinking on its head. *Phi Delta Kappan, 77*(6), 420–423.

Fusarelli, B. C., & Fusarelli, L. D. (2003, November). *Preparing future superintendents to be applied social scientists*. Paper presented at the annual conference of the University Council for Educational Administration, Portland, Oregon.

Glass, T. E. (2003). *The superintendency: A managerial imperative?* Paper presented at the annual meeting of the American Educational Research Association, Chicago.

Getzels, J. W. (1977). Educational administration twenty years later, 1954–1974. In L. Cunningham, W. Hack, & R. Nystrand (Eds.), *Educational administration: The developing decades* (pp. 3–24). Berkeley, CA: McCutchan.

Gideon, B. H. (2002). Structuring schools for teacher collaboration. *Education Digest, 68*(2), 30–34.

Hanson, E. M. (2003). *Educational administration and organizational behavior* (6th ed.). Boston: Allyn & Bacon.

Heckman, P. E. (1993). School restructuring in practice: Reckoning with the culture of school. *International Journal of Educational Reform, 2*(3), 263–272.

Henkin, A. B. (1993). Social skills of superintendents: A leadership requisite in restructured schools. *Educational Research Quarterly, 16*(4), 15–30.

Herman, J. L. (1990). *Instructional leadership skills and competencies of public school superintendents: Implications of preparation programs in a climate of shared governance.* East Lansing, MI: National Center for Research on Teacher Learning. (ERIC Document Reproduction Service No. ED328980)

Hess, F. M. (1998). The urban reform paradox. *American School Board Journal, 185*(2), 24–27.

Hess, F. M. (2003). *A license to lead? A new leadership agenda for America's schools.* Washington, DC: Progressive Policy Institute.

Howlett, P. (1993). The politics of school leaders, past and future. *Education Digest, 58*(9), 18–21.

Johnson, B. C., & Fusarelli, L. D. (2003, April). *Superintendent as social scientist.* Paper presented at the annual meeting of the American Educational Research Association, Chicago.

Kearsley, G. (1990). *Computers for educational administration.* Norwood, NJ: Ablex.

Keedy, J. L., & Björk, L. G. (2002). Superintendents and local boards and the potential for community polarization: The call for use of political strategist skills. In B. Cooper & L. Fusarelli (Eds.), *The promises and perils facing today's school superintendent* (pp. 103–128). Lanham, MD: Scarecrow Education.

Kellogg Foundation (1961). *Toward improved school administration: A decade of professional effort to heighten administrative understanding and skills.* Battle Creek, MI: Author.

Kowalski, T. J. (1995). *Keepers of the flame: Contemporary urban superintendents.* Thousand Oaks, CA: Corwin Press.

Kowalski, T. J. (1997). School reform, community education, and the problem of institutional culture. *Community Education Journal, 25*(3–4), 5–8.

Kowalski, T. J. (1998). The role of communication in providing leadership for school reform. *Mid-Western Educational Researcher, 11*(1), 32–40.

Kowalski, T. J. (1999). *The school superintendent: Theory, practice, and cases.* Upper Saddle River, NJ: Merrill, Prentice Hall.

Kowalski, T. J. (2000). Cultural change paradigms and administrator communication. *Contemporary Education, 71*(2), 5–10.

Kowalski, T. J. (2001). The future of local school governance: Implications for board members and superintendents. In C. Brunner & L. Björk (Eds.), *The new superintendency* (pp. 183–201). Oxford, UK: JAI, Elsevier Science.

Kowalski, T. J. (2003a). *Contemporary school administration* (2nd ed.). Boston: Allyn & Bacon.

Kowalski, T. J. (2003b, April). *The superintendent as communicator.* Paper presented at the annual meeting of the American Educational Research Association, Chicago.

Kowalski, T. J. (2004). School public relations: A new agenda. In T. J. Kowalski (Ed.), *Public relations in schools* (3rd ed., pp. 3–29). Upper Saddle River, NJ: Merrill, Prentice Hall.

Kowalski, T. J., Björk, L. G., & Otto, D. (2004, February). *Role expectations of the district superintendent: Implications for deregulating preparation and licensing.* Paper presented at the Annual Conference of the American Association of School Administrators, San Francisco.

Kowalski, T. J., & Brunner, C. C. (2005). The school superintendent: Roles, challenges, and issues. In F. English (Ed.), *The Sage handbook of educational leadership* (pp. 142–167). Thousand Oaks, CA: Sage.

Leithwood, K., Jantzi, D., & Fernandez, A. (1994). Transformational leadership and teachers' commitment to change. In J. Murphy & K. S. Louis (Eds.), *Reshaping the principalship* (pp. 77–98). Thousand Oaks, CA: Corwin Press.

Lipinski, A. J. (1978). Communicating the future. *Futures, 19*(2), 126–127.

Lutz, F. W. (1996). Viability of the vulnerability thesis. *Peabody Journal of Education, 71*(2), 96–109.

Manheimer, R. & Manning, R. C. (1995). System leaders apply research in their decision making. *School Administrator, 52*(6), 17–18.

Melby, E. O. (1955). *Administering community education.* Englewood Cliffs, NJ: Prentice Hall.

Morgan, C., & Petersen, G. J. (2002). The superintendent's role in leading academically effective school districts. In B. S. Cooper & L. D. Fusarelli (Eds.). *The promise and perils of the modern superintendency* (pp. 175–196). Lanham, MD: Scarecrow Press.

Murphy, J. (1991). *Restructuring schools.* New York: Teachers College Press.

Murphy, J. (1992). *The landscape of leadership preparation: Reframing the education of school administrators.* Newbury Park, CA: Corwin.

Murphy, J. (1994). The changing role of the superintendency in restructuring districts in Kentucky. *School Effectiveness and School Improvement, 5*(4), 349–375.

Murphy, J. (2002). Reculturing the profession of educational leadership: New blueprints. *Educational Administration Quarterly, 38*(2), 176–191.

Murphy, J., & Hallinger, P. (1986). The superintendent as instructional leader: Findings from effective school districts. *Journal of Educational Administration, 24*(2), 213–236.

National Center for Education Statistics (2004). *Number of public school districts enrollment, by size of district.* Retrieved February 1, 2004, from http://nces.ed.gov/programs/digest/d02/tables/PDF/table88.pdf

National Commission on Excellence in Education (1983). *A nation at risk: Imperative for reform.* Washington, DC: U.S. Government Printing Office.

Negroni, P. (2000). A radical role for superintendents. *School Administrator, 57*(8), 16–19.

Parsons, T., & Shils, E. A. (Eds.) (1951). *Toward a general theory of action.* Cambridge, MA: Harvard University Press.

Perina, K. (2002). When CEOs self-destruct. *Psychology Today, 35*(5), 16.

Petersen, G. J. (2002). Singing the same tune: Principal's and school board member's perceptions of the superintendent's role in curricular and instructional leadership. *Journal of Educational Administration 40*(2), 158–171.

Petersen, G. J., & Barnett, B. G. (2003, April). *The superintendent as instructional leader: History, evolution and future of the role.* Paper presented at the annual meeting of the American Educational Research Association, Chicago.

Peterson, K. D., Murphy, J., & Hallinger, P. (1987). Superintendents' perceptions of the control and coordination of the technical core in effective school districts. *Educational Administration Quarterly, 23*(1), 79–95.

Peterson, M. R. (1999). *Superintendent competencies for continued employment as perceived by Louisiana public school superintendents and board presidents.* Unpublished doctoral dissertation, University of Southern Mississippi, Hattiesburg.

Rice, J. M. (1893). *The public school system of the United States.* New York: The Century Company.

Riehl, C. (2000). The principal's role in creating inclusive schools for diverse students: A review of normative, empirical, and critical literature on the practice of educational administration. *Review of Educational Research, 70*(1), 55–81.

Sarason, S. B. (1996). *Revisiting the culture of the school and the problem of change.* New York: Teachers College Press.

Schein, E. H. (1996). Culture: The missing concept in organization studies. *Administrative Science Quarterly, 41*(2), 229–240.

Schlechty, P. C. (1997). *Inventing better schools.* San Francisco: Jossey-Bass.

Spring, J. H. (1994). *The American school, 1642–1993* (3rd ed.). New York: McGraw-Hill.

Streitmatter, J. (1994). *Toward gender equity in the classroom: Everyday teachers' beliefs and practices.* Albany: State University of New York Press.

Thomas, W. B., & Moran, K. J. (1992). Reconsidering the power of the superintendent in the progressive period. *American Educational Research Journal, 29*(1), 22–50.

Thwing, C. F. (1898). A new profession. *Educational Review, 25.*

Trimble, K. (1996). Building a learning community. *Equity and Excellence in Education, 29*(1), 37–40.

Tyack, D. (1974). The "one best system": A historical analysis. In H. Walberg & A Kopan (Eds.), *Rethinking urban education* (pp. 231–246). San Francisco: Jossey-Bass.

Tyack, D., & Hansot, E. (1982). *Managers of virtue: Public school leadership in America, 1820–1980.* New York: Basic Books.

Van Til, W. (1971). Prologue: Is progressive education obsolete? In W. Van Til (Ed.), *Curriculum: Quest for relevance* (pp. 9–17). Boston: Houghton-Mifflin.

Wert-Gray, S., Center, C., Brashers, D. E., & Meyers, R. A. (1991). Research topics and methodological orientations in organizational communication: A decade of review. *Communication Studies, 42*(2), 141–154.

Willower, D. J., & Forsyth, P. B. (1999). A brief history of scholarship in educational administration. In J. Murphy & K. Seashore Louis (Eds.), *Handbook of research on educational administration* (2nd ed.) (pp. 1–24). San Francisco: Jossey-Bass.

Wirt, F. M., & Kirst, M. W. (2001). *The political dynamics of American education* (2nd ed.). Berkeley, CA: McCutchan.

Zigarelli, M. A. (1996). An empirical test of conclusions from effective schools research. *Journal of Educational Research, 90*(2), 103–110.

CHAPTER 3

Conditions of Practice

KEY FACETS OF THE CHAPTER

- ○ New philosophical perspective on education
- ○ An evolving social landscape
- ○ Dissatisfaction with public education
- ○ Expecting public schools to do more with less
- ○ Status of local school districts
- ○ Organizational resistance to change

Organizational change can be initiated internally or externally. That is to say, it can emanate from persons within the organization or from persons outside the organization. In the case of public elementary and secondary education, the impetus to refashion organizational structure or operations has been predominately external; most significant changes that have occurred in districts and schools have been imposed, typically by legislation or legal decisions. Consider the following examples of such external interventions:

- *Federal legislation*—laws affecting all public institutions (e.g., the Civil Rights Act) and laws affecting schools specifically (e.g., No Child Left Behind Act)
- *State legislation*—laws or policies requiring school district compliance (e.g., outcome-based accountability programs and mandatory achievement testing)

- *Litigation*—landmark court decisions involving school desegregation (e.g., *Brown v. Board of Education*)
- *Changing societal conditions*—social problems that affect educational needs (e.g., poverty, teenage pregnancies, crime)
- *Changing political conditions*—problems that affect the distribution of power and allocation of resources (e.g., election of new school board members, failed funding referenda requiring reductions)

Because much of the consequential change in public education has been initiated and sustained by external forces, educators traditionally have not been socialized or prepared academically to assume responsibility for adapting their work environments to evolving societal needs (Hall & Hord, 2001). As a result, public schools are reactionary institutions, which standing is a disadvantage with respect to school reform.

Local school districts are vulnerable to external interventions because they are both public and political institutions. Their mission, structure, and operating procedures can be affected either by the actions of other governmental agencies or by local taxpayer decisions. In light of this political exposure, context is extremely important to understanding why school districts are at the same time similar and unique (Kowalski, 2005). Whereas they are uniformly established and structured by state laws, community context, district policies, and organizational climate are idiosyncratic (Hoyle, Björk, Collier, & Glass, 2004). Therefore, programs or administrative behaviors that are highly successful in one school district can be ineffective in other districts—a reality that serves to remind us of the shortcomings of using uniform intensification mandates to improve schools across an entire state.

This chapter explores the more significant conditions framing the context of contemporary practice for superintendents. It provides an understanding of contextual variability. The first part addresses changing social contexts, including philosophical perspectives, demographic conditions, dissatisfaction, and evolving expectations. The second part addresses workplace contexts, including the size and distribution of school districts and the nexus between organizational climate and resistance to change.

CHANGING SOCIAL CONDITIONS

During the formative years of public education, the concept of the common school was widely accepted. But as America opened its doors to immigrants at the end of the 19th century, thoughtful leaders such as John Dewey (1899) discerned that increased diversity would lead to disagreements over the purpose and content of public education. Power elites, however, saw diversity not as an asset but as a threat. Instead of allowing school districts to develop in relation to their distinctive needs, state policymakers were adamant that public education should acculturate immigrant children to values and beliefs of the white, Anglo-Saxon, Protestant majority (Spring, 1990). By pursuing the strategy of a common state curriculum, they forged public schools as agencies of control, a status that made them resistant to change and incapable of playing an instrumental role in building a new social order (Burroughs, 1974).

New Philosophical Perspectives

Prior to 1960, graduation rates were a relatively unimportant statistic for judging public education's effectiveness because most students who left school prematurely were able to gain meaningful employment. Factory jobs were plentiful and most taxpayers were satisfied if their local schools simply provided basic skills, structure, and discipline. Public elementary and secondary education essentially served as a sorting mechanism, culling from the cohort those who did not show academic promise, those who did not have the economic means to continue their education, and those who did not show an interest in education (Kowalski, 2003). Since the 1970s, world and national conditions have modified this temperament markedly. Emergence of a global economy and transition to an information-based society, for example, eradicated many factory jobs previously available to individuals with limited education and skills. In the aftermath of warnings that America's economic stability was being jeopardized by growing numbers of poorly educated individuals (e.g., National Commission on Excellence in Education, 1983) public school officials were pressured politically to pursue reforms.

As criticism of public elementary and secondary education increased in the early 1980s, state government began assuming a more central role in shaping reform initiatives (Mazzoni, 1994). State reforms almost always were imposed uniformly on all schools; the most common tactic during the mid-1980s was to seek improvement by requiring educators to do more of what they were already doing (e.g., increased graduation requirements, lengthened school years, longer school days). At the same time that this centralized approach was being deployed, however, the real educational needs among and within districts was becoming increasingly dissimilar. Divergent needs were produced by uneven demographic, social, political, and economic conditions. By the early 1990s, scholars studying reform efforts (e.g., Fullan, 1994) concluded that neither total centralization nor total decentralization could produce the required levels of improvement. This judgment was accompanied by advocacy for a hybrid reform strategy, one that urged state officials to set broad educational goals and to require local district officials to develop visions and plans to achieve those goals.

In a democratic society, values are the foundation of public education and the relevant criteria for judging the merits of school improvement initiatives (Stout, Tallerico, & Scribner, 1994). Clearly, then, the degree to which a community is divided by values has implications for its schools. Schlecty (1990) observed that educators have had considerable success operating public schools in communities where residents support a common value system; he also concluded that philosophical consensus had contributed to the success of many private schools. Most public school superintendents, however, do not practice in conditions of philosophical harmony. Instead, they administer in social settings where any new purpose or program they propose or support is likely to be challenged and resisted by community factions. The degree of opposition, however, has not been constant. In communities where negative political reactions have been strong, disagreement has usually been value driven. Although it is important for us to understand the nature, effects, and unevenness of philosophical disunity, this knowledge diminishes neither the demand for change nor the reality that public education is unlikely to improve unless meaningful reforms are implemented (Schlecty, 1990).

Evolving Social Landscape

Student learning is affected by a myriad of variables including family and community. The truth is that a growing number of students enter public schools already at risk of being educational casualties. If administrators, teachers, and policymakers do not understand social conditions affecting student learning, or if they choose to ignore them, the prospects for needed reform are reduced substantially. This is because critical school improvement steps, such as visioning and long-range planning, end up being based on incomplete information. Consequently, superintendents must keep abreast of social conditions that affect the expectations and evaluations of public education.

Demographics. The profile of American society is continuing to change both in terms of race/ethnicity and of age. More than a decade ago, Huelskamp (1993) predicted that more than any other factor, "the changing demographic makeup of the student body will have a profound effect on future educational requirements" (p. 720). Two factors are responsible for America becoming more ethnically and racially diverse: increased levels of immigration and higher birth rates in most minority groups. The federal government now considers race and Hispanic origin to be separate and distinct concepts, making direct comparisons between 2000 census data and previous census data difficult. Even so, it is clear that the percentage of population classified within racial and ethnic minorities has increased and the rate of increase has been accelerating. In 2000, approximately 98% of the population reported only one race. Within this group, 75% reported being White alone and 12% reported Black or African American alone. Approximately, 13% of the population indicated that they were Hispanic or Latino (U.S. Census Bureau, 2004).

The distribution of students of color across the states is clearly disproportionate. In several southern states, such as Mississippi, South Carolina, and Louisiana, African American students account for approximately half of the public school population (56%, 44%, and 41%, respectively) but in nine other states, they account for less than 1%. Similarly, Hispanics constitute 25% or more of the student population in 4 states—New Mexico (45%), Texas (33%), California (27%), and Arizona (26%)—but account for less than 1% of the population in 16 other states (National Center for Educational Statistics [NCES], 2004). States that have had the fastest growth rates have tended to have the highest percentage of minority students (Hodgkinson, 1992). Increases in the number of students of color enrolled in public schools, however, have not been paralleled by similar increases in the number of minority school board members and administrators (School Leaders, 1966).

Immigrant children often bring social and economic problems to the school. In addition to language difficulties, they must overcome cultural differences, personal health problems, and poverty. Consider these facts reported by NCES (2004):

- In 2000, 36% of public school children qualified for free and reduced lunch.
- African American and Hispanic children are more than twice as likely as White children to live in poverty.
- A disproportionate number of minority students constitute the 12% of all students participating in special education programs.

A majority of minority students living in poverty reside in large urban school districts that have been primary targets of critics for at least the last 25 years primarily because of poor student performance on state achievement tests (Glass, 2004). Jenks and Peterson (1991) claim that the recently created social underclass in America does not fit the traditional definition of a lower class. Many in the underclass lack job skills or the social skills necessary to retain a job. Most noteworthy here, a significant percentage of those in this underclass are students in public schools (Jenks & Phillips, 1998).

Age also is a noteworthy variable with respect to public education. According to the most recent national census, the median age in 2000 was 35.3, three years greater than it was in 1990 and the highest it has ever been. In 1990, residents younger than age 5 years constituted 7.4% of the population, but in 2000, they constituted only 6.8% of the population. Although every state experienced some growth between 1990 and 2000, the levels of growth were unequal. As examples, Nevada grew 66% and Arizona grew 40% whereas North Dakota and West Virginia grew less than 1% (U.S. Census Bureau, 2004).

Age trends are important to superintendents for a number of reasons. One of the most obvious is fluctuating enrollments. Whereas some school districts are growing rapidly, others are remaining the same size, and still others are closing schools because of fewer students. These trends also have political aspects. As the average age of the population increases, so does the percentage of residents who do not have members of their immediate families enrolled in or employed by public schools. Separation can lead to alienation, which can negatively affect support for schools. Senior citizens, owning property and living on fixed incomes, are prime examples of estranged taxpayers. In this vein, Bauman (1966) wrote:

> The "graying" of America translates to increased political power among those who do not have children in school and a concomitant lessening of the proportion of voters with school-age children. The trend has direct implications for efforts to achieve excellence in the public schools that rely on broad public support. (p. 92)

Demographic changes have produced three relevant outcomes with respect to public education. First, they have made needs among states more dissimilar than ever before. Second, they have made needs among districts within individual states more dissimilar than ever before. Third, they have made it difficult for many superintendents to gain the economic and political support they need for school improvement initiatives. Thirty years ago, many superintendents could be highly successful even though they had limited contact with the general public. Now, such isolation is intolerable because administrators are expected to know the complexity of their communities so that they can engage citizens in forging school improvement plans and gain their support to fund the initiatives included in them.

Family. In the 1950s, the typical child was reared in a family consisting of a working father, a stay-at-home mother, and two or more siblings. Additionally, the child was likely to spend a considerable amount of time with grandparents and other relatives, some of whom resided in the same community. Now many school-age children are raised in a single-parent household; in the late 1990s, 25% of all children and 60% of African American children in America lived in single-parent households (Glass, 2004).

In both single- and two-parent families, an increasing number of children are facing what Sylvia Hewlett (1991) coined a "time deficit"—decreased time parents spend with children compared to previous generations. According to the Family Research Council, the amount of time parents spend with their children (about 17 hours per week) is only half the time that was spent in 1965 (Stratton, 1995). The declining quantity and quality of family life for children directly affects public education as evidenced by programs such as preschool education, social work, and expanded food services (e.g., breakfast programs). Less obvious are a host of legal and quasi-legal issues such as guardianship, access to private records by noncustodial parents, and other policies regarding parental rights and responsibilities (Duncan, 1992).

Destructive and Antisocial Behavior. The issue of antisocial behavior is more complex than most of us realize. The term is used to describe a range of destructive behaviors commonly falling into four categories: (a) situational, (b) relational, (c) predatory, and (d) psychopathological (Van Acker, 1995). Psychologists generally agree that young children are very susceptible to violence and that the violent images they see in life and on television can warp their understanding of reality (Sauerwein, 1995). This conclusion is supported by research revealing that violence is influenced by the quantity and quality of television programs watched by students (Stratton, 1995). While discussions of antisocial behavior may appear to be theoretical and abstract, the consequences have been very real for thousands of administrators and teachers who have been confronted by students who brandished weapons or threatened them in some other manner. During the 1990s, superintendents learned that critical events reported by the media had a much greater effect on public opinion of schools than did actual performance data (Pride, 2002).

Many children no longer receive moral and ethical codes from their families, communities, and churches; instead their behavioral standards are determined by a "pop" culture and peer influence. The degree and nature of negative influence often depend on other factors mentioned here—issues such as family life and poverty. Public fears about school-based violence escalated markedly in the late 1990s as a result of media accounts of multiple murders by students at all levels of education. Although most citizens now recognize that violence is ever-present in society and in schools, superintendents and principals often are unwilling to acknowledge its occurrence on their own watch. Their reluctance stems from the fear that people will boycott communities and schools perceived to be unsafe and criticize administrators in those schools for not providing adequate discipline (Schwartz, 1996). In a climate of fear produced by nationally publicized acts of violence, many school districts adopted zero-tolerance or similar policies that led to expulsion or suspension "for minor, sometimes even noncriminal acts" (Donohue, Schiraldi, & Ziedenberg, 1999, p. 8).

Public Dissatisfaction

Discussing differing conceptions of public education purposes, Philip Schlecty (1990) described three seemingly competing objectives that have shaped curriculum, instruction, and educator behavior:

1. Preserving values and beliefs of a dominant culture

2. Preparing individuals for the workforce

3. Compensating for injustice and inequity.

Through much of the 20th century, the purposes of education were dictated by external forces (i.e., forces outside of schools and school districts). And because economic, social, and political transitions in America were often extreme, schools were required to change course abruptly. Most of these sudden transitions involved the values of excellence and equity. Excellence advocates argue that schools should nourish the assets of intelligence and ability; equity advocates argue that schools should provide equalizing opportunities (Parker & Parker, 1995). From roughly the mid-1950s to the present, rival values have shaped proposed reforms with the result that approaches to school improvement have been inconsistent. Commenting about the beginning of this era, Van Til (1971) wrote:

> With the launching of the Russian Sputnik in 1957, American social hysteria increased, and the schools proved to be a handy scapegoat. Magazines called for the closing of the "carnival" in the schools; intellectual leaders who had not been in an elementary or secondary school since their own graduations loftily condemned the schools for a lack of academic rigor. (p. 3)

Anxiety about the nation's security produced dissatisfaction with the social order. The passage of the National Defense Education Act of 1958 pushed schools toward a concept of academic excellence by advocating the more rigorous study of mathematics, science, and foreign language (Kowalski, 1981). But just a few years after schools were pushed in this direction, policymakers adopted a new political agenda as the government faced new issues such as civil rights, poverty, mounting racial tensions, and an unpopular war in Vietnam. Again the social order was disrupted, but this time, alienation, disillusionment, and distrust of government took center stage (Van Til, 1971). Much of the blame for society's imperfections was directed toward public elementary and secondary education; in the aftermath, the agenda of excellence was quickly displaced by an agenda of equity.

Reform efforts initiated during the 1970s and 1980s, however, again tipped the scales in favor of excellence. First, the "back-to-basics" movement, and then repercussions of the stinging condemnations included in the report *A Nation at Risk*, called for schools to set higher requirements and expectations. Compared to equity, excellence has been open-ended and difficult to define (Duke, 2004). In relation to school reform, the value has had two primary foci: instructional rigor and high academic standards. In the early to mid-1980s, for example, state policymakers sought to improve schooling by requiring students to do more of what they were already doing—raising graduation requirements, requiring students to take more courses in mathematics, science, and English, and extending the amount of time students attended school were characteristic of these intensification mandates. Efforts to enhance excellence, however, again sparked equity concerns; for instance, the increased requirements discouraged some marginal students to drop out of school believing that high school graduation had become improbable.

The predictable tension between excellence and equity has not resulted in one value being declared more important than the other. Each is supported in American society and rather than selecting one over the other, the preference has been to pursue both. Although parameters for achieving the necessary compromises associated with this objective have been neither clear nor consistent, the consequences have been discernible. The failure of local school boards and superintendents to balance excellence and equity has prompted state government to exercise power by imposing educational goals and the means by which they will be achieved (Bauman, 1996). Table 3.1 provides several examples of reform initiatives that have produced tensions between these values.

More recently, the federal government has assumed an active role in trying to balance excellence and equity. The No Child Left Behind Act, for example, sets district and school performance expectations (reflective of excellence) while allowing parents to transfer their children out of low-performing schools (reflective of equity). The difficulty of meeting these standards was apparent just months after the act became law; in 2003, a class action lawsuit was filed

Table 3.1   Examples of Reform-related Initiatives Creating Conflict Between Excellence and Equity

Issue	Excellence dispositions	Equity dispositions
Testing	Students must demonstrate proficiency in subject matter. Students who fail should not graduate. Schools should be judged on the basis of student test performance.	Tests often do not reveal what students really have learned. Some tests have a racial bias. Performance is often more indicative of family economic status than of the quality of education.
Charter schools	Public funds should be used to support options to traditional public schools.Competition increases school performance.	Schools of choice often separate students by wealth, race, religion, and ability. There is no evidence that competition increases school productivity.
Vouchers	Many parents are trapped in ineffective school systems. Parents and students are more committed if they have a choice in schools. Competition drives poor schools out of the market.	Vouchers will benefit families that least need them. Better schools will simply raise their tuition rates. Poor students will still be trapped and racial segregation will increase.
Full-service schools	Schools should focus on teaching and not get involved in other services.	Many students cannot succeed in school unless their psychological, social, and physiological needs are met.

against the New York City schools claiming that parents had been denied the right of transfer guaranteed under the federal law (Viteritti, 2004).

Writing about the politics of education in the 1980s, Frank Lutz and Laurence Iannaccone (1986) described *dissatisfaction theory*. They called public dissatisfaction a disease that could be predicted by monitoring changes in socioeconomic and political indicators of a community. As the illness progresses, special interest groups and others intensify efforts to influence policy; there is an increase in voter turnout for school board elections and incumbent school board members are defeated or choose not to seek another term. Ultimately, the disease causes a turnover in the superintendent's office and a disruption to the school system. The theory suggests that dissatisfaction builds over time; consequently, effective practitioners are able to identify the symptoms of discontent, to accurately measure their levels of intensity, and to understand their underlying causes. Recent research (e.g., Alsbury, 2003) reveals that the theory continues to be an effective tool for understanding instability in school districts.

In a perfect world, public opinion about education is predicated on a set of commonly accepted goals, and success is determined by an objective assessment of progress toward these purposes. Unfortunately, not even the first element, consensus of purpose, has been achieved. Consequently, perceptions formed in the arena of public opinion often are shaped by self-interests and secondhand information supplied by the media or special interest groups (Kowalski, 2001). At best, we know that America accepts two broad goals for public education: to serve the individual and to serve society. These are often described as the private and social missions for schools (Bauman, 1996).

Many Americans overlook the fact that more students today are staying in school and graduating. And while some contend they are not learning what they should learn, compared with past decades, "schools are surely doing no less" (Schlecty, 1990, p. 30). In truth, the "good old days" often are exaggerated. Contemporary critics exhibit a proclivity to focus solely on students who succeeded when they look back and to focus solely on students who did not when they look at the present. They also have ignored the fact that the development of morals, ethics, and civic responsibility occurred more naturally in the first half of the 20th century (Finn, 1991). Families, churches, neighborhoods, and other social units actively addressed the needs of youth and the positive effects of these interventions often were attributed to schools.

Disagreements over the social purposes of schooling can be traced to the establishment of public education in this country (Spring, 2001). Abrupt and consequential policy transformations, such as those described previously, occur because groups supporting competing values do not permanently dominate in political policymaking arenas (Cuban, 1988). As demonstrated in national and state politics, America is a diverse society both demographically and philosophically. Consequently, any public idea encouraging educational reform is resisted by some segment of society (Wirt & Kirst, 2001).

Although social reformers and economic conservatives often reach different conclusions about public education (Keedy & Björk, 2002), they share a concern that the next generation of adults will be unable to maintain the country's stature. Beneath their overt expressions of anxiety and discontent, however, many Americans still believe that better schools make a better society (Tyack & Cuban, 1995). Nevertheless, different and sometimes contradictory purposes for the schools emerge, even in small homogeneous communities, because informed superintendents and school board members seek to achieve both excellence and equity.

Expectation of Doing More With Less

Competing philosophical perspectives have produced two distinct reform agendas. First, there are those who emphasize that equity is a prerequisite to excellence. They believe that public education has a responsibility to provide all students with a reasonable opportunity for success by requiring educators to be sensitive to diversity and to compensate for the negative effects of poverty, abuse, and dysfunctional homes. In this vein, Natale (1992) wrote:

> One of the best hopes for improving children's lot in America, experts say, can be found in programs that link health, social, and instructional services under one roof—the schoolhouse roof. Inaccessibility of services—whether real or perceived—can keep children and their families from getting the help they need when they need it. (p. 26)

Social reformers (e.g., Garcia & Gonzalez, 1995; Kirst, 1994; Negroni, 1994) argue that meaningful reform should include reconceptualization of educational equity, additional programs for disadvantaged students, and coordinated efforts between schools and other community agencies. Believing that social and political issues must be infused into reform policies, they are generally guided by the following beliefs:

- There is a dual system of education in America—one for the poor and one for everyone else. School reform has not addressed the problems associated with having separate and unequal schools. Schools will remain ineffective as long as racism and poverty are ignored (Kozol, 1992).
- Business leaders have unfairly blamed schools for the nation's economic problems and it is unjust for them to expect schools to be reconstructed solely on the basis of economic goals (Schneider, 1992).
- Business leaders want to increase accountability and efficiency without increasing financial responsibility or equity. By imposing private-sector values on public schools, they undermine citizen responsibility for collective action to improve schools for all (Moffett, 1994).
- Many low-income and minority children do not adjust well to traditional schools that provide for them little continuity with their personal lives. Reform should focus on increased services and relevant experiences for disadvantaged students (Banks, 1993).

The nearly opposite reform position stems from beliefs that schools waste too much money, pay too little attention to nonacademic matters, lack discipline, are overdependent on government, and lack accountability. Advocates of this position argue that the application of business and economic principles will increase educational productivity without a corresponding increase in expenditures. Since the 1980s, advocates for "excellence through efficiency" have been the dominant political force in many states. In pursuing their agenda, they have portrayed students as lazy, educators as incompetent, and schools as inefficient bureaucracies. Their prescription for correcting these ills has been a mixture of intensification mandates and market-driven concepts intended to require public schools to compete for students. Vouchers, tuition tax credits, and charter schools exemplify strategies intended to push public schools away from government protection and into the marketplace where they would have to be competitive to survive (Cobb, 1992). Privatizing public schools appeals to large segments of society because it requires little or no sacrifice from taxpayers (Jacob, 2003). Such conservative critiques of public education since the early 1970s have not been peculiar to the United States; similar criticisms were voiced in Canada and Great Britain (Elliott & MacLennan, 1994).

Many who rely entirely on economic perspectives to identify academic shortcomings feel that the sole purpose of schools is to prepare dutiful workers. They charge that corporate America is paying dearly for insufficiently educated workers (e.g., Groennings, 1992). Being preoccupied with economic issues, these critics (a) are usually indifferent to moral and political contexts that extend beyond the acquisition of knowledge (Soder, 1995); (b) believe national economic problems constitute a sufficient reason for school reform (Ehrlich, 1988); (c) see evolutionary change as ineffective and demand radical reforms similar to those carried out by major corporations such as General Motors during the 1970s and 1980s (e.g., Shreve & Lidell, 1992); and (d) express pessimism about the ability and willingness of school administrators to lead a significant reform movement. Based on these dispositions, they favor strategies that impose change on schools.

Critics who combine economics, politics, and religion come at the problem somewhat differently. The Christian Right, for instance, refocused its efforts from issues such as secular humanism to topics having wider appeal during the 1980s such as multiculturalism, sex education, and outcomes-based education (Jones, 1993). Observing the growing influence of the Religious Right, George Kaplan (1994) concluded that their work had been energized by a pervasive belief that schools were failing and they had become more powerful by skillfully targeting problems that concerned most Americans.

WORKPLACE CONDITIONS

Practice in the superintendency is affected by both societal and workplace circumstances. In both contexts, politics is pervasive, thus the political issues are addressed throughout this book. In relation to school reform, however, two other workplace variables are highly influential. The first involves the continuing trend toward fewer but larger organizations in public education; the second pertains to an organizational climate resistant to change.

Status of School Districts

   Two factors highly relevant to current conditions in local school systems are their declining numbers and their contextual variability across and within states. In 1985, 39.4 million students were enrolled in public elementary and secondary schools; in 2000, that figure had increased to 47.2 million—approximately a 20% increase in that period. Yet, the number of school districts in America has continued to decline. In 1937, there were 119,001, in 1963 there were 35,676, and in 2001 there were 14,859. Less than 2% of the nation's school systems, however, have 25,000 or more students; 71% enroll fewer than 2,500 students; even more noteworthy, 48% enroll fewer than 1,000 students (National Center for Education Statistics [NCES], 2004). The decline in the number of local school districts is attributable almost entirely to school district consolidation in states that historically have had many small-enrollment districts (e.g., Illinois and Nebraska) (Ramirez, 1992).

   School district mergers, especially when coerced by state government, almost always have produced resentment; and if the mergers resulted in closing some schools, the level of bitterness was pronounced. School consolidation has been a contentious and highly emotional issue. Opposition to consolidation has been based on a mix of social, political, and economic concerns. From a social perspective, residents in small and rural districts often opposed consolidation because their school, the center of the community's identity and pride, was scheduled to be closed (Ornstein, 1993). From a political perspective, taxpayers often objected to what they perceived as a loss of power. In very small districts, residents have had more access to and influence over school board members—a condition that allowed them to protect personal interests (e.g., influencing tax rates or influencing employment decisions). From an economic perspective, school closings have been viewed negatively in relation to community development; that is, removing a school from the community often has had a detrimental influence on the future growth of taxable property.

In light of such opposition, it is reasonable to ask: Why has school district consolidation continued in many states?

Arguments favoring consolidation usually are grounded in several pervasive values that have guided education policy. They include *adequacy* (ensuring that all students receive an adequate level of education), *equality* (ensuring that all students receive reasonably equal educational opportunity), *fraternity* (ensuring that students experience and appreciate diversity and its treatment in a democratic society), and *economic development* (ensuring that schools contribute effectively to the nation's welfare) (King, Swanson, & Sweetland, 2003; Kowalski, 2003). Table 3.2 outlines the more persuasive reasons why school consolidation remains a cogent issue in some states.

Opposition to consolidation almost always has been based on another cherished value—*liberty*. Critics argue that large school districts restrict democratic participation and alienate many taxpayers who believe that ability to influence policy has been diminished (Kowalski, 2003; Post & Stambach, 1999). Recent resistance, however, has been centered on the educational merits of the guiding principle that "bigger is better." Consolidation critics point out that large school districts usually operate large schools—institutions that they believe are prone to being cold and uncaring. Moreover, some researchers (e.g., Skandera & Sousa, 2001) have found an inverse relationship between school size and parental involvement; as schools get larger, parental participation declines. Noting that there is less-than-convincing evidence that larger districts have a positive effect on student learning (Howley, 1997; Ramirez, 1992), they argue that policymakers have paid far too little attention to potential social and personal problems thought to be more prevalent in larger schools (e.g., alienation, value conflicts).

In addition to a declining number of school districts nationally, variability among states is another important dimension of local districts. As an example, Hawaii is the only state to have a single public school system. Several other states (e.g., Florida, Kentucky, Louisiana, and Nevada) have only one school district in each county. States that have a high number of small-enrollment districts (i.e., with fewer than 1,000 pupils) are predominately rural (e.g., Maine, Montana, Nebraska, Oklahoma, South Dakota, and Vermont). States also differ markedly in total expenditures per pupil; in 2000, for example, New Jersey's per pupil expenditure was 217% greater than Utah's per pupil expenditure (NCES, 2004).

Consolidation is still an issue in states that continue to operate many small districts. Mergers are also possible in urban areas where problems plaguing big-city districts can result in state government legislating these organizations out of existence (the districts would essentially be divided into pieces that are

Table 3.2   Examples of Guiding Values, Reasons, and Rationale for School Consolidation

Guiding Value	Specific Reason	Rationale
Equality	Equalization of wealth	School districts in most states vary markedly in taxable wealth; litigation and political action have resulted in efforts to neutralize the effects of wealth disparities. Having fewer but larger districts has been one option for moving in this direction.
	Equalization of opportunity	Curriculum variability often is attributable to school size; eliminating very small schools has been justified on the grounds of providing more equal educational opportunities among and within school districts.
Efficiency	Reducing operating costs	Large schools have been considered more efficient than small schools. Consolidation has been justified on the grounds that mergers reduce operating costs, including those associated with personnel.
	Economies of scale	By purchasing goods and services in larger volumes, school districts operate more efficiently and reduce per-pupil costs.
Adequacy	Expanded curriculum	As states increase graduation requirements to address needs of an information-based, high technology society, consolidation has been promoted on the grounds that some students will not have access to an adequate level of education in very small schools.
	Increased individualization	Providing adequate levels of education for all students has been problematic in some programs such as special education. Mergers have been promoted on the grounds that fewer but larger schools make it more likely that all students will receive the minimal level of required education.
Fraternity	Living in a multicultural society	Consolidation proponents have argued that larger schools are better suited to develop an understanding of living in a multicultural democratic society.
Economic development	Increasing education outputs	Some proponents have cast consolidation as an investment in human capital. They argue that students in larger schools have greater access to technology, a broad curriculum, and a more diversified faculty— attributes they associate with increased school productivity and national economic growth.

annexed by their contiguous suburban districts) (Kowalski, 1995). Overall, however, you should understand that conditions among and within states are not uniform. Moreover, you should recognize that variability reduces the accuracy of generalizations about local districts and about the roles superintendents assume in them.

Resistance to Change

One question frequently asked of superintendents is: Why has school reform been unsuccessful? This query is difficult to answer because of contextual variability; that is, reasons may differ from state to state, district to district, and even school to school. In general, however, there are certain factors that help us understand why meaningful changes are elusive.

- Educators tend to frame educational problems and develop policy largely from the perspective of social theories whereas many policymakers and legislators frame problems from the perspective of economic theories (Boyd, 1992). Thus, changes imposed on schools through statewide policies and laws do not necessarily affect the minds and hearts of educators.
- The American public has always had difficulty reaching consensus on the primary purposes of schooling (Wagner, 1993). Compromises reached in conjunction with past reforms often paper over the basic conflicts between competing values such as equity and excellence (Tyack & Cuban, 1995).
- Both public discontent and claims about the nature and severity of educational deficits have been common throughout this country's history (Harris, Hunt, & Lalik, 1986). Often policymakers and legislators mistakenly interpret this recurring condition as a unique mandate for radical change. For many parents, reform is necessary until they and their children are placed on the receiving end of it.
- The persistence of bureaucratic-like structure in many school districts reflects the fact that schools were designed to be agencies of control rather than agencies of change. Neither academic preparation nor incentives in the workplace encourage administrators to assume change agent roles (Kowalski, 2003).
- Rather than being expressions of citizen trusteeship, reform debates typically have been dominated by power elites who "have tried to persuade the public that their definition of problems and proposed solutions were authoritative" (Tyack & Cuban, 1995, p. 59). Hence, change initiatives often lack a broad base of support.

Writing about the pursuit of school reform, Haberman (1994) wrote:

The basic condition preventing significant school change is that the public doesn't want it. Using demography as a scare tactic to make the public more amenable to change doesn't work either, because there are no explicit connections made between the reforms proposed and the statistical horrors used to state the problem. (p. 692)

For the superintendent on the firing line, public discontent, excellence/equity dialectic, and demands for change have spawned a hydra-headed monster. Politically, administrators have been pushed by business and government leaders to make schools more effective and efficient and pulled by their profession, fellow educators, and their consciences to ensure that schools offer equal opportunities for every student. Unlike their business counterparts, superintendents face more explicit legal constraints, a high dependency on government for resources, less decision-making authority, and more intensive external political influences. Their decisions are judged by a public that seldom agrees on what the decisions should be (Shibles, Rallis, & Deck, 2001).

What are the consequences of these conditions? Insightful practitioners realize that excellence must be pursued without sacrificing equity. To do this, superintendents must create environments encouraging an informed and thoughtful exchange of ideas about the purposes of public education and how those purposes can be achieved in individual districts and schools (Wagner, 1993). The moral tone for governance in this process—that is, the climate in which goal setting and planning occur—is set by superintendents and school boards. Therefore, these officials often determine the dispositions toward and scope of school improvement efforts. School district employees, students, and other community members "know what is expected by seeing what is inspected and respected" (Schlecty, 1992, p. 28).

In 1971, Yale University psychologist Seymour Sarason published a thought-provoking book about public schools, *The Culture of School and the Problem of Change* (1971). After visiting schools across the nation, he concluded that the striking similarities in the roles of teachers and students across the nation were attributable to a culture that had been imposed on all public schools. Externally imposed mandates often failed to achieve their purpose, he argued, because they ignored the deeply held values and beliefs that caused teachers and administrators in rural Idaho to behave much like teachers and administrators in inner-city Boston. After again touring schools and revisiting his thesis 25 years later, Sarason (1996) remained pessimistic that educators could produce needed reforms. He found classroom structures and activities still lacking almost all the hallmarks of productive learning. In large measure, he blamed the inertia on the passivity of educators. He criticized them for not engaging in the professional responsibility of reading journals and books. Most noteworthy, he judged that internally driven change was highly unlikely because administrators and teachers understood neither organizational culture nor the process of organizational change. He also criticized them for not engaging in meaningful dialogue about their practice:

> What I find discouraging and even frightening is that school personnel rarely (if ever) raise and seriously discuss two questions. What is the over-arching purpose of schooling, a purpose which if not realized makes the attainment of other purposes unlikely, if not impossible? What are the characteristics of contexts for productive learning? (p. 379).

He adds that it is both surprising and inexcusable that the education profession has not focused on those queries.

While many educators may believe that Professor Sarason's analysis is overly pessimistic and condemning of them, few take issue with his judgment that the American public is extremely impatient. Clearly, the public has become increasingly less confident that administrators and teachers can restructure schools; as a result, they have become increasingly impatient.

FOR FURTHER REFLECTION

The landscape of practice for most school superintendents has changed markedly over the past 50 years. Today, there are fewer districts with more heterogeneous populations and schools have to respond to a growing number of social, economic, and political problems. Poverty may well be the most debilitating circumstance affecting young children in America. In the eyes of many Americans, schools have become unsafe places where expectations for learning are declining.

Not surprisingly, such perceptions spawn concern about the welfare of the nation. Are our public schools preparing students sufficiently? Will our country's economic and political stature suffer in future generations? There is growing evidence that many Americans are dissatisfied with the productivity of public education; their discontent prompts many of them to support, or at least passively accept, radical reform proposals. Pressures to reconfigure public schools or to make them compete with private schools come at a time when many taxpayers no longer have family members attending elementary and secondary education. Under these circumstances, it is not uncommon for communities to paradoxically support reform ideas but to oppose the tax increases necessary to implement them.

1. To what extent has the population in your state become more diverse? What factors contribute to diversity in your state?

2. How has diversity affected programming in local districts in your state?

3. What value(s) contributed to the development of more than 100,000 local districts in this country prior to World War II?

4. What value(s) contributed to school district consolidation and a substantial decline in the number of local districts?

5. To what extent are social problems creating new educational needs?

6. More than 50 years after the landmark decision *Brown v. Board of Education*, critics argue that schools remain racially segregated. Is this assessment accurate in your state? Is it accurate nationally?

7. What factors contribute to the public's dissatisfaction with elementary and secondary education?

8. Many public schools are being asked to do more with less. Why?

9. Why are excellence and equity considered competing values?

10. Have national media reports of violence and antisocial behavior affected public schools in your state? If so, in what ways?

Case Study

Following World War II, Tylerville became one of the fastest growing suburbs in the United States. By 1970, most available land had been developed into subdivisions and what remained was consumed by apartment complexes and strip malls. Located just 15 minutes from downtown Chicago, the community attracted primarily middle-class families. From 1950 to 1970, the school district constructed seven new schools, experienced a 175% increase in enrollment, and increased the number of employees by 160%. Most new employees were teachers who had recently graduated from college.

The district experienced its first enrollment decline in 1973. Over the next 13 years, the district's enrollment dropped from 11,500 to 6,400 and several school buildings were closed. In 1986, the pattern of decline was reversed. Slight increases, about

2% per year, have occurred ever since. The upturn in enrollments was attributable to changing demographics in the community. Many families who had lived in Tylerville in previous decades were moving to more affluent suburban communities. From 1975 to 2000, the percentage of students receiving free or reduced lunches in the district jumped from 6 to 42; the percentage of students living in one-parent families increased from 9 to 54; the percentage not completing high school before age 19 years increased from 12 to 36. Moreover, the population had become much more diverse racially and ethnically. In 1975, only 5% of the population identified themselves as people of color; in 2000, 63% did so. During the same period, the average age of the teachers increased from 29 to 52 years; however, the percentage of teachers of color only increased from 4 to 18.

Dr. Robert Stephan became superintendent of the Tylerville Community School District just about 1 year ago. He had served as superintendent of a 1,500-student school district in a small southern Illinois farming community. At age 43 years, he had 9 years of classroom experience, 6 years of building-level administrative experience, and 4 years of central office experience—all in smaller, predominately rural communities.

Dr. Stephan, his wife, and two children (ages 14 and 17 years) had mixed feelings about moving to the Chicago area. However, a $30,000 increase in salary, a lucrative benefit package, and the flexibility of not having to reside in the school district made the job sufficiently attractive. He also was impressed favorably with the fact that the school board had been very stable. Two of the members had served more than 20 years, 4 had served more than 12 years, and the remaining board member had served 4 years.

Of the many challenges he faced in Tylerville, Dr. Stephan considered the escalating dropout rate to be the most urgent. After getting settled into his new position, he appointed a special task force to study this problem. It consisted of three administrators and seven teachers. The task force's assignments were to determine the cause of the high dropout rate and to suggest ways to ameliorate the situation. After several months they issued these findings to Dr. Stephan:

1. The curriculum in the district's high school remained focused almost entirely on preparing students to enter colleges. Courses had changed very little in the last 25 years.

2. There was no school-to-work transition program.

3. Pregnancies and expulsions accounted for more than half of the dropouts. Although pregnant students could continue attending school, nearly two-thirds elected not to do so.

4. More than half of the students expelled for one semester never returned to school.

5. The most frequent reasons for expulsions were (a) illegal drugs, (b) excessive unexcused absences, (c) fighting or related acts of violence, and (d) alcohol-related offenses.

6. Students could attend classes at an area vocational school, but very few did so. Students received information about the vocational school but were not actively recruited to enroll there.

7. The percentage of high school graduates enrolling in 4-year colleges had dropped from a high of 73 in 1970 to a low of 38 in 2002.

8. Students did not have access to an alternative school program unless they qualified for special education.

9. Nearly half of the male students who dropped out of school in the past 3 years were allegedly members of gangs.

10. School district officials had little contact with other community agencies in the past, and the involvement of administrators and teachers in community activities was far less than it had been 25 years ago.

Based on these findings, the task force members presented three recommendations to Dr. Stephan:

1. The district should establish an alternative high school. Students expelled for disciplinary reasons should be eligible to attend this school.

2. The number of administrators and teachers who are persons of color should be increased. Students would benefit from having more Hispanic and African American role models.

3. The high school curriculum needs to be revised so that greater emphasis is given to school-to-work programs for students not planning to attend college.

The committee's findings and recommendations were discussed first with the district's administrators and then with the high school faculty and staff. The administrators were largely passive, expressing neither support nor opposition to the report. Many members of the high school faculty, however, reacted negatively. They perceived the report to be misguided. The chair of the English department and president of the local teachers union, for example, argued that the recommendations were an attempt to deal with symptoms and not underlying causes. She said, "Creating an alternative school, dumbing down the curriculum, and hiring staff on any basis other than qualifications will only make matters worse. I urge you not to support the task force recommendations."

Case Discussion Questions

1. Do you believe that changing demographics in Tylerville are relevant to the task force's findings and recommendations? Why or why not?

2. Is the dropout problem a critical issue in Tylerville? What is the basis of your answer?

3. Few administrators and teachers appear to be involved in community activities. Do you see this as a concern? Why or why not?

4. If you were the new superintendent in Tylerville instead of Dr. Stephan, what would you have done differently to address the dropout problem?

5. Evaluate the reaction of the president of the local teachers' union. How would you respond to her comment about the task force report if you were the superintendent?

6. Do you believe that there is a connection between the dropout rate and the declining percentage of students enrolling in 4-year colleges? Why or why not?

7. The task force appointed by the superintendent included only district employees. Given the nature of the problem and the context in which it exists, do you agree with his decision on the appointments? Why or why not?

8. What additional information would you want about the dropout problem if you were superintendent?

REFERENCES

Alsbury, T. L. (2003). Superintendent and school board member turnover: Political versus apolitical turnover as a critical variable in the application of the dissatisfaction theory. *Educational Administration Quarterly, 39*(5), 667–698.

Banks, C. A. (1993). Restructuring schools for equity: What we have learned in two decades. *Phi Delta Kappan, 75*(1), 42–44, 46–48.

Bauman, P. C. (1996). *Governing education: Public sector reform or privatization.* Boston: Allyn & Bacon.

Boyd, W. L. (1992). The power of paradigms: Reconceptualizing educational policy and management. *Educational Administration Quarterly, 28*(4), 504–528.

Burroughs, W. A. (1974). *Cities and schools in the gilded age.* Port Washington, NY: Kennikat.

Cobb, C. W. (1992). *Responsive schools, renewed communities.* San Francisco: Institute for Contemporary Studies Press.

Cuban, L. (1988). Why do some reforms persist? *Educational Administration Quarterly, 24*(3), 329–335.

Dewey, J. (1899). *The school and society.* Chicago: University of Chicago Press.

Donohue, E., Schiraldi, V., & Ziedenberg, J. (1999). School house hype: kids' real risks. *The Education Digest, 64*(6), 4–10.

Duke, D. (2004). *The challenges of educational change.* Boston: Allyn & Bacon.

Duncan, C. P. (1992). Parental support in schools and the changing family structure. *NASSP Bulletin, 76*(543), 10–14.

Ehrlich, E. (1988, September 19). America's schools still aren't making the grade. *Business Week* (3070), 129, 132, 134–136.

Elliott, B., & MacLennan, D. (1994). Education, modernity and neo-conservative school reform in Canada, Britain, and the U.S. *British Journal of Sociology of Education, 15*(2), 165–185.

Finn, C. E. (1991). *We must take charge.* New York: The Free Press.

Fullan, M. (1994). *Change forces: Probing the depths of educational reform.* Philadelphia: Falmer.

Garcia, E. E., & Gonzalez, R. (1995). Issues in systemic reform for culturally and linguistically diverse students. *Teachers College Record, 96*(3), 418–431.

Glass, T. (2004). Changes in society and schools. In T. J. Kowalski (Ed.), *Public relations in schools* (3rd ed., pp. 30–46). Upper Saddle River, NJ: Merrill, Prentice Hall.

Groennings, S. (1992). The politics of education. In T. Brothers (Ed.), *School reform: Business, education and government as partners* (pp. 15–16). New York: The Conference Board.

Haberman, M. (1994). The top 10 fantasies of school reformers. *Phi Delta Kappan, 75*(9), 689–692.

Hall, G. E., & Hord, S. M. (2001). *Implementing change: Patterns, principals, and potholes.* Boston: Allyn and Bacon.

Harris, L., Hunt, T., & Lalik, R. (1986). Are public schools failing? Assessing the validity of current criticisms. *Clearing House, 59*(6), 280–283.

Hewlett, S. A. (1991). *When the bough breaks: The cost of neglecting our children.* New York: Basic Books.

Hodgkinson, H. L. (1992). *A demographic look at tomorrow.* Washington, DC: Institute for Educational Leadership.

Hoyle, J., Björk, L., Collier, V., & Glass, T. (2004). *The superintendent as CEO.* Thousand Oaks, CA: Corwin.

Howley, C. (1997). Dumbing down by sizing up. *School Administrator, 54*(9), 24–26, 28, 30.

Huelskamp, R. M. (1993). Perspectives on education in America. *Phi Delta Kappan, 74*(4), 718–721.

Jacob, M. (2003). *The voucher veneer: The deeper agenda to privatize public education.* Washington, DC: People for the American Way Foundation.

Jenks, C., & Peterson, P. E. (1991). *The urban underclass.* Washington, DC: Brookings Institution Press.

Jenks, C., & Phillips, M. (1998). Black-white test score gap: Introduction. In C. Jenks & M. Phillips (Eds.), *The black-white test score gap* (pp. 1–54). Washington, DC: Brookings Institution Press.

Jones, J. L. (1993). Targets of the Right. *American School Board Journal, 180*(4), 22–29.

Kaplan, G. R. (1994). Shotgun wedding: Notes on public education's encounter with the new Christian Right. *Phi Delta Kappan, 75*(9), K1–K12.

Keedy, J. L., & Björk, L. G. (2002). Superintendents and local boards and the potential for community polarization: The call for use of political strategist skills. In B. Cooper & L. Fusarelli (Eds.), *The promises and perils facing today's school superintendent* (pp. 103–128). Lanham, MD: Scarecrow Education.

King, R. A., Swanson, A. D., & Sweetland, S. R. (2003). *School finance: Achieving high standards with equity and efficiency* (3rd ed.). Boston: Allyn & Bacon.

Kirst, M. W. (1994). Equity for children: Linking education and children's services. *Educational Policy, 8*(4), 583–590.

Kowalski, T. J. (1981). Organizational patterns for secondary school curriculum. *NASSP Bulletin, 65*(443), 1–8.

Kowalski, T. J. (1995). *Keepers of the flame: Contemporary urban superintendent.* Thousand Oaks, CA: Corwin.

Kowalski, T. J. (2001). The future of local school governance: Implications for board members and superintendents. In C. C. Brunner & L. G. Björk (Eds.), *The new superintendency* (pp. 183–201). New York: JAI.

Kowalski, T. J. (2003). *Contemporary school administration: An introduction* (2nd ed.). Boston: Allyn & Bacon.

Kowalski, T. J. (2005). *Case studies on educational administration* (4th ed.). Boston: Allyn & Bacon.

Kozol, J. (1992). Inequality and the will to change. *Equity and Choice, 8*(3), 45–47.

Lutz, F. W., & Iannaccone, L. (1986). *The dissatisfaction theory of American democracy: A guide for politics in local school districts.* East Lansing, MI: National Center for Research on Teacher Learning. (ERIC Document Reproduction Service No. ED274041)

Mazzoni, T. L. (1994). State policy-making and school reform: Influences and influentials. *Journal of Education Policy, 9*(5&6), 53–73.

Moffett, J. (1994). On to the past: Wrong-headed school reform. *Phi Delta Kappan, 75*(8), 584–590.

Natale, J. (1992). Growing up the hard way. *American School Board Journal, 179*(10), 20–27.

National Center for Education Statistics (2004). *Digest of Education Statistics, 2002.* Retrieved May 10, 2004, from http://nces.ed.gov/programs/digest/d02/tables/PDF/table88.pdf

National Commission on Excellence in Education. (1983, April). *A Nation at risk: The imperative of school reform.* Washington, DC: United States Government Printing Office.

Negroni, P. J. (1994). The transformation of America's public schools. *Equity and Excellence in Education, 27*(1), 20–27.

Ornstein, A. C. (1993). School consolidation vs. decentralization: Trends, issues, and questions. *Urban Review, 25*(2), 167–174.

Parker, F., & Parker, B. J. (1995). A historical perspective on school reform. *Educational Forum, 59*(3), 278–287.

Post, D., & Stambach, A. (1999). District consolidation and rural school closure: E pluribus unum? *Journal of Research in Rural Education, 15*(2), 106–120.

Pride, R. A. (2002). How critical events rather than performance trends shape public evaluations of the schools. *The Urban Review, 34*(2), 159–178.

Ramirez, A. (1992). *Size, cost, and quality of schools and school districts: A question of context.* East Lansing, MI: National Center for Research on Teacher Learning. (ERIC Document Reproduction Service No. ED361162)

Sarason, S. B. (1971). *The culture of the school and the problem of change.* Boston: Allyn & Bacon.

Sarason, S. B. (1996). *Revisiting "the culture of the school and the problem of change."* New York: Teachers College Press.

Sauerwein, K. (1995). Violence and young children. *Executive Educator, 17*(3), 23–26.

Schwartz, W. (1996). *An overview of strategies to reduce school violence.* East Lansing, MI: National Center for Research on Teacher Learning. (ERIC Document Reproduction Service No. ED410321)

Schlecty, P. (1990). *Schools for the twenty-first century: Leadership imperatives for educational reform.* San Francisco: Jossey-Bass.

Schlecty, P. (1992). Deciding the fate of local control. *American School Board Journal, 178*(11), 27–29.

Schneider, E. J. (1992). Beyond politics and symbolism: America's schools in the years ahead. *Equity and Excellence, 25*(2–4), 156–191.

School leaders (1996). *The American School Board Journal, 183*(12), A19–A21.

Shibles, M. R., Rallis, S. F., & Deck, L. L. (2001). A new political balance between superintendent and school board: Clarifying purpose and generating knowledge. In C. C. Brunner & L. G. Björk (Eds.), *The new superintendency* (pp. 169–182). New York: JAI.

Shreve, D. L., & Lidell, S. A. (1992). The GM school of reform. *State Legislatures, 18*(5), 39–41.

Skandera, H., & Sousa, R. (2001). Why bigger isn't better. *Hoover Digest: Research and Opinion on Public Policy,* (3), 1–5.

Soder, R. (1995). American education: Facing up to unspoken assumptions. *Daedalus, 124*(4), 163–167.

Spring, J. (1990). *The American school: 1642–1990* (2nd ed.). New York: Longman.

Spring, J. (2001). *American education* (10th ed.). New York: McGraw-Hill.

Stout, R. T., Tallerico, M., & Scribner, J. P. (1994). Values: The "what?" of the politics of education. *Journal of Education Policy, 9*(5&6), 5–20.

Stratton, J. (1995). *How students have changed.* Arlington, VA: American Association of School Administrators.

Tyack, D., & Cuban, L. (1995). *Tinkering toward utopia: A century of public school reform.* Cambridge, MA: Harvard University Press.

U.S. Census Bureau (2004). Overview of race and Hispanic origin. Retrieved May 15, 2004 from http://www.census.gov/prod/2001pubs/c2kbr01–1.pdf

Van Acker, R. (1995). A close look at school violence. *Update on Law-Related Education, 19*(2), 4–8.

Van Til, W. (1971). Contemporary criticisms of the curriculum. In W. Van Til (Ed.), *Curriculum: Quest for relevance* (pp. 1–8). Boston: Houghton Mifflin.

Viteritti, J. P. (2004). From excellence to equity: Observations on politics, history, and policy. *Peabody Journal of Education, 79*(1), 64–86.

Wagner, T. (1993). Systemic change: Rethinking the purpose of school. *Educational Leadership, 51*(1), 24–28.

Wirt, F. M., & Kirst, M. W. (2001). *The political dynamics of American education* (2nd ed.). Berkeley, CA: McCutchan.

PART II

*School Districts:
Governance and
Organization*

CHAPTER 4

School Districts as Organizations

KEY FACETS OF THE CHAPTER

○ The nature of local school districts

○ Differences among school districts

○ Organizational context of school districts

○ Organizational climate and politics in local districts

○ Centralized and decentralized authority

○ Directed autonomy and authority

The vast majority of superintendents in this country are employed as chief executives of local school districts. The concept of local districts is rooted in the value of liberty and is intended to provide citizens a considerable voice in controlling public education. Danzberger (1994), however, pointed out that there are two reasons why lay boards have become a fixture in public education:

> Local school boards are among the most venerable of U.S. public institutions, embodying many of our most cherished political and cultural tenets. One of these is a distrust of distant government that dates back to colonial times, when Americans were ruled from afar by governments that had little knowledge of the colonial experience and no knowledge of local conditions. Lay school boards are also valued because of Americans' ambivalence regarding experts and expertise. (p. 367)

Thus school boards have ensured that professional educators could not have free rein in designing and operating schools, a condition that has been debated frequently in the current reform environment (e.g., Danzberger, Kirst, & Usdan, 1992). This chapter explores the nature of school districts, the organizational aspects of school districts, and emerging ideas for reconfiguring this traditional institution.

NATURE OF LOCAL SCHOOL DISTRICTS

The local school district is the basic unit of government in public education's organizational structure. As noted in Chapter 3, states differ with respect to how they have formed local districts; for example, Hawaii has only one statewide system, several states have only as many districts as they have counties, and other states with relatively small populations have more than 1,000 districts. Variations are more a product of political preferences than evidence of effectiveness (Ramirez, 1992). Despite a lack of compelling evidence showing a nexus between district size or design and student learning, this basic unit of governance was largely ignored by would-be reformers during the 1980s (Hannaway, 1992). More recently, school improvement ideas, such as site-based management, charter schools, and choice, have circuitously called into question the effectiveness of local control.

Legal Status

The legal status of local school districts differs among the states. In some states, they are municipal corporations (public entities that have legal standing); more commonly, they are quasi-corporations (entities that act as if they had legal standing) (Guthrie & Reed, 1991). This latter designation indicates that districts are a special type of municipal corporation in which "local interest and advantage rather than execution of state policy are its determining characteristics" (Edwards, 1955, p. 54). Quasi-corporations have more limited authority. For this reason, school districts were often referred to as limited municipal corporations (Knezevich, 1984). In Indiana, for example, school districts are legally titled school corporations. Several states have had litigation seeking to clarify the status of school districts. Litigation of this type often has centered around the right of one unit of local government to impose its regulations on another unit of local government operating within its boundaries. For instance, can a city impose its building codes on a local school district operating within its jurisdiction? Decisions on such questions have been inconsistent across states. In some cases, the courts have ruled that municipalities have such power; in other instances, courts have ruled that school districts, as extensions of state government, are immune from municipal dictums (Campbell, Cunningham, Nystrand, & Usdan, 1990). Thus, local school districts cannot be defined precisely as either corporations or quasi-corporations. Consequently, superintendents should seek to determine conditions in their respective states.

As a subdivision of state government, local districts are subject to the state legislature's plenary powers. Provided that a legislature acts within the parameters of its constitutional provisions, it can alter a district's jurisdiction, boundaries, and powers; it can even eliminate a local district (Lunenburg & Ornstein, 1991). Because the powers granted by the state are limited to the specific purposes of public education, school districts often have less power and authority than city or county governmental units. Typically, the power granted to local districts includes (a) those expressly granted by statute, (b) those fairly and necessarily implied from powers expressly granted by statute, and (c) those that are discretionary and essential to operations (Knezevich, 1984). Because state constitutions and statutes are not uniform, the level of autonomy enjoyed by local districts differs among the states and not uncommonly among classifications of districts within a state (Campbell et al., 1990).

Between 1940 and 1980, school district consolidation, which was discussed in Chapter 3, had a tremendous effect on the number of school districts in the United States. During that period the average number of local school districts in a state declined significantly, from a high of 2,437 in 1940 to 318 in 1980 (Strang, 1987). Fewer and larger school districts transformed administrative structures and influenced administrative behaviors. As districts increased in enrollment and geographic size, they became more bureaucratic; that is, authority in them became more centralized. Centralization is intended to generate uniformity and efficiency, both widely accepted objectives. As small districts were subjected to consolidation, policymaking and administration in them became increasingly centralized (Strang, 1987).

Today, the effects of district consolidation remain controversial. In most states, rigid laws prevent reversion that would allow former school districts to secede from their current organization. In Ohio, however, several small districts were able to do just that as recently as 2004. Recognizing that dismantling district consolidation is highly improbable, if not undesirable, reformers have sought to ameliorate the negative byproducts of consolidation—derivatives such as paying insufficient attention to real student needs, political alienation, and inflexibility (Kowalski, 2003). School councils are a prime example of these efforts. Popularized in the last two decades of the 20th century, these groups are premised largely on two convictions: student needs vary among and within school districts and political support is necessary to initiate and sustain change. Integrating centralization and decentralization is yet another indication of how public education policy attempts to find middle ground among competing values such as efficiency and excellence.

Types of School Districts

Many adjectives are used to describe school systems and they are not always understood. Classifications have been based on (a) statutory provisions for creating districts, (b) fiscal independence, (c) levels of educational opportunity provided, (d) scope of territory served, and (e) geographic description. Table 4.1 summarizes classification systems for school districts.

Statutory Base. In some states, school districts are described by the law under which they were initially created. Largely because of a desire after World War II to reduce the number of local units within a state through school district

Table 4.1   Descriptors Used for School Districts

Category	Explanation
Statutory basis	Classification based on the state statute under which the school district is organized and functions, e.g., community school districts, metropolitan school districts, school city districts
Fiscal independence	Classification based on a school district's independence in determining budgets and tax rates, e.g., independent or dependent districts
Levels of education provided	Classification based on grade levels included in the school district, e.g., unit or unified districts, elementary school districts, high school districts
Scope of territory served	Classification based on a school district's relationship with townships, towns, cities, and counties, e.g., county districts, township districts
Geographic Description	Classification based on a geographic portrait, e.g., rural, urban, and suburban districts

reorganization, state governments often provided incentives and encouragements to local citizens to either merge or move away from the old township trustee system.[1] One encouragement was the provision of legal options for reorganization that allowed local officials to select the option most favorable to local citizens. In Indiana and Iowa, for example, the official name of a school district is usually indicative of the law under which the district was formed and operates, and not necessarily indicative of the geographic setting of the district: a rural district in Indiana might be called a metropolitan school district and a rural district in Iowa might be called a community school district.

Fiscal Classification. Either officially or unofficially, school districts may be referred to as *dependent* or *independent*. These words describe a local district's power (as granted by the state) to levy property taxes for the support of its operations. Approximately 90% of all districts in the United States are classified as independent; 23 states have only independent districts, 4 states have only dependent districts, and the remaining states have both (Campbell et al., 1990). Budgets and tax rates of dependent school districts must be approved by another agency of government (e.g., a county council, a city council). Proponents of dependence argue that tax rates for government services should be coordinated to protect the public from uncontrolled, unnecessary, or excessive increases. They believe that fiscal requests for public education should be weighed against all other fiscal requests for local government. Proponents for independence contend that educational needs are too important to be subjected to political battles centering on the distribution of scarce resources. In truth, few districts have plenary powers to set taxes. In most states, budgets and tax-related decisions of even independent local school boards are subjected to reviews by state agencies or restricted by statutes.

Level of Educational Programming. The *unit* or *unified district* is clearly the norm in the United States. This designation connotes that the district serves all levels of elementary and secondary education. Several states, such as California and Illinois, have both unit districts and *dual districts*. The latter designation identifies school systems that serve either elementary grades (typically preschool through grade 6 or preschool through grade 8) or secondary grades (typically grades 7 to 12 or 9 to 12). The rationale underlying dual districts is largely political. In Illinois, for example, residents in dual districts have two separate tax rates for schools, but they also have two school boards representing their interests. The maximum tax rates for the combined districts exceeded the maximum tax rate for unit districts and, consequently, opting for dual districts allowed residents to raise more revenue for public schools. Not unexpectedly, most dual districts were established in suburban areas where residents were willing to put forth additional effort to support schools and where local control was deemed highly important. In several states, such as California, Georgia, and Minnesota, community colleges, junior colleges, or technical schools serving students beyond grade 12 may also be part of a public school district.

Scope of Territory. School districts have been classified on the basis of the territory served. This classification is largely informal reflecting the relationship of the school district to townships, towns, cities, and counties. Some districts may be quite small and serve only part of a township; some may include an entire county. In most parts of the country, multiple school districts in a county are the norm; in these settings, titles such as "township district" or "city district" are common. As noted in the previous chapter, several southern states organized public education by establishing a single district in each county. The reason can be traced to colonial times when the Church of England was predominant in the southern colonies. Rather than following the pattern of community-based school districts developed in New England, these states opted for centralized government. This decision was influenced by the close relationship that existed between church affairs and public affairs in the southern colonies. Several states outside of the south, such as Utah and Nevada, also have chosen the all-county school system structure (Campbell et al., 1990).

Geographic Description. Another informal classification has been based on the geographic description of territory served. Labels such as *urban, smaller city or town, suburban,* and *rural* have been used as descriptors. These designations accommodate discussions relating to common relationships between demographic variables and educational needs in school districts. For example, urban designations often spawn perceptions of diverse populations, large-enrollment schools, high rates of poverty, and so forth. Indirectly, geographic labels also produce mental images of quality that may or may not be accurate. In several states, school districts are officially categorized according to their geographic setting by state departments of education. Such classification may be used to conduct research or to make distinctions for special funding programs.

ORGANIZATIONAL DIMENSIONS

The study of behavior in school and school districts has been conducted largely in an organizational context. All organizations are thought to share certain traits such as purpose, formal and informal structure, identifiable boundaries, social interaction, deliberate structure, and culture (Razik & Swanson, 2001). This does not mean, however, that all organizations are identical; public school districts possess characteristics that distinguish them not only from private, profit-seeking enterprises but also from other school districts—even those located in the same state (Hannaway, 1992). The common threads running through all organizations are fundamental to understanding behavior in school districts, but standing alone, they do not provide a complete picture of reality.

School Districts as Organizations

In very simple terms, organizations are "social inventions accomplishing goals through group effort" (Johns, 1988, p. 10). In virtually all definitions, two recurring themes are evident: organizations are *social units* and organizations have identifiable *goals* (Kowalski, 2003). The former refers to the fact that organizations are composed of individuals and groups who establish some level of interdependency and who inevitably have some level of interaction. People in an organization can be likened to the various cells and molecules in the human body. A problem in one area often has a systemic effect on the entire body. Identifiable goals reflect organizational purpose or mission. Organizations have differing purposes; for example, profit-seeking companies and public schools obviously have different objectives. Organizations also vary in size, environmental conditions, incentive systems, leadership and authority, and goals (Knoke & Prensky, 1984).

One of the most serious problems facing superintendents is *organizational uncertainty*. This concern stems from ambiguity in one or more of the following aspects of public education: philosophy, mission, structure, and purposes. As noted earlier, lack of clarity and consensus with regard to purpose continues to plague school reform efforts. These disagreements, however, have been positive as well as negative. Addressing this matter, Tyack and Cuban (1995) wrote, "debate over purpose in public education has been a continuous process of creating and reshaping a democratic institution that, in turn, helped create a democratic society" (p. 142). Perceptions of purpose are a complex mix of personal philosophies and societal needs. In the absence of pervasive purposes embraced by all, citizens in local districts are now being prompted to participate in critical activities such as visioning and planning. These activities will determine the need for and direction of school reform in many local districts (Kowalski, 2001). Because neither the process of examining purpose nor the outcomes are predetermined, such democratic debates over purpose contribute to organizational uncertainty—a condition that intensifies the risks of leadership, particularly in the realm of decision making (March & Simon, 1958).

Varying normative (e.g., classical theory) and descriptive theories (e.g., social systems theory) have been applied to education. Each is represented in contemporary management thinking to some extent even though they entered the mainstream of the school administration knowledge base at different historical periods (Hanson, 2003). Classical theory, or bureaucracy, emerged prior to and during the Industrial Revolution and emphasizes five control and coordination mechanisms: (a) maintaining firm hierarchical control of authority and providing close supervision of workers; (b) establishing and maintaining adequate vertical communication (top-down, one-way communication); (c) developing a myriad of rules and regulations to guide actions; (d) having clear plans and schedules for workers to follow; and (e) adding supervisory positions to the hierarchy if changing conditions or problems require additional supervision and control (Owens, 1995). Applications in school districts concentrate on predicting and controlling the behavior of teachers, students, and other employees.

Social systems theory emerged in the 1930s and was an outgrowth of the human relations approach to studying behavior in organizations. Unlike classical theory that concentrates on organizational goals, social systems theory recognizes the existence of both organizational needs and individual or group needs. Based on research and observations of groups and individuals in organizational contexts, it has served to cast doubt on some of the tenets of classical theory by demonstrating differences between ideal and real behavior. For example, social system theory helps us to understand how social acceptance often serves to influence worker behavior—a condition not recognized by classical theory. Social systems theory also explores individual behavior and power (Hanson, 2003). Individual behavior is an intricate mix of personality and role reflecting the intersection of individual needs and organizational expectations. Differences in teacher or principal behavior are often explained by the manner in which individuals choose to conform to their imposed roles or to pursue their personal needs (Chance & Björk, 2004). With respect to influence (the ability to get others to do something), social systems theory helps us to understand the relationship between formal and informal power. Formal or legitimate power is granted by the organization, typically based on position. Informal power is acquired politically, professionally, or personally. As an example, teachers or principals may have informal power either because they have access to influential people, or because they are viewed as experts, or because they are charismatic.

Open systems theory became popular in the 1960s. Unlike classical theory and social systems theory, each of which concentrate on the inner workings of the organization, open systems focuses on interactions between the organization and its wider environment (e.g., community, state). The development of open systems theory was associated with the behavior sciences approach to studying organizational behavior. Behavior is seen in the context of cycles of events describing outputs the organization gives to the environment and the inputs it receives from the environment (Hanson, 2003). For schools, open systems perspectives are especially cogent given the expectation that public institutions are highly sensitive to community needs and wants. In this frame of reference, organizational survival is more dependent on adaptability to changing social needs than the predictability of employee behaviors (Snyder & Anderson, 1986).

A number of metaphors have been used to describe organizations and to illuminate the complexity of behavior in them. The eight organizational metaphors developed by Gareth Morgan (1986) have been used widely for these purposes:

- *Organizations as machines*—seeing organizations as a set of interlocking parts with defined roles; the essence of bureaucratic theory
- *Organizations as organisms*—seeing organizations as unique social systems; examining how organizations are created, develop, able to adapt, and so forth
- *Organizations as brains*—seeing how information is processed, how learning occurs, and how knowledge is accumulated and used
- *Organizations as cultures*—seeing how values, norms, and basic assumptions determine and sustain behavior
- *Organizations as political systems*—seeing how interest, conflict, and power shape behavior
- *Organizations as psychic prisons*—seeing how people and groups become trapped by their own thoughts, ideas, or unconscious goals
- *Organizations as flux and transformation*—seeing how organizations change or re-create themselves
- *Organizations as instruments of domination*—seeing how organizations use employees, the community, or the state to achieve self-determined ends

Metaphors, like theories, help us envision the dynamic and multifaceted nature of organizational life.

Unfortunately practitioners have often treated theories and metaphors as being impractical, speculative, suppositional, or overly idealistic. This dismissive attitude is unfortunate for at least three reasons: (a) theory provides a frame of reference; (b) theorizing provides a general mode of analysis of practical events; and (c) theory guides decision making (Hoy & Miskel, 1996, p. 7). Rather than using theory, far too many administrators have become wed to a single view of organizational life that was developed primarily through personal experience and intuition. Consequently, it is virtually impossible for them to gain a full understanding of the motivations and dynamics of individual and group behavior (Bolman & Deal, 1989).

Organizational Climate

When you walk into a school, impressions immediately develop based on what you see and how you are treated. If the environment is warm and color-ful, if people are friendly and helpful, your perceptions are likely to be positive. Later, you may even refer to the school as having had a friendly atmosphere. Climate is the attribute that determines how we feel about an organization; for members of the organization, it also generates perceptions of expectations for work-related behavior (Miskel & Ogawa, 1988; Owens, 1995). Although districts and schools have myriad similarities, they are never identical. Organi-zational climate often has been used as a descriptive metaphor and an expla-nation as to why schools and school districts have defining characteristics (Miskel & Ogawa, 1988).

Frequently, climate is described as being closed or open. These terms refer to the degree to which an organization seeks to interact with its environment. Closed school districts attempt to stifle external interventions from other agencies, government, and the courts, as well as from patrons. The rationale for this behavior is a desire to avoid conflict. Allowing "outsiders" to pene-trate the organizations requires school officials to deal with competing values, beliefs, and political agendas. As an example, board meetings in a rural school district are held at 8:00 a.m. on the last Saturday of each month; no seats are provided other than for the board and administrative staff. This arrangement conveys the message, "Visitors are not welcome." By comparison, open sys-tems treat external interventions as essential to community-school district equilibrium. The rationale for this position is that schools cannot serve the public interests unless those developing policy and rules know the commu-nity's real needs and wants. In essence, philosophical and political conflict is treated as a catalyst for change (Hanson, 2003). As an example, school board meetings in a suburban school district are conducted in schools and not the administrative building. The location rotates so that at least two meetings are held in each school every year. In addition, patrons are encouraged to make statements or ask questions during the meetings and to attend after meeting receptions to converse with school officials. This arrangement conveys the message, "Your input is valued."

Organizational climate and culture are often confused and some authors even refer to them as if they were synonymous. However, most theorists identify culture as one of four elements comprising climate. The most commonly used description of climate was developed by Renato Tagiuri. His conceptualization divides climate into four elements: (a) ecology, (b) milieu, (c) organization, and (d) culture (Owens, 1995). These components are described in Table 4.2. The organizational dimension probably has received the most attention from researchers over the years. Studies in districts and schools frequently have focused on characteristics such as organizational designs (e.g., block scheduling, 12-month school calendars), formal roles (e.g., assistant principals, department chairs), and instructional designs (e.g., teaming). In the current context of school reform, however, culture has emerged as the most critical element of climate because those studying organizational change (e.g., Fullan & Stiegelbauer, 1991; Sarason, 1996) have concluded that meaningful improvements are unlikely unless the underlying values and beliefs of educators are identified, evaluated, and altered. Organizational culture is rooted in sociology and anthropology; rather than focusing on what a school district possesses, culture deals with what a school district is (Hanson, 2003). Edgar Schein (1992) formally defines a group's culture as:

A pattern of basic assumptions that the group learned as it solved its problems of external adaptation and internal integration, that has worked well enough to be considered valid and, therefore, to be taught to new members as the correct way to perceive, think, and feel in relation to those problems. (p. 12)

Organizational culture is the shared beliefs, expectations, values, and norms of conduct for individuals and groups who comprise a district or school; it is a normative structure defining "both 'what is'—knowledge, beliefs, and technology—and 'what ought to be'—values and norms—for successive generations" (Firestone & Corbett, 1988, p. 335). An organization's culture is shaped by environment (e.g., community needs and wants, competition, prevailing practices), values (shared basic concepts and beliefs), heroes (individuals who personify the shared values), rites and rituals (systematic and programmed routines), and a mechanism for disseminating shared values (network) (Deal & Kennedy, 1982). While part of a school's culture is factual, other aspects are mythical because individuals and groups establish meaning for themselves by interpreting the conditions around them (Bates, 1984).

Although some values and beliefs are commonly found across all public schools, cultures and subcultures are never identical from school to school. District and school cultures can be described on the basis of strength, that is, the degree to which organizational members adhere to the same set of values and

Table 4.2   Elements of School District Climate

Element	Description	Examples
Ecology	District's physical and material features	School buildings, equipment, technology
Milieu	District's social dimension	Interactions of administrators, teachers, students, and other employees—individually and in groups
Organization	District's formal structures	Line and staff structure, grade organization, daily schedule, calendars, and schedules
Culture	District's commonly held beliefs/values	Physical symbols of what is valued (e.g., trophies, academic award plaques), philosophy statements, assumptions about correct behavior and problem solving

SOURCE: Adapted from Kowalski (2003) and Owens (1995).

beliefs. One finds philosophical cohesiveness in a *strong culture* and considerable philosophical fragmentation in a *weak culture*. Cultures also may be described on the basis of congruence with the professional knowledge base, that is, the degree to which organizational members adhere to values and beliefs that are indicative of best practices. One finds congruence between shared values and the professional knowledge base in a *positive culture* and incongruence between shared values and the professional knowledge in a *negative culture* (Kowalski, 2003). These distinctions help us understand why so much emphasis has been placed on culture in relation to school reform. As an example, a strong negative culture would be highly resistant to adopting new organizational patterns or instructional approaches determined to be highly effective.

Accurately evaluating a district culture requires superintendents to systematically study what exists. Alluding to the nature of this task, Razik and Swanson (1995) wrote:

The integration, fragmentation, and differentiation perspectives are all available to the researcher/observer. This approach offers us a crucial illustration of the organization's "ethos," its historical purpose, power shaping, motivations, beliefs, informal settings, symbolic expression, visual data, and more. Culture is a part of the organization, and it is the organization. (p. 211)

The task of evaluating culture is intricate and time-consuming because an organization's real identity is found in varying levels ranging from tangible overt manifestations that you can see and feel to deeply embedded, unconscious assumptions that are not overtly perceptible (Schein, 1992). These layers include:

- *Artifacts*—visible structures and processes such as school buildings, the overt behavior of teacher groups, and the applications of technology
- *Espoused values*—philosophical statements, planning goals, and leadership strategies typically found in official documents (e.g., mission and vision statements) and repeated by organizational members that may or may not depict real values
- *Basic assumptions*—explicit assumptions that guide behavior and typically are not confronted or debated

A superintendent who relies solely on artifacts and espoused values is unlikely to assess district culture accurately.

When culture is defined in the context of these layers, the difficulty of changing this critical organizational characteristic is made more understandable. True change requires addressing that which is hidden from the casual observer. Moreover, the underlying beliefs shared by individuals ensconced in the culture often get sublimated, especially if these beliefs are incongruous with the professional knowledge base or with community expectations. Behavior in a school district is not random. Rather it is influenced by fundamental consistencies produced in a complex network of interactions among individuals and formal and informal groups within a cultural context (Robbins, 1986). In this vein, shared values and assumptions constitute the glue for an organization (Firestone & Corbett, 1988) and they determine the real roles assumed by organizational members (i.e., what administrators and teachers accept as their responsibility and the behaviors that are appropriate in carrying out those responsibilities) (Prestine & Bowen, 1993). Both directly and indirectly, culture affects how school districts are organized and how they function.

Nevertheless, there have been multiple cases of superintendents who tried to reconstruct school districts coercively. Almost always, their efforts were futile because they and the board members who supported them overlooked or ignored the proclivity of an organization to protect itself from intruders. As new members, including superintendents and other key administrators, become new organizational members, formal and informal processes are deployed to socialize them; that is, new members are pressured socially to accept or at least adhere to the basic assumptions that exist at the deepest level of culture (Hart, 1991). Those who are not socialized typically leave the school district or are ostracized from the organization's political power structures. Superintendents are no exception.

The failure of imposed change has been evident in large urban school districts where school board members have attempted to force change by employing a new superintendent from outside the school district. At first the legitimate power of the school board sustains the reforms initiated by the new superintendents, even if the values and beliefs underlying them are incongruous with the existing culture. When the foundation of the culture is threatened, however, political resistance to change intensifies and eventually the superintendent's legitimate power erodes (e.g., incumbent board members supporting the superintendent are defeated in elections) (Kowalski, 1995a). The existing bureaucracy almost always proves to be stronger than the new superintendent. Despite these recurring failures, school boards continue to seek imaginary "saviors"—superintendents who supposedly can transform a school district quickly and forcibly. Politics appears to be a primary reason why they do so. Often under immense community pressure to produce school improvement, the board members often become satisfied with producing an illusion of change. They first tell the public that the new superintendent is capable of producing reform and then blame the superintendent when the goal is not achieved (Kowalski, 1995a).

Local Politics

Local politics can affect the organization of school districts in two ways. First, the shared interests of patrons can influence organizational culture. As an example, biases and preferences expressed through school board members often influence what educators accept as effective practices. Second, community politics can trump organizational culture when the two forces are at odds. In either case, political pressures can play a prominent role in determining how public schools are organized and function. During the 1990s, direct community involvement in school improvement was promoted in two important ways: through federal and state legislation and policy initiatives requiring citizen involvement, and through a new citizenship movement focused on reversing declining citizen support for public organizations (Keith, 1999). Community political influence, therefore, has been neither unplanned nor disdained over the past few decades; it is construed by many as a necessary force for preventing professional control of public education and for ensuring that reforms adhere to local needs and wants (Hess, 1999).

Districts with similar institutional environments and technologies often exhibit distinct differences in organizational design and procedures for decision making. Understanding the source of these differences is important to modern practice because some policymakers have concluded incorrectly that superintendents have had the leeway to restructure schools independently. Discussing her research of local political pressures on school district design, Hannaway (1993) wrote:

> The results suggest that the assumption implicitly made by many educational reformers that schools are free to choose their organizational structure is, at least to some significant degree, overdrawn. External political pressure at the local level appears to constrain managerial arrangements. (p. 160)

Even when proposed reforms are accepted by the vast majority of teachers and administrators, a superintendent's efforts may be thwarted by community resistance. Studying attempts to decentralize authority in the Detroit, Michigan, schools, Jelier and Hula (1999) concluded that political rejection of reform ideas, no matter how well conceived and supported by best practices, produces counterpressures for reversion. Consider the example of a large city district that instituted block scheduling in secondary schools based solely on the recommendation of a new superintendent. The change was staunchly supported by teachers, principals, and the teachers' union, but opposed by a group of influential parents. They objected to the change because they concluded that block scheduling restricted course offerings for their children and, thus, put their children at a disadvantage with respect to college admissions criteria. Despite this resistance, the superintendent, supported by 6 of 7 board members, refused to rescind the program. Fourteen months later, however, two incumbent board members who supported block scheduling were defeated at the polls and the remaining board members quickly pressured the superintendent to eliminate block scheduling.

District culture and community politics are intertwined and this union requires superintendents new to their districts to foster both organizational and community relationships quickly. A California superintendent, commenting about the tendency of school boards to want change rapidly but without conflict, alluded to this necessity:

> The reality of school districts is that they are people-driven organizations, not program- or product-driven organizations. When bringing about long-term meaningful change, relationships are much more important than are innovative or creative ideas. To be successful over the long haul, a superintendent must be seen as part of the culture. In our little "us versus them" world, a superintendent must develop roots as quickly as possible. (Hewitt, 2002, p. 40)

Often the political agendas emanating from the community are at odds with initiatives proposed by educators and consequently can be highly divisive (Lugg, 1996).

ORGANIZATIONAL PARADIGMS

The distribution of authority in public education revolves around three control-related tensions: (a) tension between states and local districts, (b) tension between school districts and schools, and (c) tension between legitimate control and professionalism (i.e., administrators and teachers) (Kowalski, 1995b). Each of these plays some part in determining how authority is distributed because not all states give local districts the same level of legitimate power, not all school districts give schools the same degree of autonomy, and not all principals give teachers the same degree of independence. External variables, such as community politics and laws, and internal variables, such as organizational culture, are responsible for the variance. The distribution of power between a district and member schools traditionally has been a matter of local policy. In recent years, states, such as Kansas and Kentucky, have adopted laws requiring school-based governance councils. Through much of the 20th century, local districts emphasized centralized government, but in the past 10 to 20 years, the trend has shifted toward decentralization of authority.

Centralized Authority

School administration students who have the opportunity to observe the practice of multiple superintendents often discover that the exercise of authority among them is inconstant. Some superintendents tightly control the activities of principals whereas others are more facilitative than directive. School districts with centralized authority are characterized by a pyramidal organizational structure; that is, power and authority are concentrated in the upper echelons of the organization. As you move from the base of the pyramid to the top, the number of employees declines but the level of legitimate power increases (see Figure 4.1).

This results in superintendents having considerable authority that they use to maintain tight controls over principals who then tightly control teachers. Peterson (1987) identified six control mechanisms superintendents may use in relation to principals:

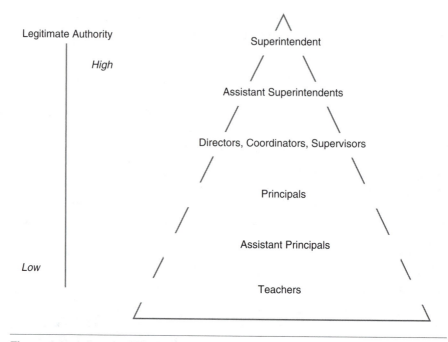

Figure 4.1   Bureaucratic Structure in a Local School District

- *Supervision control*—observing, evaluating, and directing the work of principals
- *Input control*—determining material and human resources available to principals
- *Output control*—monitoring productivity and then directing change
- *Behavior control*—developing and enforcing policy, rules, and regulations affecting principals
- *Selection-socialization control*—selecting principals who possess desired characteristics (e.g., values and beliefs) or using social pressures to make principals conform to desired characteristics
- *Environmental control*—using agents outside the organization (e.g., community power elites) to influence principal behavior

In highly centralized school districts, superintendents use many or all of these mechanisms in an effort to make principals conform to predetermined behaviors.

Centralized authority is most discernible in line and staff charts illustrating a school district's formal chain of command. Figure 4.2 shows the organizational relationships for administrators in a school district with 14,000 students.

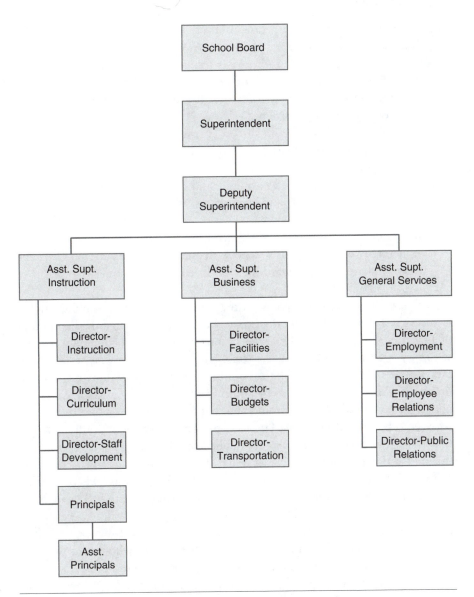

Figure 4.2   Line and Staff Relationships in a 14,000-Student District

Note that only one person, the deputy superintendent, reports directly to the superintendent. If this chain of command were strictly enforced, an elementary principal would need to get the permission of three other administrators in order to meet with the superintendent, a requirement that would be difficult to defend in most communities. Consequently, most school districts maintain a formal chain of command but protocols are typically relaxed, especially when consequential problems arise.

The concept of centralized authority is rooted in classical theory, a normative (prescriptive) theory that has been influential in shaping industrial and business organizations. The bureaucracy is identified as the ideal organization predicated on the following beliefs:

- Efficiency is the sole measure of productivity.
- Human behavior is rational.
- Work should be separated into units and closely supervised.
- Uniform policies, rules, and regulations are necessary to assure proper control.
- Individuals are not naturally inclined to work hard.
- A hierarchy of authority is necessary to establish organizational goals and to coordinate efforts toward their achievement (Hanson, 2003).

Classical theory was influential in the formation of urban school districts in the early 1900s. Because these districts were then considered the lighthouses of educational innovations, the organizational patterns they adopted were subsequently used by smaller districts (Callahan, 1962). Over time, critics have attacked the notion that public school districts should be bureaucratic-like organizations. They often did so by pointing out that some of classical theory's underlying assumptions were invalid and that there were distinctive differences between schools and factories. For example, they noted that contrary to the underlying premises of bureaucracy, public schools were not "coherent, logical, and rational institutions" and unlike manufacturing organizations they were not "designed with a clear purpose in mind, like the internal combustion engine, a jet aircraft, or even the common teakettle" (Smith, 1995, p. 587). Centralized authority in public education also has been criticized because it provides excessive administrative control at the expense of community control and because it moves decision making away from those who are in the most advantageous position to make decisions about real student needs.

The perpetuation of centralized authority in schools has often been blamed on superintendents. Detractors argue that this organizational design has been used deliberately to protect administrator self-interests (i.e., protection of their own power), to reduce conflict associated with democratic decision making, and to evade accountability. A careful analysis of history reveals the lack of sophistication in this conclusion. As detailed earlier in this chapter, local politics has and continues to play an influential role in determining how school districts get configured. Consider just three additional factors that have influenced centralization:

1. *Federal and state laws*—Many school districts were pushed toward higher levels of centralization during the 1960s and 1970s because of a growing compliance orientation that made school board members and administrators wary of litigation and state-imposed sanctions. Federal and state laws in areas such as civil rights, the rights of the handicapped, and employment discrimination prompted superintendents and school boards to adopt policies, rules, and regulations that required uniform practices (Tyack, 1990).

2. *State authority over public education*—State constitutions and statutes permit and often require legislatures and state departments of education to exercise control over local districts. The intensity of that control was elevated in the 1980s as political pressures for reform became intense. State interventions usually reinforce centralized governance structures in local districts because state authority is per se a facet of centralized government (Kowalski, 2003). School consolidation laws previously discussed provide an excellent example. Having fewer, but larger, school districts with a centralized administration made relationships between state departments of education and local districts more manageable (Strang, 1987). Complex accreditation procedures, fiscal controls, and curriculum mandates also encourage the creation of central administration and the employment of specialists who can manage these functions.

3. *Philosophical transitions*—Tensions between equity and excellence have made school boards and superintendents apprehensive about relinquishing control. Current demands for decentralization are fueled by expectations of greater quality and excellence. Advocates believe, for instance, that educational productivity suffers because bureaucratic administrators are too detached from the teaching process. But previous educational policy shifts toward quality and excellence inevitably have re-created concerns about equity and redistribution (Weiler, 1990); the history of school finance litigation demonstrates this concern.

As these examples demonstrate, centralized authority in school districts is not the result of a single cause. Social, economic, political, and legal variables all play some part in determining how school districts are organized and operate.

In school administration, centralization does not describe a specific level of authority distribution; instead, it describes a range of distributions skewed in the direction of centralized authority. Consequently, line and staff charts are insufficient to determine the actual degree of centralization; this is more accurately identified by assessment procedures such as climate audits. In many

Table 4.3   Commonly Criticized Attributes of School District Centralization

Attribute	Criticism
Concentration of authority	Decisions are limited by divisions of labor and tiers of authority; teachers are excluded from critical decisions; change can be deterred at multiple levels (Hanson, 2003).
One-way communication	Communication occurs in a top-down fashion; administrators may screen and filter information as its moves through the tiers of the district; teachers may withhold information from principals because they are excluded from critical decisions (Kowalski, 2004).
Excessive control	Principals and teachers are unable to respond appropriately to real student needs because their professional authority is restricted (Firestone & Bader, 1991).
Inflexibility	Rigid top-down structures foster an organizational incapacity to deal with unanticipated developments because most professional employees are excluded from participating in critical decisions (Hanson, 2003).

school districts, the degree of centralization shifts depending on the types of decisions that need to be made (Abbott & Caracheo, 1988).

Although there are many reasons why centralization persists, there is cause to be concerned about negative byproducts. Too much control stifles creativity and relegates principals and teachers to a status below professionals. These concerns have become increasingly disconcerting in the context of modern reform strategies. Most notably, high levels of centralization diminish the flexibility needed to execute successful improvements on a school-by-school basis and the latitude necessary to transform negative school cultures. Table 4.3 lists the possible problems stemming from centralization.

Decentralized Authority

Decentralization involves a distribution of legitimate power and authority and is intended to produce a flatter organizational configuration than does centralization. Districts claiming to be decentralized differ in the amount and types of authority granted to individual units; consequently, the term is used to describe a tendency rather than an absolute condition. For instance, a district may decentralize only those decisions involving textbook selection and instructional material acquisitions. Another district, however, may decentralize instruction, budget management, and even employment. Despite these differences, superintendents in both districts may claim to have decentralized authority.

Decentralization is not a recently developed concept. Urban growth in the 1950s and 1960s resulted in many big-city districts serving an increasingly diverse student population. Iterations of decentralization were used to mollify ethnic and racial demands for greater representation (Lunenburg & Ornstein, 1991). Recently, the concept has been promoted for both political and professional reasons. Politically, decentralization has been tied to liberty; as such, it is a widely supported concept. The notion that taxpayers ought to have greater influence over their social institutions has been repopularized in recent decades. Professionally, decentralization is linked to effective schools research suggesting that instructional effectiveness is diminished by placing educators in a quagmire of bureaucratic rules and regulations. Although professionalism more accurately relates to tensions between administrators and teachers, many policymakers have argued that this goal is unlikely to be achieved unless schools are given greater freedom from the centralized authority of school districts.

Arguments for organizational decentralization are often predicated on the anticipation of achieving the following goals: (a) increasing flexibility (schools are able to respond more quickly and directly to new needs), (b) using human resources more effectively (teachers can contribute to the decision-making process), and (c) assuring that decisions are made at the level closest to the problems (Certo, 1989). Writing specifically about schools, Brown (1991) identified three key beliefs underlying decentralization: "some variability is good; schools often know best; schools are usually trustworthy" (pp. 12–15). Interestingly, the words "some," "often," and "usually" reveal the conceptual ambiguity of decentralization. Ambivalence on the part of superintendents, however, is usually related to concerns about risk in relation to benefits. Sharing authority can make a superintendent vulnerable to criticism and legally culpable if principals make serious errors or violate laws. In addition, some superintendents question whether decentralization is truly a new standard for governance or just another in a long line of public education fads.

Reconfiguring authority relationships in a school district is laden with possible problems; Table 4.4 summarizes some of the problems. An obvious possible problem is conflict between the professional educators and the community. Consider this issue in the context of school councils, arguably the most popular iteration of decentralization. A school principal, several faculty members, and parents typically serve on these councils. If they are given

Table 4.4   Common Criticisms of School District Decentralization

Attribute	Criticism
Selective representation	School councils often are not representative of the total population; nonparents may be disenfranchised (Danzberger, Kirst, & Usdan, 1992).
Possibility of chaos	Districts that become too decentralized run the risk of becoming highly fragmented; individual schools may compete rather than collaborate and coordinate (Fullan, Bertani, & Quinn, 2004).
Democracy vs. professionalism	Excessive lay control of schools deters professionalism; when noneducators and educators serve as members of decision-making groups, their interests often are incongruous and the probability of serious conflict increases (Strike, 1993; Zeichner, 1991).
Inequities	Allowing schools to chart their own course often produces unequal educational opportunities across schools in the same district (Kowalski, 2003).
Evidence of effectiveness	Although decentralization may appeal to the political interests of taxpayers and to personal interests of teachers and principals, there is little evidence that the concept has been successful (Weiler, 1990).
Political fragmentation	Rather than resolving power-based conflict, decentralization may create new turf battles within the school; this is especially likely if decentralization does not move beyond governance to address knowledge, information, and finances (Odden, Wohlstetter, & Odden, 1995).

substantial authority to make decisions about textbooks, resource allocation, and priorities, the potential for the political interests of the community to clash with professional discretion of educators is usually high. In essence, tensions between democratic decision making and professionalism can evolve into serious conflict (Kowalski, 1995b). In addition, experience shows that decentralization efforts often fail to achieve their purposes. In Kentucky, for example, the teacher-parent-student relationship for poor families remained problematic even after schools were required to establish councils and involve parents (Björk & Keedy, 2002).

Because there are so many unanswered questions, and because school districts are such unique entities, decisions about decentralization are best made on a district-by-district basis. This is especially true with respect to pursuing school reform. Fullan (2003) argues that centralization errs on the side of overcontrol whereas decentralization errs on the side of chaos. Fullan concludes that both are necessary to some degree. Stated differently, the challenge for superintendents is not to choose centralization or decentralization; rather, it is to determine how the two need to be balanced. As examples, decentralization is highly desirable in areas related to improving instruction and centralization is highly desirable in areas related to compliance with laws and state policies.

Decentralization has presented a challenge for many experienced educators who were both prepared academically and socialized to work in highly centralized systems. Clearly, movement toward decentralization requires some degree of cultural transformation. In many districts, long-standing beliefs about efficiency, control, risk, and trust need to be revised if decentralization is to be institutionalized.

DIRECTED AUTONOMY AND DISTRICT ORGANIZATION

The nature of public schools and their relationship to state government make the complete decentralization of public education most improbable. In light of substantial evidence indicating that meaningful reform becomes more likely when schools have greater autonomy and teachers are empowered to make critical decisions in their practice, superintendents face the challenge of determining the scope and depth of necessary decentralization in their districts. Deliberations over this matter have generated interest in the concept of *directed autonomy*, an arrangement in which employees are empowered, even encouraged, to do things their own way. This empowerment, however, is not without boundaries (Waterman, 1987). Along the continuum from total centralization to total decentralization, directed autonomy is typically skewed toward decentralization.

Astute administrators realize that power already is shared in districts and schools; it just is not shared formally. That is, certain groups and individuals exercise power because of expertise, political influence, or social relationships and not because of organizational position (Chance & Björk, 2004). For example, a teacher whose sibling is on the school board in a rural district may exert considerable influence on his or her principal. Schools are not true bureaucracies; rather, they are *loosely coupled systems* because subunits in them are only partially linked to each other (Weick, 1976). From a sociological perspective, a loosely coupled system is one in which "goals are ambiguous, hierarchies of authority are not closely integrated, technologies are unclear, participation is fluid, and organizational units are partially autonomous from their social organization" (Corwin & Borman, 1988). Even in very structured schools with many rules and regulations, teachers have considerable autonomy in their classrooms because it is not feasible to monitor their practice continuously. This freedom is typically more informal than formal. That is, it is the product of processes and behaviors that are unplanned, spontaneous, and reflective of teacher needs (Hanson, 2003). Directed autonomy, however, entails a distribution of authority sanctioned, and even encouraged, by school district officials.

As peer members of the education profession, administrators and teachers who engage in directed autonomy must make decisions about authority domains. Essentially, the relevant domains for a district include (a) those responsibilities controlled exclusively by district administrators, (b) those responsibilities controlled exclusively by principals, (c) those responsibilities controlled exclusively by teachers, and (d) those responsibilities controlled mutually by administrators and teachers. As examples, school attendance boundary decisions may be controlled by the superintendent and the superintendent's staff; decisions about school building maintenance schedules may be controlled by principals; decisions about homework and grading may be controlled by teachers; decisions about the annual school calendar and fringe benefits may be decided jointly by administrators and teachers. Figure 4.3 illustrates how domains of authority may appear in a school system. In districts where professionalism and shared decision making are stressed, the most critical institutional decisions—those involving issues such as purpose, curriculum, and staff development—are in the shared authority domain.

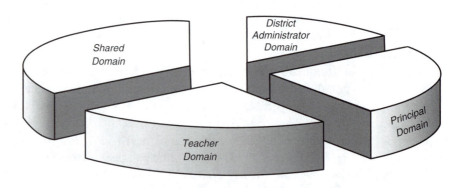

Figure 4.3   Example of Domains of Shared Authority in a School District

Admonitions to develop new authority structures in districts and schools emanate from both professional knowledge and philosophy. In the United States, proposed reforms are expected to be congruous with the principles of democracy. In this regard, three beliefs are especially noteworthy:

. . . a dedicated belief in the worth of the individual and the importance of the individual in participation and discussion regarding school life; a belief in freedom, intelligence, and inquiry; a conviction that projected designs, plans, and solutions be results of individuals pooling their intelligent efforts within communities. (Maxcy, 1995, p. 73)

Sergiovanni (1994) argues that resistance to such beliefs is prompted by our mental image of schools as organizations. He advocates that we reconsider how we perceive schools:

Life in organizations and life in communities are different in both quality and kind. In communities, we create our social lives with others who have intentions similar to ours. In organizations, relationships are constructed for us by others and become codified into a system of hierarchies, roles, and role control. (p. 4)

Articulating the need for schools to become learning communities, Barth (2000) aptly noted that the problem in public education is not that learning communities are not what they once were but that learning communities are precisely what they once were even though the world around them has changed considerably. Rather than relying on imposed policy, rules, and regulations, communities create a culture in which behavior is dependent on "norms, purposes, values, professional socialization, collegiality, and natural interdependence" (Sergiovanni, 1994, p. 4). These conditions reflect both knowledge of best practices and the real needs of learners.

Restructuring schools to become learning communities, however, is extremely difficult for at least three reasons. First, most educators and school support staff have only known the current culture of their workplace and they have been socialized to accept the basic assumptions underlying their work behavior. Even among those who prefer change, the prospect of challenging organizational culture is often seen as daunting and risk laden (Fullan, 1994).

Second, the relationship of states to local school districts—an affiliation that continues to stress efficiency and uniformity—often deters excessive autonomy for educators. But movement away from state control is unlikely. For example, concerns already have been expressed about the potential effects of fragmentation, pluralization, decentralization, and radical individualism on public education (e.g., Maxcy, 1995). Weiler (1990) argues that there is a basic tension between decentralization and "the tendency of the modern state to assert or reassert centralized control over the educational system" (p. 433). The modern state, he concludes, increasingly faces serious challenges regarding its need and value. The validity of his conclusion is supported by actions taken in many states during the 1990s by which policymakers granted leeway to local districts to determine how they would pursue school reform and then set stringent state standards and accountability measures. For example, the states imposed evaluation procedures that resulted in teachers "teaching to the test." Weiler argues that by setting the basic goals and determining how goal attainment will be measured, states really are not providing true professional autonomy. In light of the fact that the dismantling of centralized authority eventually results in centrifugal tendencies bringing into question issues of accountability, some level of state control remains inevitable (Moloney, 1989). Because of tensions between control and autonomy, some authors (e.g., Wimpelberg & Boyd, 1990) have concluded that bureaucratic and professional decision-making processes must coexist in districts and schools.

Third, school boards often set expectations that require superintendents to focus entirely or primarily on management functions. As a result, traditional dimensions of organization are perpetuated and ideas such as empowerment and shared authority are discarded as being counterproductive. The lay governance structure of districts, an expression of liberty, and the concept of learning community, an expression of professionalism, often conflict with each other. Dunn (2001) concludes that this governance structure may not provide "the optimal means for superintendents to support community-building efforts" (p. 165). The very same tensions that create a control dilemma for state government are relevant to the organizational structure of school districts. Decentralization rhetoric and policy are at the same time politically advantageous and vexatious. If schools acquire the authority to determine their own purpose, direction, and goals, are districts necessary? School districts, like states, will predictably fight to legitimize their continued existence and thus, the current governance system often inhibits decentralization and community building.

FOR FURTHER REFLECTION

School districts are at the same time legal, political, and social units of government. They are organizations characterized by their climates, especially by their cultures. Consequently, districts may appear to be identical but actually all have defining traits that make them unique. Moreover, schools comprising a district also are distinctive; the needs of students in one school may be quite different from the needs of students in another area of the school system. This is a primary reason why recent reform efforts have emphasized state deregulation and district decentralization.

The distribution of power and authority in districts is a core issue for superintendents. Although they rarely make determinations in this area unilaterally, their knowledge of organizational culture and community politics often determines the quantity and quality of influence they have. Although districts are neither totally centralized nor totally decentralized, they typically are skewed toward one of these organizational configurations. Leaders must determine the scope and depth of decentralization necessary to achieve needed school improvement (Fullan, Bertani, & Quinn, 2004). Because this must be done on a district-to-district basis, the superintendent emerges as the most important change agent involved in this decision. The challenge involves determining the right mixture of control and autonomy given a school system's climate and needs.

Taking into account what you read in this chapter, respond to the following:

1. Is public education ultimately a federal, state, or local responsibility? What evidence do you have to support your response?

2. What makes a local school district a legal entity, a political entity, and a social entity?

3. With respect to local government agencies, including public schools, what is the fundamental difference between a fiscally dependent and independent agency?

4. What are the differences between conceptualizing districts and schools as organizations and as communities?

5. What is organizational climate? Why should superintendents be concerned about climate?

6. Four elements of organizational climate were described in this chapter. What is the element of ecology? How does this element affect climate?

7. Cultures are often described along a continuum from "weak" to "strong." What are the differences between a weak and strong school district culture?

8. Cultures also are described along a continuum from "negative" to "positive." What are the differences between a negative and positive school district culture?

9. What are the advantages and disadvantages of centralizing authority in districts?

10. Can community politics really prevent school reform? Why or why not?

11. What is directed autonomy? What is the intended purpose of this concept?

Case Study

The Haddington School District is located in the heart of America's "rust belt." In 1970, the school system served just over 42,000 students; today, fewer than 23,000 are being served. Since 1980, 10 schools in the district have been closed, there have been 3 teacher strikes, and 7 different individuals have served as superintendent. These three factors are interrelated. The declining enrollments prompted school closings, which prompted reductions in force, which prompted teacher strikes, which contributed substantially to leadership instability.

Conditions in Haddington, however, started to change 2 years ago. Enrollment stabilized and for the first time in more than a decade, several new businesses opened in the community. The current superintendent, Walter Mayhew, is an experienced administrator who served as superintendent in two smaller school systems before Haddington. Because both districts were in the same state as Haddington, he was aware of the district's history when he accepted the challenging position. Dr. Mayhew's apprehensions about this school district were diminished when the school board told him they were committed to achieving excellence and to eradicating instability in the superintendent's office. The board also assured him that he would have unbridled authority to make personnel changes.

After Dr. Mayhew was named superintendent, the deputy superintendent, who also had applied for the job, announced that he would retire immediately. This permitted the new superintendent to employ his friend and long-time colleague, Helen Carey, as his deputy. She had served as a principal and assistant superintendent with Dr. Mayhew previously.

When Drs. Mayhew and Carey started their positions in Haddington, they found a rigid, highly centralized governance system that had not changed in any appreciable way since 1970. Although several central office positions had been eliminated as a result of enrollment declines, four layers of administration still existed between the superintendent and school principals.

The previous superintendent, who was promoted from within the organization, had lasted only 28 months. After having employed two successive superintendents from outside the district and seeing them fail, the board acquiesced to pressures from the teachers union and several community groups to select an internal candidate. Dr. Mayhew and Dr. Carey surmised that the previous superintendent was not committed to change and only tinkered with ecological and organizational dimensions of climate in an effort to make the board and community believe that school improvement was being pursued. As an example, he required schools to establish advisory councils but the evidence (e.g., official minutes, anecdotal comments from principals and teachers) indicated that they were perfunctory. Dr. Mayhew's predecessor essentially conducted business as usual.

Four months after arriving in Haddington, Drs. Mayhew and Carey arrived at different conclusions about improving the district. The deputy superintendent wanted to redesign the governance structure immediately, making individual schools more autonomous and accountable. She told the superintendent, "The window of opportunity to make changes is probably limited. Despite what the board members say about leadership stability, their past actions indicate they are not very patient. If we don't get things done rather quickly, we could be facing the same fate as our predecessors." She added that trying to reconfigure governance by establishing school councils was an error. Reconfiguring the administrative line and staff arrangement was her preferred starting point. More specifically, she wanted to eliminate at least three positions in the central office immediately and to then make principals more accountable for shaping a school-improvement agenda.

Dr. Mayhew disagreed. "You may be right about the time frame, but I don't believe that pursuing change so quickly is a good idea. Some previous superintendents attempted to impose change and they failed. My strategy is to first conduct a climate audit and then to engage the community in a visioning process. That may take as long as 2 years. After we finish these tasks, I think we can concentrate on developing a plan to achieve the vision. If board members are highly involved in the visioning process, they are less likely to become impatient." The superintendent added that he wanted to outline the steps toward school improvement, beginning with the climate audit and visioning, and then present it to the school board for approval.

Case Discussion Questions

1. If you were the new superintendent in Haddington, what factors would you examine to determine the extent of centralization in the district?

2. Dr. Mayhew discovers that there are several layers of authority between him and the principals. If you were he, would you be concerned about this? Why or why not?

3. What factors could prevent implementation of Dr. Carey's proposal to reconfigure the administrative staff and eliminate at least three central office positions? Based on the case study, do you find any evidence that any of the barriers are more likely than others?

4. Does the fact that Drs. Mayhew and Carey came to Haddington as "outsiders" have any relevance for how they pursue school improvement? Why or why not?

5. Based on the limited information provided, can you make any judgments about the strength of the culture in this school system? Why or why not?

6. Can you suggest an alternative for pursuing organizational change other than those offered by the superintendent and his deputy?

NOTE

1. The township trustee system, once the norm in public education, preceded school boards. Under this organizational pattern, an elected trustee in each township had jurisdiction over schools. Commonly where this pattern existed, individual districts had principals but not superintendents. Instead, the districts used the services of a county superintendent. This position served two essential functions: meeting state requirements of having a superintendent and providing assistance to both trustees and principals.

REFERENCES

Abbott, M. G., & Caracheo, F. (1988). Power, authority, and bureaucracy. In N. Boyan (Ed.), *Handbook of research on educational administration* (pp. 239–257). New York: Longman.

Barth, R. S. (2000). Building a community of learners. *Principal, 79*(4), 68–69.

Bates, R. J. (1984). Toward a clinical practice of educational administration. In T. J. Sergiovanni & J. Corbally (Eds.), *Leadership and organizational culture* (pp. 64–71). Urbana, IL: University of Illinois Press.

Björk, L. G., & Keedy, J. L. (2002). Decentralization and school council empowerment in Kentucky: Implications for community relations. *Journal of School Public Relations, 23*(1), 30–44.

Bolman, L., & Deal, T. E. (1989). *Modern approaches to understanding and managing organizations.* San Francisco: Jossey-Bass.

Brown, D. J. (1991). *Decentralization: The administrator's guidebook to school district change.* Newbury Park, CA: Corwin.

Callahan, R. E. (1962). *Education and the cult of efficiency.* Chicago: University of Chicago Press.

Campbell, R. F., Cunningham, L. L., Nystrand, R. O., & Usdan, M. D. (1990). *The organization and control of American schools* (6th ed.). Columbus, OH: Merrill.

Chance, P. L., & Björk, L. G. (2004). The social dimensions of public relations. In T. J. Kowalski (Ed.), *Public relations in schools* (3rd ed., pp. 125–148). Upper Saddle River, NJ: Merrill, Prentice Hall.

Certo, S. C. (1989). *Principles of modern management: Functions and systems* (4th ed.). Boston: Allyn & Bacon.

Corwin, R. G., & Borman, K. M. (1988). School as workplace: Structural constraints on administration. In N. Boyan (Ed.), *Handbook of research on educational administration* (pp. 209–238). New York: Longman.

Danzberger, J. P. (1994). Governing the nation's schools: The case for restructuring local school boards. *Phi Delta Kappan, 75*(5), 367–373.

Danzberger, J. P., Kirst, M. W., & Usdan, M. D. (1992). *Governing public schools: New times new requirements.* Washington, DC: The Institute for Educational Leadership.

Deal, T. E., & Kennedy, A. A. (1982). *Corporate cultures: The rites and rituals of corporate life*. Reading, MA: Addison-Wesley.

Dunn, R. J. (2001). Community and control in the superintendency. In C. Brunner & L. Björk (Eds.), *The new superintendency: Advances in research and theories of school management and educational policy* (pp. 153–168). Stamford, CT: JAI.

Edwards, N. (1955). *The courts and the public schools*. Chicago: University of Chicago Press.

Firestone, W. A., & Bader, B. D. (1991). Professionalism or bureaucracy? Redesigning teaching. *Educational Evaluation & Policy Analysis, 13,* 67–86.

Firestone, W. A., & Corbett, H. D. (1988). Planned organizational change. In N. Boyan (Ed.), *Handbook of research on educational administration* (pp. 321–340). New York: Longman.

Fullan, M. (1994). *Change forces: Probing the depths of educational reform*. Philadelphia: Falmer.

Fullan, M. (2003). *Change forces with a vengeance*. London: Routledge/Falmer.

Fullan, M., Bertani, A., & Quinn, J. (2004). New lessons for districtwide reform. *Educational Leadership, 61*(7), 42–46.

Fullan, M., & Stiegelbauer, S. (1991). *The new meaning of educational change*. New York: Teachers College Press.

Guthrie, J. W., & Reed, R. J. (1991). *Educational administration and policy: Effective leadership for American education*. Boston: Allyn & Bacon.

Hannaway, J. (1992). *School districts: The missing link in education reform*. East Lansing, MI: National Center for Research on Teacher Learning. (ERIC Document Reproduction Service No. ED359644)

Hannaway, J. (1993). Political pressure and decentralization in institutional organizations: The case of school districts. *Sociology of Education, 66*(3), 147–163.

Hanson, E. M. (2003). *Educational administration and organizational behavior* (5th ed.). Boston: Allyn & Bacon.

Hart, A. W. (1991). Leader succession and socialization: A synthesis. *Review of Educational Research, 61*(4), 451–474.

Hess, G. A. (1999). Community participation or control? From New York to Chicago. *Theory into Practice, 38*(4), 217–224.

Hewitt, P. (2002). Rapid change? Only the name on your office door. *School Administrator, 59*(9), 40–41.

Hoy, W. K., & Miskel, C. G. (1996). *Educational administration: Theory, research, and practice* (5th ed.). New York: McGraw-Hill.

Jelier, R. W., & Hula, R. C. (1999). A house divided: Community politics and education reform in Detroit. *Urban Review, 31*(1), 3–29.

Johns, G. (1988). *Organizational behavior: Understanding life at work* (2nd ed.). Glenview, IL: Scott, Foresman.

Keith, N. Z. (1999). Whose community schools? New discourses, old patterns. *Theory into Practice, 38*(4), 225–234.

Knezevich, S. J. (1984). *Administration of public education: A sourcebook for the leadership and management of educational institutions* (4th ed.). New York: Harper & Row.

Knoke, D., & Prensky, D. (1984). What relevance do organizational theories have for voluntary associations? *Social Science Quarterly, 65*(1), 3–20.

Kowalski, T. J. (1995a). *Keepers of the flame: Contemporary urban superintendents.* Thousand Oaks, CA: Corwin.

Kowalski, T. J. (1995b). Preparing teachers to be leaders: Barriers in the workplace. In M. O'Hair & S. Odell (Eds.), *Educating teachers for leadership and change: Teacher education yearbook III* (pp. 243–256). Thousand Oaks, CA: Corwin.

Kowalski, T. J. (2001). The future of local district governance: Implications for board members and superintendents. In C. Brunner & L. Björk (Eds.), *The new superintendency: Advances in research and theories of school management and educational policy* (pp. 183–204). Stamford, CT: JAI Press.

Kowalski, T. J. (2003). *Contemporary school administration: An introduction* (2nd ed.). Boston: Allyn & Bacon.

Kowalski, T. J. (2004). School public relations: A new agenda. In T. J. Kowalski (Ed.), *Public relations in schools* (pp. 3–29). Upper Saddle River, NJ: Merrill, Prentice Hall.

Lugg, C. A. (1996). Calling for community in a conservative age. *Planning and Changing, 27*(2), 2–14.

Lunenburg, F. C., & Ornstein, A. C. (1991). *Educational administration: Concepts and practices.* Belmont, CA: Wadsworth.

March, J. G., & Simon, H. A. (1958). *Organizations.* New York: John Wiley.

Maxcy, S. J. (1995). *Democracy, chaos, and the new school order.* Thousand Oaks, CA: Corwin.

Miskel, C. & Ogawa, R. (1988). Work motivation, job satisfaction, and climate. In N. Boyan (Ed.), *Handbook of research on educational administration* (pp. 279– 304). New York: Longman.

Moloney, W. J. (1989). Restructuring's fatal flaw. *Executive Educator, 11*(10), 21–23.

Morgan, G. (1986). *Images of organization.* Beverly Hills, CA: Sage.

National Center for Educational Statistics (1993). *Digest of educational statistics: 1993.* Washington, DC: U.S. Government Printing Office.

Odden, A., Wohlstetter, P., & Odden, E. (1995). Key issues in effective site-based management. *School Business Affairs, 61*(5), 4–16.

Owens, R. G. (1995). *Organizational behavior in education* (5th ed.). Boston: Allyn & Bacon.

Peterson, K. D. (1987). Administrative control and instructional leadership. In W. Greenfield (Ed.), *Instructional leadership: Concepts, issues, and controversies* (pp. 139–152). Boston: Allyn & Bacon.

Prestine, N. A., & Bowen, C. (1993). Benchmarks of change: Assessing essential school restructuring efforts. *Educational Evaluation and Policy Analysis, 15*(3), 298–319.

Ramirez, A. (1992). *Size, cost, and quality of schools and school districts: A question of context.* East Lansing, MI: National Center for Research on Teacher Learning. (ERIC Document Reproduction Service No. ED361162)

Razik, T. A., & Swanson, A. D. (1995). *Fundamental concepts of educational leadership and management.* Upper Saddle River, NJ: Merrill, Prentice Hall.

Razik, T. A., & Swanson, A. D. (2001). *Fundamental concepts of educational leadership and management* (2nd ed.). Upper Saddle River, NJ: Merrill, Prentice Hall.

Robbins, S. P. (1986). *Organizational behavior: Concepts, controversies, and applications* (3rd ed.). Englewood Cliffs, NJ: Prentice Hall.

Sarason, S. B. (1996). *Revisiting the culture of the school and the problem of change.* New York: Teachers College Press.

Schein, E. H. (1992). *Organizational culture and leadership* (2nd ed.). San Francisco: Jossey-Bass.

Sergiovanni, T. J. (1994). *Building community in schools.* San Francisco: Jossey-Bass.

Smith, F. (1995). Let's declare education a disaster and get on with our lives. *Phi Delta Kappan, 76*(8), 584–590.

Snyder, K. J., & Anderson, R. H. (1986). *Managing productive schools: Toward an ecology.* Orlando, FL: Academic Press.

Strang, D. (1987). The administrative transformation of American education: School district consolidation, 1938–1980. *Administrative Science Quarterly, 32*(3), 352–366.

Strike, K. A. (1993). Professionalism, democracy, and discursive communities: Normative reflections on restructuring. *American Educational Research Journal, 30*(2), 255–275.

Tyack, D. (1990). Restructuring in historical perspective: Tinkering toward utopia. *Teachers College Record, 92*(2), 170–191.

Tyack, D., & Cuban, L. (1995). *Tinkering toward utopia: A century of public school reform.* Cambridge, MA: Harvard University Press.

Waterman, R. H. (1987). *The renewal factor: How the best get and keep the competitive edge.* New York: Bantam Books.

Weick, K. E. (1976). Educational organizations as loosely coupled systems. *Administrative Science Quarterly, 21*(1), 1–19.

Weiler, H. N. (1990). Comparative perspectives on educational decentralization: An exercise in contradiction? *Educational Evaluation and Policy Analysis, 12*(4), 433–448.

Wimpelberg, R. K., & Boyd, W. L. (1990). Restructured leadership: Directed Autonomy in an age of educational reform. *Planning and Changing, 21*(4), 239–253.

Zeichner, K. M. (1991). Contradictions and tensions in the professionalization of teaching and the democratization of schools. *Teachers College Record, 92*(3), 363–379.

CHAPTER 5

School Boards

KEY FACETS OF THE CHAPTER

- ○ Legal status and authority of boards
- ○ Ideal and real roles
- ○ Differences in school board composition
- ○ Political contexts
- ○ Criticisms and recommended reforms

S ince the early 1990s, school reform has focused more intently than in the past on governance issues in public education. The added attention has included scrutiny of lay school boards in an effort to determine whether they are an asset or liability in relation to needed change (Todras, 1993). For many, challenging the authority of school boards is tantamount to challenging liberty because the idea of local control is "deeply embedded in grassroots American political values" (Danzberger, Kirst, & Usdan, 1992, p. 1). Consequently, the citizenry is likely to oppose efforts to eliminate local school boards, even if their eradication promised to expedite school restructuring.

This chapter examines the role and responsibilities of school boards and their functions in contemporary contexts. With respect to the latter issue, special attention is given to the critical issue of school board and superintendent relationships. Both positive and negative aspects of these associations are reviewed. The chapter concludes by examining the future of school district governance.

LEGAL STATUS AND AUTHORITY

Statutes pertaining to the regulation of public education by local boards vary from state to state; even so, "all states dictate such matters as the corporate nature and size of local boards as well as the powers delegated to them" (Russo, 1994, p. 7). Although the context of public education has changed markedly over the past 100 years, many regulating statutes have remained unchanged. Despite massive alterations in the social, economic, and political structure of American society, despite substantial population increases, and despite having fewer but larger school districts, the present arrangement for local control in public education—a system through which states delegate authority to elected or appointed school boards—remains very much like it was in the early 20th century (Danzberger & Usdan, 1994). The press for school reform, however, has created a sense of emergency in some quarters; as a result, state policymakers are more willing to experiment. Legally and politically, unproductive or fiscally troubled local districts can become serious problems for a state government because public education is ultimately a state responsibility.

During the 1980s and 1990s, legislative actions in Illinois, Kentucky, and Massachusetts demonstrated that distressed districts may induce drastic measures. Chicago's public schools, for example, had long been a source of growing public dissatisfaction when a coalition of parents, activists, and business leaders lobbied to get the Illinois Legislature to pass the Chicago School Reform Act of 1988. The legislation required every school in the city's school system to establish a local school council—an elected body of parents, teachers, and neighbors—that was given control over principals' contracts and part of the school budget. After this extreme attempt failed to produce desired results, Chicago's mayor successfully lobbied to have the law amended in 1995. The changes gave the mayor the power to appoint a new school board and superintendent and also gave the newly appointed board and superintendent sweeping powers not granted to their predecessors. In less than a decade, the Illinois legislature imposed extreme and seemingly contradictory governance structures on one of the nation's largest school systems, first by decentralizing authority and then by giving the mayor essentially plenary powers. In similar fashion, the Massachusetts legislature first abolished Boston's elected school board and then gave the city's mayor authority to appoint new board members (Todras, 1993). The most sweeping example of change, however, occurred in Kentucky. Responding to a lawsuit challenging that state's public education system, the legislature enacted a massive reform act that took effect in 1990; all laws, policies, and regulations pertaining to public education were rewritten and local districts were mandated to increase citizen participation in governance while being held accountable by the state for the results.

States also are able to exercise control over local districts by virtue of their existing authority. In 1989, for example, New Jersey's state government directly took control of the Jersey City schools. "Takeover statutes" permit state government to assume administrative responsibility for troubled local districts; Arkansas, Georgia, Kentucky, New Jersey, New Mexico, Ohio, South Carolina, Texas, and West Virginia are examples (Pancrazio, 1994). States also may have statutory authority to assume financial control of districts while not otherwise usurping school board authority. In Indiana, for example, districts determined to be operating with fiscal deficits must have all financial decisions approved by the state's Property Tax Control Board. School boards in these controlled districts, however, continue to formulate policy, approve employment, and so forth.

The focus on school district governance has sparked a myriad of questions about the functions of school boards and the statutes that grant them power. Studying this issue, Pancrazio (1994) predicted that more states were likely to pass laws formalizing their authority to assume complete control of stressed local districts. Moreover, virtually all states have taken measures to strengthen accountability standards for local districts. Many observers (e.g., Harrington-Lueker, 1993) concluded that momentum is building for overhauling the governance system for public elementary and secondary education. Because statutes related to state authority are dynamic, superintendents should determine the applicability of state control statutes to their school districts.

IDEAL AND REAL BOARD ROLES

Historically the literature has included a great deal of information about public school boards, especially in relation to their policymaking role and to legal and ethical behavior. Yet, considerable confusion and controversy persist with regard to the ideal role of these officeholders (Campbell & Greene, 1994). As an agency of state government, the local school board assumes a control function that is actualized through policy decisions. This responsibility has external and internal dimensions. Externally, the school board's decisions should represent the will of the district's patrons—an expectation requiring board members to discern real community needs and wants. Internally, board responsibilities include ensuring proper administrative control through the office of the superintendent, making primary fiscal decisions about budgets and taxes, and examining of the district's outputs (Campbell, Cunningham, Nystrand, & Usdan, 1990). In light of persisting disagreements about board member roles, the National School Boards Association attempted to define these responsibilities concisely. More than two dozen specific duties were identified in these four broad categories:

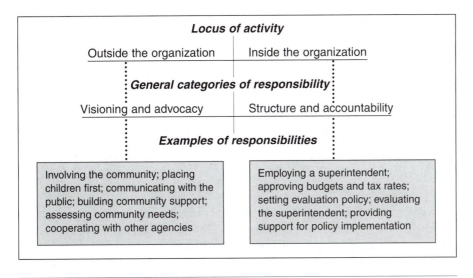

Figure 5.1   Role Expectations for School Boards

- Establishing a long-term vision for the school system
- Establishing and maintaining a basic organizational structure for the school system, including employment of a superintendent, adoption of an annual budget, adoption of governance policies, and creation of a climate that promotes excellence
- Establishing systems and processes to ensure accountability to the community, including fiscal accountability, accountability for programs and student outcomes, staff accountability, and collective bargaining
- Functioning as advocates for children and public education at the community, state, and national levels. (Campbell & Greene, 1994, p. 392)

Figure 5.1 provides an outline of role expectations.

For both external and internal role expectations, there is a fine line separating what superintendents usually interpret as appropriate and inappropriate school board member behavior. For example, board members are expected to maintain two-way communication with the public. Through this process, they frequently receive positive feedback about programs and employees; occasionally, however, they uncover perceived problems or negative attitudes. Although accessing negative information clearly falls within the parameters of appropriate board member behavior, choosing to act on this information rather than relaying it to the superintendent does not. When board members elect to assume administrative duties, conflict between the superintendent and board members becomes highly probable.

Preferred board member roles also have been examined in relation to actual behaviors. The Iowa Association of School Boards (2004), for example, developed the following list of characteristics of highly effective board members:

- They focus on serving all children.
- They understand their basic role and responsibilities.
- They work well as team members.
- They act professionally and with integrity.
- They commit the necessary time and effort.

Role conflict for school board members is often framed by having to choose between two distinctively different conceptualizations: being a *trustee* and being a *delegate*. The former is grounded in the belief that board members are obliged to act rationally in serving broad public interests; the latter is grounded in the belief that board members are obliged to protect their personal interests and the interests of groups supporting them. Therefore, trustees tend to make independent judgments regarding a superintendent's policy recommendations and their decisions reflect a concern for the entire community. Delegates tend to make political judgments regarding a superintendent's policy recommendations and their decisions reflect personal and special interest group concerns (McCurdy, 1992). Many board members try to avoid making a choice between acting as a trustee and acting as a delegate, making their behavior more unpredictable. They meander between the two roles, typically selecting behavior based on contextual variables, that is, the conditions surrounding a given decision.

From the earliest decades of the 20th century, the trustee role was established as the ideal. In addition to behaving rationally and not politically, ideal board members have been expected to respect the demarcation between policy development and policy implementation. Whereas promulgating policy is the domain of the school board, implementing policy is the domain of professional administrators (Zeigler, Jennings, & Peak, 1974). The ideal conceptualization, however, has never been fully understood or accepted by many citizens. Especially since the 1960s, "local boards have evolved back into politicized boards, increasingly involved in the operations and administration of their school districts" (Danzberger & Usdan, 1994, p. 366). Citizens often believe that they should have unrestricted access to their school board members and that board members should be their personal advocates who listen, respond, and intervene when called upon to do so. Studying the responsiveness of New Jersey school board members to parents and community groups, Kenneth Greene (1990) found that the amount of responsiveness among these individuals varied considerably and that their behavioral differences were affected by "[t]he level of electoral competition in the district, the complexity of the district, and whether or not they [board members] plan to run for reelection" (p. 374). Summarizing the determinants of board member behavior, he concluded that neither the entreaties of professional associations nor the aura of expertise surrounding educational administration were sufficiently convincing to overcome pragmatic, political considerations.

Recently, reformers have focused on content-centered role conflict. That is to say, they have become increasingly interested in topics that are either ignored or insufficiently addressed by board members. This scrutiny has produced a list of common criticisms, including (a) not spending sufficient time on educational matters, (b) not working effectively with other community agencies, (c) not providing adequate policy oversight, (d) not effectively communicating outcomes to the community, and (e) failing to provide a long-term vision for the school system (Danzberger, 1994). To some degree, these oversights are caused by community expectations that school board members devote themselves to the issues of the day rather than becoming preoccupied with abstract, long-term projects such as visioning and planning. As a result, some school boards spend virtually all of their time ameliorating day-to-day issues that have little consequence for improving teaching and learning.

Recent studies of school board behavior indicate that superintendent policy recommendations are approved approximately 90% of the time (Glass, 2001). At first glance, this finding appears to invalidate convictions that many board members behave as delegates continuously or occasionally. This statistic, however, does not reveal the extent to which board member pressures may influence a superintendent's recommendations. To get their recommendations approved, superintendents often must make accommodations and reach compromises (Lashaway, 2002). Neither superintendents nor board members want to be mired in public conflict. Board members who do not support a superintendent's initial recommendation may make their feelings known prior to having to vote publicly. If a sufficient number of board members are opposed, superintendents may change their recommendation to fit the board's preference. By doing so, the superintendent gives the community the impression that the board and administration are in harmony and protects the superintendent's political standing with the board. In a national study (Glass, Björk, & Brunner, 2000), only 43% of the superintendents said that they took the lead in developing policy—a finding that supports the contention that the approval rate of superintendent policy recommendations does not reflect philosophical congruence between superintendents and board members accurately.

Delegate board members mired in the political realities of community conflict often view superintendents as managers and not professional leaders—a perspective reflecting previously described tensions between professionalism and democracy (Kowalski, 2004). These board members are aware of and sensitive to the public's reluctance to relinquish control over schools to administrators (Blumberg, 1985). They are reminded repeatedly by their constituents that no single person, no matter the person's level of education and experience, should control school district decisions. Given this context, a delicate compromise between the professional role of the superintendent and the desire of taxpayers to influence critical decisions through school board members has evolved. At the same time that communities overtly accept the trustee role, there is a less discernible but undeniable demand for board members to be political delegates. Recognizing tensions between professionalism and democracy, school board members often refuse to treat policy and administration as completely separate functions (Trotter & Downey, 1989).

COMPOSITION OF SCHOOL BOARDS

There are substantially fewer school board members in the United States today than there were 75 years ago. In 1930, there were approximately 200,000 school boards and 1 of every 500 citizens was a school board member. In 2003, the number of school boards declined to less than 15,000 and only 1 in every 20,000 citizens was a board member (Meier, 2003). Consequently, most school board members probably represent diverse populations. Local boards differ in size, selection methods, authority, and composition.

Size and Selection

The size of school boards varies across and within states. Typically, the number of school board members is determined by a general state statute or by a specific statute under which the district was established. Almost always, the number of board members is odd rather than even to prevent recurring tie votes. Some school boards have as few as 3 members whereas others have as many as 15 members. The norm, however, is 5 or 7 members.

Basically, school board members are either appointed or elected to office. Each option can occur in several ways as detailed in Table 5.1.

State statutes either detail selection methods or provide a range of options for local districts. In rare instances, school boards may have several members who are elected and several members who are appointed. In many states, boards are allowed to appoint a person to complete the unexpired term of a

Table 5.1   Methods for Selecting School Board Members

Category	Options	Explanation
Appointment	By an external official or group	Appointments to the school board are made by a mayor, city council, county council, judge, or some other person or official agency (depending on relevant laws and policies).
	By the school board	In a number of states, school boards are given the authority to replace a school board member who leaves office prior to the expiration of his or her term of office. If board members are not elected to office initially, then appointments for unexpired terms are often made by the person or group making the initial appointment.
Elected	Partisan or nonpartisan	The vast majority of school board elections are conducted on a nonpartisan basis; in some districts, however, individuals are the official candidates of political parties.
	At-large or districted candidacy	In some school districts, some or all seats on the board are legally associated with specified areas or districts; that is, candidates can only seek the seat(s) on the school board that is designated for their specific area of residence. The concept of districted candidates is the same as the one used to elect representatives to the United States House of Representatives. Elections involving districted candidates may be based on at-large or districted voting (depending on relevant laws and policies).
	At-large or districted voting	At-large voting allows all voters in a school district to vote for all contested seats, even if the seats themselves are districted.

board member who has resigned or otherwise vacated his or her seat. Persons appointed to an elected board, however, must be elected when the term expires if they wish to remain in office. Regionally, appointed boards are more common in the south than in other areas of the country; according to district enrollment, appointed boards are more likely in larger school systems (Campbell et al., 1990).

Appointive systems are becoming slightly less popular, possibly because some voters believe appointed board members are less responsive to constituent needs and wants. In 1992, Virginia, the only state that did not allow school board elections, changed its statutes (Underwood, 1992). Movement away from appointed school boards, however, has been very gradual. From the early 1970s to the early 1990s, the percentage of appointed boards declined by 1% or less; in the early 1990s, just over 94% of all boards were elected (Glass, 1992). Hess (2002) reported that 93% of school boards reported that all members were elected. Having partisan elections for school board members has clearly been the exception; nearly 90% of all school board elections have been nonpartisan elections (Campbell et al., 1990). Not only are most school board elections nonpartisan, they are basically apolitical affairs characterized by low levels of campaign spending, few incumbent defeats, and relatively little competition among candidates (Hess, 2002).

Both appointed and elected boards have their proponents; Table 5.2 outlines common arguments for each option.

Support for appointed school boards is often dependent on the specifications of a law, especially that part of the law identifying the person and group who is to make the appointment. In large cities, for example, superintendents often have been wary of mayoral appointments that could give city hall added political leverage over the public schools (Kowalski, 1995).

Despite recent concerns about politics deterring school reform, transition in board member selection almost always has moved from an appointed board to an elected board. Although a fairly substantial number of school districts over the past four or five decades have made this change, relatively little is known about political consequences. Moving from appointing board members to electing them can intensify instability because incumbents who had been appointed may not seek election or they may be defeated in an election. In addition, this transition in selection methods often produces new political alliances within the community and new political arrangements for policymaking (Godfrey, 1987).

School board elections, like all other elections, may be influenced substantially by the activities of political action committees or similar pressure groups. During the past few decades, some of these coalitions have changed their tactics in an effort to obscure their motives; for example, they have selected and financed "stealth" candidates—individuals who do not disclose their affiliation or true agenda until elected (Ledell, 1993). Describing the efforts of Christian fundamentalist groups during the early 1990s, Arocha (1993) wrote:

Table 5.2   Perceived Advantages and Supporting Arguments for Appointed and Elected School Boards

Category	Perceived Advantage	Supporting Argument
Appointment	Greater emphasis on credentials	The person making the appointment may may be more inclined than the voting public to examine issues such as academic credentials, relevant experiences, philosophy, and intentions.
	Greater likelihood of being a trustee	Because appointees are less indebted to political groups, they may be more inclined to support the broad interests of the public rather than the narrow interests of individuals or groups.
	Improved pool of candidates	Some who are well-prepared to serve on school boards do not want to subject themselves to the elective process; the appointment system may be more appealing to influential citizens.
	Greater likelihood of collaboration	Because appointments are often made by key governmental officials or groups, appointees may be less inclined to be territorial; they may exhibit a greater willingness to collaborate with other community agencies.
	Less likely to intrude in administration	Appointees are not politically obligated to individuals who may urge them to get involved in administrative matters; their reappointment is more likely to be based on an assessment of the total service rather than their vote on a single incident.
Election	Congruence with democracy	In a democratic society, election is the preferred mechanism for selecting public representatives.
	Accountability	The schools belong to the people and those governing should be answerable to the people.
	Representative boards	Elections are more likely to produce a school board that is representative of the total community.

(Continued)

Table 5.2 (Continued)

Category	Perceived Advantage	Supporting Argument
	Public awareness	The election process makes citizens aware of issues and needs in education and aware of differing philosophies and critical issues.
	Public participation	The school board election is one avenue of citizen involvement in schools; with approximately 75% of the voters not having children enrolled in the public schools, this is an important issue.

. . . religious fundamentalists are using the democratic process effectively, sometimes joining forces with taxpayers, senior citizens, and other conservative religious groups that share their agenda. They are winning seats on local and state school boards and they are using hard-won power to reshape educational policy. (p. 9)

Battles fought in school board elections reflect the philosophical differences that exist in American society. Members of the most zealous groups believe that the country is engaged in a cultural war, and clearly, they have decided to make the public schools a battleground. These tactics have produced intense emotional struggles, tensions, and even open hostility. But despite concerns about pressure groups and stealth candidates, public preference for elected boards remains strong. Perhaps the major reason is that this process is more likely to increase board member responsiveness to parents and community groups seeking to influence policy or administrative decisions (Greene, 1990).

Demographic Profile

During much of the first half of the 20th century, school board members were White males who were often politically powerful in their communities. This was especially true in the most prominent districts—the large city systems (Kowalski, 1995). Since then, the demographic profile of board members has become less homogeneous. In 1989, approximately 32% of board members were females and this percentage increased to just over 40% in 1994 (Educational Vital Signs, 1994) and remained at this level in 2001 (Vail, 2001). In 1989, 94% of all board members were White and this figure decreased slightly to just over 90% in 1994 (Educational Vital Signs, 1994); by 2001, it had dropped to 86% (Vail, 2001). Among non-White board members, approximately 8% identified themselves as African Americans and approximately 4% as Hispanics (Hess, 2002).

Despite continuing concerns about the demographic composition, school boards are more ethnically diverse than most other state and national elective bodies (Hess, 2002). Moreover, 2 of 3 superintendents nationally indicated that their board members were aligned with the common interests of the citizens represented. Only 19% said that the board was aligned with a distinct community faction, and slightly less than 3% said the board was dominated by community elites (Glass et al., 2000).

Compensation

Nationally, school board members report spending about 25 hours per month on board-related tasks. A substantial number of them, however, report spending as much as 20 hours per week. The greater time commitment is especially likely in large districts (i.e., those with more than 25,000 students) (Hess, 2002). The amount of time devoted to board activities has generated questions about compensation for the officeholders.

Many, but not all, school board members are entitled to receive salaries—that is, compensation for their service—in addition to expense reimbursements. Statutes vary among the states, and laws concerning compensation for school board members generally fall into one of three broad categories: (a) states permitting all board members to be compensated, (b) states permitting some board members to be compensated, and (c) states not permitting compensation (Needham, 1992). Approximately two-thirds of board members nationally receive no salary; only 4% reported receiving $10,000 or more in 2001. Large school districts are the most likely to provide compensation and the most likely to provide compensation at a level of $10,000 or more (Hess, 2002).

CRITICISMS AND RECOMMENDED REFORMS

By the late 1980s, most educational reformers had become convinced that intensification mandates could only produce slight improvement in student performance. Consequently, their attention shifted toward more radical reform proposals such as school restructuring. When this transition in strategy occurred, school and school district governance were drawn into the school reform debate. In 1992, two national reports, *Facing the Challenge* (funded by the Twentieth Century Fund and Danforth Foundation) and *Governing Public Schools* (produced by the Institute for Educational Leadership), found the current system of school governance to be inadequate; both reports recommended "sweeping changes in the ways school boards are organized and operate" (Harrington-Lueker, 1993, p. 31). Since these reports, the attention given to the governance of school districts has escalated.

Criticisms

Critics of local school boards have become more vocal in recent years. As an example, an article questioning the future of school boards (Elizabeth, 2003) quoted Chester Finn, a former assistant secretary of education and advocate for major governance reform, as saying: "School boards are an aberration, an anachronism, an educational sinkhole." Such stinging criticisms are only one of several reasons why the time-honored tradition of local school boards is now being questioned. Consider two reasons.

- *Instability.* Many observers believe that the current governance structure is resulting in leadership instability—a condition that deters reform. Critics argue that because the tenure of both board members and superintendents is declining, leadership teams in many districts are not in office long enough to implement needed changes. In truth, the tenure of superintendents has declined only in small rural and large urban districts; the national average for all districts (approximately 6 years) has remained relatively constant for several decades (Glass et al., 2000; Kowalski, 2003). Nevertheless, it is likely that as districts have become larger, boards have become more divided politically and philosophically, which is not especially favorable to reform.
- *Incompatibility with modern reforms.* Ideas such as charter schools, choice, and district decentralization have generated questions both about the need for boards and about their appropriate roles. Site-based management, for example, has required many boards and superintendents to reconsider the distribution of power among the state, district, and individual school and the effects of this redistribution on their roles. Changing conditions have prompted some scholars (e.g., Danzberger, 1994) to advocate that boards spend more time on issues such as curricular frameworks, bridging reform initiatives with district policy, assuring adequate and equitable experiences across the school district, and evaluation, and less time on management functions. Other critics (e.g., Finn, 1997) argue that school boards help to perpetuate the monopolistic status of public education—a condition that prevents meaningful competition and reform based on market forces.

admit that they are concerned about their
e... ...onducted by the Institute for Educational
L... ...at "boards, by their own admission, are not
f... ...nning and goal-setting policy bodies"
(Danzberger...

...sed by two perceived conditions: local
sc... ...esent them and local school boards no
lo... ...ufficiently (Danzberger et al., 1992).
Re... ...l districts in this country probably has
inc... ...ong many taxpayers. Even so, discontent
als... ...political conditions. For most of the 20th
cen... ...ommunity elites exerted the most influ-
enc... ...962; Wirt & Kirst, 2001) and because
thes... ...as community leaders, the public may
hav... ...interventions. In the 1970s, however,
teac... ...dable opponent. Their affiliation with
nati... ...r direct involvement with schools, and
their... ...ve role in school board elections made
them... ...many districts. Commenting on organized... ...(2001) noted that in local politics, "the
teac... ...osition of being able to determine who
sits o... ...with whom they will be bargaining"
(p. 43... ...or obstacle to school reform, he argues
that t... ...leverage to control public education has been enhanced by
their ability to seize control of local boards (Moe, 2003a). As an example, a
recent California study found that 92% of school board incumbents endorsed
by teachers unions were elected (Moe, 2003b). This is not surprising in light
of the fact that teachers unions are the largest outside contributors and the
most active campaigners in school board elections (Elizabeth, 2003). Even so,
there are still many local districts where community power elites yield considerable power, including the ability to influence school board elections and
key policy decisions.

Negative images of school boards have been exacerbated by the public's perception that conflict is pervasive, not only between board members and the
superintendent, but also among board members themselves (Danzberger et al.,
1992). Even superintendents are beginning to question whether the current
governance structure is appropriate. In a national survey of superintendents,
Glass (2001) found that 68% felt that the school board system needed to be
"seriously restructured" or "completely replaced."

Recommended Changes

More than 100 years ago, school boards were "separated from municipalities and the political patronage system to better serve the needs of children and youth, without the encumbrances of unsavory political influence (Norton, Webb, Dlugosh, & Sybouts, 1996, p. 111). Recently, however, this arrangement has been questioned by reformers and despite its apparent imperfections, most policymakers appear unwilling to tamper with the status quo. Nevertheless, some analysts continue to argue that the primary role of local boards should be reconfigured. Danzberger (1994), for example, believes that needed school restructuring is improbable unless it is accompanied by a restructuring of governance. Debates on this topic are often contentious and reveal opposing dispositions nested in values and politics.

If the governance structure of local districts is to improve, we must first identify effective and ineffective behavior. Schlechty (1992) argues that the best boards create a consensus vision, develop and implement a plan for engaging the community in discussion about the vision, empower leaders to achieve the vision and evaluate the extent of implementation, and assure that policies and regulations contribute to achieving the vision. At the same time, they do not engage in micromanagement, act as advocates for narrow parochial interests, or separate themselves from teachers and administrators for political protection from public criticism. The separation issue is especially compelling because it divides the policymaking body of the organization from the administrative body of the organization—a separation that inevitably leads to serious problems in superintendent and board member relationships.

Examining the role of local boards in school improvement, the Institute for Educational Leadership recommended that state legislatures repeal all current laws regarding school boards and that these bodies should be officially renamed "Local Education Policy Boards" (Danzberger et al., 1992, p. 87). The Institute's report identified a policy board's activities as visioning, planning, curriculum development, community interactions, and budget and contract approvals. These reconfigured boards would no longer serve a quasi-judicial function (e.g., presiding over appeals or other hearings), have a fiduciary responsibility (e.g., approving claims, purchase orders), engage in budget management, manage details of construction projects, be involved in personnel matters other than those pertaining to the superintendent, or approve routine travel requests such as field trips.

Interestingly, the term *policy board* also has been used by individuals advocating a more direct role for school board members in day-to-day governance. Advocates of this position claim that a lack of progress in school reform is attributable to existing school cultures that resist lay interventions and to superintendents who treat board members as subordinates. As an example, one school board member authored an article calling for school boards to become policy boards but in a way that was quite different from the Institute for Educational Leadership's recommendation. She wrote:

Traditionally, few boards ever have meetings without the superintendent physically present: they are much like children relying on a parent—or students relying on a teacher. Just as we see kids in a classroom, when excellence is not demanded, when thoughtfulness is not valued, and when self-directed meaningful work is not required, then apathy and mediocrity result. Is it any wonder trustees have abdicated their responsibilities over the years? (Zlotkin, 1993, p. 24)

This board member advocated (a) that superintendents should occasionally take a back seat (i.e., to get out of the way and let board members lead), (b) that board members attend seminars and conferences on school administration (so they could be more effective in administrative activities), and (c) that trustees should build relationships with staff members other than the superintendent.

The two very different perspectives reveal why it will be extremely difficult to change state laws affecting local school boards. At one end of the philosophical spectrum are reformers who want to restrict board intrusions into administration so that members can devote their time to critical policy issues (e.g., vision, mission, and curriculum). These reformers see superintendents as professionals who should be allowed to implement policy and to manage the school system without direct board member interventions. At the other end of the spectrum are reformers who view superintendents largely as political appointees or domesticated public employees. They believe that political interests, common sense, and their own wisdom trump a superintendent's recommendations. Ideas espoused by these antiprofessionalists actually have existed from the earliest days of school administration and they reflect an inescapable tension between professionalism and democracy (Kowalski, 2004). An indifference toward the value of superintendent policy recommendations and interventions into administration are two reasons why social and political factors, and not research and theory, were the most influential variables shaping professional study and practice in school administration for much of the past century (Goldhammer, 1983).

In the final analysis, the primary purpose of school boards should be to transform community needs into a coherent and achievable vision that gives direction to school improvement. In meeting this goal, boards "must represent the best and finest thinking in the community regarding the purposes of education in a democracy" (Schlechty, 1992, p. 28). The development of these essential visions, unique for each school district, becomes more probable when school board members assume leadership in developing policy and cease managing policy implementation. On the other hand, reform becomes more likely when school administrators understand that they must apply their professional knowledge in highly political contexts (Wirt & Kirst, 2001). Thus, they should neither treat board members as subordinates nor should they expect that their recommendations will be consistently and automatically approved.

FOR FURTHER REFLECTION

This chapter reviewed the duties and responsibilities of school boards and school board members, and profiled the contemporary school board. Of special note is the distinction between the concept of *trustee* and the concept of *delegate*. Ideally, board members are expected to be trustees acting in the interests of the entire community; in reality, some board members are political delegates acting in the interests of selected pressure groups. Philosophical and political reasons determining which role board members embrace were discussed.

Focused attention was given to the critical issue of the relationship between the board and the superintendent. Sustained efforts to achieve school reform have placed greater attention on practices that enhance or destroy these associations. Superintendents often have been advised to restrict their social contact with board members and to insist on absolute distinctions between policy making and policy implementation. This division, however, is far less clear in practice than it is in the professional literature.

The future of school boards also was discussed. Some analysts advocate rescinding existing laws for school boards and then reconfiguring these legislative bodies as education policy boards. Others advocate that board members take an even more direct role in running schools. To date, state policymakers appear to be uninterested in changing any dimension of this long-standing institution.

As you consider the content of this chapter, address the following issues:

1. What are the differences between developing policy and implementing policy?

2. What are the fundamental differences between the concepts of a board member as a "trustee" and a board member as a "delegate"?

3. In your experience, have most board members been delegates or trustees?

4. Some board members rely heavily on the superintendent for leadership and information; others prefer to immerse themselves in problems and to collect their own information. What factors may cause a board member to behave in one manner or the other?

5. Common wisdom suggests that telling an interviewer what the interviewer wants to hear is a good way to enhance your chances of the getting the job. Is it advisable in a superintendent interview? Why or why not?

6. How can superintendents destroy their integrity?

7. Because the vast majority of school board members have not had formal preparation for their role prior to entering office, what types of orientation experiences can superintendents provide for them?

8. In your opinion, should states change laws to raise requirements for serving on school boards? Why or why not?

9. What are the advantages and disadvantages of electing school boards?

10. What questions would you ask during an interview to determine the values and beliefs of the board members concerning the superintendent's role?

Case Study

In the 3 years that Dr. Elaine Conklin has been superintendent of Green River School District, she has established a positive working relationship with the teachers' union. The union president, Mark Udell, has publicly praised her for working closely with teachers and with the community. Elaine's predecessor, Dr. Evan Strack, resigned after only 2 years in office, telling the board members that the union's leadership constituted an insurmountable barrier to school improvement. Needless to say, Superintendent Strack's personal relationship with Mr. Udell was not positive.

Unlike her predecessor, Dr. Conklin was patient and saw reform as a long-term process. She decided that she had to make the union an ally in pursuing change, so she recommended to the board that the union be permitted to appoint one teacher to each of four key district committees. Although two of these committees already had a teacher representative, the appointments had been made by the school board. Neither of the teachers who had been appointed were union members. Superintendent Conklin's recommendation on including union representatives turned out to be more controversial than she imagined. Three of the school board members told her privately that they would not support the recommendation and urged her to drop the issue before it became public. Among the remaining four board members, two reacted favorably to the recommendation and two made no comment. Convinced that the recommendation was in the district's best interests, she presented it to the board in a public meeting. After more than 30 minutes of discussion, the recommendation was approved by a margin of 4 to 3.

The terms of two of the board members who did not support the superintendent's recommendation were expiring. Both announced that they were seeking re-election and neither expected more than token opposition. Initially, Mr. Udell announced that the teachers' union would not support the incumbents and publicly urged "more progressive" residents to challenge them. Two weeks later, the union issued a press release that they were supporting two challengers—one a teacher who lived in Green River but worked in a neighboring district and the other a retired teacher and former union president in Green River.

Although Superintendent Conklin had no active role in either encouraging the incumbents to seek re-election or encouraging the union to find challengers, she was pulled into the political quagmire by the candidates. The incumbents argued that her cozy relationship with the teachers' union had encouraged that group to broaden its political power. The challengers praised the superintendent and argued that the incumbent board members, by virtue of voting against the superintendent's recommendation on union representation on district committees, exhibited that they were the real obstacles to school reform.

Reporters from the local media repeatedly asked Dr. Conklin to comment on the election and the statements about her made by the four candidates. She refused. The board president who had been her most ardent supporter met with her privately and told her that her political capital with the school board was being rapidly depleted. At least three of the board members, including the two incumbents, already had told the board president privately that they would not vote to renew the superintendent's contract when it expired the following year. The day after meeting with the board president, Mr. Udell met with the superintendent at his request. He told Dr. Conklin that he had learned from a reliable source that she would be dismissed if the two incumbents were elected. He urged her to publicly support the two challengers and pledged that the teachers' union would play an active role in protecting her job.

Case Study Questions

1. Given the circumstances surrounding the departure of her predecessor, should Dr. Conklin have pursued a relationship with the teachers' union? Why or why not?

2. Although the superintendent knew that her recommendation to appoint union members to each of the four district committees was controversial and divisive, she presented it to the board anyway. Was her action appropriate ethically and politically?

3. What would have been the advantages and disadvantages of acquiescing to the three board members and withdrawing the recommendation?

4. If you were the superintendent, would you listen to the board president or to Mr. Udell?

5. Do you think the two incumbents are treating the superintendent fairly? Why or why not?

6. Local teachers' unions have been successful in getting their representatives elected to school boards in many districts. Has their success had a positive or negative effect on public education?

7. Identify the options the superintendent has in dealing with this matter. Which option would you choose?

REFERENCES

Arocha, Z. (1993). The Religious Right's march into public school governance. *School Administrator, 50*(9), 31–34.

Blumberg, A. (1985). *The school superintendent: Living with conflict.* New York: Teachers College Press.

Callahan, R. E. (1962). *Education and the cult of efficiency: A study of the social forces that have shaped the administration of public schools.* Chicago: University of Chicago Press.

Campbell, D. W., & Greene, D. (1994). Defining the leadership role of school boards in the 21st century. *Phi Delta Kappan, 75*(5), 391–395.

Campbell, R. F., Cunningham, L. L., Nystrand, R. O., & Usdan, M. D. (1990). *The organization and control of American schools* (6th ed.). Columbus, OH: Merrill.

Danzberger, J. P. (1994). Governing the nation's schools: The case for restructuring local school boards. *Phi Delta Kappan, 75*(5), 367–373.

Danzberger, J. P., Kirst, M. W., & Usdan, M. D. (1992). *Governing public schools: New times new requirements.* Washington, DC: The Institute for Educational Leadership.

Danzberger, J. P., & Usdan, M. D. (1994). Local education governance: Perspectives on problems and strategies for change. *Phi Delta Kappan, 75*(5), 366.

Educational Vital Signs. (1994). A supplement to the *American School Board Journal, 181*(12), A1–A31.

Elizabeth, J. (2003, November 30). School boards' worth in doubt. *Pittsburgh Post-Gazette.* Retrieved June 12, 2004, from http://www.post-gazette.com/local-news/20031130boardsmainloca12p2.asp

Finn, C. E. (1997). Learning-free zones: Five reasons America's schools won't improve. *Policy Review, 85.* Retrieved June 15, 2004, from http://www.policyreview.org/sept97/learning.html

Glass, T. E. (1992). *The 1992 study of the American school superintendency.* Arlington, VA: American Association of School Administrators.

Glass, T. E. (2001). *Superintendent leaders look at the superintendency, school boards, and reform.* Denver, CO: Education Commission of the States.

Glass, T., Björk, L., & Brunner, C. (2000). *The 2000 study of the American school superintendency.* Arlington, VA: American Association of School Administrators.

Godfrey, M. (1987). *Case study in change: Appointed to elected school board.* East Lansing, MI: National Center for Research on Teacher Learning. (ERIC Document Reproduction Service No. ED300926)

Goldhammer, K. (1983). Evolution in the profession. *Educational Administration Quarterly, 19*(3), 249–272.

Greene, K. R. (1990). School board members' responsiveness to constituents. *Urban Education, 24*(4), 363–375.

Harrington-Lueker, D. (1993). Reconsidering school boards. *American School Board Journal, 180*(2), 30–36.

Hess, F. M. (2002). *Schools boards at the dawn of the 21st century: Conditions and challenges of district governance.* Washington, DC: National School Boards Association.

Iowa Association of School Boards (2004). *Traits of effective school board members.* Retrieved June 4, 2004, from http://www.ia-sb.org/boardbasics/traits.asp

Kowalski, T. J. (1995). *Keepers of the flame: Contemporary urban superintendents.* Thousand Oaks, CA: Corwin.

Kowalski, T. J. (2003). Superintendent shortage: The wrong problem and wrong solutions. *Journal of School Leadership, 13*, 288–303.

Kowalski, T. J. (2004). The ongoing war for the soul of school administration. In T. J. Lasley (Ed.), *Better leaders for America's schools: Perspectives on the manifesto* (pp. 92–114). Columbia, MO: University Council for Educational Administration.

Lashaway, L. (2002). *The superintendent in an age of accountability.* East Lansing, MI: National Center for Research on Teacher Learning. (ERIC Document Reproduction Service No. ED468515)

Ledell, M. A. (1993). Taking the steam off pressure groups. *School Administrator, 50*(9), 31–34.

McCurdy, J. (1992). *Building better board-administrator relations.* Alexandria, VA: American Association of School Administrators.

Meier, D. (2003). The road to trust. *American School Board Journal, 190*(9), 18–21.

Moe, T. M. (2001). A union by any other name. *Education Next, 1*(3) 40–45.

Moe, T. M. (2003a). Reform blockers. *Education Next, 3*(2), 56–61.

Moe, T. M. (2003b, October). *Teachers' unions and school board elections.* Paper presented at the School Board Politics Conference, Kennedy School of Government, Harvard University.

Needham, J. D. (1992). To pay or not to pay? *American School Board Journal, 179*(3), 40–41.

Norton, M. S., Webb, L. D., Dlugosh, L. L., & Sybouts, W. (1996). *The school superintendency: New responsibilities, new leaders.* Boston: Allyn & Bacon.

Pancrazio, S. B. (1994). State takeovers and other last resorts. In P. First & H. Walberg (Eds.), *School boards: Changing local control* (pp. 71–90). Berkeley, CA: McCutchan.

Russo, C. J. (1994). The legal status of school boards in the intergovernmental system. In P. First & H. Walberg (Eds.), *School boards: Changing local control* (pp. 3–20). Berkeley, CA: McCutchan.

Schlechty, P. C. (1992). Deciding the fate of local control. *American School Board Journal, 178*(11), 27–29.

Todras, E. (1993). *The changing role of school boards.* East Lansing, MI: National Center for Research on Teacher Learning. (ERIC Document Reproduction Service No. ED357434)

Trotter, A., & Downey, G. W. (1989). Many superintendents privately contend school board "meddling" is more like it. *American School Board Journal, 176*(6), 21–25.

Underwood, K. (1992). Power to the people. *American School Board Journal, 179*(6), 42–43.

Vail, K. (2001). Teamwork at the top. *American School Board Journal, 188*(11), 23–25.

Wirt, F. M., & Kirst, M. W. (2001). *The political dynamics of American education* (2nd ed.). Berkeley, CA: McCutchan.

Zeigler, L. H., Jennings, M. K., & Peak, W. G. (1974). *Governing American schools: Political interaction in local school districts.* North Scituate, MA: Duxbury.

Zlotkin, J. (1993). Rethinking the school board's role. *Educational Leadership, 51*(3), 22–25.

CHAPTER 6

Superintendent and School Board Relationships

KEY FACETS OF THE CHAPTER

- Importance of positive relations

- Building positive relationships

- Common problems associated with board members

- Common problems associated with superintendents

- Maintaining positive relations

- Managing conflict

One of the most unsettling realities in the practice of school administration is that one election can change everything. Although top executives in many private companies face similar uncertainties, the probability of rapid radical change is not nearly as great as it is in public education. Even more important, the relationships that a superintendent establishes and maintains with board members not only affect personal survival, they shape organizational effectiveness (Björk & Keedy, 2001; Petersen & Fusarelli, 2001). When friction occurs, our first inclination is to conclude that the parties have performed inappropriately, that they hold different philosophies, or that they have different political goals. Several authors who have examined this issue (e.g., Carter, 2000; Dawson & Quinn, 2000) have arrived at a different conclusion: The fundamental problem, they say, is that the current governance culture not only tolerates role ambiguity, it actually causes it. In this cultural context, roles are often reversed: superintendents spend considerable time developing policy and boards immerse themselves in administrative functions.

As discussed in Chapter 5, the prospect of reconfiguring school boards is remote. Consequently, aspiring superintendents need to prepare themselves to build positive relationships in unaccommodating climates. The task is somewhat like trying to grow tomatoes in an outdoor garden in New England during the winter; it would be foolish to attempt because of the inhospitable climate. To succeed, the grower must be creative and plant in an environment having proper temperatures, light levels, and moisture (e.g., a greenhouse environment). Similarly superintendents who rely on happenstance to develop positive relationships in the prevailing negative climates make a poor choice. The task requires imagination and effort. Referring to successful practice, Shibles, Rallis, and Deck (2001) noted that the most effective superintendents are those who "work with their board members to build a team that clarifies purpose and makes decisions based on data that have been analyzed and interpreted according to shared definitions and criteria to become common information" (p. 180).

This chapter explores the nature of board-superintendent relationships and examines the reasons why those relationships affect both individuals and school districts. Positive and negative actions related to relationships are also discussed, and a summary of conflict resolution activities is provided.

IMPORTANCE OF POSITIVE RELATIONSHIPS

Probably no relationship in a school district has a greater effect on successful education than that between a board and its superintendent. Much like a solid marriage, good relationships weather power struggles, misunderstandings, and competing needs that are manifestations of inevitable conflict found in all organizations (Hanson, 2003). If personal associations are negative or weak, superintendents and board members consume time and energy sniping at each other rather than addressing the district's real needs (Vail, 2001). Disharmony is especially damaging in school districts making a genuine effort to implement change because division between the superintendent and board members casts doubts in the minds of citizens that the proposed alterations are essential.

A lack of leadership stability has made relationships more important than ever. Both school board and superintendent turnover make it difficult to implement reforms because reforms that may take 5 years or longer to develop often get eliminated or pushed aside when changes occur at the top of a district's hierarchy (Kowalski, 1995). Poor relations between a superintendent and school board members have been identified as a major cause of leadership volatility (Weller, Brown, & Flynn, 1991). Examining this issue, Carter (2000) concluded that both parties usually share some blame when natural role tensions are not addressed properly and allowed to breed animosity:

> I have seen firsthand the damage done to the CEO role and to superintendents personally by board behavior we have come to accept as normal. School governance is fraught with the ironic combination of micromanagement and rubber stamping, as well as an array of tradition-blessed practices that trivialize the board's important public policy role. (p. 6).

Recently, several policy scholars (e.g., Danzberger, Kirst, & Usdan, 1992; Petersen & Fusarelli, 2001) have examined the effects of poor relations on school improvement efforts. Unsurprisingly, they concluded that such associations thwart this objective. For example, political battles and superintendent instability attenuate critical functions such as collaborative visioning and long-range planning; not corrected, they diminish the effectiveness of both the board and administration (Petersen & Fusarelli, 2001).

Although the literature commonly refers to board-superintendent relations, several studies (Blumberg, 1985; Kowalski, 1995) have shown that superintendents are inclined to characterize these relationships as individual associations rather than associations with the board as a unit. Three factors appear to contribute to this tendency. First, school boards today are often more factional than pluralistic (Shibles et al., 2001), a condition that intensifies political behavior and attenuates unity. Consequently, talking about the board collectively is impractical, if not impossible, for many superintendents because the members do not commonly share a single agenda (Kowalski, 1995). Second, the superintendent's reputation and job survival are largely dependent on the superintendent's ability to influence critical policy decisions. Most often, efforts to sway votes occur on a one-to-one basis between the superintendent and an individual board member (Blumberg, 1985).

A multitude of ethical, moral, professional, and social issues frame the relationship between a superintendent and school board members. For instance, superintendents have the professional and ethical obligation to make recommendations to the board on policy matters. While board members are ethically bound to listen, they certainly are not obligated to follow the superintendent's recommended course of action. Hence, communication, both formal and informal, becomes an essential process in policymaking, and effective communication is certainly at the core of positive relationships (Kowalski, 2004). In their studies of superintendent and board member relationships, Petersen and Fusarelli (2001) cited three variables that may have made these associations increasingly more difficult: changing demographics in school districts, demands for school reform, and changes in the preparation, socialization, and experiences of superintendents.

During much of the past century, board and superintendent relationships were framed by community power structures because these configurations often determined the composition and philosophical agenda of local boards. Researchers hypothesized that superintendents would align their leadership role to fit board expectations and, hence, to fit the expectations of the community power structure (Keedy & Björk, 2002). McCarty and Ramsey (1971) identified four types of power structures and the likely effects of each on board member and superintendent behavior:

- *Dominated structure*—A few individuals (elites), by virtue of wealth or historical prominence, possess most of the power. This structure often produced a dominated board; that is, a board that treated the superintendent as a domesticated government employee. Under these circumstances, the superintendent became a functionary and not professional leader.
- *Factional structure*—Power is distributed between or among community factions having competing religious, philosophical, economic, social, or political agendas. Board members typically represent major factions and because board members are divided, superintendents engage more directly in political behavior to survive.
- *Pluralistic structures*—Power is dispersed and emerging issues produce coalitions. Unlike factions, coalitions are focused on an issue and dissolve once their task is completed. Boards in these communities also tend to be issue-oriented; they formulate opinions based on an objective analysis of the matter at hand. Unlike factions, however, they are not rigidly bound by ideology or long-range objectives. Superintendents in these situations tend to play a facilitative role offering information and professional recommendations.
- *Inert structures*—Community power is rarely exercised in relation to public schools. Little interest is shown in school board elections and board members tend to approve administrative recommendations routinely. Superintendents in these situations are often the dominant decision maker in the organization.

Unfortunately, superintendents typically find it difficult to apply such models objectively to their own practice. As an example, 97% of superintendents participating in the most recent national study conducted by the American Association of School Administrators identified their primary role as either professional advisor (47.7%) or dominant decision maker (49.5%); only 1.2% said they were functionaries and only 1.6% said they were political strategists (Glass, Björk, & Brunner, 2000). Clearly, these results are more indicative of the roles superintendents think they should be assuming than of the roles they are actually assuming because thousands of school boards still exist in communities with dominated or factional power structures. Discrepancies between normative and actual behavior help us understand the tremendous potential that exists for board-superintendent friction. Although the vast majority of superintendents prefer to see themselves as professional decision makers, many are coerced to accept subordinate or political roles.

BUILDING POSITIVE RELATIONSHIPS

Because healthy relations between a superintendent and board members cannot be taken for granted, those aspiring to this position need to ask: How do I build and maintain positive relationships? Two factors that loom large in answering this critical query are *thoughtful planning* and *effective human relations skills* (Norton, Webb, Dlugosh, & Sybouts, 1996). A third factor that nurtures positive relationships is *philosophical congruence*.

Planning

Relationship building begins with the employment process—a time when the foundation is constructed—and is continuous. Before an effective plan can be developed, the superintendents must have a vision of what is to be accomplished. This mental image should be based on accurate self-assessment and contain attainable objectives. Foremost, it should identify normative standards for leadership and management behavior and ideal associations between the superintendent and board members. The mental image should detail mutual role expectations, communication, and problem-solving behavior, and it should be discussed with the board before it is formally adopted. Not sharing mutual expectations in this manner is a major cause of conflict between board members and superintendents (McCurdy, 1992). After the discourse, the vision may need to be modified.

Once a mutually acceptable vision of board-superintendent relations is in place, the superintendent can develop a strategy for achieving it. The plan should include both process tactics and outcome goals. The former include procedural behaviors that characterize how the superintendent will treat board members and be treated by them. The most critical include the following:

- *Honesty*—Misrepresentations can occur as early as the employment process; when this happens, positive relations become even more difficult. Superintendents and board members often find it advantageous to espouse certain values they really do not embrace. For example, a superintendent may claim to be democratic to gain board member approval when in actuality the superintendent is highly dictatorial. Dishonesty is almost always unmasked after the parties begin interacting and its disclosure diminishes or even destroys credibility.

- *Continuous two-way communication*—In many districts, administrators continue to be socialized to accept bureaucratic communication procedures. Accordingly, they believe that information should only flow in one direction, top-down. By exchanging information with the board instead of disseminating it—a process that entails both distributing and collecting information (Kowalski, 2004)—superintendents avoid alienation.

- *Fairness*—If superintendents want board members to express goodwill, they must do the same. This means being fair, just, and caring in their associations. When superintendents use different standards to relate to board members, they can expect to receive the same treatment.

- *Cooperation*—Too often, board members and superintendents view their relationship as competitive. That is, they perceive it as a power struggle. Effective relationships, however, are more often reflective of cooperation—the parties focus on how they can help each other rather than on jurisdictional conflicts.

- *Assistance*—Board members generally respond positively to superintendents who attempt to help them be effective. This is especially true if the assistance occurs in a subtle diplomatic manner. Providing orientation for new board members is one example. For many individuals, public office is a task for which they have had no formal preparation. Yet, only about 1 in 4 superintendents (26%) involved in a national study said that their board members had attended orientation workshops sponsored by national or state organizations. Over twice as many (55%), however, said they provided this assistance (Glass et al., 2000).

Once a superintendent has identified positive behaviors, attention can be given to specific outcomes. The most common goals include the following:

- *Mutual respect*—As noted earlier, superintendent role expectations are not constant; some possess almost complete power and others possess literally no power. Neither of these options is healthy with regard to board-superintendent relationships because mutual respect and not dominance is the primary bonding element. This means that the parties honor each other's role, avoid usurping authority, and never behave dictatorially. Superintendents should have high regard for the local school board as an American institution of representative governance (Shannon, 1996).

- *Trust*—In its absence, suspicions, misinterpretations, accusations, insecurity, and political behavior flourish. Not surprisingly, studies have repeatedly found that superintendents and board members cite trust as the most important element in their working relationship (McCurdy, 1992).

- *Effectiveness*—Relations are important because of the effect they have on a school district's programs and subsequently on student achievement. Congenial relations, although preferable, are in and of themselves insufficient; these associations must also be effective. Therefore, superintendents should make a conscious effort to link their relations with the board to the district's productivity.

- *Commitment to continuous improvement*—When administrators evaluate teachers, they ideally engage in both formative and summative evaluation. The same should be true of a board relations plan. The superintendent should focus on how annual evaluations will contribute to improved personal performance, improved board performance, and improved relationships.

Figure 6.1 illustrates a model for building and retaining positive relationships.

Human Relations

Interpersonal skills—that is, how we treat other people—involve our disposition toward interacting with others and our ability (skills) for doing so (Egan, 1976). The best intentions of superintendents and the value of their knowledge can be diminished by poor communication or by treating others inappropriately. This is why effective superintendents constantly focus on the human relations dimension of their contact with others and especially with board members (Eadie & Houston, 2003). They believe that positive working relations enhance personal and organizational performance.

Clearly, communication is the most relevant dimension of human relations. As noted in a previous discussion of communication (see Chapter 2), school administrators often have been socialized to communicate for efficiency rather than for relationship building. For much of the last century, management science has advocated a classical communication model in which instructions and commands are transmitted down a chain of command and only from one person to the person or persons below (Luthans, 1981). In the early 1960s, for example, Thayer (1961) identified only four functions of administrative communication: informing, instructing or directing, evaluating, and influencing.

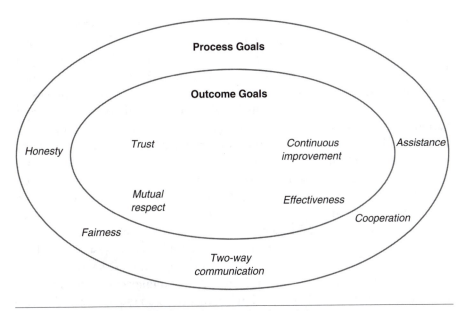

Figure 6.1   A Model for Building Positive Board Relations

Within this normative context, managers frequently believed that communication effectiveness depended solely on the quality of the messages *they* composed and transmitted (Clampitt, 1991). Superintendents emulating corporate managers often treated subordinates, as well as board members, in this impersonal manner, convinced that their major priority was to control information (Achilles & Lintz, 1983).

Beginning in the 1980s, the classical communication model, long deemed the ideal for managers (Luthans, 1981), was increasingly criticized across organizations, and in public school systems specifically. In the case of school districts, discontent centered on the apparent ineffectiveness of this model in relation to developing shared understandings (Hoy & Miskel, 1996), implementing modern reform strategies (Kowalski, 1998b), administering in an information-based society (Hanson, 2003), and engaging in moral and ethical practice (Sergiovanni, 2001). At the same time, empirical evidence indicated a nexus between the communication style of administrators and perceptions of their effectiveness (e.g., Richmond, McCroskey, Davis, & Koontz, 1980; Snavely & Walters, 1983). As a result, administrators were encouraged to pursue harmony between the detached nature of management and the moral dimension of dealing with people (Sergiovanni, 2001) and to employ relational communication to achieve this objective with both employees and board members (Kowalski, 2004).

Relational communication pertains to both the manner in which information is exchanged and interpersonal perceptions of the exchange (Littlejohn, 1992). Although *interpersonal communication* has been defined broadly to include one-way symbolic transmissions by some authors (e.g., Ehling, White, & Grunig, 1992), the term is restricted here to define a two-way process in which persons influence one another's behavior over and above their organizational role, rank, and status (Cappella, 1987). Relation communication is symmetrical, meaning that the process is intended to benefit all interactants (Grunig, 1989) and meaning that the interactants behave similarly, and minimize their differences, including those involving legitimate (position-based) power in the organization (Burgoon & Hale, 1984). Put another way, superintendents and board members avoid situations in which one party is subordinated. In comparison, complementary communication—behavior promoted by classical theory and found historically in most public school systems—reduces opportunities for mutual influence and information sharing (McGregor, 1967). Whereas relational communication is intended to minimize interactant differences, complementary communication is intended to do the opposite; that is, it is intended to establish one party as dominant and the other as submissive (Burgoon & Hale, 1984).

Wiemann (1977) defined communication competence as "the ability of an interactant to choose among available communicative behaviors in order that he (she) may successfully accomplish his (her) own interpersonal goals during an encounter while maintaining the face and line of his (her) fellow interactants within the constraints of the situation" (p. 198). This definition has a distinctive behavioral tone indicating that competence and performance are entangled. To be competent a superintendent must know not only which behavior is appropriate, but must demonstrate competency in performing the behavior. McCroskey (1982) cautioned, however, that judging competence solely on behavior is insufficient because competent communicators do not always succeed and incompetent communicators do not always fail when pursuing interpersonal goals. Accordingly, McCroskey concluded that communication competence spans three knowledge domains:

- *Cognitive domain*—To be deemed an effective communicator, individuals must demonstrate that they know and understand the basic field of communication (Larson, Backlund, Redmond, & Barbour, 1978). As an example, superintendents should have conceptual knowledge about the relationship between communication and organizational culture.
- *Psychomotor domain*—To apply interpersonal communication, superintendents must demonstrate an ability to apply knowledge and understanding (Wiemann, Takai, Ota, & Weimann, 1997); they must develop

specific skills. As an example, superintendents cannot meet role expectations if they are unable to encode and decode messages, use correct grammar, listen effectively, apply principles of nonverbal communication, communicate in context, work effectively with print and broadcast media, build credibility and trust, resolve conflict, and use appropriate technology.

- *Affective domain*—To apply interpersonal communication, superintendents must possess supportive attitudes and feelings about the process (McCroskey, 1982). Put another way, they must want to communicate in ways that build interpersonal relationships rather than in ways that make them dominant or submissive.

McCroskey's framework for competence is nearly identical to one offered several years later by Spitzberg and Cupach (1984). The three components of their paradigm are knowledge (recognizing the appropriateness of a communication practice), skill (the ability to perform the selected practice), and motivation (desire to communicate in an appropriate and effective manner). These models provide a relevant framework for evaluating superintendent competence and in fact, they are integral to standards used to evaluate professional preparation.

Philosophical Compatibility

Board member and superintendent underlying values and beliefs about governance and administrative style frequently do not surface until these individuals face a serious problem. At that point, their perceptions of each other are tested and they discover whether they share similar philosophical dispositions. Value compatibility may not be essential to a good relationship but more often than not, it is. For example, a husband and wife having very dissimilar religious and political views usually have to work hard to overcome tensions and disagreements stemming from the philosophical differences. Unless they are inclined to respect each other's views and unless they have the skills necessary to demonstrate this respect, their relationship may be an endless cycle of tension and overt hostilities.

Failing to discuss personal philosophy and misrepresentation are the two most common causes of value incompatibility. In the former, a superintendent and board members avoid discussing values and beliefs, either because they are uncomfortable doing so or because they fail to recognize their importance. In the latter, individuals purposefully mislead each other. As an example, a job applicant may claim to be highly democratic and facilitative in order to be employed when in fact the applicant is highly autocratic. A person's true dispositions, however, are exposed by overt behavior once the parties begin interacting.

Real board member and superintendent behavior can be revealed and categorized by studying decision-making behavior. Tallerico (1989), for example, found that board members and superintendents exhibited distinct behaviors when making decisions. Board member behavior was categorized as (a) refusing to engage in administration and relying substantially on the superintendent's leadership, (b) cultivating a wide range of information sources and engaging in oversight and management activities, and (c) cultivating a wide range of information sources but deferring to the superintendent's authority. Superintendent behavior was categorized as (a) high control orientation and inclination to persuade board members to accept their position, and (b) lesser control orientation and inclination to have board members seek a wide range of information and present divergent views. Before entering into a formal relationship, both administrators and board members should consider the extent to which their dispositions (and hence their behavior) are compatible. For example, highly control-oriented superintendents are unlikely to work well with board members who cultivate their own information sources and intrude into administration routinely.

Recognizing the importance of philosophical congruence, Katz (1993) formulated a typology for board members and superintendents. He described school board member behavior along a continuum from "corporate board style" to "familial board style." The former was characterized by reliance on the superintendent for data and recommendations, formality, and commitment to standards; the latter was characterized by informality, informal communication, and extreme loyalty to the community. Katz categorized superintendent behavior along a continuum from task orientation to relationship orientation (a distinction commonly found in leadership theory). He concluded that productive relationships occurred when task-oriented superintendents were matched with corporate-type board members or when relationship-oriented superintendents were matched with familial-type board members.

The relevance of philosophical compatibility is especially evident among factional school boards. Studying divided boards, Newman and Brown (1992) found that superintendents most often aligned themselves with factions that shared their values and beliefs on critical issues such as policy decisions and governance boundaries. Yet, politics and not ideology guides the behavior of some administrators. For these superintendents, aligning with the most powerful faction is more judicious than aligning with the most compatible faction. Although this strategy may be effective in the short-term, philosophical differences between the superintendent and faction members eventually become known (Kowalski, 1995).

MANAGING CONFLICT WITH BOARD MEMBERS

Even the best planned and intentioned relationships are subjected to difficult times when individuals function under stress. During these challenging periods, all parties share a responsibility to preserve their positive association but professional stature makes the superintendent most responsible. Consequently, administrators need to know the conditions most likely to produce serious conflict and effective techniques for managing these situations.

Common Problems Attributed to School Board Members

In the eyes of the law, the authority of a school board member is restricted to actions taken by the board as a whole (Norton et al., 1996). As previously mentioned superintendents usually view board relationships individually rather than collectively. Consequently, they usually describe them from a sociopolitical rather than a legal perspective (Blumberg, 1985). These assessments are based on expectations stemming from an intricate mix of ethical, moral, legal, social, and political standards that are learned during their socialization, both in graduate school and in practice. The following are the criticisms of board member behavior most commonly voiced by superintendents.

- *Pursuing single issues.* This problem is characterized by a board member who shows little or no interest in general community. needs because the board member is focused on only one issue. Often, the board member is affiliated with a special interest group or is pursuing revenge individually against one or more district employees (e.g., seeking to get a principal or a coach dismissed).
- *Pursuing personal gain.* This problem is most frequently characterized by two situations: (a) viewing a position on the school board as a stepping stone to a higher political office and (b) using the office to advance self-interests, such as gaining employment for family members and friends.
- *Rejecting the professional status of the superintendent.* This problem is characterized by a board member who treats the superintendent as a domesticated public employee. At best, the superintendent is viewed as a manager or politician, but never as a true professional leader.
- *Satisfying a need for power.* This problem is characterized by a board member who has a need to dominate and control others. This person purposefully creates conflict and prefers to be part of a factional board because the board member cannot exercise a sufficient level of power to satisfy personal needs when the board operates as a unit.

- *Failing to maintain confidentiality.* This problem is characterized by a board member who discloses confidential information about personnel, legal matters, or delicate problems. This offense is most frequently committed in matters related to personnel issues or collective bargaining; both legal and ethical problems may be created.
- *Intruding into administration.* This problem, clearly the most commonly cited in the literature, is characterized by a board member who consistently and egregiously engages in administrative responsibilities. This person typically spends an inordinate amount of time with routine school matters; visit schools often, and encourages employees and community residents to contact her when they are dissatisfied.

Not being adequately prepared to serve on a school board is another complaint registered by superintendents. The idea of setting high educational requirements for this office, however, remains controversial (Danzberger, 1994) and consequently, most states simply have age and residence criteria.

Common Problems Attributed to Superintendents

Because most board members neither complete a course of study in school administration nor share the socialization experiences of administrators, their initial perceptions of superintendent behavior are regularly shaped by personal convictions. Consequently, their mental images may or may not be in accord with the educational administration's professional knowledge base. As an example, a national survey of superintendents found that board members were nearly divided over whether they wanted them to be educational leaders or managers (Glass et al., 2000). While some board members modify their perceptions after acquiring experience on the school board, others cling to their fundamental beliefs about appropriate superintendent behavior. Even so, many of the recurring complaints voiced by board members are cogent to the education profession's standards for ethical practice. The following concerns are those most frequently voiced by school board members.

- *Lacking respect for board members.* This concern is characterized by superintendents who believe that their professional knowledge trumps the voice of the people. Superintendents come to expect board members to "rubber stamp" every recommendation—typically without asking questions. These administrators often appear aloof and condescending.

- *Lacking integrity.* This concern is characterized by superintendents who are not trustworthy. They typically divulge information that is supposed to be confidential, including private conversations with board members.
- *Subordinating rather than cooperating.* This concern is characterized by superintendents who question the board's legitimate authority. Rather than viewing the board as a legislative body, they see it as a political entity. The concern is similar to a lack of respect but differs in that the focus is legitimacy rather than competence.
- *Failing to provide leadership.* This concern is characterized by superintendents who fail to provide direction, either with respect to advising the board on what needs to be done or with respect to providing recommendations for controversial or difficult policy decisions. Offenders encourage the board to act independently as a means of reducing personal political risk.
- *Failing to manage.* This concern, one of the most prevalent, is characterized by superintendents who are either incapable or unwilling to manage the district's resources appropriately. Offenders may fail to properly advise the board of critical issues (e.g., a budget deficit) or to deal with problems after they emerge (e.g., correcting a hazardous condition in a school building).
- *Failing to be accessible.* This concern is characterized by superintendents who do not make themselves available to board members; for example, they do not return telephone calls or e-mail promptly, or do not agree to appointments in a timely manner. Some board members, unfortunately, believe that superintendents have no responsibility more important than responding immediately to board member queries.
- *Failing to communicate.* This concern is characterized by superintendents who control information and disseminate material selectively. Moreover, they exhibit little interest in exchanging information with others.
- *Failing to comply with ethical and moral standards.* This concern is characterized by superintendent behavior that violates the law, community standards, or professional ethics.

Research indicates that the nature of these concerns varies across types of districts. In rural school systems, for example, superintendents generally get dismissed because of personal shortcomings such as financial mismanagement, financial malfeasance, poor communication, and marital immorality (see, e.g., Chance & Capps, 1992). In urban districts, superintendents generally get dismissed for political reasons such as not mollifying critics who demand radical change and power transitions on the school board as a result of elections (Kowalski, 1995).

Monitoring Relationships

Board member-superintendent relationships often deteriorate if they are not properly monitored. To avoid this problem, superintendents and boards should periodically evaluate their relationship. This increases the probability that problems will be detected early and encourages interventions to correct the situation (Castallo, Greco, & McGowan, 1992). Periodic retreats are a good format for this function because it allows the parties to focus on the issue without being interrupted constantly by day-to-day problems. Some school boards establish a standing committee on superintendent relationships to ensure that the topic receives appropriate attention (Eadie, 2003).

Often it is helpful to begin evaluating relationships by collecting individual perceptions. For example, the board president could ask each board member to complete a brief questionnaire regarding the superintendent's performance and ask the superintendent to provide feedback about the board's performance. The responses become a starting point for periodic discussions. Informal conversations should not replace a superintendent's formal annual evaluation; instead, they should be designed to contribute to that more formal process. In essence, the discussions constitute periodic "checkups" that prevent problems from festering until the annual evaluation occurs (Castallo et al., 1992).

Although formal annual evaluations are crucial to managing positive relationships, the overall purpose of both superintendent and board assessments should be to increase school district effectiveness (Kowalski, 1998a). Whereas school boards commonly evaluate superintendents, the opposite is rarely true. Therefore, school boards have been encouraged to conduct self-evaluations and then share the results with the superintendent. Board self-assessment should focus on group and not individual performance. In addition to examining the working relationship between the board and superintendent, self-assessment can encompass the following purposes:

- Identifying and clarifying the purpose of the board as a policymaking body
- Identifying operational strengths and weaknesses
- Assessing past successes and failures
- Exhibiting accountability to the public
- Providing a mechanism for avoiding abuses of power
- Providing a framework for goal setting
- Enhancing an understanding of and appreciation for the process of performance evaluation (Kowalski, 1981)

Additionally, board self-evaluation helps to build credibility and aids board members to distinguish properly between administration and policymaking (Robinson & Bickers, 1990).

Even though many observers assume that school boards consistently evaluate superintendents within the normal course of performing their duties, this is not necessarily true. Two studies conducted during the 1990s in individual states (see Simpson, 1994; Koryl, 1996), revealed that approximately one-fourth of the superintendents were not evaluated by the board formally. More recently, both national and states studies have indicated a slight improvement. In 2000, 80% of the superintendents in a national study (Glass et al., 2000) and 84% of superintendents in a three-state study (Indiana, Illinois, and Texas) (Sharp, Malone, & Walter, 2003) said they were evaluated formally.

Conflict Resolution Strategies

Conflict is defined by two conditions: the presence of two or more viewpoints on an important issue and the incompatibility of those views (Hanson, 2003). The common perception in our society is that it is always destructive; consequently, administrators often do not know that it also can be constructive. Constructive conflict encourages open communication that prompts district officials to identify and then test their values and beliefs so that a coherent agenda for needed change can be pursued. In this vein, conflict can be a valuable catalyst for school improvement. Conflict evolves into hostility when the parties believe that their opponents are pursuing one or more of the following objectives: (a) to reduce their resources, (b) to reduce their power, or (c) to destroy their reputation (Cheldelin & Lucas, 2004). Hostility is most common when conflict becomes malevolent—that is, the parties have the specific goal of hurting their opponents. In these situations, participants typically use hateful language, make dogmatic statements instead of asking questions, exhibit inflexibility, and act emotionally (Hanson, 2003).

The challenge for the superintendent is not to eliminate conflict because conflict is inevitable in all organizations including school districts. Instead the superintendent's task is either to use conflict productively (i.e., to produce a positive outcome) or to control potential damage through effective management. Using conflict productively begins with this question: How can I use this situation to benefit the school district? As an example, assume that the board and superintendent are divided over increasing funding for an elementary music program. The disagreement provides an opportunity for the parties to explore in depth the total curriculum and to find ways to improve it.

Effective conflict management requires an accurate diagnosis and proper selection of resolution strategies. Spaulding and O'Hair (2004) identified five basic types of conflict: philosophical (value differences); resource-based (competition for scarce resources); interpersonal (e.g., personality clashes); territorial (power and jurisdiction disputes); and perceptual (e.g., unvalidated assumptions). Some strategies work well for certain types of conflict but not for others. For example, providing more money can settle resource disputes but is unlikely to ameliorate philosophical or interpersonal conflict. Using a mediator or outside facilitator may help resolve interpersonal and perceptual conflict but is unlikely to resolve philosophical or resource disputes. Both Harvey and Drolet (1994) and Spaulding and O'Hair (2004) provide in-depth information about selection of resolution strategies on the basis of conflict type.

FOR FURTHER REFLECTION

This chapter examined the important issue of board-superintendent relations. The importance of these associations and the reasons why they are difficult to build and maintain were discussed. Although the separation of administrative and board roles is primarily legal and professional, practitioners tend to focus on the social and political elements of their relationships. They do so not with the board as a whole, but with individual board members. As a result, the association is really a series of relationships between the superintendent and each board member.

Common problems detracting from positive relations were discussed from both superintendent and board member perspectives. Suggestions were made for building and maintaining positive interactions. The former involves visioning an ideal relationship, planning a strategy for achieving it, and then monitoring through periodic evaluations. The latter depends heavily on dealing with conflict. Inevitable disputes should either be used to produce positive outcomes or they should be managed skillfully so that the negative outcomes are minimized.

As you consider what you have read, answer the following questions:

1. Why do superintendents tend to discuss their relations with board members individually rather than collectively?

2. Why are board-superintendent relations important to the district?

3. Board members are supposed to set policy and superintendents are supposed to enforce policy. Does this dichotomy of responsibilities add to or detract from positive relations?

4. In your school district, what complaints have superintendents had of board members? What complaints have board members had of superintendents?

5. How can conflict between a board and superintendent be used to improve conditions in a school district? Can you cite any examples of this occurring in your school district?

6. Why is communication essential to building positive relationships?

7. What is the purpose of developing a vision of an ideal relationship?

8. When is conflict most likely to be destructive?

9. Is it a good idea to use the same resolution strategies for all types of conflict? Why or why not?

10. What is philosophical compatibility? Why is it an important issue in board-superintendent relations?

Case Study

George Collins has been an educator for 20 years, including 7 years as a classroom teacher, 8 years as an elementary principal, and just over 5 years as a director of curriculum. Recently, he decided to become a school superintendent. Judging that this position would not become vacant in his current place of employment, he applied for six vacant positions in a 100-mile radius of his current residence. He was invited to interview for two of them.

George's first interview was with the Hampton Unified District #1, a predominately rural district serving slightly more than 1,000 students. During the interview, George was asked to characterize his leadership style and personal strengths. He responded in the following manner:

When I was a teacher and principal, I respected administrators who involved me in important matters. Therefore, I try to involve others. I also believe the community should participate in critical decisions affecting their schools. We, the board and administration, have the responsibility of creating opportunities for citizens to do that. I believe the board and superintendent are partners, not adversaries. Your job is to approve policy; my job is to recommend policy to you and then to ensure that it is followed. With respect to principals and teachers, I view them as peer professionals. Therefore, I try to give them autonomy but I insist they accept responsibility for their decisions. If they don't perform to our standards, I intervene. Finally, I favor partial decentralization of authority. Principals and teachers should be given greater control over curriculum and instruction. This permits them to individualize their work to the real needs of their students.

The board members reacted positively to George's message and the board president commented, "Mr. Collins, I think we agree with your philosophy. It is a pleasure to hear an administrator tell us what he believes." George was flattered and left the interview thinking that he would be offered the position.

Less than a week after his interview in Hampton, George interviewed with the board in the Rogers City Unified Schools, a district with about 1,800 students. While the two districts were not that different in size, they were dissimilar in most other ways. Whereas Hampton served a rural, farm-based population, Rogers City served an industrial community where most families had some link to the mining industry.

During the Rogers City interview, George was not asked to state his leadership style and philosophy, but he volunteered that information anyway. He told the board, "Ladies and gentlemen, I think you need to know who I am and what I believe about education." He then stated the same beliefs and values he had articulated a few days earlier in Hampton. But the reaction in Rogers City was different. One board member commented, "There are a lot of fancy ideas and dreams about the way things should be, but the fact is that superintendents don't survive unless they are good managers and stay on top of things. We have had more than our share of employee problems in this district and the taxpayers are fed up. Our last superintendent didn't know how to deal with the teachers' union and people began to see him as unwilling to deal with difficult problems."

Another board member offered her views: "We expect the superintendent to be fair but tough. If you don't demand that people work hard, they probably won't. Our biggest problems here are money and facilities; we don't have enough money and our buildings desperately need attention. Quite frankly, I don't think we have an interest in experimenting with your ideas about decentralization."

The board president spoke next. "Mr. Collins, we are not shy about saying what we believe. Now, we don't always agree but we feel free to express our views. Personally, I think a superintendent and school board learn to work together—there is no such thing as 'love at first sight' when it comes to running a school district. So, I'm not that concerned that we may not all think alike. If my wife and I had to agree on everything, we would have been divorced long ago. We all dream, but the reality is that we must work together. Neither you nor we have all the answers. But I do think you should know, most of us are not really ready to try a lot of new ideas. Our first priority should be to get the public to support the school system more than they do."

George left the interview in Rogers City believing that the board was not interested in him and he was not particularly interested in them. He was confident he would be offered the position in Hampton. Four days following his interview in Rogers City, the board president in Hampton notified him the board had decided to hire another person as superintendent. George was clearly disappointed. Several hours later, he received another call, this one from the board president in Rogers City. "Mr. Collins, this is Fred Drover, president of the school board in Rogers City. We had a special meeting this morning and decided to offer the superintendent job to you. We are aware you are a finalist for the job in Hampton and may be highly interested in that job. Personally, I think we offer a better opportunity. To convince you of that, I'm offering a $95,000 salary for the first year, a 3-year contract, and a very nice fringe benefit package that includes a leased automobile. In case you don't know, the salary would be $9,000 higher than we were paying the previous superintendent."

George was stunned. "I really did not expect to be offered the job in Rogers City. The discussion during the interview gave me the impression that several board members disagreed with my views."

The board president responded, "Well, that's perceptive of you. You are not the first choice of two board members but the other four members and I very much want you to be our superintendent. As I said in the interview, people worry too much about their disagreements and not enough about what they might have in common. The five-member majority is prepared to do what it takes to get you to come to Rogers City."

George asked for and was granted a three-day period to consider the offer. During that time, he discussed his options with his wife. While he was concerned that two board members may not be supportive of him, he worried that he might not be offered another superintendent position. He was currently making $70,000 and the salary in Rogers City was a primary attractor for him. His wife told him that she would support whatever decision he made. George decided to counter Mr. Drover's offer as a way of determining how much support he might have. He called the board president. "Mr. Drover, this is George Collins calling. My wife and I have discussed your offer and I am interested. However, I have two requests. First, I would like the salary for the first year increased to $98,000. Second, I want the school district to reimburse me for my relocation expenses."

Without hesitating, Mr. Drover responded affirmatively to both requests. Six weeks later, George Collins was the new Rogers City superintendent.

Within 1 month after starting his new job, George discovered that the division over his employment as superintendent was reflective of deep philosophical and political differences that had separated the board into factions. Five to two votes had been the norm for the past 18 months. The dominant faction led by Mr. Drover expected George to be loyal to them; the other two board members told him that he should remain neutral and not get involved in board disputes.

The first regularly scheduled school board election occurred approximately 1 year after George became superintendent. The terms of two board members, both in the Drover faction, were expiring and they were seeking re-election. The incumbents were opposed by two candidates handpicked by the two board members outside the Drover faction. Everyone in Rogers City realized that the election could change the balance of power on the school board. Three weeks before the election, the local newspaper surprised everyone by endorsing the two challengers. Mr. Drover was furious and visited with George after the editorial appeared.

As I see it, George, we both have a lot at stake here. You realize that if the challengers get elected, I'm out as president. That could mean trouble for you. You would have a new majority to deal with and one of the two board members who didn't vote to hire you would be board president. These people want to run the show and your life would become miserable. You have impressed a lot of people in the short time you've been here. The teachers' union president likes you and the teachers are backing the incumbents. I checked and two incumbents have supported every one of your recommendations. How would you feel about doing an interview with a reporter attesting the great job done by these board members? Your comments could sway some votes. Our backs are against the wall. We can help each other. Will you do it?

Case Discussion Questions

1. What could George have done to learn more about the Rogers City school board before accepting the position?

2. When George asked for additional salary and relocation expenses, the board president immediately agreed. What if any conclusions could you draw from the board president's behavior?

3. Would you have accepted the position in Rogers City knowing that two of five board members did not support you? Why or why not?

4. If you were George, what else would you have done before making a decision about the job in Rogers City?

5. Was it ethical for the board president to expect that George would be loyal to his faction? Why or why not?

6. Should superintendents become involved in school board elections? Why or why not?

7. If George agrees to be interviewed by a reporter about the two incumbents, would he be getting involved in the election or only meeting his duty to communicate with the public? Defend your response.

REFERENCES

Achilles, C. M., & Lintz, M. N. (1983, November). *Public confidence in public education: A growing concern in the 80s.* Paper presented at the Annual Meeting of the Mid-South Educational Research Association, Nashville, Tennessee.

Björk, L. G., & Keedy, J. (2001). Politics and the superintendency in the U.S.A.: Restructuring in-service education. *Journal of In-service Education, 27*(2), 275–302.

Blumberg, A. (1985). *The school superintendent: Living with conflict*. New York: Teachers College Press.

Burgoon, J. K., & Hale, J. L. (1984). The fundamental topic of relational communication. *Communication Monographs, 51*, 193–214.

Cappella, J. N. (1987). Interpersonal communication: Definitions and fundamental questions. In C. R. Berger & S. H. Chaffee (Eds.), *Handbook of communication science* (pp. 184–238). Newbury Park, CA: Sage.

Carter, J. (2000). Toward coherent governance. *The School Administrator, 57*(3), 6–10.

Castallo, R. T., Greco, J., & McGowan, T. (1992). Clear signals: Reviewing working relationships keeps board and superintendent on course. *American School Board Journal, 179*(2), 32–34.

Chance, E. W., & Capps, J. L. (1992). *Superintendent instability in small/rural schools: The school board perspective*. East Lansing, MI: National Center for Research on Teacher Learning. (ERIC Document Reproduction Service No. ED350121)

Cheldelin, S. I., & Lucas, A. (2004). *Conflict resolution*. San Francisco: Jossey-Bass.

Clampitt, P. G. (1991). *Communicating for managerial effectiveness*. Newbury Park, CA: Sage.

Danzberger, J. P. (1994). Governing the nation's schools: The case for restructuring local school boards. *Phi Delta Kappan, 75*(5), 367–373.

Danzberger, J. P., Kirst, M. W., & Usdan, M. D. (1992). *Governing public schools: New times new requirements*. Washington, DC: The Institute for Educational Leadership.

Dawson, L. J., & Quinn, R. (2000). Clarifying board and superintendent roles. *The School Administrator, 57*(3), 12–14, 16, 18.

Eadie, D. (2003). High-impact governing. *American School Board Journal, 190*(7), 26–29.

Eadie, D., & Houston, P. (2003). Ingredients for a board-savvy superintendent. *The School Administrator, 60*(2), 56–57.

Educational Vital Signs. (1994). A supplement to the *American School Board Journal, 181*(12), A1–A31.

Egan, G. (1976). *Interpersonal living*. Monterey, CA: Brooks/Cole Publishing.

Ehling, W. P., White, J., & Grunig, J. E. (1992). Public relations and marketing practice. In J. E. Grunig (Ed.), *Excellence in public relations and communication management* (pp. 357–393). Hillsdale, NJ: Lawrence Erlbaum Associates.

Glass, T., Björk, L., & Brunner, C. (2000). *The 2000 study of the American school superintendency*. Arlington, VA: American Association of School Administrators.

Glass, T. E. (1992). *The 1992 study of the American school superintendency*. Arlington, VA: American Association of School Administrators.

Glass, T. E. (2001). *Superintendent leaders look at the superintendency, school boards, and reform*. Denver, CO: Education Commission of the States.

Grunig, J. E. (1989). Symmetrical presuppositions as a framework for public relations theory. In C. H. Botan (Ed.), *Public relations theory* (pp. 17–44). Hillsdale, NJ: Lawrence Erlbaum Associates.

Hanson, E. M. (2003). *Educational administration and organizational behavior* (5th ed.). Boston: Allyn & Bacon.

Harvey, T., & Drolet, B. (1994). *Building teams, building people*. Lancaster, PA: Technomic.

Hess, F. M. (2002). *Schools boards at the dawn of the 21st century: Conditions and challenges of district governance*. Washington, DC: National School Boards Association.

Hoy, W. K., & Miskel, C. G. (1996). *Educational administration: Theory, research, and practice* (5th ed.). New York: McGraw-Hill.

Katz, M. (1993). Matching school board and superintendent styles. *School Administrator, 50*(2), 16–17, 19–20, 22–23.

Keedy, J. L., & Björk, L. G. (2002). Superintendents and local boards and the potential for community polarization: The call for use of political strategist skills. In B. Cooper & L. Fusarelli (Eds.), *The promises and perils facing today's school superintendent* (pp. 103–128). Lanham, MD: Scarecrow Education.

Koryl, M. (1996). *Formal evaluation of Indiana school superintendents: Practices and superintendent perceptions*. Unpublished doctoral dissertation, Ball State University.

Kowalski, T. J. (1981). Why your board needs self-evaluation. *American School Board Journal, 168*(7), 21–22.

Kowalski, T. J. (1995). *Keepers of the flame: Contemporary urban superintendents*. Thousand Oaks, CA: Corwin.

Kowalski, T. J. (1998a). Evaluation: Critiquing the CEO. *American School Board Journal, 185*(2), 43–45.

Kowalski, T. J. (1998b). The role of communication in providing leadership for school reform. *Mid-Western Educational Researcher, 11*(1), 32–40.

Kowalski, T. J. (2004). School public relations: A new agenda. In T. J. Kowalski (Ed.), *Public relations in schools* (3rd ed., pp. 3–29). Upper Saddle River, NJ: Merrill, Prentice Hall.

Larson, C. E., Backlund, P. M., Redmond, M. K., & Barbour, A. (1978). *Assessing communicative competence*. Falls Church, VA: Speech Communication Association and ERIC.

Littlejohn, S. W. (1992). *Theories of human communication* (4th ed.). Belmont, CA: Wadsworth.

Luthans, F. (1981). *Organizational behavior* (3rd ed.). New York: McGraw-Hill.

McCarty, D. J., & Ramsey, C. E. (1971). *The school managers: Power and conflict in American public education*. Westport, CT: Greenwood.

McCroskey, J. C. (1982). Communication competence and performance: A research and pedagogical perspective. *Communication Education, 31*(1), 1–7.

McCurdy, J. (1992). *Building better board-administrator relations*. Alexandria, VA: American Association of School Administrators.

McGregor, D. (1967). *The professional manager*. New York: McGraw-Hill.

Newman, D. L., & Brown, R. D. (1992). Patterns of school board decision making: Variations in behavior and perceptions. *Journal of Research and Development in Education, 26*(1), 1–6.

Norton, M. S., Webb, L. D., Dlugosh, L. L., & Sybouts, W. (1996). *The school superintendency: New responsibilities, new leaders*. Boston: Allyn & Bacon.

Petersen, G., & Fusarelli, L. (2001, November). *Changing times, changing relationships: An exploration of the relationship between superintendents and boards of education*. Paper presented at the annual meeting of the University Council for Educational Administration, Cincinnati, OH.

Robinson, G. E., & Bickers, P. M. (1990). *Evaluation of superintendents and school boards*. Arlington, VA: Educational Research Service.

Richmond, V. P., McCroskey, J. C., Davis, L. M., & Koontz, K. A. (1980). Perceived power as a mediator of management communication style and employee satisfaction: A preliminary investigation. *Communication Quarterly, 28*(41), 37–46.

Sergiovanni, T. J. (2001). *The principalship: A reflective practice perspective* (4th ed.). Boston: Allyn & Bacon.

Shannon, T. A. (1996). Lessons for leaders. *American School Board Journal, 183*(6), 19–22.

Sharp, W. L., Malone, B. G., & Walter, J. K. (2003, October). *Superintendent and school board evaluation: A three-state study*. Paper presented at the Annual Meeting of the Mid-Western Educational Research Association, Columbus, Ohio.

Shibles, M. R., Rallis, R. F., & Deck, L. L. (2001). A new political balance between superintendent and board: Clarifying purpose and generating knowledge. In C. C. Brunner & L. G. Björk (Eds.), *The new superintendency* (pp. 169–181). New York: JAI.

Simpson, E. H. (1994). *Practices and procedures used in the evaluation of public school superintendents in South Carolina as perceived by superintendents and school board chairpersons*. Unpublished doctoral dissertation. University of South Carolina, Columbia.

Snavely, W. B., & Walters, E. V. (1983). Differences in communication competence among administrative social styles. *Journal of Applied Communication Research, 11*(2), 120–135.

Spaulding, A., & O'Hair, M. J. (2004). Public relations in a communication context: Listening, nonverbal, and conflict-resolution skills. In T. J. Kowalski (Ed.), *Public relations in schools* (pp. 96–122). Upper Saddle River, NJ: Merrill, Prentice Hall.

Spitzberg, B. H., & Cupach, W. R. (1984). *Interpersonal communication competence*. Beverly Hills, CA: Sage.

Tallerico, M. (1989). The dynamics of superintendent–school board relationships: A continuing challenge. *Urban Education, 24*(2), 215–232.

Thayer, L. O. (1961). *Administrative communication*. Homewood, IL: Richard D. Irwin.

Vail, K. (2001). Teamwork at the top. *American School Board Journal, 188*(11), 23–25.

Weller, L. D., Brown, C. L., & Flynn, K. J. (1991). Superintendent turnover and school board member defeat: A new perspective and interpretation. *Journal of Educational Administration, 29*(2), 61–71.

Wiemann, J. M. (1977). Explication and test of a model of communication competence. *Human Communication Research, 3*, 195–213.

Wiemann, J. M., Takai, J., Ota, H., & Wiemann, M. O. (1997). A relational model of communication competence. In. B. Kovacic (Ed.), *Emerging theories of human communication* (pp. 25–44). Buffalo: State University of New York Press.

CHAPTER 7

School District Policy

KEY FACETS OF THE CHAPTER

O Nature of school district policy

O Purposes of policy in public education

O Development of policy statements

O Political environment of policy development

O Role of values in school district policy

O Professional input in developing policy statements

O Policy implementation

O Policy versus rules and regulations

As noted in Chapter 5, school boards are expected to set policies in areas not covered by state laws and regulations and administrators are expected to enforce policy. This separation of powers is blurred by the fact that *policy* has many different meanings and in the absence of a universal understanding, persons, including board members and superintendents, self-define this key word. In addition, distinctions between developing and implementing policy can be ambiguous. For example, superintendents clearly play a critical role in policy development by providing board members with recommendations and supporting information; board members support enforcement by adjudicating problems that are policy based.

As national and state reform agendas were being forged during the mid-1980s, surprisingly little attention was given to the importance of district policies on the quality of educational experiences. Since then, however, reformers have focused on how district policy affects efforts to restructure governance, curriculum, and instructional strategies (Bauman, 1996), largely because the locus of reform activity has shifted from the state to the district as well as to school levels (Björk & Keedy, 2002; Kowalski, 2003).

This chapter explores the meaning of policy and how it is developed, analyzed, and evaluated. Particular attention is given to the school board's responsibilities and leadership expectations placed on superintendents. Distinctions are made between policy statements and administrative regulations. The chapter places school-district policymaking in the context of school reform and shows that superintendents do play a critical role in policy development.

ESSENCE OF POLICY

Defining policy has been a challenging task for education authors because the concept is broad and defined in many different ways. Consequently, most definitions found in textbooks are long, confusing, and abstract. In simple terms, policy establishes both expectations and constraints for members of a school district and serves one of the following purposes:

- Setting district goals and objectives
- Determining the recipients of district educational services
- Determining the amount of investments in district operations
- Allocating resources to and among district sub-units
- Determining the means by which district personnel will deliver services (King, Swanson, & Sweetland, 2003)

District policies most familiar to both district employees and community members pertain to student discipline, transportation (busing), extracurricular programs, school facilities (e.g., public use of building during nonschool hours), and taxation.

Defining Policy

Descriptions of policy may be formal or informal. In the former category, laws, regardless of whether they are derived from state constitutions, statutes, or legal decisions, are prime examples. For instance, a superintendent might refer to a law requiring school districts to provide transportation to students living at least 1 mile from school as a state policy. In the latter category, the prevailing behavior of a person or agency may be described as policy (Anderson, 1990). For instance, a principal might tell a teacher that it is the superintendent's policy not to see employees unless they have an appointment. Policy promulgated by district school boards is most commonly distinguished as *public policy*—a term that refers more directly to "the action of government and the intentions that determine those actions" (Cochran, Mayer, Carr, & Cayer, 1986, p. 2). Fowler (2000) referred to public policy as "the dynamic and value-laden process through which a political system handles a public problem" (p. 9). In the case of school districts, the process of policymaking focuses largely on setting parameters for determining what services are to be provided, to whom they are to be provided, and the manner in which they should be provided.

A school board's powers to create and enforce policy is granted by the state legislature, and all board policy decisions must conform to the limitations of relevant constitutional provisions, statutes, federal and state regulations, and common law (Imber & Van Geel, 1993). Formal policy decisions made by school boards produce *policy statements*—written policy adopted at an official meeting and subsequently placed in the district policy manual. Appropriately developed, policy statements provide administrators and others "a guide for discretionary action, a statement of purpose rather than a prescription for action" (Clemmer, 1991, p. 20).

Interpretations of policy, however, vary for at least four reasons. First, policy can either describe a general course of action or describe a specific decision. As an example, a person might refer to board policies on pupil conduct and discipline by saying: "The board's discipline policies are really strict" (a judgment about the board's overall disposition). Or a person might say: "The board's truancy policy is very rigid" (a judgment about a specific disposition). When policy is discussed broadly, it is seen as a series of more or less related activities (Anderson, 1990).

Second, ambiguity is caused by ill-defined distinctions between what is intended (*policy as stated*) and what actually occurs (*policy in use*) (Anderson, 1990). Assume that a school board establishes a policy that mandates an automatic expulsion for a second offense involving possession of an illegal drug. The board, however, has made exceptions to its own policy on several occasions because of what the superintendent and board members considered extenuating circumstances. When asked about the school board's policy on penalizing students for illegal drug possession, one principal in this school system told parents: "A second offense results in an automatic expulsion." This administrator referred to the policy in its official form—the way in which it appears in the policy manual or policy as stated. Another principal, however, answered the same query differently: "Usually students are expelled under board policy for a second offense." This principal's response was based on policy application or policy in use. Policy in use is created as "guidelines are interpreted, mandated characteristics are weighed, differential priorities are assigned, action theories are applied, and ideas come to life in the form of implementing decisions and professional practice" (Sergiovanni, Burlingame, Coombs, & Thurston, 1992, p. 59).

Third, confusion typically surrounds differences between policy and regulations (or rules). Assume that a school board adopts the following policy statement: "Principals shall be responsible for evaluating the performance of all school employees annually." The high school principal subsequently sends a memorandum to faculty stating the following: "Either the principal or an assistant principal shall observe each teacher formally at least twice each semester. The observation reports shall be incorporated into the teacher's annual performance evaluation." Is the principal's statement on observations a policy or a regulation? Most teachers and even some principals may view the statement as policy, largely because they either do not understand distinctions between policy and regulations or because they ignore the distinctions and use the terms interchangeably. Although textbooks distinguish policy as a school board prerogative and rule/regulations as an administrative prerogative, the line between these two actions is very murky (Sergiovanni et al., 1992).

Fourth, confusion often is created with respect to *actual* and *de facto policy*. Must a policy become an actual policy statement before it is official? Both practically and legally, the answer is no. Assume a school district has no policy statement concerning student eligibility for extracurricular participation. Even so, the board has consistently approved the superintendent's recommendations to bar students who received two or more failing grades in one semester from participating; their decisions on the recommendations are part of official board meeting minutes. If challenged legally on this matter, the courts might determine that the school board knowingly and consistently approved these administrative decisions and in so doing, the board established de facto policy. De facto policy creates the possibility that not all legal policy is found in the district's policy manual.

Benefits of Good Policy

Properly developed school district policy provides *direction* to decision makers and *information* to those who may be affected. Direction has legal connotations in that administrators and other employees may be evaluated with respect to whether they followed board policy. A superintendent, for example, may be dismissed for repeatedly ignoring the board's policy on allowing community groups to use school facilities. Policies also are a source of information in that they enlighten persons new to the school district about the school board's objectives, values, beliefs, and priorities. In this vein, policy has symbolic value (Rebore, 1984).

Clemmer (1991) noted that effective policy can "save time, clarify objectives, promote consistency, and assign responsibility" (p. 12). Conversely, poorly developed policy can be unduly restrictive and prevent professional educators from exercising appropriate judgments. This negative potentiality is most apparent in school reform. Current efforts to restructure schools, for instance, are rooted in a belief that meaningful improvement occurs when changes are based on real student needs identified by teachers and administrators and not when they are based on generic changes identified by state policymakers (Fullan, 2001). Consequently, superintendents and board members face the difficult task of determining a proper mix of control and freedom. If there is too little control, the result may be unequal educational opportunities across the district's schools, or even chaos, as individual schools move in distinctively different directions. Conversely, too much policy control defeats the purpose of decentralizing school improvement.

POLICY STATEMENTS

Generally, school boards are allowed to set policies in areas of expressed and implied power, provided that such policies are not unconstitutional, in discord with existing laws, or contrary to state regulations. Policy decisions made by school boards may be shaped by four critical considerations: laws; politics and political behavior; values; and organizational and professional influences (see Figure 7.1).

Legal Influences

Although policy does not need to restate existing laws and school boards cannot legally rewrite laws via policy, laws are an essential consideration in policy formation. This is especially true with regard to new statutes affecting or potentially affecting students or school employees. Cogent examples include laws pertaining to civil rights, legislation for disabled individuals, and equal

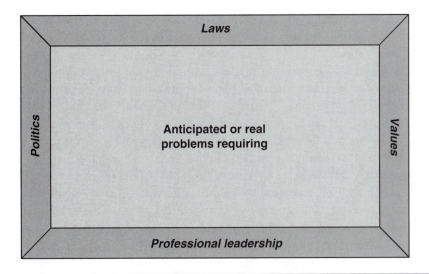

Figure 7.1   Variables Affecting School District Policy

opportunity employment. Even though these laws are relatively explicit, there may be a need for school districts to develop policy statements to assure compliance. Broader legal matters, such as court rulings, also set policy parameters. Anderson (1990) noted, "public policy, at least in its positive form, is based on law and is authoritative" (p. 8). For example, taxation is a binding matter. Unlike policies developed for private companies, policy in education has an authoritative and legally binding quality.

School reform has made the legal dimension of policymaking even more evident. During much of the 1980s, state legislatures had the most prominent role in establishing school improvement laws. Since then, the center of legal activity has shifted to the courts both because state statutes and local policies are being challenged (Heise, 1995). Disputes over state standards for district accreditation and over testing for high school graduation exemplify this transition. As the courts rule, both statutes and existing policy may require revisions.

Political Influences

Political behavior is a recurring element in public policy development. Competition for fiscal resources, power, participation, and prestige exemplify considerations that influence school board decisions. In making these important decisions, board members typically have the latitude to use their own criteria. Therefore, they may elect to ignore evidence and the superintendent's recommendation and rely entirely on emotion or political conditions (e.g., bowing to public opinion, pressure group interventions, or the judgment of influential others).

Ideally, board members are trustees acting independently to serve the interests of the entire community. This role prompts them to give due consideration to less powerful citizens and to respect and appropriately weigh minority opinions. This disposition, known as *public spirit*, is a political form of altruism that comes in two distinguishable forms: an emotional attachment to others and community (love); a rational commitment to a set of principles (duty) (Mansbridge, 1994). As communities become more diverse, and as political pressures placed on school board members intensify, the proclivity for board members to act as delegates rather than trustees increases; in urban districts, for instance, boards are often factional, reflecting major economic, ethnic, social, political, and philosophical divisions (Björk & Keedy, 2001; Kowalski, 1995).

Objectively and accurately determining the public's best interests is one of the major policy development tasks. Among the alternatives a superintendent and board members can choose to complete this assignment, four are especially noteworthy.

1. *Identifying areas of intense conflict.* Policymakers gain a better understanding of divergent, and often competing, constituent positions.

2. *Identifying shared community interests.* Policymakers are able to establish common ground for shaping policy.

3. *Identifying effective procedures for making decisions in the context of competing interests.* Policymakers are able to be inclusive in setting policy (Anderson, 1990).

4. *Identifying community needs and interests.* Policymakers are able to address matters of real concern (Glass, 1997).

These actions restrict political influence that often results in policy being promulgated in the interests of select groups rather than in the interests of the entire community.

Ideological, Institutional, and Personal Values

The political aspects of policymaking are related to deeply held values that have influenced public education in America from its very origin (Stout,

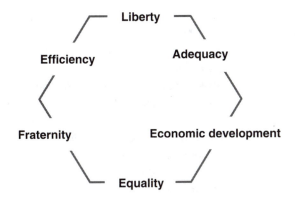

Figure 7.2   Ideological Values Influencing Education Policy in a Democratic
Society

Tallerico, & Scribner, 1994). Values are basically enduring beliefs about what
is desirable (Razik & Swanson, 2001). Historically, education policy has been
the product of constant interplay among the values of *equality, efficiency,* and
liberty (Guthrie & Reed, 1991). King et al. (2003) identify three other values
that have been given increasing attention in the past few decades: *adequacy, fraternity,* and *economic development.* Although adequacy has often pertained to
minimum standards (i.e., How much education is sufficient?), it often has been
associated with excellence in the context of school reform (see Figure 7.2).

   The simultaneous pursuit of social meta values inevitably creates tension in
relation to education policy. For example, states that permitted local districts
tremendous latitude to determine both tax rates and levels of educational spending encountered serious equity problems among local districts (i.e., wealthy districts had to put forth much less effort than did poor districts to support schools
and they often outspent the poor districts by a substantial margin). Despite such
inherent tensions, neither the court of public opinion nor state courts have been
willing to sacrifice one value to make another dominant in education policy
(King et al., 2003). Consequently, major reform policy has often included a
combination of values. In the mid-1960s, for example, federal programs aimed
at education simultaneously emphasized equity and efficiency, which constituted a form of bureaucratic elitism. In the mid-1980s, however, reform efforts
were characterized by the pursuit of excellence (adequacy) and efficiency, which
also constituted a form of bureaucratic elitism (Sergiovanni et al., 1992).

   Although tensions associated with the simultaneous pursuit of social values
have been most evident at the national and state levels, they also have existed

locally. Currently many superintendents and board members are trying to decide a proper balance between liberty (giving individual schools, teachers, and parents autonomy) and equity (ensuring reasonably equal educational opportunities across a school district). Although the value ingredients in a policy decision may be consistent across states and districts, the proportions certainly are not. Urban districts, for example, are prone to emphasize equity more than liberty, whereas small rural districts are prone to do the opposite.

Institutional values—that is, beliefs about the normative nature of organizations embedded in institutional culture—also may influence policy. In the case of public education, these values typically are viewed as inherently defensive of professional interests or inherently defensive of bureaucratic interests (Kogan, 1975). Educators, for example, may oppose a proposed policy statement that would reduce their professional discretion with regard to assigning homework. If a school board is inclined to give preference to the institutional value of professionalism, the board is likely to be affected by the stated opposition. If the board is inclined to give preference to technical efficiency and controlled uniformity (attributes of a true bureaucracy), it is likely to be unaffected by the stated opposition. In other words, both ideological and institutional values influence policy decisions. The potency of institutional values can be tempered by the distribution of power in a district. Even though the school board's institutional values may lean toward efficiency and uniformity, the board may be reluctant to follow its convictions in setting policy if board members are confronted by powerful groups harboring different values (Kowalski, 2003).

Personal values are associated with personal needs and they also can shape education policy (Anderson, 1990). Consider a board member who has publicly opposed the idea of charging a rental fee to community groups for using school facilities. However, after receiving considerable cost and liability information from the superintendent, the board member concludes that opposing such fees is probably an incorrect position to maintain. Even so, the board member votes against the superintendent's recommendation to adopt a user-fee policy simply because the board member wants to avoid being viewed by voters as indecisive. Critics have pointed out that board members increasingly view their role as being a political representative and not a true trustee (Land, 2002). This pattern elevates the prominence of personal values in relation to social meta values.

Judging board member behavior related to policy is not a simple matter of labeling a board member as either being altruistic or being self-centered. Policy positions emerge from an intricate mix of ideological, institutional, and personal values, and superintendents often underestimate the extent to which board members see themselves as being altruistic, even in situations in which self-interests may appear obvious (Mansbridge, 1994). Scholars who have studied major reforms in public education during the 20th century (e.g., Guthrie & Reed, 1991) point out that in making critical decisions, such as those eliminating segregated schools and those providing more equity in state school finance programs, policymakers typically have been guided by ideological values and altruism.

Professional Influences

There are two primary sources of professional input that may influence policy decisions: education and administrative input provided by superintendents, and legal input that is usually provided by the board's attorney or by special legal consultants.

A superintendent's recommendation on policy should reflect both an accurate analysis of pertinent information from the professional knowledge base and an accurate analysis of contextual variables (conditions in which the policy will be implemented). No issue should receive greater consideration in policy than the welfare of students and, therefore, superintendent recommendations should be nested in best practices in pedagogy, educational psychology, and school administration. The need for theoretical and practice-based knowledge in these critical areas is one reason why superintendents should be licensed members of the education profession. Context analysis is equally important. Here variables such as prevailing student needs, leadership strategies and styles, school district climate (including culture), and human and material resources are analyzed and explained in a supporting policy rationale. When professional educators fail to recommend policy, policymakers act largely on their own mix of values, an outcome demonstrated by many of the reform initiatives enacted by political elites during the 1980s and early 1990s (Katz, 1993).

Legal guidance constitutes the second type of professional influence for policy, and studies (e.g., McKinney & Drake, 1994) often reveal that school attorneys are highly involved in policy development. Advice from an attorney may relate to the board's authority to set policy or to legal interpretations that affect the statement being developed. The advice can be given in two ways: directly to board members or indirectly through the superintendent. The latter approach is preferable for at least two reasons. First, it permits the integration of the superintendent's professional advice with the attorney's legal advice; second, it encourages a leadership team approach and discourages competition between the superintendent and attorney. Legal advice passing through the superintendent should never be altered before it is shared with the school board; if the superintendent disagrees with the legal advice, the superintendent should state the objection and encourage the board to seek a clarification from the attorney or to seek a second opinion. Access to school attorneys, even by board members, occurs most often through the superintendent (Painter, 1998).

Research often reveals a disparity between the ideal school attorney role espoused in the literature and actual attorney behavior as reported by superintendents (Haberl & Zirkel, 2001). Friction between a superintendent and the board's attorney can lead to serious conflict and confusion for board members. This negative condition is most likely to occur when the superintendent believes that the attorney is attempting to influence policy in areas outside the attorney's expertise or when the attorney and superintendent do not have a positive personal relationship. A Pennsylvania study (Haberl & Zirkel, 2001) revealed that most districts did not have a formal policy addressing the role of school attorneys; however, the absence of a formal policy did not determine whether attorneys had a favorable working relationship with superintendents. This finding should not be construed to mean that such a policy is not necessary; rather, it illuminates the critical nature of personal relationships to positive attorney-superintendent relations. Consequently, school boards should directly involve superintendents in retaining school attorneys and they should expect the attorney to be part of a leadership team rather than an independent expert who deals exclusively with board members (Thune, 1997).

Not all board members believe that they require recommendations from professionals prior to making policy decisions (McCurdy, 1992). Noting that policy is their domain, some board members believe that this arrangement diminishes the intentions of a representative democracy. This concern is yet another manifestation of the inherent tensions between professionalism and democracy (Kowalski, 2003). Ideally, superintendents should understand and accept that their professional knowledge must be applied in political contexts (Wirt & Kirst, 2001). Likewise, board members should understand and accept the fact that they continuously have to consider both the professional and political dimensions of their policy decisions. In the healthiest situations, superintendents and board members trust each other and respect each other's roles and responsibilities (McCurdy, 1992). When this ideal relationship exists, board members properly integrate professional guidance with values and political realities, and both the superintendent and board members place the interests of students above all else.

POLICY FORMULATION

Policy development does not occur in a uniform manner across all school districts. While some superintendents use an elaborate process that ranges from needs assessment to impact forecasts, others build policy extemporaneously as it becomes necessary to do so. In the same vein, the extent to which policy is developed is uneven across districts. Many possible causes can be associated with this lack of uniformity. Past practices, size of the district, and experiences with litigation are just a few examples. Nevertheless, there are certain barriers that board members often cite. A national study of board members produced the following list of obstacles: lack of time; lack of staff; poor administrative leadership; trepidation stemming from the belief written policies may be too restrictive; lack of knowledge related to the task; lack of leadership or board member continuity; lack of resources for consultants; and a lack of information (First, 1992).

Policy statement decisions can focus on developing new policy statements, revising existing policy, rescinding existing policy, and interpretations and enforcement of policy. Table 7.1 provides examples for each of these categories. Recurring problems in the third category usually indicate that a policy needs to be revised. In addition, there are five stages to shaping and using school district policy: problem formation/identification; policy formulation; policy adoption; policy implementation; and policy evaluation (Portney, 1986).

Table 7.1   Examples of Policy Initiatives

Type of Action	Example
Development of new policy statements	A school district is experiencing problems with requests to place students in accelerated classes; previous decisions were made solely by principals and teachers. The potential for litigation leads the superintendent to recommend a policy to insure uniformity of practice.
Modification of existing policy statements	A school district has a policy allowing community groups to rent school buses; an insurance audit raises questions about the district's liability for this practice. The current policy is revised to address insurance concerns.
Deletions of policy statements	A school district decides to rescind a policy concerning student conduct because a court ruling brings into question the legal status of the policy.
Policy interpretation and enforcement	A school district has a policy concerning student clubs. A new superintendent interprets the policy differently than did the prior superintendent. The principals disagree with the new superintendent's interpretation and ask the school board to determine whether the past or current interpretation is correct.

Framing a Problem

School district policy should be grounded in a real or potential problem. Problem identification ideally occurs through planned, purposeful activities such as opinion polling or needs assessment studies. Unfortunately, some superintendents fail to anticipate problems and wait for problems to surface naturally, such as when there is a crisis or emergency situation. Problem definition is perhaps the most difficult and complex stage of policy development because it reveals what a superintendent sees as public issues and how the superintendent thinks and talks about these concerns (Rochefort & Cobb, 1994). Personal bias, philosophical dispositions, emotion, and politics usually play some part in determining the nature and legitimacy of a problem, but ideally, these influences are controlled by objectivity. Consider a school district that has a dropout rate of 12%. Some superintendents may see this as an unacceptable rate, whereas others view the statistic positively because the state dropout average is 19%.

The superintendent's purpose should be to frame the problem accurately and objectively because the policy adopted inevitably is subjected to political discourse. Rochefort and Cobb (1994) note that problem statements can serve at least four functions: explanation, description, preference, and persuasion. Although it may be advantageous to state a problem in a manner that appeals to a majority of the community, doing so when the majority position is inaccurate virtually assures that proposed solutions pursued through a policy statement will fail (Dery, 1984). Imagine superintendents who are dealing with poor test scores in elementary schools. Many taxpayers not directly associated with the schools have concluded that the problem is rooted in lax discipline. Although the superintendents disagree, they are unwilling for political reasons to state their true convictions that social conditions (namely poverty and a lack of parental support) are the real issues. Stating the problem to mollify the majority leads to policy that only exacerbates the test score problem.

One way a superintendent can enhance objectivity is to involve others in problem framing. The participants should engage in a communicative approach to decision making—that is, they state and then are allowed to test their perceptions and beliefs (St. John & Clemens, 2004). Having a cross section of perceptions also reveals preferences. Consider a district in which the superintendent is attempting to reduce expulsions. Teachers may urge the superintendent to propose an alternative high school, whereas taxpayer groups may urge the superintendent to pursue a lower cost option, such as establishing an in-school suspension program. By presenting the problem in several different ways, the superintendent is better able to identify alternative solutions and the degree of support for each of them (Cochran et al., 1986).

Once a problem has been framed, the superintendent can develop a list of possible solutions so that they can be analyzed and, in some instances, tested. Cooper, Fusarelli, and Randall (2004) identified four critical dimensions of policy implementation:

1. *Normative.* The proposed policy statement should be clear and acceptable to major stakeholder groups. In most school districts today, this ideal seems remote; superintendents in politically diverse districts often seek sufficient, rather than total, support.

2. *Structural.* The problem being addressed must be solvable and the proposed policy should provide either the most rational solution or at least parameters for rational solutions.

3. *Constituentive.* The proposed policy will be implemented successfully if there is a strategic balance of pressure and support. Pressure serves to validate the need for policy; support is essential to implementation.

4. *Technical.* The district has the necessary human and material resources to implement the proposed policy.

Adopting Policy

Once the dimensions of policy have been considered, the superintendent can draft a policy statement and use the following criteria to evaluate it.

- *Completeness*—The statement is sufficiently instructive to communicate purpose and rationale.
- *Flexibility*—The statement has provisions for review and amendments; it can be modified rather easily (Clemmer, 1991).
- *Clarity*—The statement is sufficiently clear to guide the decision maker and to inform those who may be affected; the statement will have high reliability in interpretation and implementation (Conran, 1989).
- *Brevity*—The statement includes essential information but is not unduly prescriptive or descriptive.
- *Stability*—The statement does not become less effective because of personnel changes (Rebore, 1984).

Once a policy statement has been approved formally by the school board, the superintendent must consider informing all relevant publics. To some extent, persons are informed by media coverage of the school board meeting; such information, however, is often general and vague. Consequently, the superintendent should provide a communication to all interested and affected parties detailing the content of the policy statement, its intent, and pertinent information related to its implementation.

Evaluating Policy

Arguably, evaluation is the most ignored aspect of school district policy. All too often, school boards adopt statements and then literally leave them unaltered unless a major crisis evolves. New policy should be evaluated within one year of adoption; after a policy has proven to be effective, the rate of evaluation recurrence can be reduced to once every two or three years depending on the nature of the policy and frequency of its use. Evaluation should address both the effectiveness of the policy statement and the effectiveness of implementation procedures. In both domains, the process should serve formative and summative functions (see Figure 7.3). The former is focused on improvement and is framed by the following questions: How can the wording of the policy statement improve? How can enforcement procedures improve? The latter is focused on making judgments related to stated goals and is framed by the following questions: Has the policy statement achieved its objective? Have enforcement procedures ensured that the policy statement was implemented properly?

A superintendent cannot evaluate a policy properly unless the purposes of the statement are known and validated (Cooper et al., 2004). As noted earlier, policy often develops in relation to a real or anticipated problem; hence, the objective typically is to eliminate, avoid, or diminish the effects of the problem. As an example, a school board adopts a policy requiring community groups to pay a user fee for meetings held in school buildings. This policy could have several different objectives such as offsetting operating costs, reducing the use of buildings by community groups, or increasing district revenues. Unless the real purpose or purposes are known, an accurate and valid evaluation is unlikely.

Effective evaluation also depends on separating the statement from enforcement activities. Policy can fail to meet its objective either because the wording is inappropriate or because the decisions related to implementation are flawed or inconsistent. Even the best worded policy statement can be rendered ineffective by poor enforcement procedures. Consequently, purpose and process need to be examined separately. Assume that the school board that adopted a facility user fee did so specifically to offset rising operating costs. The policy statement requires the superintendent to recommend a fee schedule for each school

FUNCTION

	Formative Evaluation	*Summative Evaluation*
Policy Statement	**Purpose: Improving the policy statement**	**Purpose: Judging the effectiveness of the policy statement**
Policy Enforcement	**Purpose: Improving policy enforcement**	**Purpose: Judging the effectiveness of policy enforcement**

SCOPE (labeled on left between the two rows)

Figure 7.3   Dimensions of School District Policy Evaluation

year based on estimates of insurance, custodial, and utility costs. After the first year of enforcement, the district's business manager calculates that the user fees covered only approximately 50% of the district's costs. Unless the statement is separated from enforcement, the superintendent would be unable to determine whether the policy statement lacks sufficient specificity or whether the problem stems from underestimating user fee revenues (an enforcement problem).

POLICY ADMINISTRATION

The effectiveness of policy is determined by both the quality of the statement (e.g., clarity, relevance, and flexibility) and the quality of administration used to enforce it. The responsibility for policy compliance belongs to the district superintendent. In this vein, the superintendent (or designees) has two essential obligations: the development and maintenance of a school district policy manual and establishing rules and regulations to facilitate compliance.

District Policy Manual

Board policies should be maintained and codified in a notebook commonly called a policy manual. Two codification systems are widely used for this purpose: The Davies-Brickell System and the National Education Policy Network of the National School Board Association (Norton, Webb, Dlugosh, & Sybouts, 1996). Codification involves assembling, numbering, and indexing policies so they can be accessed and referenced by users (Clemmer, 1991). Describing the ideal policy manual, Glass (1992) wrote that it should be "a living document that serves as the chief guide for district management and, therefore, is a signpost for administrators, board members, teachers, and other staff who are responsible for carrying out their duties" (p. 237).

Because board policy serves to inform decision making, each district employee should be able to use the manual as a reference; parents, students, and the general public also should have access to the document. Typically, employee access is accomplished by having manuals in school libraries, principal offices, and faculty workrooms; citizen access is typically accomplished by placing manuals in public libraries, district administrative offices, and community centers. To ensure currency, the superintendent should revise the manual as policy is added, deleted, or altered. In addition, either the superintendent or designee should conduct an annual review of the policy manual to determine if the content has remained complete and accurate (Conran, 1989). Developing a policy manual and keeping it current can be time consuming tasks and for this reason, many superintendents opt to retain consultants to perform these functions. Efficiency, however, should not be the sole criterion for deciding how policy manuals will be maintained. As an example, superintendents who avoid policy revisions after the manual has been developed so that updates are not necessary are really defeating the purpose of having the document (Jones, 1995).

Administrative Rules and Regulations

Distinctions between policy and regulations are often ambiguous, both legally and definitively. From a legal perspective, "regulation" is often used to describe non-constitutional and non-statutory rules promulgated by public departments, agencies, or bureaus (Imber & Van Geel, 1993). Norton et al.

(1996) describe policy as being legislative in nature and as goal assertions focused on aims and not procedures; they described regulations as being executive in nature and as being focused on *how* to implement policy. In school districts, regulations most commonly refer to administrative directives developed in conjunction with or in the absence of policy statements. Regulations do not require formal board approval but often, regulations are approved by the school board to ensure their legality. As an example, superintendents routinely recommend that school boards approve individual school student handbooks prior to the start of each school year.

Board policy and administrative regulations can be easily intermingled if proper steps are not taken to separate them. For example, a superintendent may add regulations to a policy manual without properly distinguishing this subject matter from official board policy statements. Regulations are extensions of policy and placing them in the policy manual can be advantageous if they are not misconstrued as being part of the policy statement.

The manner in which regulations and policy are stated gives decision makers various degrees of freedom. This is a critical factor that superintendents should acknowledge when they draft or approve relevant statements. In this vein, regulations may fall into one of the following categories:

- *Mandatory regulations* identify an issue requiring administrative action and do not allow decision-maker discretion. They are intended to ensure absolute consistency; the emphasis is on following a prescribed action, not on encouraging professional judgment. Zero-tolerance policies and regulations fall into this category. As an example, a principal may develop the following regulation: Students caught smoking in a school building shall be suspended for three days.
- *Directory regulations* identify an issue requiring administrative action and allow a limited level of decision-maker discretion. They are intended to promote consistency but acknowledge that contextual variables and professional judgment may need to be considered. As an example, a principal may develop the following regulation: Students caught smoking in a school building normally will be suspended for three days; however, extenuating circumstances may merit a lesser or more severe punishment that must be approved by the superintendent.
- *Discretionary regulations* identify an issue requiring administrative action and give the decision maker considerable discretion. The intent is to place considerable emphasis on contextual variables and the professional judgment of the decision maker. As an example, a principal may develop the following regulation: Students caught smoking in a school building should be disciplined as deemed appropriate by the school principal.

- *Proscriptive regulations* identify an issue requiring administrative action and give the decision maker complete discretion to handle the matter. The intent is to allow administrators to base their decision completely on contextual variables and professional judgment. As an example, a principal may develop the following regulation: Board policy prohibits smoking in all areas of all school buildings; principals are expected to take necessary enforcement action (Clemmer, 1991).

The trend toward increased legal intervention in public education has served to limit the jurisdiction of administrators to impose rules and regulations; this trend has been most evident in the area of student discipline. In the 1960s, superintendents and principals typically had considerable discretion to develop codes of conduct and to enforce them; today, administrators are largely restricted to enforcing regulations intended to promote legitimate educational goals (Imber, 2002). As an example, the passage of Pub. Law No. 103-382, commonly called the Gun-Free Schools Act, required local districts to adopt a zero-tolerance policy on guns or face forfeiture of their eligibility to federal funds under the Elementary and Secondary School Education Act. In the months following passage of this federal law, states adopted complementary laws requiring a minimum of a one-year expulsion (Pipho, 1998). Although administrators typically communicate the nature of regulations to relevant publics, they less commonly explain the reasons underlying these rules. Doing so is especially important when the regulations are required by law or when they pertain to student discipline (Shore, 1998).

FUTURE CONSIDERATIONS

Although policymaking continues to be accepted as the board's most essential function, surprisingly little attention has been given to the effects of district policy on student learning (Land, 2002). Neglect of this issue is one reason why the role of these governing bodies has been called into question. Critics have charged that boards spend far too much time with political and noneducational matters while largely ignoring critical policy issues that relate more directly to education programs (e.g., Danzberger, Kirst, & Usdan, 1992). In fact, several state studies (e.g., Hange & Leary, 1991; Van Alfen & Schmidt, 1996–1997) have shown that boards typically spend only a small portion of their formal meetings dealing with any type of policy. Reformers fear that unless greater emphasis is placed on setting, implementing, and evaluating instructional and curricular policies, reform at the district and school levels will be attenuated.

One alternative for improving the functions of school boards is to transform them to be educational policy boards (Danzberger et al., 1992). This change would require some state deregulation so that greater discretion concerning what is taught and how it is taught could be exercised by local district officials. Once reconfigured, policy boards would relinquish their quasi-judicial and fiduciary responsibilities and concentrate on providing broad goals and directions for educational programs (Danzberger, et al., 1992). The notion that boards should spend less time on financial and managerial matters is likely to be opposed by many taxpayers who would view this change as a transfer of power from trustees to professional administrators. The idea that boards should devote more time to educational matters, however, is far less controversial. A 1992 statement issued by the National School Boards Association identified four major school board functions: (a) envisioning a community's future educational program, (b) establishing facilitative organizational structures and community environments, (c) ensuring performance assessment systems to enhance accountability, and (d) serving as paramount child advocates (Fisher & Shannon, 1992). While these functions are widely accepted as normative standards, critics argue that they are not put into practice when board members opt to spend their time managing the district.

Another proposed alternative is the elimination of school boards. Proponents (e.g., Chubb & Moe, 1990; Whitson, 1998) argue that the present governance system has been ineffective and perpetuates public schools as quasi-monopolies. Three concepts have been suggested in relation to eliminating boards. The first pertains to parental choice and is predicated on the belief that vouchers provided by the state would allow schools to function independently under the general jurisdiction of state government. The strategy is rooted in the assumption that market forces would force schools either to improve or to close. The second concept moves in an opposite direction by allowing a larger governmental unit to take over public education. For example, a city school system would become part of city government and be under the general authority of the mayor. This strategy is rooted in the assumption that greater coordination of governmental services would be beneficial. The third proposal is similar to the previous proposal in that it involves consolidating public schools with other governmental agencies already providing services to school-age children (e.g., mental health clinics). This proposal is rooted in the assumption that students can be better served and that operating costs can be controlled through agency coordination (Land, 2002).

The current political climate suggests that neither changing the role of school boards significantly nor eliminating them is likely. Instead, gradual incremental changes are more likely. As an example, the current pattern of states setting broad educational goals and then holding local district officials accountable for attaining them is having three visible effects. First, school boards (and superintendents) have to devote more attention to curriculum and instruction; second, they have to provide greater involvement for both employees and community members in critical functions such as visioning and planning; third, they have to focus more directly on the real needs of district students. Collectively, these emerging expectations make school boards more dependent on the professional knowledge and experience of superintendents (Kowalski, 2001).

FOR FURTHER REFLECTION

This chapter examined the meaning of policy and how it can be developed, implemented, and evaluated at the school district level. These tasks have become increasingly important in a political environment in which local district officials are being asked to assume greater responsibility for school reform. As such, expectations that superintendents can provide professional leadership grounded in pedagogy and effective administrative practices also is increasing.

As you consider the importance of school-district policy and the superintendent's responsibility to exert leadership in this function, respond to the following questions.

1. What purposes are served by local district policies?

2. What is the relationship between district policy and state laws and policies?

3. How can ideological values, institutional values, and personal values influence policy decisions in local districts?

4. What are the primary differences between school board policy statements and administrative regulations?

5. What is a policy manual?

6. What is codification as it pertains to policy?

7. Who should have access to district policy manuals and how can this access be provided?

8. From a legal perspective, what is *de facto policy*?

9. What causes variance in the way in which individuals frame problems? How do these differences affect policy development?

10. Many states have attempted to shift the focus of school reform to local districts in an effort to address the real needs in individual schools. How has this trend affected the role of superintendent as a professional educator?

Case Study

Bill Davis acquired his first superintendency in Buffalo Falls School District last July. After having been a middle school principal in another school district for 12 years, he accepted his current position in this predominately rural district of 1,350 students knowing that the previous superintendent had been dismissed. At age 47, he was willing to incur risk to become a superintendent. Although Buffalo Falls has had three superintendents in the last nine years, Bill concluded that he could work effectively with the board members and administrators. He had met all of them while being interviewed for his job and felt that they would be supportive of him.

The issue of school board policy was never discussed by Bill or the school board prior to his assuming the superintendency. Bill had assumed that the district had a policy manual and he planned to evaluate it once he became oriented to his new position. His assumption about the existence of a manual, however, was incorrect. He discovered that previous superintendents and the board members had used the official minutes of school board meetings as the official record of policy statements. Superintendent Davis thought that this was a precarious practice and he urged the board president to support the development of a policy manual. He noted that a manual would provide three essential services: it would inform administrative and faculty decisions; it would provide a codified reference document allowing persons to access policy statements more rapidly; it would provide a framework for conducting policy evaluations.

Mr. Williams did not disagree with any of the superintendent's contentions and indicated he thought developing the manual was a good idea. At the next board meeting, Superintendent Davis recommended that the district retain the services of a consultant to develop the manual. The cost to the district would be approximately $9,000. All five board members voted in favor of the recommendation.

After the consultant had reviewed board minutes for the past 12 years, he met with Superintendent Davis and identified several areas where policy had not been promulgated. For example, the school district had no policies on the use of school buildings or buses by community groups. In total, the consultant's list of policy voids totaled 15 areas. The consultant recommended that the district adopt policies in these areas as soon as possible.

Superintendent Davis shared the consultant's recommendation with Mr. Williams and indicated that he agreed with the consultant. The board president, however, seemed surprised by the suggestion. "Are you sure we need policy in these areas? We haven't had any problems in these areas so why should we tinker with them now? The superintendent responded that there were potential problems and having policy statements would reduce risk to the district. Mr. Williams said that he would discuss the matter with the school attorney, Madeline McDougal.

After reading the consultant's recommendation, Ms. McDougal told the board president that the issue of developing these policies was more philosophical than legal. Clearly, the board had the authority to set policy in these areas, but she was not convinced that it was necessary to do so. She pointed out that in many of the identified areas, the board either had never had to take action or the action was taken on a case-by-case basis. She cited bus rental as an example. Such requests were processed individually and the board approved some of them and not others. Ms. McDougal cautioned Mr. Williams that a policy could reduce the board's discretion in these matters or, even more noteworthy, the authority for bus rentals could be transferred from the board to the superintendent.

Mr. Williams conveyed the attorney's opinions to Superintendent Davis. The superintendent pointed out that the attorney was speculating about his objectives; that is, she was guessing as to why the superintendent wanted to develop these policies. In an effort to counteract this situation, he suggested that the board delay making a decision on the consultant's recommendation until he drafted policy statements in each of the 15 areas. Mr. Williams quickly responded: "Why should you be developing policy recommendations? Policy is the board's responsibility. Our two previous superintendents complained that board members got involved in administration. If you start making policy recommendations, won't you be intruding into our domain?"

"No I won't," Bill answered. "My responsibility is to make recommendations on all policy matters. You have the authority to approve or not approve the recommendations."

Mr. Williams indicated that the issue needed to be discussed with the full board in an executive session prior to the next board meeting. After summarizing the situation and focusing heavily on Ms. McDougal's assessment, Mr. Williams asked the other board members to comment. None appeared anxious to do so. Mr. Williams then said to Superintendent Davis, "It's easy to say that we don't have to follow your recommendations, but if we don't, several negative outcomes are possible. First, I'm sure you won't be pleased if the board keeps rejecting your recommendations. Second, following your recommendations may lead to the public perception that we're a 'rubber stamp' school board. My opinion is that we shouldn't try to fix something that is not broken."

"Well, where do we go from here?" Bill inquired.

Mr. Williams immediately answered, "Bill, we don't need these new policies, and even if we did, developing them is a board responsibility. Most of these areas the consultant identified have nothing to do with teaching and learning. I can see where your counsel is important if we are setting policy on matters that affect teaching; but, quite frankly, when it comes to making decisions about school buildings and buses, we know the community much better than you do. We want you to succeed and be our superintendent for a long time. So let's not get off on the wrong foot."

Two other board members indicated that they agreed with Mr. Williams; the remaining two members said they felt that the superintendent should make policy recommendations as suggested by Superintendent Davis. The four also were divided as to whether they should follow the consultant's recommendation and adopt policy statements in the 15 areas.

Case Discussion Questions

1. Evaluate the consultant's recommendation that the school board should adopt policy in the 15 areas. Do you agree with the consultant or with the school board president?

2. To what extent is Superintendent Davis responsible for causing the problems discussed in the case?

3. Is Mr. Williams correct when he asserts that superintendents should not interfere in policy development? Explain your answer.

4. Identify the options available to Superintendent Davis at this point. If you were he, which would you select?

5. The board members are divided on the issue of policy development. To what extent is this issue relevant to the superintendent's decision on this matter?

6. If a school board relies almost entirely on state statutes and regulations, what policy inputs are going to be ignored?

7. What are the purposes of a policy manual?

8. Who should have access to a policy manual?

REFERENCES

Anderson, J. E. (1990). *Public policymaking: An introduction.* Boston: Houghton Mifflin.

Bauman, P. C. (1996). *Governing education: Public sector reform or privatization.* Boston: Allyn & Bacon.

Björk, L. G., & Keedy, J. L. (2001). Politics and the superintendency in the U.S.A.: Restructuring in-service education. *Journal of In-service Education, 27*(2), 275–302.

Björk, L. G., & Keedy, J. L. (2002). Decentralization and school council empowerment in Kentucky: Implications for community relations. *Journal of School Public Relations, 23*(1), 30–44.

Chubb, J. E., & Moe, T. M. (1990). *Politics, markets, and America's schools.* Washington, DC: Brookings Institute.

Clemmer, E. F. (1991). *The school policy handbook.* Boston: Allyn & Bacon.

Cochran, C. E., Mayer, L. C., Carr, T. R., & Cayer, N. J. (1986). *American public policy* (2nd ed.). New York: St. Martin's Press.

Conran, P. C. (1989). *School superintendent's complete handbook.* Englewood Cliffs, NJ: Prentice Hall.

Cooper, B. S., Fusarelli, L. D., & Randall, E. V. (2004). *Better policies, better schools: Theories and applications.* Boston: Allyn & Bacon.

Danzberger, J. P., Kirst, M. W., & Usdan, M. D. (1992). *Governing public schools: New times new requirements.* Washington, DC: Institute for Educational Leadership.

Dery, D. (1984). *Problem definition in policy analysis.* Lawrence: University of Kansas Press.

First, P. F. (1992). *Educational policy for school administrators.* Boston: Allyn & Bacon.

Fisher, E. H., & Shannon, T. A. (1992). Some good ideas despite pernicious and unsubstantiated negativism. *Phi Delta Kappan, 74*(3), 230–231.

Fowler, F. C. (2000). *Policy studies for educational leaders.* Upper Saddle River, NJ: Merrill, Prentice Hall.

Fullan, M. (2001). *The new meaning of educational change* (3rd ed.). New York: Teachers College Press.

Glass, T. E. (1992). The district policy manual. In P. First (Ed.), *Educational policy for school administrators* (pp. 234–238). Boston: Allyn & Bacon.

Glass, T. E. (1997). Using school district public opinion surveys to gauge and obtain public support. *School Community Journal, 7*(1), 101–116.

Guthrie, J. W., & Reed, J. R. (1991). *Educational administration and policy: Effective leadership for American education* (2nd ed.). Boston: Allyn & Bacon.

Haberl, W. E., & Zirkel, P. A. (2001). The working relationship of the attorney with the superintendent and the school board in Pennsylvania: Recommended versus actual practice. *Catalyst for Change, 30*(3), 20–27.

Hange, J. E., & Leary, P. A. (1991, November). *The leadership function of school boards: West Virginia data.* Paper presented at the Annual Meeting of the Southern Regional Council for Educational Administration, Auburn, Alabama.

Heise, M. (1995). The courts vs. educational standards. *Public Interest, 120,* 55–63.

Imber, M. (2002). Rules for rules. *The American School Board Journal, 189*(9), 67-68.

Imber, M., & Van Geel, T. (1993). *Education law.* New York: McGraw-Hill.

Jones, R. (1995). Manual labor: Keeping school board policies current. *The American School Board Journal, 182*(12), 21–24.

Katz, L. G. (1993). *Trends and issues in the dissemination of child development and early education knowledge.* East Lansing, MI: National Center for Research on Teacher Learning. (ERIC Document Reproduction Service No. ED360102)

King, R. A., Swanson, A. D., & Sweetland, S. R. (2003). *School finance: Achieving high standards with equity and efficiency* (3rd ed.). Boston: Allyn & Bacon.

Kogan, M. (1975). *Educational policy-making.* Hamden, CT: Linnet Books.

Kowalski, T. J. (1995). *Keepers of the flame: Contemporary urban superintendents.* Thousand Oaks, CA: Corwin.

Kowalski, T. J. (2001). The future of local district governance: Implications for board members and superintendents. In C. Brunner & L. Björk (Eds.), *The new superintendency: Advances in research and theories of school management and educational policy*. Stamford, CT: JAI.

Kowalski, T. J. (2003). *Contemporary school administration: An introduction* (2nd ed.). Boston: Allyn & Bacon.

Land, D. (2002). Local school boards under review: Their role and effectiveness in relation to students' academic achievement. *Review of Educational Research, 72*(2), 229–278.

Mansbridge, J. (1994). Public spirit in political systems. In H. Aaron, T. Mann, & T. Taylor (Eds.), *Values and public policy* (pp. 146–172). Washington, DC: Brookings Institute.

McCurdy, J. (1992). *Building better board–administrator relations*. Alexandria, VA: American Association of School Administrators.

McKinney, J. R., & Drake, T. L. (1994). The school attorney and local educational policymaking. *West's Education Law Reporter, 93*, 471–480.

Norton, M. S., Webb, L. D., Dlugosh, L. L., & Sybouts, W. (1996) *The school superintendency: New responsibilities, new leaders*. Boston: Allyn & Bacon.

Painter, S. R. (1998). School district employment practices regarding school attorneys. *Journal of Law & Education, 27*(1), 73–87.

Pipho, C. (1998). Living with zero tolerance. *Phi Delta Kappan, 79*(10), 725–726.

Portney, K. E. (1986). *Approaching public policy analysis*. Englewood Cliffs, NJ: Prentice Hall.

Razik, T. A, & Swanson, A. D. (2001). *Fundamental concepts of educational leadership* (2nd ed.). Upper Saddle River, NJ: Merrill, Prentice Hall.

Rebore, R. W. (1984). *A handbook for school board members*. Englewood Cliffs, NJ: Prentice Hall.

Rochefort, D. A., & Cobb, R. W. (1994). Problem definition: An emerging perspective. In D. A. Rochefort & R. W. Cobb (Eds.), *The politics of problem definition* (pp. 1–31). Lawrence: University Press of Kansas.

Sergiovanni, T., Burlingame, M., Coombs, F., & Thurston, P. (1992). *Educational governance and administration* (3rd ed.). Boston: Allyn & Bacon.

St. John, E., & Clemens, M. M. (2004). Public opinions and political contexts. In T. J. Kowalski (Ed.), *Public relations in schools* (3rd ed., pp. 47–67). Upper Saddle River, NJ: Merrill, Prentice Hall.

Shore, R. M. (1998). Personalizing the school environment. *Thrust for Educational Leadership, 28*(1), 30–31.

Stout, R. T, Tallerico, M., & Scribner, J. P. (1994). Values: The "what?" of the politics of education. *Journal of Education Policy, 9*(5–6), 5–20.

Thune, G. R. (1997). Was that a red flag? *The School Administrator, 54*(11), 12–15.

Van Alfen, C., & Schmidt, S. M. (1996–1997). Leadership and rural school boards: Utah data. *Rural Educator, 18*(2), 1–4.

Whitson, A. (1998). Are local boards obsolete? *Childhood Education, 74*, 172–173.

Wirt, F. M., & Kirst, M. W. (2001). *The political dynamics of American education* (2nd ed.). Berkeley, CA: McCutchan.

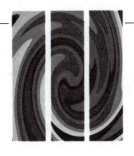

PART III

*Superintendent
Leadership and
Management
Responsibilities*

CHAPTER 8

*Providing Leadership
at the District Level*

KEY FACETS OF THE CHAPTER

○ Importance of leadership in contemporary practice

○ Understanding leadership

○ Leadership functions

○ Leadership dispositions

○ Normative perspectives on leadership

During the last two decades of the 20th century, widespread concern for the condition of public schooling launched what is arguably the most concentrated, comprehensive, and continual effort to reform public education in America's history. National commission and task force reports examined the purpose and condition of schooling, demanded accountability and higher expectations for student performance, and challenged conventional assumptions about how schools are structured, managed, and governed (Björk, 2001). Closely entwined themes of leadership and learning, as well as increasing demands for participation in decision- and policymaking venues, heightened expectations that superintendents provide leadership needed to reinvent schools (Odden, 1995). In the past, most superintendents focused on acquiring "knowledge about" organizational and managerial issues to enhance their effectiveness. During the 1980s and 1990s, however, superintendents saw the need to acquire "knowledge for" improving learning and teaching, establishing inclusive patterns of governance, and distributing leadership. Recently, however, the need to adequately address issues related to ensuring that all children learn pressed them to acquire "knowledge for" improving instruction, decision-, and policymaking, "knowing why" these changes are needed and "knowing how" to accomplish these goals. "Knowing why" reforms are central to the fundamental purpose of schooling in a democratic society and to ensuring social and organizational justice. "Knowing how" to accomplish these important goals requires political acuity as well as communication and interpersonal skills in working with and through others (Björk, Lindle, & Van Meter, 1999). As the landscape of district leadership unfolds, superintendents are compelled to acquire a wider range of theoretical and practical information about schools and districts to accomplish their goals. This chapter explores (a) leadership as an administrative role expectation, (b) leadership functions, (c) instructional leadership, and (d) normative leadership perspectives.

UNDERSTANDING LEADERSHIP

Leadership has been defined in different ways and consequently, perceptions of this role have not been uniform. This fact continues to present problems for practitioners who confuse this term with *administration* and *management*. Three topics are especially relevant to understanding leadership appropriately: (a) distinctions between leadership and management, (b) distinctions between leadership style and strategy, and (c) the determinants of leadership behavior.

Leadership Versus Management

Aristotle distinguished between knowledge necessary to make things and knowledge necessary to make right choices. The former is largely rational and technical; the latter is more practical and embedded in values and beliefs. Historically, the school administration profession has given much more attention to technical knowledge, largely because the realities of practice required superintendents to concentrate on managerial tasks. Many practitioners considered management and leadership synonymous until the late 1970s when scholars began to distinguish between these roles (Bass, 1985; Bennis & Nanus, 1985; Burns, 1978; Rost, 1991). This line of inquiry produced a paradigm shift away from industrial-management to postindustrial leadership perspectives. Nanus (1989), for example, wrote that, "Managers are people who do things right and leaders do the right things" (p. 21). Burns' (1978) seminal work, which focused on transactional versus transformational behavior, also contributed to a more precise understanding of administration (Gronn, 2000). According to Burns, transactional administrators believed that people are motivated primarily by self-interests. Thus they do what they are asked to do largely because of rewards and punishment. Jaques (1989) characterized transactional administration as management. Transformational administration by comparison focuses on working with and through others in accomplishing shared goals (Bass, 1985). This type of behavior is commonly associated with leadership (Kowalski, 2003).

Rost (1991) also viewed management and leadership as separate roles. Management was described as an "authority relationship between at least one manager and one subordinate who coordinate their activities to produce and sell particular goods and/or services" (p. 145). The relationship between the supervisor and employee is asymmetrical; that is, the supervisor has the authority to manage the exchange of labor for wages and retains the power to use coercive means to sanction unacceptable worker behavior. In other words, the relationship "is primarily top-down as to the directives given and bottom-up as to the responses given" (Rost, 1991, p. 147). Management exists in hierarchical and democratic organizations as the raison d'être of organizations (i.e., the need to maintain organizational efficiency, coordinate activities, and accomplish goals). By contrast, Rost (1991) defined leadership as "an influence relationship among leaders and followers who intend real changes that reflect their mutual purposes" (p. 162). This transformational view is predicated on a symmetrical relationship between supervisor and employee; that is, both parties communicate freely and benefit from their interactions (Kowalski, 2003).

Bennis and Nanus's (1985) notion that transformational behavior "is morally purposeful and elevating" (p. 218) underscores the importance of incorporating moral and ethical standards in a superintendent's practice. Moral leadership seeks to influence others by appealing to "higher ideals and moral values such as liberty, justice, equality, peace, and humanitarianism" (Yukl, 1989, p. 210) in pursuit of commonly held, higher-level goals. These ideals and values empower others to improve their work, to increase their professional competency through reflection, and to promote a sense of community, ownership, and commitment (Bennis, 1984; Burns, 1978). Transformational leadership may occur at both a personal level (e.g., exchanges between two individuals) and an organizational level (e.g., cultural change) (Yukl, 2002). At the school district level, a transformational superintendent can build a professional community within a school or district by valuing "the ideal of group solidarity and a commitment to norms of care and responsibility" (Power, 1993, p. 159).

In summary, management is a function that focuses primarily on how to do things. Leadership is a function that focuses primarily on making decisions about what to do. Administration is a broad term that encompasses both roles (Kowalski, 2003). In modern practice, both management and leadership are considered essential for superintendents. Even so, leadership has assumed much more prominence in the context of societal changes and sustained demands for school reform.

Leadership Strategy and Style

Superintendent leadership strategies and styles are influenced by a wide array of factors including role expectations, personal needs, and work contexts. For example, as discussed in Chapter 2, superintendents are expected to assume five separate role characterizations. Although the importance of each varies depending on social trends and conditions within school districts (Sergiovanni, Burlingame, Coombs, & Thurston, 1992), all remain relevant to practice (Brunner, Grogan, & Björk, 2002; Callahan, 1966; Kowalski, in press). In addition to organizational roles, a superintendent's behavior is influenced by personal characteristics. Getzels and Guba (1957) referred to these two behavior determinants as the sociological (nomothetic) and psychological (idiographic). In brief, behavior was described as the product of the intersection of organizational expectations and personal dispositions.

Leadership *strategy* refers to long-term, comprehensive patterns of leadership behavior (Bassett, 1970) formed through organizational socialization—formal and informal processes by which the culture of the organization and ways of doing administration are transmitted to new members (Etzioni, 1969; Van Maanen & Schein, 1979). The nexus between strategy and socialization has become especially cogent in the context of school reform because it helps us understand why superintendents and principals often resist being change agents. Historically, public schools were agencies of stability (Spring, 1990) with the result that most administrators were socialized to avoid failure; that is, they were rewarded for dodging conflict and preventing problems from reaching higher levels of the organization. Even when this strategy conflicted with personal convictions, many practitioners accepted "their role entirely in symbolic terms. In doing so they become dependent upon the organization for their very character, with the result that they put themselves at its mercy" (Bassett, 1970, p. 223). Clearly, leadership strategy is a deeply embedded and culturally transmitted pattern of behavior that persists over time and is difficult to change.

Leadership *style,* on the other hand, refers to a superintendent's motivational system that determines how the superintendent interacts with subordinates (Bass & Stogdill, 1990; Bassett, 1970; Hoy & Miskel, 2005). Variation in style is usually described along continua such as from autocratic to democratic and from task orientation to people orientation. In essence, style is an intricate mix of personal philosophy, professional knowledge, experience, and situational variables. For the modern superintendent, effective style choices often depend on selecting behaviors that best fit circumstances (Leithwood, 1995).

To appreciate the difficulty of changing administrative practice, it is necessary to distinguish between leadership strategy and style. Whereas leadership strategy may be culturally embedded and organizationally imposed, leadership style remains largely a matter of personal conviction. As expected, congruity between organizational strategy and individual style often benefits an administrator because conflict between the two variables is reduced. Nevertheless, inappropriate strategies often deter necessary organizational development.

Determinants of Leadership Behavior

Among the most widely recognized and used human relations models explaining administrative behavior are McGregor's (1960) *Theory X* and *Theory Y.* These models posit that a superintendent's perspective of people determines how subordinates will be treated. Theory X is framed by three pessimistic assumptions: (a) people generally dislike work and try to avoid it; (b) because of a negative disposition toward work, employees must be pushed and controlled if they are to attain organizational goals; and (c) because they lack personal responsibility, employees seek managerial control (McGregor, 1990a). Theory X is commonly associated with traditional management behavior. Theory Y is framed by very different assumptions: (a) conditions in the workplace affect employee commitment, responsibility, and productivity; (b) in positive environments, employees often become committed to organizational goals and work diligently toward their attainment; and (c) employees possess the ability to solve problems they encounter, but this potential is either not recognized or not used in many organizations (McGregor, 1990b). McGregor stressed the importance of leaders questioning their subconscious assumptions about employees and the effects of those assumptions on relationships and organizational productivity. In essence, McGregor's theories help us understand how our convictions about human nature shape our behavior as school administrators.

Administrative behavior also is affected by predispositions toward tasks and people. Seminal work in this area was developed at Ohio State University by

Hemphill and Coons (1950). They identified two behavioral dispositions: *initiating structure* and *consideration*. The former is associated with employee productivity and organizational effectiveness and it can have considerable impact on group performance when tasks in a school district are poorly defined. Consideration, however, involves building trust, respect, and friendship and showing concern for the well-being of employees. Halpin (1967) found that highly effective superintendents scored high on both initiating structure and consideration dimensions whereas ineffective superintendents scored low on both. Although individuals may be naturally inclined to emphasize tasks over people, the most effective administrators develop the skill to emphasize both (Hoy & Miskel, 2005).

During the 1980s *situational leadership* and *contingency leadership* became increasingly attractive as the complexity of school reform increased and national attention focused on leader effectiveness. Four separate, yet related, variables are relevant: context, leader traits, behavior, and effectiveness. Behavior is determined by a mix of personal traits and skills; effectiveness is determined by the extent to which traits and skills are adapted appropriately to a given situation (Hoy & Miskel, 2005). In summary, the belief that contextual variability requires different leadership styles supplants the belief that there is one best administrative style. This perspective partially explains why some superintendents have been highly successful in some settings but not in others.

INSTRUCTIONAL LEADERSHIP

During the late 1980s, interest in large-scale, systemic reform shifted the focus to districts, and the instructional leadership role of superintendents was acknowledged as being central to district educational reform initiatives. Many educators, however, regard this function as an unachieved ideal because they do not see these administrators engaged with teachers in their classrooms. In part, this perception is predicated on the assumption that superintendent and principal roles in instructional leadership are identical. In fact, they are often quite different.

Scholars have found that when superintendents are involved in instructional matters, serve as transformational leaders, and use managerial levers at their disposal to support learning and teaching, they can indirectly improve instruction (Björk, 1993; Bridges, 1982; Cuban, 1984; Fullan, 1991; Hord, 1993; Petersen & Barnett, in press). Although district size may affect how superintendents enact instructional leadership, several pervasive activities have been documented (Murphy & Hallinger, 1986).

- *Staff recruitment and selection.* Hiring effective teachers and principals is both substantive (e.g., building school capacity) and symbolic (e.g., conveying the importance of learning and teaching to all stakeholders) (Brown & Hunter, 1986).
- *Principal supervision and evaluation.* Superintendents affect principal priorities through the performance evaluation system and through ongoing supervision linked to that system.
- *Articulating clear goals for curriculum and instruction.* Superintendents play a pivotal role in visioning and planning, and they subsequently assume major responsibility for reinforcing the goals established through these processes.
- *Financial planning for instruction.* Superintendents often determine the distribution of financial resources; consequently, they have some power to determine the priority given to instruction (Gamoran & Dreeben, 1986; Murphy & Hallinger, 1986).

Superintendents also function as instructional leaders when they create a climate that emphasizes the importance of improving teaching and learning (Björk & Gurley, 2003), function as transformational leaders (Pajak & Glickman, 1989), and provide high-quality, research-based and proficiency-oriented professional development (Daresh, 1991). In sum, a superintendent's instructional leadership role is viewed as a form of proactive administration focused on enabling and facilitating the practice of principals and teachers.

The most recent American Association of School Administrators study of superintendents (Glass, Björk & Brunner, 2000) found that the instructional leadership is a primary role expectation expressed by school boards. More precisely, school board members anticipate that superintendents will assess learner outcomes, accommodate multiple teaching paradigms, encourage new educational programs needed to meet student needs, and cope with changing curricular priorities.

The extent to which superintendents opt to be instructional leaders depends on several variables. For instance, superintendents are socialized to school administration in both graduate school and the workplace (Goodlad, 1990). Professional networks that span school district organizations affirm existing norms, as well as allow new normative leadership styles to diffuse and be adopted. These socialization forces have contributed to the standardization of instructional programs, institutional rules of what society defines as school (Bacharach & Mundell, 1993), structural similarities of school and district organizations (Ogawa, 1992), and conformity in ways of administering (Hoy & Miskel, 2005). As a result, providing leadership to produce substantial change in the way that instruction is organized and delivered has not been a natural characteristic for many experienced superintendents.

Public dissatisfaction and reform initiatives have challenged conventional assumptions about leaders and leadership (Björk, 1996), and in literally thousands of school districts, superintendents have been changing their behavior. Conventional views centered on control, power, and authority are being replaced by emerging views centered on collegiality and collaboration (Brunner et al., 2002; Elmore, 1999; Neuman & Simmons, 2000). Alluding to the nexus between increased demands for instructional improvement and reconfigurations of normative administrator behavior, Elmore (1999) concluded that in a knowledge-intensive enterprise such as teaching and learning, complex tasks are not likely to be completed unless leadership responsibility is widely distributed among organizational roles.

Education reform reports released during the early 1980s focused on improving curriculum and classroom instruction; however, by the middle of the decade emphasis shifted to teacher professionalism and the role of principals in supporting school transformation and enhancing student achievement (Barth, 1990; Schletchty, 1990). Many education commission reports note that to accomplish systemic and lasting reform, principals and teachers have to directly engage in transformative processes to improve student learning (Hallinger, Bickman, & Davis, 1996). During the 1980s and 1990s, proposals for supporting reform and enhancing student achievement were advanced by shifting decision making to the school level through site-based management and school-based decision-making councils (Fullan, 1991), as well as by promoting the concept of teacher leadership. Distributed leadership requires educators to think differently "about the purposes of their work, [but also] . . . the skills and knowledge that go with these purposes" (Elmore, 2000, p. 35).

Research findings on instructionally effective schools (Lezotte, 1994) indicate that administrators who work with and through others tend to be more successful in improving school climate, learning, teaching, and parental involvement. Consequently, sharing authority with those who have been historically excluded from participation in school governance and decision making is arguably beneficial to authentic school reform (Jenni & Maurriel, 1990).

LEADERSHIP FUNCTIONS

A recurring theme in this book is that a superintendent's practice is focused on large-scale, systemic reform and institutional development. Unlike their predecessors who devoted much of their time to managing and protecting the status

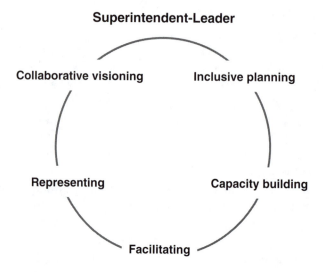

Figure 8.1   Superintendent Leadership Functions

quo, current practitioners face the challenges of determining how schools should be restructured to meet a wider array of student needs, to ensure that every student learns, and to reconcile policy conflict generated by increasing levels of social and political diversity. In this vein, visioning, planning, capacity building, facilitating and representing are essential functions as illustrated in Figure 8.1.

Visioning

The belief that a superintendent should determine a district's future unilaterally is conceptually flawed and inconsistent with prevailing thought on organizational development. Creating a district vision should be neither a solitary act nor a short-term endeavor. Visions are instrumental in that they provide parameters for long-term action (a symbolic statement that helps stakeholders to give meaning to action) (Conger, 1989), and a sociological force that generates the shared commitment essential to intended change (Björk, 1995). In essence, a vision represents a collective sense of the possible. Rather than creating an illusion of change (Kowalski, 1995), shared visions serve a critical and pragmatic school reform function.

Ideally, a school district's vision represents shared values and beliefs about the purpose of schooling and consensus about future directions. Ideally, it is formalized in a written document called a vision statement—a one- or two-page narrative that paints a picture of what the school district wants to achieve in the future (Winter, 1995). To be effective, this statement should be realistic, credible, and attractive to most administrators, teachers, students, and parents, and it should state how the future is an improvement over prevailing conditions (Bennis & Nanus, 1985). Frequently, vision is a manifestation of organizational culture, a representation of shared values and beliefs about teaching, learning, citizenship, democracy, and life. As a context for adopting change strategies, vision is more effective when it is broad enough to integrate the personal visions of many, reflects the needs of individuals and community, is congruous with the existing knowledge base in education, and is compatible with the personal vision of those who lead the organizations.

Cunningham and Gresso (1993) noted that vision also is important because it can be the basis for planning (visionary planning). When this occurs, "[t]he visionary model focuses stakeholders' thinking and direction on the ideal school they wish to create. This opposes traditional deficit models that focus attention on correcting the problems that exist within the school system" (p. 75). In essence, a school district vision provides a foundation for planning the future. Not only does a widely supported vision often influence district culture, it also programs subconscious thinking about preferred behaviors for goal achievement (Tice, 1980). In essence, the vision becomes a daily guide for employees.

Developing a vision can be viewed as a generative process that enhances and enlarges the organization's capacity to shape its future by providing richer meaning to the collective experiences of exploring school district problems, needs, and strengths; it is a reference point against which day-to-day activities can be tested against shared future directions (Senge, 1990). Visionary leadership takes on new meaning in the context of groups and collaboration. Instead of the superintendent determining and then imposing a vision on others, the superintendent leads and facilitates discussions and decisions that produce a collective vision. More directly, "[t]he major task of the superintendent and other administrators is to create shared visions" (Lilly, 1992, p. 5).

Planning

Planning is essentially a mechanism for moving a school district from its current state to a desired state—that is, it is a process for achieving a vision. District data are analyzed and then integrated with mission and evolving social conditions so that informed resource allocation decisions can be made (Cunningham & Gresso, 1993). Consensus in planning, just as consensus in visioning, helps build a sense of ownership in a change process (Fullan, 2004). Unfortunately, contextual variability precludes any one approach to reaching consensus from being equally effective across all districts. Noting this fact, Fullan (2004) advises that superintendents should gather relevant information by visiting schools, meeting with community groups, and studying problems before plunging into visioning and planning activities that require changes in organizational culture and structure.

There are two distinguishable but interrelated dimensions to planning: *process* and *technique*. Process details the sequence of the stages (i.e., ordering what is to be accomplished), whereas technique identifies approaches used at each stage (i.e., methods for reaching goals) (Nutt, 1985). Sergiovanni (1991) described planning as setting goals and objectives and developing blueprints or strategies for their implementation. These two basic features of planning can be addressed in different ways, which is one reason why there are multiple planning paradigms. Nutt (1985) described a five-step continuous planning cycle: (a) formulation (the interface of existing and visionary states); (b) conceptualization (breaking needs into small components and selecting a paradigm appropriate to the task); (c) detailing (identifying and refining contingency approaches to meeting needs); (d) evaluation (identifying costs, benefits, potential pitfalls, and contingency approaches); (e) implementation (setting strategies to gain acceptance and identifying implementation techniques).

Planning is often described as being long-range or strategic. Both adjectives typically refer to processes that extend two or more years; consequently, some observers believe the terms are interchangeable. McCune (1986), however, defined long-range planning as a more restrictive process—one that is closed (i.e., not involving the community) and concerned primarily with resource management. Strategic planning, by comparison, has a broader connotation. It emerged from military applications (Stone, 1987) and involves systematically evaluating opportunities and potential impacts of environmental changes on the organization itself. Environmental scanning (i.e., monitoring the environment consistently), broad participation, and visioning are defining characteristics of strategic planning (Justis, Judd, & Stephens, 1985; Verstegen & Wagoner, 1989). As an example, a superintendent engaging in strategic planning would identify and analyze environmental changes (those outside of the district's organizational boundaries), assess district strengths and weaknesses, develop and implement operational plans, and motivate employees to work toward achieving specific long-term goals. Such planned change is more likely to be supported if it is incremental and guided by annual operational objectives (Winter, 1995).

Planning paradigms also can be broadly categorized as integrated or nonintegrated. Nonintegrated planning refers to a process carried out in isolation by a limited number of specialists. This iteration, especially now that there is so much uncertainty about how information and technology will transform the process of education, increases the risk of producing a flawed product. Conversely, integrated planning requires broad participation and is nested in a social system perspective (Schmidt & Finnigan, 1992). As a result, both the district and the environment in which it functions are thought to influence outcomes. Thus integrated planning requires information on (a) school district philosophy, vision, and mission; (b) constituent groups; (c) legal and financial restrictions; (d) professional knowledge and expertise; (e) school district needs and values; (f) learner needs and values; and (g) community needs and values. However, because decisions are affected by emotions and politics (the human element of planning), outcomes are subject to some error regardless of sophistication (Banghart & Trull, 1973). Integrated planning is preferable for school districts because:

- Both the organization and community are engaged in the process.
- Real needs get aligned with community philosophies.
- Conflict is recognized as an inherent part of planning and appropriate management interventions are deployed.
- Participants are exposed to data that increases their knowledge of the school district and enhances their ability to make rational decisions about goals and strategies.
- Participation nurtures a sense of ownership that almost always has a positive political effect.

These likely benefits are noteworthy because the success of change efforts often hinges on support and cooperation from those most affected (James, 1995). Such commitment becomes less probable when school officials, insulated from the general public, impose their goals on others.

Planning paradigms are also categorized broadly as linear or nonlinear. Linear models are prescriptive, providing the planner a sequential path. The underlying assumption is that each task builds on the previous task. Planning participants concentrate on a single stage supposedly making the process less complex and more efficient. Despite being simple, linearity can be problematic in several ways. The process can stall at a particular stage causing considerable time delays, systems failure, and even the cessation of planning. In addition, information sharing may be curtailed if separate committees are assigned to complete each stage. This often is done in more bureaucratic organizations in an effort to emphasize divisional jurisdiction and technical expertise. For example, the assistant superintendent for curriculum and principals may be assigned to work on instructional goals and the assistant superintendent for business and the assistant superintendent's employees are assigned to work on the budget phase.

Because several or most stages can be pursued concurrently in nonlinear models, these models tend to be more flexible than linear approaches. Advocates argue that the idiosyncratic nature of institutions and communities should dictate planning's starting point and they believe that formative adjustments should be an inherent part of the process (Murk & Galbraith, 1986). Because nonlinear approaches are less orderly, they usually require more facilitation and management.

Capacity Building

Effective superintendent leadership is focused on building the capacity of principals, teachers, and parents to improve student learning. Firestone (1989) defines capacity as "the extent to which the district has knowledge, skills, personnel, and other resources necessary to carry out decisions" (p. 157). Duke (2004) identified three general elements associated with building organizational capacity for change, including (a) a supportive organizational structure, (b) a culture that embraces change, and (c) adequate resources to support capacity-building efforts. Numerous authors (e.g., Berliner & Biddle, 1995; Björk, 1993; Duke, 2004; Hopkins, 2001; Short & Greer, 1997; Short & Rinehart, 1992) have identified the following conditions as underlying capacity building:

- Altering governance and decision-making structures to institutionalize distributed and transformational forms of leadership
- Aligning and delivering professional development activities with distributed leadership and instructional improvement tasks to enhance the capacity of teachers and principals to successfully implement change initiatives
- Recruiting and selecting teachers, principals and key central office staff whose views on the future of schooling are consistent with district goals
- Providing adequate resources to support planned change initiatives
- Valuing and the use of data in improving learning and teaching
- Building community capacity

These factors promote collective action and nurture a district culture conducive to change. In addition, Björk (1993) and Firestone (1989) advance the notion that district superintendents occupy a strategic position in the organization and have managerial levers at their disposal that can be employed to launch and sustain education reform.

Successful change requires a district culture in which teachers and principals value learning and invest time and effort to improve education for all children. Without involving professional staff in developing, implementing and modifying curricula and pedagogical strategies, a superintendent's probability of achieving school improvement is bleak (Barth, 1991). Although structures such as site-based management and school-based decision making provide platforms for broadening participation, they do not assure this outcome. Consequently, superintendents must monitor implementation to ensure that these new structures function as intended (Björk, 1993).

Enabling others to be productive also includes staff development because the complexity of the education process and the challenges of educational change make it unlikely that necessary skills will be acquired without planned interventions (Duke, 2004). In recent years, professional development has been moving away from short-term venues that emphasize "seat time" and "credit hours." The preferred models are research based, continuous, and performance assessed (Björk, Kowalski, & Browne-Ferrigno, in press). Joyce and Showers (1983) found that different professional development configurations produced different outcomes on learners. The highest level of transfer from professional development to practice occurs when mentoring is added to the theory-demonstration-practice-feedback professional development configuration. Unfortunately, most professional development programs tend to focus on concepts, some demonstration, little practice, and scant attention to either feedback or mentoring, which are highly effective (Gottsman, 2000).

School improvement in general, and organizational problem solving in particular, are dependent on the commitment, creativity, and intelligence of the district's employees (Astuto & Clark, 1992). In this vein, superintendents function as enablers when they make wise investments in human capital; that is, they recruit, hire, and support new teachers committed to instructional improvement. Such decisions help erect a culture of learning and innovation (Smylie & Hart, 1999; Sykes, 1999). Resource allocation decisions, both for employing staff and for supporting their practice once employed, are equally pertinent (Duke, 2004).

Because school districts are dependent on local communities for political and financial support, superintendents must assess and nurture community capacity to ensure support for educational initiatives (Duke, 2004; Hoyle, Björk, Collier, & Glass, 2005). Their interaction with parents, citizens, interest groups, business leaders, and other local government officials expands citizen knowledge about district education programs and creates opportunities for inclusive decision making (Kowalski, 2004; Odden & Odden, 1994). Districts derive substantial benefits from working with community citizens, including (a) increased financial support (political capital) (Valenzuela & Dornbush,

1994), (b) positive dispositions and interrelationships among citizens (social capital) (Smylie & Hart, 1999), and (c) increased citizens' knowledge and skills (human capital) (Bourdieu, 1986; Coleman, 1990).

Facilitating

A central function of superintendents as transformative leaders is facilitating organizational change, including altering decision and governance structures (Murphy & Louis, 1999). In this regard, facilitative leadership is associated with increasing teachers' involvement in and commitment to democratic decision-making processes. Facilitative approaches promoted by superintendents and principals—including building trust, democratic decision making, empowerment, innovation and risk taking—contribute to teachers' sense of efficacy in initiating and sustaining change (Rollow & Bryk, 1995). Superintendents and central office support staff also are instrumental in protecting implementation efforts from interference (McCarthy & Still, 1993). Moreover, highly effective superintendents rely on consensus rather than coercion, and they lead through facilitation rather than through commands and tight controls (Murphy, 1995).

A superintendent's first task as a school-improvement facilitator is to develop a sense of collegiality among administrators and teachers by nurturing their continuing professional growth (Cunningham & Gresso, 1993) and by creating a climate of shared commitment, mutual trust, and understanding (Razik & Swanson, 2001). In addition, the superintendent is expected to (a) identify participants' talents, knowledge, and skills; (b) encourage creative thinking; (c) ensure that information essential to framing and solving relevant problems is accessible; (d) acquire necessary resources; and (e) model group process skills (Cunningham & Cordeiro, 2000).

Representing

Superintendents are the visible leaders of their school districts and this responsibility has both formal and informal dimensions (Blumberg, 1985); that is, they symbolically represent their districts both when they are serving in an official capacity and when they are not. Therefore the symbolic relevance of their appearance and behavior becomes no less relevant when they are shopping at the mall or having dinner at a local restaurant. In most communities, superintendents live in a virtual fishbowl and their school boards expect them to project an image congruous with the district's espoused philosophy (Kowalski, 1995).

NORMATIVE LEADERSHIP DISPOSITIONS

Leadership in the superintendency also is studied in relation to ideal strategies and styles. For at least the last three decades, superintendents have been encouraged to be democratic, ethical, and transformational. Collectively, these expectations provide a mosaic of normative standards related to instructional leadership and organizational improvement.

Democratic Leadership

Increased demands for citizen participation as an expression of community control have rekindled expectations that superintendents epitomize democratic, moral, and ethical leadership (Beck & Foster, 1999). Burns (1978) observed that democratic leadership is anchored in three beliefs:

1. Relationships between a leader and the organization's members are bound by collaborative efforts to achieve mutual goals.

2. Leaders recognize that the organization's members grant them the authority to act on their behalf and further, this authority may be withdrawn.

3. Leaders have a moral responsibility to fulfill social contracts with the organization's members.

In addition, democratic leaders value the public's lawful claim to its schools (Björk & Gurley, 2005) and exhibit the capacity to create one community out of many voices. Unlike conditions affecting practitioners in most other professions, superintendents must apply their professional knowledge in a context where political acceptance is essential (Kowalski, 2003). That is, superintendents face conflicting expectations that their practice is guided by a professional knowledge base and that their practice is guided by the will of the people (Wirt & Kirst, 2001).

Moral and Ethical Leadership

Moral leadership is framed by the unending scrutiny of an administrator's use of power and decision choices (Greenfield, 1991). Superintendents who embrace this concept commit themselves to represent all citizens, including parents, other taxpayers, and students. Equally noteworthy, they attempt to meet the needs of all students and resist temptations to engage in political actions that compromise this essential commitment (Sergiovanni, 1994). They abide by the ethical codes of their profession and the ethical standards set by the communities they serve.

Ethical constructs are commonly perceived in legal contexts, but the meaning of administrative ethics is broader than this. Referring to administrators in all types of organizations, Blanchard and Peale (1988) proposed a simple, three-part "ethics check" for leaders:

1. Is it legal?

2. Is it balanced?

3. How will it make me feel about myself? (p. 27).

In school administration, ethics extend beyond legalities to such issues as bias, discrimination, nepotism, violating confidentiality, commitment to work responsibilities, and playing politics for purposes of self-interest (Howlett, 1991; Kimbrough & Nunnery, 1988). Starratt (1995) formulated three foundational themes for ethical practice: the ethic of critique, the ethic of justice, and the ethic of caring. The first addresses issues such as hierarchy, privilege, and power (e.g., Who controls public schools? Who defines the future of public education?). The second addresses issues such as democratic participation and equal access to programs and resources (e.g., How are scarce resources allocated? How are critical decisions made?). The third addresses issues focusing on human relationships such as cooperation, shared commitment, and friendship (What do personal relationships demand from superintendents, other administrators, and teachers?). While the first two themes have received some attention in school administration literature, the third has been largely ignored (Starratt, 2003). Moral leadership requires attention to what schools are all about and what they do, how decisions are made, as well as the nature of those decisions. Sergiovanni (1992) referred to this process as *purposing*. Purposing allows members of the school community to identify goals and strategies that can be supported by all.

Transformational Leadership

As noted previously in this chapter, transformational leadership emphasizes morally purposeful and elevating behavior that is accomplished by working with and through others (Bennis & Nanus, 1985) to meet shared organizational improvement goals (Rost, 1991). The central idea of transformational leadership is empowering others for the purpose of bringing about significant change (Bennis & Nanus, 1985; Burns, 1978; Leithwood, Begley, & Cousins, 1994). Thus it involves promoting the belief that reform is a total organization phenomenon and motivating school personnel and clients to assume responsibility for pursuing pertinent goals (Ogawa & Bossert, 1995).

Transformational leadership entails building both capacity and commitment for change. Leithwood (1994) describes the following operational elements of this concept:

- Building a shared vision of the school
- Creating and aligning school and district goals
- Creating an intellectually stimulating environment
- Nurturing a positive, learning-oriented culture
- Providing individual support and development opportunities
- Modeling best practices and learning-oriented organizational values
- Creating authentic organizational structures that support shared decision-making venues
- Establishing and reifying high expectations for student and adult learning.

Research (e.g., Bogler, 2001) demonstrates that the behavior of transformational administrators can directly and indirectly influence teacher job satisfaction by virtue of affecting their perceptions of their profession and their perceptions of their professional responsibilities. When principals and teachers see school improvement as a shared responsibility, they are more inclined to participate in visioning and planning, to enthusiastically pursue implementation, and to assume ownership for school reform initiatives.

FOR FURTHER REFLECTION

This chapter examined the leadership roles of the superintendent within the school district. The quest for school renewal has placed added emphasis on change initiatives, elevating the importance of functions such as visioning, planning, collaboration, teamwork, and transformational leadership. These new ways of leading are directly focused on increasing the effectiveness of superintendents as instructional leaders.

As you consider what you read in this chapter, answer the following questions:

1. What is the difference between visioning and planning?

2. School boards often seek superintendents who are "visionary leaders." Does this mean that new superintendents should be expected to impose their vision on their school districts? Why or why not?

3. What are the advantages and disadvantages of integrated and nonintegrated planning?

4. What are the advantages and disadvantages of linear planning and nonlinear planning?

5. What are differences between leadership strategy and leadership style?

6. What is democratic leadership? Based on your observations, do most superintendents embrace this concept?

7. Superintendents who reach administrative decisions by consensus may be accused of being weak; that is, detractors will conclude that they are unwilling to make difficult choices alone. Would you defend consensus decision making? Why or why not?

8. What is your image of a superintendent as an instructional leader? Is this the same image you have of principals as instructional leaders?

9. Assume you are advising a school board that is preparing to interview superintendent candidates. What questions would you recommend that the school board ask about a candidate's leadership style?

10. What is ethical leadership? What factors may deter a superintendent from behaving ethically?

11. How do transactional and transformational leaders differ in their perceptions of employees?

Case Study

Dr. Raymond Bernelli was preparing to leave town for a second interview with the Oak Meadow School District board. If he were selected as the district's next superintendent, he would be assuming his fourth superintendency in 19 years. As the chief executive officer, he was able to implement new programs in three different districts and did so with the enthusiastic support of administrators, teachers, and the community. His accomplishments contributed to his reputation as a visionary leader and change agent.

The Oak Meadow School District is located in a suburb of a large midwestern city. The following demographic statistics describe this system:

- The overall enrollment is 22,386.
- The average annual family income is the highest in the state.
- The average teacher salary is the second highest in the state.
- The average annual expenditure per pupil is second highest in the state.
- Eighty-three percent of the district's high school graduates enroll in 4-year institutions of higher education.
- The racial-ethnic composition of the school district includes a 5% African American population and a 3% Hispanic population.

When Dr. Jacob Eddelman announced his retirement after having served as superintendent for 13 years, the Oak Meadow school board was inundated with inquiries about the position. Even so, they employed Dr. Rita Morales, a nationally known search consultant, to assist them with finding a new leader. Together the board and Dr. Morales looked at more than 125 applications. They interviewed six semifinalists, narrowed the field to two, and conducted second interviews with the finalists.

The seven-member school board reflected the composition of the community. By occupation, three were business executives, one was a surgeon, one was an attorney, one was a retired teacher, and one was a retired electrical engineer. The board president, Ronald Barrin, was vice president of a brokerage firm and the senior board member, having served continuously for 17 years.

During the first interview, Dr. Bernelli was asked a number of questions about his career and his philosophy of education. He elected to tell the board members about the specific programs that he had implemented in each of three districts. The board members were uniformly impressed and they evaluated his personal appearance, communication skills, and self-confidence positively. Although he was one of two finalists, he entered the second interview as the school board's leading candidate.

The second interview took place in the district's boardroom located adjacent to the superintendent's office. All seven board members were present; however, Dr. Morales, the board's consultant, was not. After about 15 minutes of informal discussion, the board president asked a challenging question:

"Dr. Bernelli, we are impressed by all the accomplishments you outlined in your previous interview. While this is not a district seeking a total makeover, many of us feel that some new ideas would prevent stagnation. Quite frankly, we are highly interested in employing you. You have a vision and obviously you're not afraid to pursue change. You have had several weeks since our last meeting to reflect on us, the community, and the school system. What changes would you pursue if you became our superintendent?"

Without hesitation, Dr. Bernelli responded, "I don't know."

Silence filled the room. After a series of glances among the board members, Mr. Barrin spoke again.

"Maybe I didn't ask the question very clearly. Let me try again."

But before he could do so, Dr. Bernelli spoke. "I understood your question. Allow me to explain my answer. To respond intelligently, I need to know much more about your school district."

One of the other board members asked, "Aren't there certain school reform initiatives that all school districts should be pursuing? Aren't there governance and education improvements that would be beneficial regardless of community and district contexts?"

"Perhaps," Dr. Bernelli responded, "but effective change requires specificity. This is a reputable school district that no doubt employs many outstanding educators. I believe change should be pursued through the collective power of district stakeholders. Your principals and teachers know the students and the community. Until I have opportunities to communicate with them and until I am able to study this district's prevailing culture, my suggesting specific changes would be precarious."

One of the board members then asked, "How long will it take you to do these things?"

"That depends on the degree to which open communication can be pursued, but given the size of the organization, I would estimate a minimum of two years."

The board president spoke next. "Dr. Eddelman, our retiring superintendent, also has a reputation for getting things done. He has not been a dictator, but on the other hand, he has never backed away from making difficult decisions. Over time he has made some enemies, but what executive doesn't? Most principals and teachers have been highly supportive of him, but all principals and teachers respect his courage. He often asked others for input, but he openly stated that important decisions were his responsibility."

Dr. Bernelli responded. "I have met Dr. Eddelman and I know that he is respected by other superintendents. He clearly has been very successful in this district. Keep in mind, however, that yesterday is not necessarily the same as tomorrow. What was needed in the past may not work in the future; leadership styles that worked in the past may not work in the future. It would be very easy for me to articulate a change agenda today, but if I did, I would mislead you about my administrative philosophy. If I am honored to be your next superintendent, I will work diligently to forge a climate in which the community and all district employees will work collaboratively to ensure that this remains a first-rate school system."

Case Discussion Questions

1. Assess Dr. Bernelli's philosophy about change from (a) a professional perspective, (b) a managerial perspective, and (c) a transformational leadership perspective.

2. Board members are likely to react in different ways to Dr. Bernelli's comments. Why?

3. In your opinion, did Dr. Bernelli err in stating his convictions about pursuing change? Why or why not?

4. Is it possible for a superintendent to be both decisive and collaborative?

5. Why might some observers view collaboration and consensus decision making as administrator weaknesses?

6. Many board members are under pressure to produce change. In light of this fact, do you agree with Dr. Bernelli's attitude about the way in which change should be pursued? Why or why not?

7. Would you like to be one of Dr. Bernelli's assistant superintendents? Why or why not?

8. Do you believe that the occupations of the board members affect their dispositions toward an ideal superintendent? Provide a rationale for your response.

9. Should Dr. Bernelli be concerned about replacing Dr. Eddelman? If so, what concerns should he have?

REFERENCES

Astuto, T., & Clark, D. (1992). Challenging the limits of school restructuring and reform. In A. Lieberman (Ed.), *The changing contexts of teaching: Ninety-first yearbook of the National Society for the Study of Education (NSSE)* (pp. 90–109). Chicago: University of Chicago Press.

Bacharach, S., & Mundell, B. (1993). Organizational politics in schools: Micro, macro and the logics of action. *Educational Administration Quarterly, 29*(4), 423–52.

Barth, R. (1990). A personal vision of a good school. *Phi Delta Kappan, 71*(8), 512–616.

Barth, R. (1991). Restructuring schools: Some questions for teachers and principals. *Phi Delta Kappan, 73*(2), 123–128.

Bass, B. M. (1985). *Leadership and performance beyond expectations.* New York: Free Press.

Bass, B., & Stogdill, R. (1990). *Bass & Stogdill's handbook of leadership.* New York: Simon & Schuster.

Bassett, G. A. (1970). Leadership style and strategy. In L. Netzer, G. Eye, A. Graef, R. Drey, & J. Overman (Eds.), *Interdisciplinary foundations of supervision* (pp. 221–231). Boston: Allyn & Bacon.

Banghart, F. W., & Trull, A. (1973). *Educational planning.* New York: Macmillan.

Beck, L., & Foster, W. (1999). Administration and community: Considering the challenges, exploring the possibilities. In J. Murphy & K. S. Louis (Eds.), *Handbook of research on educational administration* (2nd ed., pp. 337–356). San Francisco: Jossey-Bass.

Bennis, W. G. (1984). The four competencies of leadership. *Training and Development Journal, 38*(8), 14–19.

Bennis, W. G., & Nanus, B. (1985). *Leaders: The strategies for taking charge.* New York: Harper & Row.

Berliner, D., & Biddle, B. (1995). *The manufactured crisis: Myths, fraud, and the attack on America's public schools*. Reading, MA: Addison-Wesley.

Björk, L. (1993). Effective schools effective superintendents: The emerging instructional leadership role. *Journal of School Leadership, 3*(3), 246–259.

Björk, L. (1995). Substance and symbolism in the education commission reports. In R. Ginsberg, & D. Plank (Eds.), *Commissions, reports, reforms and educational policy* (pp. 133–149). New York: Praeger.

Björk, L. (1996). The revisionists' critique of the education reform reports. *Journal of School Leadership, 7*(1), 290–315.

Björk, L. (2001). Preparing the next generation of superintendents: Integrating formal and experiential knowledge. In C. C. Brunner & L. Björk (Eds.), *The new superintendency: Advances in research theories of school management and educational policy* (pp. 19–54). Greenwich, CT: JAI.

Björk, L., & Gurley, D. K. (2003). Superintendents as transformative leaders: Schools as learning communities and communities of learners. *Journal of Thought, 38*(4), 37–78.

Björk, L., & Gurley, D. K. (2005). Superintendent as educational statesman and political strategist. In L. Björk & T. J. Kowalski (Eds.), *The contemporary superintendent: Preparation, practice and development*. Thousand Oaks, CA: Corwin Press.

Björk, L., Kowalski, T. J., & Browne-Ferrigno, T. (in press). Learning theory and research: A framework for changing superintendent preparation and development. In L. Björk & T. J. Kowalski (Eds.), *The contemporary superintendent: Preparation, practice and development*. Thousand Oaks, CA: Corwin Press.

Björk, L., Lindle, J. C., & Van Meter, E. (1999). A summing up. *Educational Administration Quarterly, 35*(4), 657–663.

Blanchard, K., & Peale, N. V. (1988). *The power of ethical management*. New York: William Morrow.

Blumberg, A. (1985). *The school superintendent: Living with conflict*. New York: Teachers College.

Bogler, R. (2001). The influence of leadership style on teacher job satisfaction. *Educational Administration Quarterly, 37*, 662–683.

Bourdieu, P. (1986). The forms of capital. In J. Richardson (Ed.), *Handbook of theory and research for sociology education* (pp. 141–258). New York: Greenwood.

Bridges, E. (1982). Research on the school administrator: The state of the art, 1967–1980. *Educational Administrator Quarterly, 18*(3), 12–33.

Brown, F., & Hunter, R. (1986, April). *A model of instructional leadership for schools*. Paper presented at the Annual Meeting of the American Educational Research Association, San Francisco, CA.

Brunner, C., Grogan, M., & Björk, L. (2002). Shifts in the discourse defining the superintendency: Historical and current foundations of the position. In J. Murphy (Ed.), *The educational leadership challenge: Redefining leadership for the 21st century: Ninety-ninth Yearbook of the National Society for the Study of Education (NSSE)* (pp. 211–238). Chicago: University of Chicago Press.

Burns, J. M. (1978). *Leadership*. New York: Harper Torchbooks.

Callahan, R. E. (1966). *The superintendent of schools: A historical analysis.* East Lansing, MI: National Center for Research on Teacher Learning. (ERIC Document Reproduction Service No. ED0104410)

Coleman, J. (1990). *Foundations of social theory.* Cambridge, MA: Harvard University Press.

Conger, J. A. (1989). *The charismatic leader. Behind the mystique of exceptional leadership.* San Francisco: Jossey-Bass.

Cuban, L. (1984). Transforming the frog into a prince: Effective schools research and practice at the district level. *Harvard Educational Review, 54*(2), 129–151.

Cunningham, W., & Cordeiro, P. (2000). *Educational administration: A problem-based approach.* Boston: Allyn & Bacon.

Cunningham, W., & Gresso, D. (1993). *Cultural leadership: The culture of excellence in education.* Boston: Allyn & Bacon.

Daresh, J. C. (1991). Instructional leadership as a proactive administrative process. *Theory into Practice, 30*(2), 109–112.

Duke, D. (2004). *The challenges of education.* Boston: Pearson Education.

Elmore, R. (1999, September). *Leadership of large-scale improvement in American education.* Paper prepared for the Albert Shanker Institute.

Elmore, R. (2000). *Building a new structure for school leadership.* Washington, DC: The Albert Shanker Institute.

Etzioni, A. (1969). *The semi-professions and their organizations: Teachers, nurses, social workers.* London: Free Press.

Firestone, W. (1989). Using reform: Conceptualizing district initiative. *Educational Evaluation and Policy Analysis, 11*(2), 151–164.

Fullan, M. (1991). *The meaning of educational change.* New York: Teachers College Press.

Fullan, M. (2004). *Leadership and sustainability.* Thousand Oaks, CA: Corwin Press.

Gamoran, A., & Dreeben, R. (1986). Coupling and control in educational organizations. *Administrative Science Quarterly, 31*(4), 612–632.

Getzels, J. W., & Guba, E. G. (1957). Social behavior and the administrative process. *School Review, 65,* 423–441.

Glass, T., Björk, L. B., & Brunner, C. C. (2000). *The 2000 study of the American superintendency: A look at the superintendent of education in the new millennium.* Arlington, VA: American Association of School Administrators.

Goodlad, J. I. (1990). *Teachers for our nation's schools.* San Francisco: Jossey-Bass.

Gottsman, B. (2000). *Peer coaching for effectiveness* (2nd ed.). Lanham, MD: Scarecrow Press.

Greenfield, T. B. (1991). Foreword. In C. Hodgkinson (Ed.), *Educational leadership: The moral art* (pp. 3–9). Albany: State University of New York.

Gronn, P. (2000). Distributed properties: A new architecture for leadership. *Educational Management & Administration, 28*(3), 317–338.

Hallinger, P., Bickman, L., & Davis, K. (1996). School context, principal leadership and student achievement. *Elementary School Journal, 96*(5), 527–550.

Halpin, A. (1967). Change and organizational climate. *Journal of Educational Administration, 5,* 5–25.

Hemphill, J., & Coons, A. (1950). *Leader behavior description questionnaire.* Columbus: Ohio State University Press.

Hopkins, D. (2001). *Improvement for real.* London: Routledge/Falmer.

Hord, S. (1993). Smoke, mirrors or reality: Another instructional leadership. In D. Carter, T. Glass, & S. Hord (Eds.), *Selecting, preparing and developing the school district superintendent* (pp. 1–19). Washington, DC: Falmer Press.

Howlett, P. (1991). How you can stay on the straight and narrow. *Executive Educator, 13*(2), 19–21, 35.

Hoy, W., & Miskel, C. (2005). *Educational administration: Theory, research and practice* (7th ed.). New York: McGraw-Hill.

Hoyle, J., Björk, L., Collier, V., & Glass, T. (2005). *The superintendent as CEO: Standards-based performance.* Thousand Oaks, CA: Corwin.

James, J. (1995). Negotiating the Grand Canyon of change. *The School Administrator, 52*(1), 22–29.

Jaques, E. (1989). *Requisite organization: The CEO's guide to creative structure and leadership.* Arlington, VA: Cason Hall.

Jenni, R., & Maurriel, J. (1990, April). *An examination of the factors affecting stakeholders' assessment of school decentralization.* Paper presented at the annual meeting of the American Educational Research Association, Boston.

Joyce, B. R., & Showers, B. (1983). *Power in staff development through research on training.* Alexandria, VA: Association for Curriculum and Staff Development.

Justis, R. T., Judd, R. J., & Stephens, D. B. (1985). *Strategic management and policy.* Englewood Cliffs, NJ: Prentice Hall.

Kimbrough, R. B., & Nunnery, M. Y. (1988). *Educational administration: An introduction.* New York: Macmillan.

Kowalski, T. J. (1995). *Keepers of the flame: Contemporary urban superintendents.* Thousand Oaks, CA: Corwin Press.

Kowalski, T. J. (2003). *Contemporary school administration: An introduction.* Boston: Allyn & Bacon.

Kowalski, T. J. (2004). School public relations: A new agenda. In T. J. Kowalski (Ed.), *Public relations in schools* (3rd ed., pp. 3–29). Upper Saddle River, NJ: Merrill, Prentice Hall.

Kowalski, T. J. (in press). Evolution of the school district superintendent position. In L. Björk, & T. J. Kowalski, (Eds.) *School district superintendents: Role expectations: Professional preparation, and development.* Thousand Oaks, CA: Corwin Press.

Leithwood, K. (1994). Leadership for school restructuring. *Educational Administration Quarterly 30*(4), 498–518.

Leithwood, K. (1995). Cognitive perspectives on school leadership. *Journal of School Leadership, 5*(2), 15–35.

Leithwood, K., Begley, P., & Cousins, B. (1994). The nature, causes and consequences of principals' practices: An agenda for the future. *Journal of Educational Administration, 28*(4), 5–31.

Lilly, E. R. (1992). *Superintendent leadership and districtwide vision.* East Lansing, MI: National Center for Research on Teacher Learning. (ERIC Document Reproduction Service No. ED343222)

Lezotte, L. (1994). The nexus of instructional leadership and effective schools. *School Administrator, 51*(6), 20–23.

McCarthy, J., & Still, S. (1993). Hollibrook Accelerated Elementary School. In J. Murphy & P. Hallinger (Eds.), *Restructuring schooling: Learning from on-going efforts* (pp. 63–83). Newbury Park, CA: Corwin.

McCune, S. D. (1986). *Guide to strategic planning for educators.* Alexandria, VA: Association for Supervision and Curriculum Development.

McGregor, D. (1960). *The human side of enterprise.* New York: McGraw-Hill.

McGregor, D. (1990a). Theory X: The integration of individual and organizational goals. In J. Hall (Ed.), *Models of management: The structure of competence* (2nd ed., pp. 11–18). Woodlands, TX: Woodstead.

McGregor, D. (1990b). Theory Y: The integration of individual and organizational goals. In J. Hall (Ed.), *Models of management: The structure of competence* (2nd ed., pp. 19–27). Woodlands, TX: Woodstead.

Murk, P. J., & Galbraith, M. W. (1986). Planning successful continuing education programs: A systems approach model. *Lifelong Learning, 9*(5), 21–23.

Murphy, J. (1995). Restructuring in Kentucky: The changing role of the superintendent and district office. In K. Leithwood (Ed.), *Effective school district leadership: Transforming politics into education* (pp. 117–133). Albany: State University of New York.

Murphy, J., & Hallinger, P. (1986). The superintendent as instructional leader: Findings from effective school districts. *Journal of Educational Administration, 24*(2), 213–236.

Murphy, J., & Louis, K. (Eds.). (1999). *Handbook of research on educational administration* (2nd ed.). San Francsico: Jossey-Bass.

Nanus, B. (1989). *The leader's edge.* Chicago: Contemporary Books.

Neuman, M., & Simmons, W. (2000). Leadership for student learning. *Phi Delta Kappan, 82*(1), 9–12.

Nutt, P. C. (1985). The study planning processes. In W. G. Bennis, K. D. Benne, & R. Chin (Eds.), *The planning of change* (4th ed., pp. 198–215). New York: Holt, Rinehart & Winston.

Odden, A. R. (1995). *Educational leadership for America's schools.* New York: McGraw-Hill.

Odden, A., & Odden, E. (1994, April). *Applying the high involvement framework to local management of schools in Victoria, Australia.* Paper presented at the annual meeting of the American Educational Research Association, New Orleans.

Ogawa, R. (1992). Institutional theory and examining leadership in school. *International Journal of Educational Management, 6*(3), 14–21.

Ogawa, R., & Bossert, S. (1995). Leadership as an organizational property. *Educational Administration Quarterly, 31*(2), 224–243.

Pajak, E. F., & Glickman, C. D. (1989). Dimensions of school district improvement. *Educational Leadership, 46*(8), 61–64.

Petersen, G., & Barnett, B. (in press). The superintendent as instructional leader: Current practice, future conceptualizations and implications for preparation. In L. Björk, & T. J. Kowalski, (Eds.). *School district superintendents: Role expectations, professional preparation and development.* Thousand Oaks, CA: Corwin Press.

Power, F. C. (1993). Just schools and moral atmosphere. In K. Strike and P. Ternasky (Eds.), *Ethics for professionals in education* (pp. 148–161). New York: Teachers College Press.

Razik, T. A., & Swanson, A. D. (2001). *Fundamental concepts of educational leadership* (2nd ed.). Upper Saddle River, NJ: Merrill, Prentice Hall.

Rollow, S., & Bryk, A. (1995). Politics as a lever for organizational change. In S. Eston, D. Kerbow, & P. Sebring, *Democratic participation and organizational change: The Chicago experience* (pp. 43–92). Boulder, CO: Westview.

Rost, J. C. (1991). *Leadership for the twenty-first century.* Westport, CT: Praeger.

Schlechty, P. (1990). *Schools for the 21st century.* San Francisco: Jossey-Bass.

Schmidt, W., & Finnigan, J. (1992). *The race without a finish line: America's quest for total quality.* San Francisco: Jossey-Bass.

Senge, P. (1990). *The fifth discipline: Mastering the five practices of the learning organization.* New York: Doubleday.

Sergiovanni, T. J. (1991). *The principalship: A reflective practice perspective* (2nd ed.). Boston: Allyn & Bacon.

Sergiovanni, T. J. (1992). *Moral leadership: Getting to the heart of school improvement.* San Francisco: Jossey-Bass.

Sergiovanni, T. J. (1994). *Building community in schools.* San Francisco: Jossey-Bass.

Sergiovanni, T. J., Burlingame, M., Coombs, F. S., & Thurston, P. W. (1992). *Educational governance and administration* (3rd ed.). Boston: Allyn & Bacon.

Short, P., & Greer, J. (1997). *Leadership in empowered schools: Themes from innovative efforts.* Upper Saddle River, NJ: Merrill, Prentice Hall.

Short, P., & Rinehart, J. (1992). School participant empowerment scale: Assessment of the level of participant empowerment in the school. *Educational and Psychological Measurement, 54*(2), 951–960.

Smylie, M., & Hart, A. (1999). School leadership for teacher learning and change: Human and social capital development. In J. Murphy & K. S. Louis (Eds.), *Handbook of research on educational administration* (2nd ed., pp. 421–441). San Francisco: Jossey-Bass.

Spring, J. (1990). *The American school 1642–1990: Varieties of historical interpretation of the foundations and development of American education* (2nd ed.). New York: Longman.

Starratt, R. J. (1995). *Leaders with vision: The quest for school renewal.* Thousand Oaks, CA: Corwin Press.

Starratt, R. J. (2003). *Centering educational administration: Cultivating meaning, community, responsibility.* Mahwah, NJ: Lawrence Erlbaum Associates.

Stone, S. C. (1987). *Strategic planning for independent schools.* Boston: National Association of Independent Schools.

Sykes, G. (1999). The "new professionalism" in education: An appraisal. In J. Murphy & K. S. Louis (Eds.), *Handbook of research on educational administration* (2nd ed., pp. 227–249). San Francisco: Jossey-Bass.

Tice, L. (1980). *New age thinking for achieving your potential.* Seattle, WA: The Pacific Institute.

Van Maanen, J., & Schein, E. (1979). Toward a theory of organizational socialization. *Research in Organizational Behavior, 1,* 209–264.

Valenzuela, A., & Dornbush, S. (1994). Familism and social capital in the academic achievement of Mexican origin and Anglo high school adolescents. *Social Science Quarterly, 75,* 18–36.

Verstegen, D. A., & Wagoner, J. L. (1989). Strategic planning for policy development: An evolving model. *Planning and Changing, 20*(1), 33–49.

Winter, P. A. (1995). Vision in school planning: A tool for crafting a creative future. *School Business Affairs, 61*(6), 46–50.

Wirt, F., & Kirst, M. (2001). *The political dynamics of American education.* Berkeley, CA: McCutchan.

Yukl, G. A., (1989). *Leadership in organizations* (2nd ed.). Englewood Cliffs, NJ: Prentice Hall.

Yukl, G. A. (2002). *Leadership in organizations* (5th ed.). Upper Saddle River, NJ: Prentice Hall.

CHAPTER 9

*Material Resources
Management*

KEY FACETS OF THE CHAPTER

○ Fiscal management

○ Facility planning and management

○ Transportation services

○ Food Services

Superintendents are often criticized for being preoccupied with the political and managerial aspects of their work and for spending too little time providing leadership for instructional programs. Such rebukes are increasingly noteworthy because of pressures placed on local district officials to develop a vision for effective schooling and to plan a coherent reform agenda for reaching that vision. Critics, however, often ignore the reasons why management became and remains an integral part of administrative work.

Management emerged as an essential role of the superintendent during and immediately following the American Industrial Revolution. As discussed in Chapter 2 on role conceptualizations, pressure to reconfigure administrators as business executives was driven primarily by a quest for technical efficiency (Brunner, Grogan, & Björk, 2002). Several decades later, efforts to make management the sole or even primary superintendent function came under attack, especially from progressive philosophers, such as William Heard Kilpatrick and George Sylvester Counts. These critics viewed the obsession with scientific management as a manifestation of a broader infusion of business values into public education (Van Til, 1971). Their criticisms and changing social concerns shifted attention to schools as democratic institutions and to superintendents as political leaders. In the 1960s and 1970s, however, the public's demand for accountability and cost-effective management reestablished an emphasis on managerial efficiency (Tyack & Cuban, 1995).

During the past two decades, the superintendent's role as organizational manager has often been demeaned and devalued, which is unfortunate given the realities of practice. As an example, many members of our profession, especially those working in higher education, now prefer to call this specialization "educational leadership" rather than school administration or educational administration. While the term leadership has become politically preferable, taken literally this label actually is misleading and counterproductive in relation to the realities of practice in the superintendency. The truth is simply this: *administration, whether in business or in education, inescapably entails both leadership and management functions* (Kowalski, 2003). Management and leadership are distinctive but not mutually exclusive; in fact, they are interdependent roles (Adamchik, 2004). Sadly, these two core functions have not been defined uniformly in the literature and the lack of consistency has produced two recurring errors. First, some members of the profession believe that leadership and administration are synonymous (Yukl, 1989); second, the concepts of administration, leadership, and management are frequently misused in modern literature, mostly because authors have not defined them or defined them correctly (Shields & Newton, 1994). Starratt (1990) appropriately characterized the school administrator as an actor who must play the parts of both managers and leaders. As a manager, a superintendent makes and enforces rules, controls material and human resources, strives for objectivity and rationality, and pursues efficiency. As a leader, a superintendent focuses on philosophy, purpose, and school improvement. Although leadership is clearly more essential to the central purposes of schooling, management is neither unimportant nor counterproductive to effective education.

Contrary to what some observers may believe, effective superintendents exhibit neither disdain for nor indifference toward their management duties. They recognize that they must assume several roles and transition among them as circumstances dictate. This chapter and the next are devoted to management responsibilities. The topic is divided into two parts: material resources management, which is discussed in this chapter, and human resources management, which is discussed in the next. As you read these chapters, remember that the ascendancy of leadership as a superintendent role does not make effective management any less essential than in the past (Sergiovanni, Burlingame, Coombs, & Thurston, 1992).

FISCAL MANAGEMENT

Oversight of fiscal operations clearly is the most visible management role performed by most superintendents. This is true largely for two reasons. First, a substantial portion of revenues still are derived from local taxes and this prompts citizens to closely monitor financial operations. Second, budgetary decisions and business operations are closely scrutinized by state government and when management deficiencies are identified (e.g., via state audits), they are made public and reported in the media (King, Swanson, & Sweetland, 2003). In the public's eye, the fiduciary responsibility of the school board and superintendent is at or near the top of their responsibilities. Yet, many novice superintendents enter practice believing that their preparation for this responsibility is marginal (McAdams, 1995). Apprehensions about being prepared to manage vast fiscal resources are connected to professional preparation and licensing. In the absence of a national curriculum to prepare superintendents and because of inconsistent state licensing requirements, some practitioners actually become superintendents without having completed academic courses in either the economics of education or school business management. Others have completed just one generic course in which the curriculum was not practice based.

The fiscal management role is further complicated by inconsistent conditions of practice. In relatively small districts (i.e., with fewer than 1,500 students), rarely do we find professional support staff operating a separate business division of the organization. Because these districts continue to be the norm, their superintendents often are forced to function as the business manager. In comparison, superintendents in larger districts often have support staff specialists, and the larger the district, typically the greater the number of professional personnel assigned to this division. Some states (e.g., Ohio) also require local school boards to employ a full-time treasurer and to have the treasurer report to the board and not to the superintendent (a dubious organizational concept based on the belief that instruction and financial management should be conducted as mutually exclusive functions). Because of conditions in larger districts and in states that diminish superintendent control over financial operations, some observers incorrectly concluded that superintendents do not need to know much about financial management. This conclusion is myopic, partly because these conditions are not relevant to thousands of practitioners and partly because all superintendents realize that they can relegate functions but not ultimate responsibility.

Business management in public education is a complex responsibility. Many functions need to be performed, each requiring different types of information and skills. In addition, the parameters for executing the functions are inconsistent from state to state; as an example, requirements for audits in two neighboring states, Illinois and Indiana, are substantially different. Therefore, a superintendent must not only be prepared to manage an array of fiscal functions, a superintendent must also be prepared to apply this knowledge within the parameters of a given state's laws. Table 9.1 lists primary business management responsibilities. In smaller school districts, several of these functions consume an inordinate amount of a superintendent's practice.

Planning and Budgeting

Budgets should be a compilation of three plans: an *education plan,* a *revenue plan,* and an *expenditure plan* (Hack, Candoli, & Ray, 1995). Decisions about anticipated spending ought to be predicated on meeting the needs of students and on reasonably accurate revenue estimates. Therefore, the education plan should be developed prior to either revenue or expenditure plans and this is done by identifying needs, establishing goals, organizing objectives, and describing programs to meet these objectives (Burrup, Brimley, & Garfield, 1996). Once completed, the education plan should be interfaced with the revenue plan; the latter document includes both anticipated income and cash balances. If discrepancies between the two plans are identified, the superintendent has three choices before developing or approving an expenditure plan.

1. The superintendent can ignore discrepancies between planned programs and resources available to pay for them. Although this clearly is a poor choice, it is made by some superintendents as evidenced by the fact that there are school districts approving deficit-producing budgets each year. Before opting to develop and recommend such a budget, superintendents should know pertinent state laws and the consequences of outspending their financial resources. In Indiana, for instance, a district operating in arrears can be placed under the direct control of a state property tax control board—an action that requires all local district fiscal decisions to be approved by the state.

2. The superintendent can opt to reduce the scope of the education plan to ensure that it can be funded completely. This option may be necessary if there are no viable alternatives for increasing revenues.

Table 9.1   Fiscal Management Responsibilities

Responsibility	*Explanation*
Financial planning	Pertains to long-range planning about revenues and expenditures, especially to infusing these considerations into comprehensive strategic plans.
Budgeting	An annual process of developing a document that details program needs, estimated costs of programs, and estimated revenues.
Accounting	A process that determines the fiscal condition of a school district; usually mandated by state law, the process serves as both a measure of accountability and a source of public information.
Debt management	Entails estimates of debt capacity, the structuring of debt, payment on debt obligations, and other matters associated with indebtedness of the school district.
Auditing	A process mandated by state law that serves as a means of determining the financial status of a school district and determining whether transactions have been executed in compliance with existing laws and regulations; audits can be internal or external, and some form of external auditing is usually required.
Purchasing	An ongoing process of procuring necessary equipment and materials for the operation of the school district; includes specific functions such as preparing bids, cost analysis, and recommendations for board action.
Inventory management	Controlling and storing equipment and materials that will be used at some future date.
Materials distribution	Disseminating equipment and materials from storage areas to specific sites as such materials are requisitioned.
Risk management	Involves the procurement and management of insurance policies protecting the school district and its property; specific functions include developing specifications, obtaining competitive bids, selecting insurance carriers, and actual management.
Salary and wage management	A function that includes record keeping and the dissemination of checks to employees; also includes management of fringe benefit programs (e.g., insurance, retirement).

3. If possible, the superintendent can opt to increase revenues. This often is a difficult decision because it usually requires a tax increase. Such increases may require passing a tax referendum but even when it can be done simply by school board approval, it is subject to controversy. As an example, disgruntled taxpayers may disagree about the necessity to deliver all services and material items in the education plan.

After program needs and projected revenues are balanced, the expenditure plan can be developed and the three plans are then fused to become the school district's budget. Properly developed, annual budgets provide a planning resource, a document that communicates educational intentions to the broader community, a legal justification for expending public dollars, a control mechanism for revenue and expenditure decisions, and a guide for evaluating fiscal performance (Hartman, 1988).

Despite the fact that an education plan should be the nucleus of budgeting, district financial plans are often developed without it. When a superintendent fails to provide a programmatic foundation, the superintendent produces a *mechanical budget*—a document that may comply with state law but is basically irrelevant to serving the real needs of students (Hack et al., 1995). Moreover, budgeting in many districts has been an exclusive rather than inclusive function: The document is developed exclusively by the superintendent and the superintendent's support staff and approved by the school board; input from principals, teachers, and other stakeholders is bypassed. This approach results in an *administration-dominated and highly centralized budget* (Hack et al., 1995). This practice has become increasingly troublesome in a reform environment in which decentralization, teacher professionalism, and democratic decision making are being stressed.

Accounting and Auditing

Whereas a budget provides a plan for administrative decision making, accounting and auditing are intended to produce efficiency and effectiveness in fiscal operations. Accounting systems should protect public funds from losses resulting from carelessness, inappropriate expenditures, theft, embezzlement, or malfeasance on the part of administrators. They also should provide (a) a systematic process for interfacing fiscal expenditures with educational goal attainment, (b) a process for meeting requirements established by local and state governmental units, and (c) a means for providing accountability data to district patrons (Hack et al., 1995). Additionally, accounting procedures are de facto a decision-making tool for board members and administrators. During a budget cycle, for example, information from the accounting process contributes to budget control; that is, district officials are able to make decisions within the established parameters specified in the budget.

In general, the superintendent's responsibility is to guarantee that the accounting process is properly executed and supervised. This includes ensuring that:

- prescribed procedures are congruous with legal mandates and governmental regulations;
- various functions are assigned to workers who are properly prepared to execute their responsibilities;
- appropriate records are maintained;
- records are adequately protected against loss and damage;
- the work of one employee serves as a check on the work of another employee;
- all involved employees have property surety bonds;
- cash receipts are properly handled;
- safety practices are used for check writing and recording financial transactions;
- two or more individuals must share the responsibility of disbursing funds; and
- results of the accounting process are properly communicated to taxpayers (Drake & Roe, 1994).

In essence, proper control of an accounting system serves two critical purposes: a mechanism for properly recording financial transactions and a means of supplying adequate safeguards against errors or the misuse of public funds.

Auditing is an extension of the accounting process that verifies the accuracy and completeness of financial transactions as they relate to the general budget and specific accounts within it (Hack et al., 1995). Generally, audits are either internal (conducted by school district officials) or external (conducted by persons not employed by the district). The latter category can further be divided into two groups: required examinations by specified auditors (e.g., by state appointed auditors) and examinations performed by independent third parties retained by school district officials (e.g., an audit by an independent accounting firm that is not required by law). Internal audits are often used to provide information for the superintendent, school board, or larger community. Because they are not usually mandated, those conducting the audit have greater degrees of freedom to determine the process and foci. External audits, especially when mandated by state law, are much more structured. Year-end, external audits usually include:

- a study of school board minutes in conjunction with a financial transaction to determine if proper approvals were obtained;
- verification of revenue receipts of all types;
- verification of expenditures via examination of requisitions, purchase orders, vouchers, and canceled checks;
- a review of journal and ledger entries;
- reconciliation of bank statements, accounts, and investments; and
- a review of subsidiary documents (e.g., deeds, inventory statements, trusts, sinking funds) (Burrup et al., 1996).

In many states, the audit also includes specific judgments regarding the degree to which the school district's financial transactions comply with state laws and regulations.

Over the past few decades, the trend has been to require more stringent and frequent audits. In many states, higher demands for accountability have led to "open door" or "sunshine" laws that require public officials to report financial data more comprehensively, more frequently, and more openly. Within many school districts, trends toward decentralization and participative decision making also have contributed to increased emphasis on financial reporting (Hack et al. 1995). Although audits are intended to reveal serious errors and potential wrongdoing, only a small percentage actually finds these problems. A less recognized purpose of audits is to build public confidence by verifying good practice, efficiency, and observance of laws and regulations (Burrup et al., 1996).

Debt Management

School districts, just like families, incur periodic debts that may be either short-term or long-term obligations. Short-term debts (commonly considered to be one year or less) usually involve loans secured to address financial emergencies created by cash flow problems (e.g., late tax payments). These obligations account for about one-fourth of all debt in the municipal markets (i.e., debt incurred by governmental agencies). Long-term debts are more commonly associated with capital development projects (e.g., new school buildings, renovations, and land acquisition) or the expenditure of large sums of money for equipment (e.g., purchase of school buses or computers).

The administrative responsibilities associated with debt management have always been complex, as evidenced by integral functions such as estimating tax impact, determining advantageous structures for debts, securing loans, and selling bonds. Debt management also has been made more intricate by changes in federal and state tax laws that restrict arbitrage (investing bond proceeds at a higher rate of interest than is being paid by the issuer of the bonds) and the sale of municipal bonds (Rebore & Rebore, 1993).

Risk Management

Risk management is a process by which administrators make decisions that reduce the school district's exposure to financial loss. It is the "total overview of establishing the best possible manner of minimizing potential risks while protecting the public assets of the school district and taxpayer" (Thompson, Wood, & Honeyman, 1994, p. 479). The scope of potential risks within a school district is quite broad. Possible losses range from lawsuits over student accidents to natural disasters (e.g., the destruction of buildings by fire or tornadoes). Today, risk management extends beyond purchasing insurance and filing claims to include preventive measures. This expansion is a result of both rising insurance premiums and insurance carrier expectations that clients take proactive steps to prevent losses.

According to Hack et al. (1995), superintendents can control risk in four meaningful ways. First, they can avoid exposure or eliminate exposure if it already exists; for example, they can remove or replace dangerous playground equipment. Second, they can recommend prevention policy and practices; for example, they can develop and implement school crisis safety plans. Third, they can take steps to lessen the financial impact of losses that cannot be prevented; for example, they can structure insurance packages to provide more comprehensive coverage. Fourth, they can transfer all or part of the risk to another party; for example, they can require community groups using school buildings or buses to provide their own insurance coverage.

Even though many districts assign risk management to a person other than the superintendent, experts agree that the superintendent's support remains essential because so many areas of risk prevention require districtwide coordination (Burrup et al., 1996). Consider the following examples of possible contributions a superintendent can make.

- The identification of risk is a critical first step to building an effective program. The superintendent can commission a comprehensive study involving a broad-based committee that includes representatives of all segments of the school community. The product can be reviewed annually to assure accuracy.

- The risk management program will not function well unless it is assigned to a capable individual and given an adequate budget. Both of these decisions usually require superintendent support.
- Prevention is often predicated on support programs. For example, a superintendent may initiate a wellness program as a means of reducing employee health insurance claims.
- Prevention is also enhanced by effective policies that protect the school district from risk. For example, a superintendent may recommend revisions of policy relating to the use of school buildings during evenings and weekends.
- Implementation of a risk management program is dependent on effective two-way communication between the school district and the community and between the individual schools and central administration. The superintendent is often instrumental in developing and maintaining effective communication.

Purchasing and Inventory Management

Purchasing materials and equipment is an ongoing fiscal function in all school districts. Because public funds are used for these purchases, the responsibility is controlled by federal and state laws, governmental regulations, and local district policies. The controls typically mandate uniform practices in the following areas:

- *Competitive bidding.* Many states require school districts to receive sealed bids for purchases that exceed a certain amount; laws also may require acceptance of the "lowest and best bid."
- *Requisitions and purchase orders.* School districts commonly require employees to fill out a state-approved requisition form and/or purchase order for procuring supplies or equipment.
- *Filing and paying claims.* Financial transactions between school districts and vendors usually require administrators to follow established procedures and the use of approved forms; the manner in which the claims are processed and approved is usually specified by law, policy, or regulations.

Purchasing decisions can lead to conflicts between the school district's interests and a public official's pecuniary or personal interest. When conflicts of interest appear to exist, a superintendent has the responsibility to investigate the matter and to inform the board and thus the public of the results. When the conflicts are real, the superintendent must take steps to resolve the issue legally. Many states now have statutes requiring all public employees and school board members to disclose possible conflicts. For example, a board member who is an employee of a bank that serves as a depository for school funds would have to disclose that fact. Determining what constitutes a conflict unfortunately is not simple; courts in different states have issued very dissimilar rulings on this matter (Hack et al., 1995). Consequently, superintendents should consult with the school attorney to ascertain the nature of existing laws for conflicts of interest in the superintendent's state.

Inventory management is a related but separate administrative function. Cost savings and immediate availability are the two common reasons why school districts warehouse supplies and equipment. With regard to the former, purchasing commonly used items in large quantities (e.g., computer ink cartridges and printer paper) almost always lowers unit costs. With regard to the latter, providing needed materials as quickly as possible increases the efficiency and quality of education programs. In small school districts, decisions about the extent of warehousing may be influenced by space availability and the reliability and speed of vendor deliveries. Intermediate districts or other confederations of local districts may serve to offset the disadvantages faced by small districts by providing both collaborative purchasing and collaborative warehousing.

When making decisions about inventory management, a superintendent should answer the following questions:

- How much space is needed for warehousing?
- How will supplies and equipment be distributed from the warehouse?
- What are the estimated costs for warehousing (including utilities, insurance, and personnel) and for distribution (including equipment, personnel, insurance, and fuel) and how do these costs compare to estimated cost savings from bulk purchasing?
- How will security and inventory control be provided?
- What, if any, supplies and equipment will continue to be stored in individual schools or district buildings?
- What are the minimum and maximum quantities of equipment and supplies that will be warehoused?

Economic efficiency is clearly a prime objective of inventory control and warehousing. Often, effective operations in these areas produce savings in ways that are not readily observed by the public or district employees. For example, effective management in this area can prevent unnecessary purchases (e.g., duplicating purchases), reduce theft (e.g., providing highly secure areas for costly items), facilitate cost analysis (e.g., studies of purchasing decisions), and promote the evaluation of widely used products. Efficiency, however, ought not be the sole criterion; providing timely replacement of equipment or getting supplies to teachers when they are needed can be even more important.

Even when the superintendent is not the purchasing agent (which typically is the case except in very small districts), the superintendent is responsible for ensuring effectiveness and efficiency. This can be accomplished in many ways, including emphasizing the need for rational and objective decisions, insisting on vendor competition, and requiring operational analysis and program evaluation. Most importantly, the superintendent is the person who must ensure that service to the education process does not get minimized by other considerations. *The true measure of success for an inventory management program is the degree to which it meets the needs of district employees and students.* For this reason, superintendents should try to involve school-based personnel in the process. Some examples of how school-based personnel can participate in the process include principals and teachers giving input for equipment and material specifications, being invited to product demonstrations, evaluating products after they have used them, and evaluating the effectiveness of the distribution system.

Salary and Wage Management

Even though administrators now use modern technologies for business management, managing payroll and fringe benefit programs is a complex and demanding responsibility. Often, districts have multiple compensation and fringe benefit programs to cover employee categories. As an example, professional staff members receive annual contracts that stipulate salaries (a set amount of money to be paid for a certain period of time); other employees are usually paid on the basis of hourly or daily wages (Rebore & Rebore, 1993). Moreover, the process and substance of employee-group compensation is subject to annual changes required by policy revisions, changes in state laws, or modifications to collective bargaining agreements.

Salary and wage management is inextricably tied to the personnel function in school districts. Policies and practices pertaining to structuring compensation programs and to fringe benefit packages exemplify this point. Personnel benefit decisions often have ramifications; they can affect employee morale, generate political tensions (e.g., causing taxpayers to take sides in a collective bargaining dispute), or result in legal problems (e.g., making errors in payroll deductions). Generally, the structure of a salary and wage program is shaped by multiple forces, including organizational philosophy, state and federal laws, existing master contracts with unions, employment conditions in the geographic area (i.e., prevailing wages, unemployment rates), and common practices in other school districts in the state.

FACILITY MANAGEMENT

School buildings constitute a sizable investment of public funds, and their development and maintenance are cogent administrative responsibilities. Providing adequate facilities is often cited as one of the most essential responsibilities of superintendents (e.g., Hoyle, 1999; Witcher, 1994). Since 1980, this task has been given added attention for the following reasons:

- A national study conducted in the late 1980s (Lewis, 1989) indicated that at least 25% of the nation's school buildings were in poor physical condition and provided inappropriate learning environments. By the mid-1990s, updates indicated that this percentage had increased to about 33% (General Accounting Office, 1996).
- Many school districts have had unstable enrollments that have affected them in varying ways. In states such as Florida and Georgia, districts keep growing, requiring their superintendents to be engaged in school construction continuously. In other states, such as the Dakotas, superintendents also are devoting attention to school facilities, but for different reasons. Declining enrollments have intensified pressures for school consolidation and school closings—actions that result in having to determine the fate of unused facilities.
- The need to introduce technology into instructional environments has presented challenges for superintendents because they have had to devise ways of infusing computers into spaces that were not designed to accommodate them. Both the design of new buildings and the renovation of existing buildings are more complex because of technology (Kowalski, 2002).
- Equity issues in school finance have been contested in the courts in more than 40 states. Although the primary focus of the lawsuits has been operating funds, funding capital outlay also been injected in a number of them (Thompson et al., 1994). States that continue to require districts to fund all or most of the cost of school construction with local property tax revenues are especially vulnerable to litigation (Kowalski & Schmielau, 2001).
- In many school districts, superintendents have experienced an increased demand for services and an increased demand for accountability and efficiency. In essence, the public wants administrators to do more with less.

This dilemma extends to school buildings. At the same time that operating costs (e.g., utilities, insurance) are increasing, taxpayers are expecting school buildings to be more fully used, especially for community functions.

- School reforms have produced processes and programs that affect school buildings. Examples include expanded school years (including mandatory summer school), curricular modifications that affect course enrollment and building use (e.g., required remedial programs, decreased emphasis on elective courses), and extended services (e.g., individual testing, social work) Thus master planning for school facilities is now integral to school improvement efforts (Smith, 2003).

Collectively, issues such as these have made school facility management a more pervasive activity in the work lives of superintendents.

Planning

Because capital outlay investments have both political and economic implications, they require extensive planning and substantial community support. Success with these two critical tasks is made more probable when superintendents (a) develop a long-range plan, (b) build support for the plan, and (c) plan specific facility projects (Castaldi, 1994). Recognizing the political nature of facility development and maintenance in states where funding is totally or highly dependent on local tax revenues, many superintendents involve a significant number of citizens in facility planning. While inclusive planning can generate conflict as individuals with different values participate, this approach usually engenders a sense of ownership and pride among the involved citizens.

Planning participants often become ambassadors, helping school officials garner broad community support for proposed projects. Citizen involvement also makes it more likely that real needs will be assessed accurately and that all relevant alternatives for addressing those needs are identified (Kowalski, 2002). Although participation often intensifies conflict, the advantages outweigh the difficulties. By involving a broad spectrum of the community and reaching consensus, a superintendent views conflicting priorities and disagreements as opportunities to build necessary political support for planning outcomes (Erwood & Frum, 1996). All too often, superintendents and their school boards develop facility plans alone and then discover that their goals are not shared by a majority of taxpayers.

A common error made in facilities management is to treat individual projects independently. Systems theory reveals that doing so is precarious because

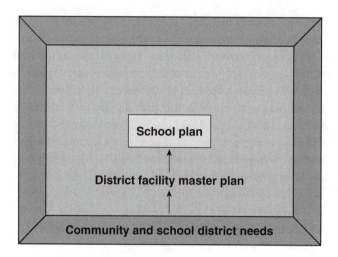

Figure 9.1   Relationship of District Facility Plan to Individual School Plans

elements of a school district (e.g., individual schools) are not autonomous. A decision to replace a high school building, for example, potentially affects every other building in the district. Why? Because the high school project expends both economic and political capital. If other buildings in the district need to be improved or replaced, the superintendent's ability to gain support for these projects may be attenuated by the high school project. Consequently when done properly, facility planning and management are far more complex tasks than they appear on the surface. Decisions about individual projects should be made using a systems perspective—a district planning approach that looks at community needs and educational needs across all facilities simultaneously (Smith, 2003). Only when a long-range district facility plan is in place is the superintendent really prepared to make decisions related to individual projects (Kowalski, 2002). Figure 9.1 illustrates that district facility master plans should be framed by real needs and that individual school plans are extensions or components of the master plan.

Deciding who will be on the project planning team is one of the superintendent's most important decisions (Bell, 2003). Unless an administrator has a general understanding of facility planning, the administrator will struggle to identify the scope of professional assistance needed (McClure, 2002). Replacing, renovating, or enlarging a school can require the services of architects, construction managers, building contractors, educational planning consultants, financial consultants, and bond counsel. A superintendent's decisions about the scope of services needed and about selecting who will provide those services should be shaped by professional knowledge about school facilities and planning (Kowalski, 2002) and about the role of physical environments in educational programming and outcomes (Ryland, 2003). In addition, a superintendent faces the equally important question of determining personal involvement. In large school systems, superintendents may have a very limited role because of specialized support staff—in some cases, staff that even includes an in-house architect. In most school systems, however, superintendents get deeply immersed in facility projects requiring them to adjust their priorities and time commitments.

Approval of Facility Projects

Public approval for facility projects is required in many states either by referenda or by some form of petition process. This requirement is linked to the long-standing practice of having local tax revenues fund all or a portion of school construction costs. Three issues often emerge when superintendents seek to gain voter approval for construction projects under these conditions. First, some citizens believe that the property tax is unfair and therefore, they voice their philosophical objections when increases in this tax are proposed. Second, some taxpayers argue that school buildings are unimportant to student learning and therefore, they contend that scarce resources should not be used for bricks and mortar. Third, some voters oppose any form of tax referenda because they believe they already are overtaxed (Kowalski, 2002). In light of these sentiments, school officials often find it difficult to get sufficient voter approval for funding facility projects. Consequently, both planning and public relations are integral aspects of facility management.

Maintenance

In addition to planning and building support for building projects, superintendents have oversight responsibilities for facility maintenance. This duty spans many managerial activities such as:

- Providing an organizational format for maintenance and custodial services
- Ensuring that maintenance and custodial employees have relevant job descriptions
- Ensuring that maintenance and custodial employees are properly supervised and their job performance objectively evaluated
- Evaluating the extent to which the entire maintenance program supports educational programs

- Ensuring that the maintenance department has appropriate policies, rules, and operating procedures
- Promoting the importance of safe and well-maintained school facilities
- Creating an effective balance of centralized and decentralized controls for the district's maintenance program

Recent crisis situations have exhibited the reality that superintendents, even in large school systems, are held accountable for maintaining adequate, efficient, flexible, adaptable, healthful, and safe learning environments.

Aspects of facility maintenance have changed substantially over the past three decades. In large measure, technology has resulted in more sophisticated mechanical, electrical, and air control systems. Additionally, modern schools are designed to provide students and staff with access to information via computers and other technologies that integrate voice and video. Distance learning, for example, is now being used extensively across the country. These advancements have had a profound effect on staffing needs in maintenance departments. When buildings were less sophisticated, superintendents could—and often did—elevate a successful maintenance worker to a management position such as director of buildings and grounds. In the early 1980s, for example, just over 67% of all such directors in the United States did not possess a college degree (Abramson, 1981). Even though such positions still do not require a college degree or a license in most states, the scope of responsibilities and the sophistication of operations has prompted a growing number of superintendents to employ persons with college degrees in management or engineering (Kowalski, 2002).

PUPIL TRANSPORTATION

In small towns and rural areas, the image of superintendent as manager is usually more conspicuous than in other communities because in these settings, the local school district commonly operates the largest transportation service in the immediate area. But even in these smaller districts, many taxpayers ignore or underestimate the amount of management required to make this operation effective and efficient. Two questions frame the management of pupil transportation: How will the function be organized? How will the service be capitalized?

Organizational Options

Superintendents must decide how they structure the transportation program in the broader organization. Most generally, the superintendent has two options: to supervise the program directly or to relegate the responsibility to another administrator. In the former arrangement, the person responsible for the transportation program, typically called the *transportation director*, reports to the superintendent. This configuration is common in very small districts. In the latter arrangement, the transportation director reports to a designated member of the superintendent's cabinet (typically an assistant or associate superintendent). This configuration is the norm across all districts.

In larger districts, transportation directors typically require both managerial and technical skills. Managerially, the director must have knowledge and experience to supervise personnel, administer budgets, develop schedules, and so forth. Technically, the director needs to understand topics such as bus maintenance, routing, bus safety, and fuel efficiency.

Capitalization Options

Determining how services will be capitalized refers to capital outlay decisions. The decision is somewhat analogous to the decision a family makes about lodging. They can buy a house, rent a house, or rent an apartment; each option has advantages and disadvantages depending on the family circumstances (e.g., their geographic location, their assets and liabilities, and their long-term plans). Similarly, superintendents usually have options with regard to how they will obtain buses for pupil transportation. In broadest terms, they have two choices as shown in Table 9.2: ownership or contracting.

Outright ownership is the norm among school districts in the United States. Although initially expensive, many experts believe it is the best choice for two reasons. Economically, ownership can be less expensive in the long-term and ownership ensures the owner greater control. In this vein, deciding to own buses or to engage private contractors is much like deciding to buy or lease a new car. Whether leasing is a better option depends on the buyer's economic status, amount of vehicle usage, ability to care for the vehicle, and length of time it will be in the buyer's possession.

Efficiency aside, many superintendents prefer owning buses because it provides them the ability to make adjustments when necessary and to control the number and quality of program employees. Advocates of private contracting or *outsourcing* (e.g., Hunter, 1995; Lieberman, 1986), by comparison, point out that their preferred approach can reduce both management responsibilities and labor-related problems: district administrators do not have to manage transportation personnel, maintain buses, develop route schedules, and so forth. Skeptics, however, argue that private contractors can be insensitive to student and parent needs and all too often they are focused entirely on the bottom line

Table 9.2   Options for Operating a Transportation Program

Option	Explanation
District ownership and maintenance	District purchases all of its own buses and maintains the fleet with employees; only major mechanical problems may be contracted out for services.
District ownership and contracted maintenance	District purchases all of its own buses but enters into a contract with a private company for maintaining the fleet.
Partial ownership and partial contracting	District owns some buses but enters into contracts with private parties or companies for other routes; generally, each party maintains its own buses.
Outsourcing by routes	District develops bus routes and advertises for bids by predetermined routes; under this option, the school district has no capital outlay; individual contractors buy and maintain their own buses.
Outsourcing entire program	District enters into a single contract with a company that provides total transportation services; under this option, the school district has no capital outlay or management responsibility for day-to-day operations.

(i.e., profit). Outsourcing also may generate political problems in the local community, especially if it causes current employees to lose their jobs (Saks, 1995). Historically, many rural districts opted to provide pupil transportation via individual contracts based on predetermined routes because resident farmers with flexible schedules were able to supplement their income. Although outsourcing on an individual route basis saves capital outlay (the contractors own and maintain their buses), the option can be expensive in the long-term, especially if competition is limited or nonexistent. When this is the case, superintendents basically have no choice other than to pay what the contractors demand. To move from outsourcing to district ownership is difficult financially because few districts have the resources necessary to buy a fleet of buses at one time (Daneman, 1998; Fickes, 1998).

Research comparing options for operating pupil transportation programs (e.g., Page & Davis, 1994) reveal that generalizations about ownership versus outsourcing are precarious. Because of their differing situations, each district must examine contextual variables to assess and evaluate the two options. The following are some of the most cogent considerations for determining how to operate a transportation program:

- *Statutory provisions*—Are all options allowable? To what extent do laws favor one approach in relation to the others?
- *State funding*—Does the current state funding formula favor one approach over the others?
- *Policy*—Are there any policy provisions restricting choices?
- *Past practice*—To what extent do current and past practices present potential political problems in relation to the options?
- *Liability costs*—What differences exist with regard to tort liability?
- *Overall cost*—How do the options compare with respect to initial costs and operating costs?
- *Program scope*—To what extent are buses used beyond taking students to and from school? How will the scope of programming be affected by the options?
- *Maintenance*—How will maintenance be provided under each option? Will maintenance costs vary among the options?
- *Control*—To what extent does each option diminish the superintendent's control over pupil transportation? How much control is the district willing to relinquish?
- *Political acceptance*—Will some of the alternatives cause political problems?
- *Fleet replacement*—How often are buses replaced? How do the options compare with respect to long-term replacement costs.

Special Considerations

The responsibility of managing a transportation system has been made even more complex by federal and state legislation protecting the rights of disabled individuals. Special needs students cannot be denied transportation services offered to students in regular programs and they may require transportation services even when they do not meet criteria for transporting students in regular programs (Bright, 2003). Under the Individuals with Disabilities Education Act (IDEA) of 1997, transportation for these students includes:

- Travel to, between, and from schools
- Travel in and around school buildings
- Travel from the student's house to a vehicle
- Travel to a caretaker if the child does not return to the child's home after school

Both direct costs for such services (e.g., mileage, taxi fares) and indirect costs (e.g., tolls, parking fees) must be assumed by school districts (Bluth & Hochberg,

1994). Because many disabled students are educated in schools other than the one they would normally attend, and because some disabled students cannot be transported on regular school buses, a myriad of special accommodations are necessary.

Unfortunately, far too many taxpayers apply inappropriate criteria when judging the effectiveness of pupil transportation programs. Most notably, they identify efficiency and economy, and not safety and convenience, as the primary criteria (Zeitlin, 1989). Consequently, superintendents need to remind the school board, employees, and the general public that effective pupil transportation is determined by a mix of safety, adequacy (responsiveness to real needs and wants), and efficiency.

FOOD SERVICES

Managing a food services program includes specific tasks, such as establishing operational structures, determining the scope of services provided, and establishing an appropriate format for delivering services. For superintendents, the essential challenge is to balance nutrition, consumer wants, and efficiency—a task made difficult by changing government standards and increasingly diverse consumer demands. Historically, superintendents have relied on state guidelines and professional counsel to make nutrition-related decisions and they have relied on school principals to advise them on consumer demands. With respect to efficiency, many superintendents have treated food services programs with a polite indifference; if the programs did not have a serious deficit, they were left alone. This disposition was myopic; as an example, long-term operating costs such as large equipment items were often never considered.

Management Dimensions

Proper management of a food service program requires adequate supervision to ensure productivity, cost controls, cost-benefit analysis, and a reinvestment of resources to fund necessary improvements (Boehrer, 1993). The issue of supervision is especially noteworthy because in many schools first-level management is provided by persons without formal management training, namely head cooks (Anderson & Durant, 1991). Consequently, the superintendent has to take steps to provide selected managers with essential basic skills in areas such as purchasing, inventorying, record-keeping, performance assessment, and accounting.

Issues related to managing food services are broader than most people realize. Consider the following examples of issues that explicate this fact.

- With a few exceptions, school districts provide student lunch programs; an increasing percentage of districts, prompted by federal subsidies, also are providing breakfast programs; in 2000, more than 71,000 schools participated in the federal school breakfast program (Coles, 2000).
- Choice has emerged as a major concern as many parents and students are dissatisfied with regular school meals. The number of children requiring or requesting special menus, such as vegetarians, continues to increase (Jones, 1996). Consequently, a very large percentage of schools now offer salad bars and à la carte options in addition to their traditional lunch menu.
- The potential for litigation related to food services keeps increasing. Illustrative of this fact, a small rural district in the state of Washington was ordered to pay a nearly $5 million judgment to the families of 11 children who became ill after being served undercooked taco meat in an elementary school cafeteria (Cook, 2003).
- Food services outside the school day are another consideration. In thousands of schools, community groups, clubs, and even businesses use school facilities for meetings, many of which involve meals (Kowalski, 2002).

Organizational and Operational Options

Outsourcing, a concept already discussed in relation to pupil transportation, also is relevant in the area of food services. Major companies have entered the school food services market and in a highly competitive environment, they offer attractive incentives to superintendents. Even so, political resistance to using private contractors remains high in many communities, largely for two reasons. First, a majority of cafeteria employees are district residents; in many cases, residents of the neighborhoods served by the school in which they work. Any change that threatens their employment is almost certain to generate political resistance. Second, many parents feel more comfortable knowing that local residents are employed in the food services program.

Despite concerns about relinquishing control and political backlashes, contracting for food services can have several benefits. For example, this option can diminish union-related problems, the need for direct management, and infuse efficiency measures (e.g., large volume purchasing of equipment and staples).

Another reason why private contracting has increased in importance has to do with management itself. Many superintendents believe that private contracting frees principals to focus more directly on curriculum—a noteworthy issue in light of increasingly complex federal and state rules (Van Wagner, 1995). The trend toward private contracting became discernible in the late 1980s; between 1989 and 1993, nearly 300 school districts dropped out of the National School Lunch Program (a federally subsidized program) both because of fast food providers entering this market and because of the increasing complexity of in-house management (Van Wagner, 1995). Despite its growing popularity, outsourcing continues to be rejected by a high percentage of superintendents. Studies conducted by the U.S. General Accounting Office indicate that this rejection may be merited; as many as two-thirds of private contracts were found to be in less than full compliance with federal requirements, and many of them fell short in critical areas such as adequate monitoring and evaluation criteria (Many school lunch contracts go sour, 1996).

In districts not engaging in outsourcing, organizational structure is an important decision, usually made by the superintendent. One dimension of organization pertains to control. Will the district's food services program be centralized (under the jurisdiction of a central authority) or decentralized (under the jurisdiction of each building principal)? Another dimension involves food preparation in relation to service. During the 1960s and 1970s, a time when many new school buildings were being built to accommodate increasing enrollments, district officials often opted to engage in food satellite programs. Under this concept, meals are prepared at a central site and delivered to the school where they are served in the cafeterias. The primary intents are to reduce capital outlay costs by eliminating the need for full kitchens in every school and to reduce operating costs by virtue of fewer employees. Satellite program proponents also argue that the concept produces a better product (via quality control achieved by having fewer but more specialized personnel) and standardization (via consistency in the quality of product served in every school) (Van Egmond-Pannell, 1983). Despite these claims, many school districts retain an organizational structure in which food is prepared and served separately in each school.

Supervisory Responsibilities

Although superintendents ultimately are accountable for managing food services, they rarely supervise the function directly, even in small districts. Districts leaning toward centralized management typically have directors possessing specialized knowledge in both food services and management (e.g., a dietician who has a management background). Whether a food services director reports to the superintendent depends on the size of the district. When there are one or more assistant superintendents, it is more likely that the director will be supervised by one of these support staff members.

In districts where the function is decentralized, principals generally assume management responsibility (especially the financial dimensions) and designate a head cook to oversee the food preparation and service. Because many of the school-based employees are inexperienced and because turnover can be rather high, principals often must provide orientation and staff development for the employees. This configuration has become increasingly subject to criticism from detractors who argue that principals spend too much time running the food services program at the expense of more essential functions demanding professional leadership (e.g., curriculum development, instructional leadership, and teacher evaluation).

FOR FURTHER REFLECTION

This chapter examined major managerial responsibilities assumed by district superintendents. The functions discussed included finance, facilities, pupil transportation, and food services. As you think about the content of this chapter, answer the following questions:

1. What factors have contributed to a negative perspective of a superintendent's management role?

2. What basic functions are included in fiscal management?

3. Do superintendents in large districts assume the same fiscal management roles as superintendents in small districts? Why or why not?

4. What factors have made facility management a more complex and time-consuming task for many superintendents?

5. Many problems encountered by superintendents in relation to facility management are political. Why?

6. What is outsourcing? What are the perceived advantages and disadvantages of this concept in relation to transportation and food services?

7. What is a satellite food service program? What is the intended purpose of this concept?

8. What factors could be considered in deciding whether to outsource transportation or food services?

Case Study

Over the past seven years, the Dalton Township School District has increased approximately 20% in enrollment. Currently, there are about 1,750 students in grades kindergarten through 12. This growth has presented a number of challenges for the district's superintendent, John Zeemer. When he became superintendent 5 years ago after having been an elementary principal in the district for 12 years, he had expected the district's enrollment to remain stable. At the time, however, he was unaware that a large electronics company was planning to build a factory in the neighboring school district. Soon after the plan to build the factory was announced, two local home builders gained approval for large subdivisions in Dalton Township. The builders believed that professional personnel, comprising nearly half of the factory's employees, would prefer to live in Dalton Township because of its rural setting and low property taxes.

Over the past three years, Dalton Township school enrollments have increased by approximately 1% per year and recently completed enrollment studies project an increase of approximately 2% per year for at least the next five years. Superintendent Zeemer quickly realized that he had a serious facility problem. The district's four schools (two elementary schools, a middle school, and a high school) were now operating between 105% (the high school) and 120% (one of the elementary schools) of designed capacity. If the enrollment forecasts were accurate, serious overcrowding would occur. Consequently, the superintendent initiated contact with several superintendents in districts with growing enrollments to seek their advice. He also began a series of discussions with the school board.

Working privately with the school board members, Superintendent Zeemer concluded that the best solution to the district's facility need was to build a third elementary school. The district's organizational plan would then change. The three elementary schools would serve grades K–6 instead of K–5; the middle school enrollment would be reduced by one-third by virtue of the sixth grade returning to the elementary schools; the high school would continue serving grades 9–12. The change would alleviate crowding in the elementary and middle schools where the problem was most serious. The estimated cost of the project was $14 million. Despite mixed reactions from taxpayers, the board approved Superintendent Zeemer's recommendation. The bond referendum for the project passed by a narrow margin: 52% in favor and 48% opposed.

From its founding 45 years ago, the Dalton Township Schools have had only one professional administrator at the district level, the superintendent. Three nonprofessional employees also worked in the district office: a treasurer/bookkeeper, a secretary, and a receptionist. Once the building project started, Superintendent Zeemer had to devote considerable time to working with the architects and principals. As a result, he became increasingly dependent on his three staff members and the four principals to assume some of his normal duties. As an example, one elementary principal helped manage the transportation program. As more work was relegated to the three central office employees, they became disgruntled. Two of them hinted that they may quit unless an additional person was hired.

Superintendent Zeemer began to realize that even after the building program was completed, workloads would never return to their former levels. The district would have to operate one more school, the transportation program would increase, and there would be more teachers and administrators. He concluded that the answer was to hire an assistant superintendent. Making this recommendation in the aftermath of the tax increase for the building program, however, was a politically precarious decision.

Case Discussion Questions

1. In a district the size of Dalton Township, what tasks would a superintendent have to perform in relation to planning and building a new elementary school?

2. Did Superintendent Zeemer act appropriately by relegating more duties to the principals and three central office staff members?

3. The superintendent conferred with several superintendents and then worked privately with the board to develop a plan to alleviate enrollment growth problems. Would you have used this approach? Why or why not?

4. The superintendent concludes that he really needs an assistant superintendent. Do you concur? Why or why not?

5. The bond referendum for the new school passed by a narrow margin. In the aftermath of the tax increase for construction, the superintendent fears that a recommendation to add an assistant superintendent will not be approved by the school board. Do you concur? Why or why not?

REFERENCES

Abramson, P. (1981). The superintendent of buildings and grounds: His job, his status, his pay. *American School and University, 54*(2), 66–71.

Adamchik, W. (2004). *Leadership vs. management.* Retrieved August 13, 2004, from http://www.beafirestarter.com/id24.html

Anderson, K. M., & Durant, O. (1991). Training managers of classified personnel. *Journal of Staff Development, 12*(1), 56–59.

Bell, D. L. (2003). A team approach to building a new school. *School Administrator, 60*(4), 32.

Bluth, L. F., & Hochberg, S. N. (1994). Transporting students with disabilities: Rules, regs and their application. *School Business Affairs, 60*(4), 12–17.

Boehrer, J. M. (1993). Managing to meet the bottom line. *School Business Affairs, 59*(11), 3–8.

Bright, K. L. (2003). Resource utilization. In R. Weaver, M. Landers, T. Stephens, & E. Joseph (Eds.), *Administering special education programs: A practical guide for school leaders* (pp. 129–150). Westport, CT: Praeger

Brunner, C. C., Grogan, M., & Björk, L. G. (2002). Shifts in the discourse defining the superintendency: Historical and current foundations of the position. In J. Murphy (Ed.), *The educational leadership challenge: Redefining leadership for the 21st century* (pp. 211–238). Chicago: University of Chicago Press.

Burrup, P. E., Brimley, V., & Garfield, R. R. (1996). *Financing education in a climate of change* (6th ed.). Boston: Allyn & Bacon.

Castaldi, B. (1994). *Educational facilities: Planning, modernization, and management* (4th ed.). Boston: Allyn & Bacon.

Coles, A. D. (2000, November 22). Federal breakfast program feeds record numbers. *Education Week, 20*(12), 6.

Cook, G. (2003). Food safety questions continue in wake of ruling. *The American School Board Journal, 190*(11), 10–12.

Daneman, K. (1998). Ins and outs of privatization. *American School & University, 71*(1), 16, 18.

Drake, T. L., & Roe, W. H. (1994). *School business management: Supporting instructional effectiveness.* Boston: Allyn & Bacon.

Erwood, D., & Frum, R. D. (1996). Forming a united front. *American School & University, 68*(8), 84–86.

Fickes, M. (1998). Making the buses run. *School Planning and Management, 37*(5), 39–42.

General Accounting Office (1996). *School facilities: America's schools report differing conditions.* Report to congressional requesters. East Lansing, MI: National Center for Research on Teacher Learning. (ERIC Document Reproduction Service No. ED397508)

Hack, W., Candoli, I., Ray, J. (1995). *School business administration: A planning approach* (5th ed.). Boston: Allyn & Bacon.

Hartman, W. T. (1988). *School district budgeting.* Englewood Cliffs, NJ: Prentice Hall.

Hoyle, J. (1999). The triumphant superintendent. *School Administrator, 56*(6), 6–9.

Hunter, R. C. (1995). Private procurement in the public sector and in education. *Education and Urban Society, 27,* 136–153.

Individuals with Disabilities Education Act. (1997). Retrieved August 10, 2004 from http://www.ed.gov/offices/OSERS/Policy/IDEA/index.html

Jones, R. (1996). Salad daze. *The American School Board Journal, 183*(2), 20–22.

King, R. A., Swanson, A. D., & Sweetland, S. R. (2003). *School finance: Achieving high standards with equity and efficiency* (3rd ed.). Boston: Allyn & Bacon.

Kowalski, T. J. (2002). *Planning and managing school facilities* (2nd ed.). Westport, CT: Bergin & Garvey.

Kowalski, T. J. (2003). *Contemporary school administration: An introduction* (2nd ed.). Boston: Allyn & Bacon.

Kowalski, T. J., & Schmielau, R. E. (2001). Potential for states to provide equality in funding school construction. *Equity and Excellence in Education, 34*(2), 54–61.

Lewis, A. (1989). *Wolves at the schoolhouse door: An investigation of the condition of public school buildings.* Washington, DC: Education Writers Association.

Lieberman, M. (1986). *Beyond public education.* New York: Praeger.

Many school lunch contracts go sour, says government report. (1997). *American Teacher, 81*(2), 12.

McAdams, P. (1995). Everything you always wanted to know about the superintendency, but were afraid to ask. *NASSP Bulletin, 79*(570), 86–90.

McClure, R. (2002). Choosing your team. *American School & University, 75*(3), 370–372.

Page, P. R., & Davis, L. D. (1994). Leave the driving to us. *The American School Board Journal, 181*(11), 43–45.

Rebore, W. T., & Rebore, R. W. (1993). *Introduction to financial and business administration in public education.* Boston: Allyn & Bacon.

Ryland, J. (2003). Fads, fancies and fantasies: An educator's perspective on current educational facility issues. *School Planning & Management, 42*(6), 16–24.

Saks, J. B. (1995). Exercising your options. *American School Board Journal, 182*(10), 38–40.

Sergiovanni, T., Burlingame, M., Coombs, F., & Thurston, P. (1992). *Educational governance and administration* (3rd ed.). Boston: Allyn & Bacon.

Shields, C., & Newton, E. (1994). Empowered leadership: Realizing the good news. *Journal of School Leadership, 4*(2), 171–196.

Smith, S. J. (2003). Design: The visionary master plan. *American School & University, 75*(12), 142–145.

Starratt, R. J. (1990). *The drama of schooling, the schooling of drama.* Bristol, PA: Falmer Press.

Thompson, D. C., Wood, R. C., & Honeyman, D. S. (1994). *Fiscal leadership for schools: Concepts and practices.* New York: Longman.

Tyack, D., & Cuban, L. (1995). *Tinkering toward utopia: A century of public school reform.* Cambridge, MA: Harvard University Press.

Van Egmond-Pannell, D. (1983). Satelliting school lunch production. *School Business Affairs, 49*(11), 20, 42–43.

Van Til, W. (1971). Prologue: Is progressive education obsolete? In W. Van Til (Ed.), *Curriculum: Quest for relevance* (pp. 9–17). Boston: Houghton Mifflin.

Van Wagner, L. R. (1995). Fed up. *The American School Board Journal, 182*(5), 39–41.

Witcher, A. E. (1994). Expanding school facilities: The superintendent holds the key. *The Clearing House, 68*(5), 35–36.

Yukl, G. A. (1989). *Leadership in organizations* (2nd ed.). Upper Saddle River, NJ: Merrill, Prentice Hall.

Zeitlin, L. S. (1989). Pupil transportation and fiscal responsibility. *School Business Affairs, 55*(4), 35–39.

CHAPTER 10

Human Resources Management

KEY FACETS OF THE CHAPTER

○ Human resources administration in school districts

○ Working with employee unions

○ Special education

○ Pupil personnel services

○ Legal services

In addition to being responsible for material resources, superintendents also are expected to manage the human dimensions of schools districts. Setting parameters for this topic is difficult because districts and schools are distinctively different from most industrial organizations and somewhat different from each other. Two of the most relevant characteristics that contribute to individuality are the human-intensive nature of schools and the human processes of teaching and learning (Harris & Monk, 1992). Moreover, most employees in the typical school district are professional personnel; that is, they are licensed practitioners who have a certain degree of independence and authority and a need to engage in continuous learning.

Rather than trying to provide an exhaustive list of management tasks involving school district employees, this chapter highlights five functions that require considerable attention from superintendents: *human resources administration, working with employee unions, special education, pupil personnel services,* and *legal services*. Clearly, the first topic (formerly referred to as personnel management) is the most encompassing and complex.

MANAGING PERSONNEL

Basically human resources administration includes human labor, the physical abilities of individuals and groups in an organization, and the mental abilities relevant to the services provided by a school district (Rebore, 2001). Three terms merit clarification in relation to this function: *human resources management* (HRM), *human resources development* (HRD), and *human resources administration* (HRA). HRM generally has a narrower connotation than the other two, referring to organizational functions such as determining staffing needs, employee recruitment, employee selection, and orientation to the organization that were previously encompassed by "personnel management." HRD typically refers to a broader range of functions, including activities such as career development, staff development, employee wellness programs, and formative performance evaluation. HRA is generally synonymous with HRD but is used commonly in relation to education. Webb and Norton (2003) define HRA as follows:

> . . . those processes that are planned and implemented in the organization to establish an effective system of human resources and to foster an organizational climate that enhances the accomplishment of educational goals. (p. 4)

This more global perspective is used in this chapter.

Scope of Human Resources

Even small school districts are relatively large organizations. A school system with only 1,500 students, for example, may have more than 100 employees—far more employees than would be found in most small businesses. Although the public readily recognizes that superintendents have to deal with personnel management functions, the public is less inclined to discern that the quality of management provided is a critical determinant of how human resources are developed and deployed (Lipiec, 2001) and that the quality of management in districts affects educational programs (Seyfarth, 2002). With respect to the latter point, employee selection, induction, and staff development can influence teacher knowledge and motivation; the work environment, compensation programs, and grievance policies can influence teacher motivation; personnel evaluations can inform and remind employees of the school district's expectations (Seyfarth, 2002).

Human resources administration in a school district includes a number of distinct functions; the following are among the more pertinent ones:

- *Planning*—formally preparing for future qualitative and quantitative staffing needs
- *Personnel recruitment*—encouraging persons with desired qualifications to seek employment in the district
- *Personnel selection*—conducting paper screening, interviews, postinterview applicant evaluations, and other related selection procedures
- *Orientation*—helping new employees to become acclimated to the school district
- *Defining position requirements*—maintaining relevant job descriptions for all employees
- *Performance evaluation*—ensuring that formative and summative employee appraisal systems are developed and used
- *Staff development*—providing growth experiences essential to professional practitioners to ensure that current theory, research, and practice is integrated
- *Compensation programs*—managing salary and benefit programs
- *Wellness programs*—providing opportunities and services related to preventing employee physical, psychological, or emotional problems
- *Employee relations*—ensuring that relationships between district officials and employees are positive and legal

As is the case with all management functions, however, the size of the school district typically determines the nature and depth of the superintendent's direct involvement in any or all of these functions. Yet, three goals are constant across school systems: "to hire, retain, develop, and motivate personnel in order to achieve the objectives of the school district, to assist individual members of the staff to reach the highest possible levels of achievement, and to maximize the career development of personnel" (Rebore, 2001, p. 11).

As districts became larger, HRA became more complicated and demanding. Work roles became more specialized and employees were divided into categories or groups based on their employment status (e.g., professional or nonprofessional) or assignments (e.g., administrative or teaching). Two other critical developments also made HRA more demanding. First, school administrators, like administrators of other organizations that employ primarily professional personnel (e.g., hospital managers), were expected to provide staff development programs essential to maintaining high levels of employee performance (Harris & Monk, 1992). This necessity was driven primarily by the constant evolution of new knowledge and the corresponding requirement for skill improvement. The infusion of microcomputers into schools during the 1980s, for instance, placed pressures on teachers to transform their instructional activities. Many of the teachers (and administrators), however, were computer illiterate. Consequently, superintendents had to provide relevant learning experiences for employees to ensure that schools would be on the cutting-edge of instructional innovations. Second, personnel administration was affected by federal and state laws addressing employment practices and the treatment of employees (Webb & Norton, 2003). Topics such as equal employment opportunity, sexual harassment, and age discrimination became cogent issues for superintendents. Interestingly, these laws prompted many superintendents to centralize personnel functions in an effort to exert greater control over potential legal infractions (Tyack & Hansot, 1982).

Collectively then, the growing size of school districts, the increasing need to provide staff development, and new employment laws have combined to make personnel management more difficult and complicated. Although every activity that touches an employee is arguably related to HRA, four categories are particularly cogent for superintendents:

1. *Employment practice*—spanning recruitment, selection, and job placement issues

2. *Human resources development*—spanning planning activities, induction, staff development, and employee assistance programs

3. *Employment management*—spanning performance appraisals, record keeping, and compensation programs

4. *Employee relations*—spanning collective bargaining, grievances, and litigation

   Table 10.1 provides examples of specific functions, grouped under these headings.

Organizational Dimension

The actual role a superintendent plays in personnel management may range from indirectly supervising administrators who are directly responsible for HRA to directly supervising the implementation of HRA. Variance in the

Table 10.1   Elements of Personnel Management

Category	Specific Functions	Examples
Employment Practices	Needs assessment	Determining the number and types of positions needed
	Recruitment	Posting vacancies and securing applicants
	Screening applicants	Both written materials and job interviews
	Selection	Developing procedures for making employment decisions
	Contracting	Issuing employment contracts
	Evaluating outcomes	Determining effectiveness of employment practices
Human Resources Development	Induction	Providing orientation and adjustment to the school and to the work role
	Staff development	Planning and providing workshops, seminars, professional leaves
	Performance evaluation	Conducting formative and summative evaluation and providing clinical supervision
	Assistance programs	Providing special assistance programs for employees (e.g., wellness programs)
Employment Management	Record keeping	Maintaining personnel files
	Payroll	Working with fiscal management to provide necessary information for compensation
	Fringe Benefit programs	Managing insurance, vacation, sick leave, and other types of employee benefits
	Legal problems	Working with attorneys to resolve legal problems affecting employees or the school district
	Environment control	Ensuring healthy and safe work environments for employees; providing accommodations for disabled employees
	Employee severance	Making retirement, layoffs, reduction-in-force, and dismissal decisions
Employee Relations	Employee morale	Providing social activities such as picnics, group trips, and opportunities for travel
	Collective bargaining	Negotiating contracts with employee unions
	Grievance management	Handling formal and informal employee complaints

superintendent's direct participation, however, does not diminish the need to apply several general principles across all school districts:

- All employees should be considered in organizing the program; personnel management is not a responsibility that only pertains to professional staff.
- Because personnel management is so broad, duties are commonly shared between central-office and building administrators and among divisions within the central office. A key facet of successful programming is determining which operations should be centralized and which should be decentralized.
- Because responsibilities are shared among a number of administrators, it is important to identify and communicate specific role expectations to those who assume duties and responsibilities.
- Duties and responsibilities ought to be designated on the basis of knowledge, skill, and experience (Castetter, 1992).

In addition, all superintendents assume primary responsibility for four specific personnel management tasks: policy development, policy implementation, general control of the personnel program, and improvement of the personnel program (Castetter, 1992). To ensure a proper level of accountability in larger districts, the superintendent should maintain two-way communication with persons assigned to manage the various personnel functions. Such interaction is an effective means for detailing problems, needs, and recommendations for program improvement.

Three factors are influential in determining the actual role of a superintendent in HRA. The first is district size. Obviously, a more direct management role is unlikely in very large districts, and in very small districts, superintendents may not have the financial resources to hire support staff to manage this responsibility. The second factor is personal philosophy. Administrators often tilt toward being task oriented or people oriented (Kowalski, 2003). Those who pay more attention to issues such as employee satisfaction and morale are apt to make HRA a high priority—a decision likely to make a superintendent engage more directly in managing human resources. The final factor is the distribution of power and authority in the district. In a highly centralized district, either the superintendent or the superintendent's designee is apt to control the HRA process; in a highly decentralized district, much of the authority and responsibility for HRA is relegated to principals. The more centralized the system, the more likely that a superintendent will have a direct management role.

Decentralization of school district governance, a popular concept exemplified by site-based management, sparks a number of novel questions regarding policy, program control, and program improvement in areas such as employment, staff development, and performance evaluation (Sergiovanni, 2001). How much autonomy can and should be given to individual principals and school-based governance councils to select new employees? What legal risks are incurred if decentralized decision making leads to processes or outcomes that are incongruous with state law or school district policy? Primarily because of such legal concerns, complete decentralization of personnel management (i.e., relegating the responsibility entirely to principals) is unlikely. Fortunately, technology has made a mix of centralized and decentralized management more feasible, efficient, and effective.

MANAGING RELATIONSHIPS WITH EMPLOYEE UNIONS

When collective bargaining gained a foothold in public education circa 1960, many superintendents were unprepared to deal with this process and reluctant to engage in it (Campbell, Cunningham, Nystrand, & Usdan, 1990). The greatest apprehensions were visible in relation to dealing with teacher unions. Previously, both administrators and teachers were members of the National Education Association (NEA) and the organization's state affiliates. In fact, superintendents were the most prominent NEA members for much of the first half of the 20th century and they controlled much of the organization's power (Callahan, 1964). Teacher unionization not only altered relationships between superintendents and teachers, it affected relationships among administrators. Principals, for example, often tried to maintain positive relationships with the superintendent and school board on the one hand and with faculty on the other hand (Kowalski, 2003). Many principals tried to avoid being cast as either "management" or "labor." Their attempts to remain neutral often generated considerable conflict as boards and superintendents began to demand their absolute loyalty. In some larger urban districts, principals actually followed the teachers' lead and formed their own unions—an action that further divided leadership and management personnel.

Collective Bargaining

The growth of collective bargaining was swift; by the early 1980s, 85% of the states either required or permitted school boards to engage in collective bargaining with employee unions (Lunenburg & Ornstein, 1996). Generalizations about state laws are difficult because they are diverse; as an example, collective bargaining legislation applies only to select employee groups (e.g., to teachers but not other employees) in some of them. By the mid-1990s, 22 states had established public employee relations boards with the responsibility of implementing relevant laws and providing third-party services for mediation, fact finding, and arbitration (Rebore, 2001).

Throughout much of the 1970s and 1980s, attention to union-related matters became a time-consuming activity for superintendents. In some districts, as many as six or seven separate employee unions negotiated contracts with the school board. Simply managing these master contracts (e.g., handling grievances) required an inordinate amount of the superintendent's time and energy.

During the late 1980s and 1990s, policymakers and scholars began questioning the effects of unionism on school reform. Evidence as to the influence of collective bargaining is conflicting. For example, critics of unions argued that collective bargaining fosters greater centralization of authority and animosity between administrators and teachers. By contrast, union proponents argued that collective bargaining forces boards and superintendents to be less bureaucratic and more attentive to real problems in the schools (Shedd & Bacharach, 1991). Despite such mixed views, many observers believe that traditional collective bargaining has been counterproductive. Consequently, two alternatives have been promoted more recently: *collaborative bargaining* and *consensus bargaining*. Whereas conventional negotiations almost always place teachers and administrators in an adversarial relationship, these concepts are designed to build trust and to nurture shared decision making. Collaborative bargaining seeks to focus on real problems affecting schools; consensus bargaining strives to increase rationality by reducing emotion and extreme positions (Misso, 1995). Their intent is to produce "win-win" situations; that is, an association designed to provide both parties with victories.

New concepts for bargaining, however, have not eradicated concerns about dealing with unions. Some labor relations specialists have warned school officials that collaborative approaches often lead people to become infatuated with process rather than objectively evaluating outcomes. Further, they have pointed out that the greatest successes with collaboration have been achieved in wealthy school districts, where ample resources have been available to mollify union leaders (Harrington-Lueker, 1990). Because competition for scarce resources is the essence of political behavior, the nexus between wealth and collaboration is understandable.

Explanations for teacher unionism have varied from feelings of helplessness (e.g., Lieberman, 1986) to justifiable quests for autonomy (Newman, 1990). Although educators view themselves as professionals, most of them work in highly bureaucratic organizations; hence, they are denied even the most basic trappings of a legitimate profession (Kowalski, 2004). Consequently, many teachers and administrators remain ambivalent about unions and collective bargaining. Role conflict has been intensified in recent years by reform proposals that seek to give teachers greater autonomy and stronger voice in governance (e.g., site-based councils). Teacher empowerment, however, is not really compatible with traditional unionism because teachers who participate in making critical decisions actually become school leaders. At the least, the current protracted quest for school improvement has generated consequential questions about the role and status of educators in American society. In the absence of major changes, many superintendents continue to face two seemingly contradictory tasks: taking a traditional management disposition toward unions and building the trust and confidence of teachers by treating them as colleagues.

Superintendent's Direct Role in Bargaining

Regardless of what type of bargaining approach is used, a superintendent must address one essential question: Should I be involved directly with negotiating union contracts? Across the country, many superintendents, and especially those in small school districts, either continue to serve as the board's chief negotiator or they sit at the bargaining table as a member of the board's team (Glass, Björk, & Brunner, 2000). Many superintendents are forced to do so because small district school boards are often reluctant to employ a chief negotiator. Their disinclination to employ consultants to handle bargaining has both political and economic roots. Politically, they do not want to alienate the union by bringing an "outsider" to the table to represent them and they want to make sure that the union understands that the superintendent is on the board's side. Economically, they do not want to incur the cost associated with hiring a professional negotiator (Sharp, 1989). Regardless of why superintendents may find themselves at the bargaining table, they face the distinct possibility that their involvement in this activity is reflected in their performance evaluation (Norton, Webb, Dlugosh, & Sybouts, 1996).

The likelihood of the superintendent being at the bargaining table increases when collaborative approaches are used because gaining the necessary level of confidence and trust from both the school board and the union becomes essential to success (Attea, 1993). Yet, some critics (e.g., Ficklen, 1985; Pennella & Philips, 1987) argue that putting the superintendent at the bargaining table is unwise under any circumstance because doing so detracts from more important leadership and management responsibilities and raises the possibility of personal conflict between the superintendent and union officials. Because each school district is unique with respect to past practices, union relationship, philosophy, needs, culture, milieu, and resources, there is no universally accepted practice with regard to direct superintendent involvement in collective bargaining. Consequently, aspiring superintendents should first decide whether they are willing and able to engage in collective bargaining and then determine potential employer expectations in this regard.

MANAGING SPECIAL EDUCATION PROGRAMS

The amount of time superintendents devote to special education has grown incrementally in the past several decades. Legislation for students with disabilities requires school districts to provide a wide range of programs and accommodations to serve pupil needs even at the preschool level. These requirements are based on federal and state laws and disputes over compliance have had to be adjudicated, either through specified administrative procedures or through the courts.

Legal Requirements

Although public schools historically have been required to serve disabled students, the scope and descriptions of these services broadened substantially in the 1970s. Three pieces of federal legislation were largely responsible: the Rehabilitation Act of 1973; Public Law 93–380; and Public Law 94–142 (Lunenburg & Ornstein, 1996). Public Law 94–142, the Education for All Handicapped Children Act, required states to adopt policies that assured that public schools would provide a free, appropriate education predicated on the needs of individual students. Such services could include classroom instruction, physical education, home instruction, and instruction in special institutions (residential care facilities, hospitals). Section 504 of the Rehabilitation Act, as amended in 1974, stated that schools could not exclude a student from participation in programs on the basis of the student's handicapping condition. To do so constituted discrimination. Provisions extended a student's rights to areas such as accessing school buildings. The Handicapped Act Amendments of 1990 gave P.L. 94–142 a new title, the Individuals with Disabilities Education Act. This legislation officially changed basic terminology by substituting the term "disability" for "handicap" (LaMorte, 1996). The most discussed aspect of special education laws has been the concept of *least restrictive environment* (originally called *mainstreaming,* but more recently referred to as *inclusion*). This facet of the law specifies that handicapped children—to the maximum extent possible—were to be educated with children who are not disabled, and that removal of a special needs student from the regular classroom can occur only when the nature or severity of the disability makes education in the regular classroom unsatisfactory as specified in a student's individual education program (IEP). In considering litigation in the area of special education, the courts have been decisive and protective of the rights of students and their parents (Williams & Macmillan, 2003); in particular, they have been rather consistent in enforcing the concept of inclusion (Berger, 1995).

Implications for Superintendents

Compliance with the numerous laws and court decisions protecting the rights of disabled students is an obvious concern for school superintendents. The concept of related services, for example, affects the management responsibility of superintendents very directly. Under this provision, school districts are required to supply special accommodations in areas such as transportation and developmental, corrective, or support services such as therapy (speech, language, occupational, physical, psychological), recreation, diagnostic and evaluative medical services, and counseling (Campbell et al., 1990). The only limit is that medical services are exempted unless they are required for diagnostic or evaluative purposes (Russo & Osborne, 2003). For even highly experienced superintendents, though, such distinctions are neither obvious nor commonly understood. Consequently, situations that call for related services often must be evaluated on a case-by-case basis and the superintendent must seek counsel from both legal and special education experts.

Four specific responsibilities frame the superintendent's management role in special education.

1. *Team building*—Both the letter and spirit of special education laws are unlikely to be met unless the program is supported by district administrators. Principals are especially instrumental because of their direct role in the diagnostic and prescriptive stages of student placement (Weaver & Landers, 2003). Superintendents, by setting the tone for legal compliance, often determine principal dispositions. Negative, resistant attitudes are not only unprofessional and unethical, they are unproductive. Individual students are potentially harmed by negative attitudes because they do not receive required services and the school district is potentially harmed because the prospects for litigation increase.

2. *Adjudication of potential and actual conflict*—Superintendents are drawn into special education disputes by district employees seeking advice, by due process procedures, or by litigation. The net effect is that superintendents are spending more time on special education than ever before.

3. *Policy recommendations*—Superintendents play an instrumental role in recommending policy on special education and in establishing rules and regulations that ensure that the policies are managed appropriately.

4. *Determining organization for compliance*—One of the most critical decisions made by superintendents relates to how the district will meet its special education obligations. For larger districts, the process begins by deciding whether to provide services independently or in conjunction with one or more other school districts. Once a decision is made on this issue, superintendents must decide issues related to staffing and administrative responsibility such as how many personnel must be employed by the district and who will supervise these employees.

Because school districts have options with regard to delivering special education, superintendents must know and understand the pertinent laws and prevailing conditions relating to special education so that they can recommend appropriate policies and organizational structure. When this knowledge is missing, these essential decisions are apt to be made for purely political and economic reasons. Consider the example of a superintendent in a rural district who convinced the school board to withdraw from the local special education cooperative simply because the superintendent and the cooperative director could not work together effectively. Without properly weighing the consequences, the superintendent jeopardized the education programs of involved students, increased costs to the district substantially, and made the district more vulnerable to litigation.

Many administrators have entered practice not fully committed to the concepts they must enforce. As an example, a study of superintendents in Texas (Hooper, Pankake, & Schroth, 1999) found that many of them were ambivalent about the pedagogical effectiveness of inclusion. Moreover, novice superintendents either have been unprepared to deal with the legal and educational dimensions of special education or underestimated the amount of time they needed to devote to this program (DiPaola & Walther-Thomas, 2003). As a result, they often have been overwhelmed by parental complaints, hearings, and lawsuits—experiences that nurtured negative dispositions toward special education laws. The most common disputes between administrators and special education parents (or their advocates) have centered on the development

Table 10.2   Key Considerations With Regard to Special Education

Responsibility	*Examples of Critical Questions*
Program organization	What options exist with regard to providing services? What are the advantages and disadvantages of membership in a joint services venture? What factors may change organizational structures? If the school district becomes part of a joint services venture, what authority/role will the school district have in the governance of the joint services entity?
Supervision of services	How will programming be supervised? How much supervision must or should be provided by the superintendent?
Personnel management	How many individuals will be directly employed by the school district? How many will be employed by the special education cooperative? What legal issues are raised in the area of employment (e.g., tenure status of teachers who work in the district but are employed by the cooperative)?
Adjudicating problems	What role will the superintendent play in disputes? What policies need to be developed with regard to adjudicating problems for disabled students?

of the IEPs; interpretations of IEPs with regard to programming; suspension or expulsion of disabled students; parental dissatisfaction with programming decision (especially as related to inclusion); and student placements in special schools or institutions (e.g., placement of a student in hospital requiring substantial financial payments by the school district). Table 10.2 is a guide to critical issues pertaining to the superintendent's management role in special education.

Special Education Cooperatives

In an effort to provide the legally required comprehensive services, many school districts belong to joint ventures, often called special education cooperatives. These entities became common in the 1970s for several reasons. First, most school districts could not afford to operate low-incidence programs required by federal and state laws independently. As an example, some small districts faced the requirement of providing a special program for a single student with a diagnosed disability. Second, many small districts could not justify or afford employing their own special education director; not having such an administrator was de facto a problem because the pertinent laws and state policy required oversight from such an administrator. Third, the number of students qualifying for special programs increased dramatically after new laws redefined what constituted a disability. Hence superintendents had to expand existing programs or create new ones. Collectively these conditions made membership in a joint services venture prudent professionally and economically. The legal and operational dimensions of such ventures were discussed previously in Chapter 1.

MANAGING PUPIL PERSONNEL SERVICES

A commonly overlooked area of a superintendent's management responsibilities is in student personnel services. Historically, many superintendents were indifferent toward this function, largely because a nexus between supplemental services and student learning was not recognized or well established (Wentling & Piland, 1982). Societal and economic changes, however, have required superintendents to increase both the quantity and quality of support services. As an example, school reform has spawned new expectations regarding how schools should address mental health and psychosocial concerns; today, greater attention is being given to prevention programs, which has reshaped the goals and foci of student personnel services (Adelman & Taylor, 2000).

Components

Generally, student personnel services have included administrative and supervisory tasks concerned with enrollment-related issues (e.g., admission, registration, classification) and student support services (e.g., services focused on the development of student abilities, interests, and needs) (Knezevich, 1984). In small school districts, duties associated with these undertakings were typically dispersed among available personnel, with much of the responsibility assigned to principals and assistant principals. In larger districts, these functions were typically more centralized and placed under the jurisdiction of an assistant superintendent or director.

Even today, there is no universally established boundary for student personnel services. In some districts, special education and student personnel services are combined but this arrangement has become less common. The most readily recognized elements of pupil personnel administration are as follows:

- *Attendance services:* Included here are matters pertaining to student enrollment and attendance. This could include legal matters governing residency, verification of age, compliance with state laws and district policy concerning attendance, maintenance of attendance records, and the preparation and filing of required attendance reports.
- *Services of the economically disadvantaged:* Federal assistance programs such as Title I and Head Start are often housed within student personnel services in large school systems. Responsibilities include the development, management, and evaluation of relevant programs.
- *Guidance and counseling services:* With the expansion of counseling services in schools, greater attention is being given to providing coordination and support from the central office. Common services include standardized testing programs, support for building level counselors and teachers, a referral service for serious problems, and resources for vocational and academic counseling.
- *Administration of pupil conduct:* Although most student discipline issues are handled at the level of the individual school, central administration commonly becomes involved in certain aspects of this function. These might include: providing suspension and expulsion hearings, dealing with legal matters pertaining to student conduct, policy analysis and evaluation, consultation for administrators, teachers, parents, and students, and staff development.
- *Student health service:* The primary purposes of this function are the assessment and diagnosis of health problems, compliance with state laws and district policies relative to health screening tests (e.g., vision tests), and wellness programs and preventive measures.
- *Social work:* Largely because of expanding social and economic problems, many school districts are employing social workers. These professionals usually address student needs that extend beyond the school. Issues such as dysfunctional families, child abuse, and community-based problems are the primary foci.
- *Standardized testing programs:* This segment of pupil personnel services is arguably the fastest growing responsibility. The expansion of state required testing programs during the past two decades is the reason. This element of testing differs from individualized testing that is typically administered under the jurisdiction of special education programs.

Organization

The need for student personnel services has increased markedly largely because of societal conditions. As examples, a growing number of students in America live in poverty and negative effects of poverty on student academic performance are well established (Glass, 2004); there is growing awareness that social, physical, psychological, economic, and emotional problems prevent students from learning (Dryfoos, 2002). In many districts, appropriate responses to these conditions have not been coordinated and the result has been additional organizational stress (Kowalski, 2003). When responsibilities for student personnel services are dispersed and unplanned, superintendents find it extremely difficult to take advantage of opportunities (e.g., potential federal grants), to respond to emerging needs (e.g., a need for intervention programs to deal with gang-related violence), and to provide appropriate supervision. A lack of supervision almost always results in coordination problems; for example, allowing social workers to function independently (i.e., purely as school-based personnel) is almost certain to produce substantial variance in case loads because needs are not evenly distributed across schools.

Superintendent challenges related to managing pupil personnel services are probably greatest in districts not sufficiently large to merit a separate division for this program. In these situations, superintendents assume much of the direct management responsibility. As such, they must decide which services will be provided, who will provide them, who will supervise them, and how they will be funded.

MANAGING THE LEGAL DIMENSIONS OF SCHOOL DISTRICTS

The potential for legal problems in school administration is one reason why districts have routinely employed or retained the services of attorneys. These professionals provide counsel on issues ranging from the acquisition of property to liability lawsuits and represent their clients in legal proceedings. Consequently, the personal relationship between a superintendent and the school attorney is extremely important. Unfortunately, many practitioners have entered the superintendency not knowing much about the role and responsibility of a school attorney. Three management dimensions of school attorneys are covered here: attorney selection and evaluation; compensation options; ideal versus actual roles.

Attorney Selection and Evaluation

Like all decisions in public organizations, ones involving school attorneys are not always rational or objective. In some instances, school board members have placed more emphasis on politics than on professionalism; for example, they have been more concerned with retaining a local resident than with retaining an experienced school law practitioner. Such myopic choices are most likely to occur when superintendents fail to provide professional direction for the school board. This direction should include an objective analysis of (a) potential legal risks to the district, (b) attorney responsibilities in relation to those risks, (c) qualifications required of a school attorney, and (d) options for finding a person who meets those qualifications.

The National School Boards Association (1997) offers several suggestions for selecting a school attorney. One suggestion is to define the role before beginning the search. Attorney roles can vary substantially based on state law, district past practices, and current board member expectations. The superintendent should recommend to the board answers to the following questions: Must the attorney attend board meetings regularly? Will the attorney be expected to litigate routine lawsuits? What relationship will the attorney have with district personnel and the school board? How accessible should the attorney be to the superintendent and board members? After the desired role is defined, selection criteria and their relative importance need to be established. At this stage, the superintendent should pose another series of questions that need to be answered collectively by board members and the superintendent. Must the school attorney be a resident of the school district? Should preference be given to district residents? Must the attorney have previous school law experience? After the role and selection criteria are established, the superintendent should make recommendations on the selection process. Most notably, the following questions should be addressed: What role will the board and superintendent each play in the selection process? Will other individuals be involved in the selection process? In some districts, superintendents have been given the authority to select an attorney; in other situations, school boards have made this decision without superintendent participation. Given the importance of the school attorney's relationship to both the school board and superintendent, neither of these approaches is advisable. The most productive situations have involved the mutual approval of the superintendent and school board (National School Boards Association, 1997).

Attorney Compensation

Deciding how to compensate a school attorney is another key superintendent decision related to managing legal issues. A variety of approaches are used across and within states. Geiger and Cantelme (2002) identified the following options:

- *Unrestricted hourly rate*—The attorney submits a billing and is compensated on the basis of an agreed upon hourly rate (e.g., $100 per hour).
- *Hourly rate with an annual ceiling*—The attorney submits a billing and is compensated on the basis of an agreed upon hourly rate until an annual earnings ceiling is reached; after that point, services are rendered for the remainder of the year without additional compensation (e.g., $45,000 per year cap).
- *Retainer with hourly fee*—The attorney receives a fixed amount as a retainer and then is compensated on an hourly basis for services actually rendered; typically the hourly rate is lower than customary rate because of the retainer (e.g., a $20,000 retainer and a $50 per hour rate).
- *Retainer, hourly fee, and reimbursable expenses*—The attorney receives a fixed amount as a retainer, is compensated on an hourly basis for services actually rendered, and is reimbursed for customary expenses (e.g., a $15,000 retainer, a $40 per hour fee, and reimbursements for expenses).
- *Annual contract*—The attorney agrees to perform all duties specified in the contract for a fixed annual amount (e.g., $35,000 per year).

Another option being used by larger districts is to employ a full-time in-house attorney.

Universally determining the best option for retaining a school attorney is impractical because of the less-than-uniform circumstances facing local districts. For example, some school systems have more exposure to risk and are more likely to become involved in litigation. In general, however, making a compensation decision solely on the basis of initial cost may not be the best choice because the potential for conflict and administrative costs have not been weighed. As an example, using an hourly rate with an annual ceiling may appear prudent because the district would only have to pay for services actually rendered. In practice, however, the attorney and school officials may disagree over billings and the district's business official may have to devote considerable time to monitoring claims and payments. When any option other than an annual contract is being contemplated, superintendents should conduct a thorough cost analysis before making a specific recommendation.

Ideal Versus Actual Attorney Roles

Analyzing the literature on school attorneys, Haberl and Zirkel (2001) identified normative standards for effective deployment:

- *Policy statements*—board policy should stipulate the school attorney's role and a requirement for evaluating the school attorney's performance.
- *Performance*—school attorneys should be expected to attend board meetings; they should have frequent contact with the superintendent (typically at least twice a week); and they should advise the superintendent and school board on statutes, regulations, procedures, and policy.
- *Operating procedures*—the school attorney represents the school board and not specifically the superintendent; acting in concert, the superintendent and board president give direction to the attorney; and communication between the attorney and school board members should go through the superintendent.

As these standards demonstrate, the personal relationship between the superintendent and attorney is really an association among the superintendent, attorney, and school board. Neither the school board nor the superintendent should unilaterally determine, control, or evaluate the attorney.

Perhaps the greatest potential for conflict between superintendents and school attorneys lies in the area of district policy. Since World War II, the courts have assumed an increasingly aggressive role in shaping educational policy (Kirp & Jensen, 1985; Tyack, James, & Benavot, 1987) and this trend has affected the manner in which local districts approach policy. Judicial activism blurs the fine line separating policy making from legal analysis at the district level. To be more precise, some school attorneys exhibit a proclivity to emulate activist judges; that is, they see their role as one of establishing the spirit and language of school board policy rather than as rendering legal opinions on proposed and existing policy. When attorneys function as policymakers and not legal analysts and advisors, they impose their personal values and biases into subject matter for which they have little or no formal expertise (e.g., curriculum, student discipline). Past practice indicates that many attorneys do not clearly understand what is expected of them, with the result that they self-define their role (McKinney & Drake, 1995).

FOR FURTHER REFLECTION

A superintendent's management responsibilities extend to the organization's human resources. Over time, these assignments have become broader, more time-consuming, and more complicated. Fine of the most prevalent management functions—human resources administration, employee unions, special education, pupil personnel services, and legal counsel—were addressed here. As you think about what you have read concerning these topics, answer the following questions.

1. What functions are commonly included in human resources administration in a school district?

2. How do small and large school districts typically differ in the way that human resources administration is organized?

3. In your school district, which employee groups are unionized? To what extent does the superintendent manage relationships with these unions?

4. What are the differences between traditional and collaborative bargaining?

5. Why has special education become a more challenging management responsibility of superintendents?

6. What factors lead many administrators to develop negative attitudes toward compliance with special education laws?

7. What functions are typically included in student personnel services? Are these functions requiring more or less management?

8. What options do school districts have for compensating superintendents? What option is used in your school district?

9. Is it advisable for a superintendent to select a school attorney without school board member involvement? Why or why not?

10. What role should a school attorney play in policy development?

Case Study

Range County is one of 37 school districts in this western state. Despite its vast geographic size, the district serves fewer than 5,000 students; however, the general population is increasing and total student enrollment is rising approximately .1% per year.

Last year, veteran superintendent John Oley retired and the school board selected Dr. Clair Montgomery to replace him. Dr. Montgomery was an assistant superintendent in a large suburban district outside of St. Louis, Missouri.

Once in office, Dr. Montgomery began attacking the district's most serious challenge—adequate finances. Her predecessor had blamed the condition on the state's finance system, arguing that increases in state support were inadequate in relation to enrollment increases. Prior to leaving office, Mr. Oley had twice attempted to pass a referendum to gain funding for a new middle school that would alleviate crowded classroom conditions. Both efforts were defeated by wide margins. Although Dr. Montgomery did not disagree with Mr. Olney's contention about state financing, she concluded that he had ignored other contributing problems that prompted district voters to reject proposed tax increases. One of these problems involved the school attorney.

Wilbur Bascom has been the school attorney for the Range County School District for 23 years. Born and raised in Yellow River, the county seat, he has outlasted five superintendents. In reviewing conditions related to his employment, Dr. Montgomery highlighted the following facts:

- He is retained on annual contract with his compensation set at $55,000.
- He is required to attend all school board meetings.
- If he represents the school district in litigation, he receives additional compensation based on an hourly rate.
- During the previous school year, he was compensated a total $108,000; the additional compensation coming from three lawsuits involving a student expulsion, a bus accident, and a student injury in football.
- In addition to his compensation, he was reimbursed more than $40,000 for expenses, nearly half of the amount being reimbursement for attendance at professional meetings, including the national meetings for superintendents and school board members.

Dr. Montgomery was surprised by the figures. In the district where she was previously employed, the school attorney received an annual contract of only $22,000 and the district served approximately six times as many students.

Dr. Montgomery discussed the school attorney's employment with the board president, Emil Prescott. He was surprised that she raised the issue and he immediately became defensive. "Wilbur's an institution here. He has saved our necks a number of times. We pay him only about half as much as we pay you—and he's a lawyer."

The superintendent then raised the question about reimbursements. Mr. Prescott's answers suggested that Mr. Bascom functioned more like a board member than as a school attorney. He regularly attended professional meetings attended by one or more of the board members and he justified doing so on the basis that he advised the board on all policy matters. Learning this did not comfort the new superintendent. The meeting ended with the board president advising the superintendent to forget about trying to save money by restructuring the school attorney's employment contract.

After her meeting with Mr. Prescott, Dr. Montgomery sat quietly in her office staring out the window. She had met Mr. Bascom several times; he was always present when she met with the school board, her employment interviews included. He was a charming individual who clearly had a great deal of political influence. He recently invited her and her husband to dinner at his ranch. The easy alternative would be to overlook the issue but doing so troubled her. The district had so many needs and she was convinced that both the attorney's compensation and his traditional role were inappropriate.

Case Discussion Questions

1. If you were the new superintendent in Range County would you be concerned about the compensation provided for the school attorney? Why or why not?

2. Evaluate the apparent role played by the school attorney. Is his involvement in all policy matters troubling to you? Why or why not?

3. What are the advantages and disadvantages to the superintendent if she decides to discuss this issue with the school attorney?

4. What are the advantages and disadvantages to the superintendent if she decides to recommend that the board restructure the school attorney's contract?

5. What options might the superintendent pursue to deal with this matter?

6. Should a new superintendent attempt to deal with this type of problem during the first few months of the superintendent's employment? Why or why not?

REFERENCES

Adelman, H. S., & Taylor, L. (2000). Shaping the future of mental health in schools. *Psychology in the Schools, 37*(1), 49–60.

Attea, W. (1993). From conventional to strategic bargaining: One superintendent's experience. *School Administrator, 50*(10), 16–19.

Berger, S. (1995). Inclusion: A legal mandate, an educational dream. *Updating School Board Policies, 26*(4), 1–4.

Callahan, R. E. (1964). *The superintendent of schools: An historical analysis.* Final report of project S-212. Washington, DC: U. S. Office of Education, Department of Health, Education, and Welfare.

Campbell, R. F., Cunningham, L. L., Nystrand, R. O., & Usdan, M. D. (1990). *The organization and control of American schools* (6th ed.). Columbus, OH: Merrill.

Castetter, W. B. (1992). *The personnel function in educational administration* (5th ed.). New York: Macmillan.

DiPaola, M. F., & Walther-Thomas, C. (2003). *Principals and special education: The critical role of school leaders.* Gainesville, FL: Center on Personnel Studies in Special Education.

Dryfoos, J. (2002). Full-service community schools: Creating new institutions *Phi Delta Kappan, 83*(5), 393–399.

Ficklen, E. (1985). Whoa there! By stationing the superintendent at the bargaining table, you could be gunning for trouble. *The American School Board Journal, 172*(5), 32–33.

Geiger, P. E., & Cantelme, D. (2002). Choosing and paying for legal services: There is a way to get and pay for what you need and can afford! *School Business Affairs, 68*(10), 22–24.

Glass, T. (2004). Changes in society and schools. In T. J. Kowalski (Ed.), *Public relations in schools* (3rd ed., pp. 30–46). Upper Saddle River, NJ: Merrill, Prentice Hall.

Glass, T., Björk, L., & Brunner, C. (2000). *The 2000 study of the American school superintendency.* Arlington, VA: American Association of School Administrators.

Haberl, W. E., & Zirkel, P. A. (2001). The working relationship of the attorney with the superintendent and the school board in Pennsylvania: Recommended versus actual practice. *Catalyst for Change, 30*(3), 20–27.

Harrington-Lueker, D. (1990). Some labor relations specialists urge caution. *The American School Board Journal, 177*(7), 29.

Harris, B. M., & Monk, B. J. (1992). *Personnel administration in education* (3rd ed.). Boston: Allyn & Bacon.

Hooper, H. H., Pankake, A., & Schroth, G. (1999). Inclusion in rural school districts: Where is the superintendent? *Rural Special Education Quarterly, 18*(1), 23–27.

Kirp, D., & Jensen, D. (1985). *School days, rule days: The legislation and regulation of education.* Philadelphia: Falmer.

Knezevich, S. J. (1984). *Administration of public education: A sourcebook for the leadership and management of educational institutions* (4th ed.). New York: Harper & Row.

Kowalski, T. J. (2003). *Contemporary school administration: An introduction* (2nd ed.). Boston: Allyn & Bacon.

Kowalski, T. J. (2004). The ongoing war for the soul of school administration. In T. J. Lasley (Ed.), *Better leaders for America's schools: Perspectives on the manifesto* (pp. 92–114). Columbia, MO: University Council for Educational Administration.

LaMorte, M. W. (1996). *School law: Cases and concepts* (5th ed.). Boston: Allyn & Bacon.

Lipiec, J. (2001). Human resources management perspective at the turn of the century. *Public Personnel Management, 30*(2), 137–146.

Lieberman, M. (1986). *Beyond public education.* New York: Praeger.

Lunenburg, F. C., & Ornstein, A. C. (1996). *Educational administration: Concepts and practices* (2nd ed.). Belmont, CA: Wadsworth.

Misso, J. D. (1995). Consensus bargaining: A step toward rational thinking. *School Business Affairs, 61*(12), 26–28.

McKinney, J. R., & Drake, T. L. (1995). The school attorney and local educational policy making. *West Education Law Quarterly, 4*(1), 74–83.

National School Boards Association (1997). *Selecting and working with a school attorney: A guide for school boards.* Alexandria, VA: Author.

Newman, J. W. (1990). *America's teachers.* New York: Longman.

Norton, M. S., Webb, L. D., Dlugosh, L. L., & Sybouts, W. (1996). *The school superintendency: New responsibilities, new leadership.* Boston: Allyn & Bacon.

Pennella, M., & Philips, S. (1987). Help your board negotiate: Stay off the bargaining team. *Executive Educator, 9*(4), 28–29.

Rebore, R. W. (2001). *A human relations approach to the practice of educational leadership* (6th ed.). Boston: Allyn & Bacon.

Russo, C. J., & Osborne, A. G. (2003). Legal issues in special education. In H. R. Weaver, M. F. Landers, & E. A. Joseph (Eds.), *Administering special education: A practical guide for school leaders* (pp. 25–48). New York: Praeger.

Sergiovanni, T. J. (2001). *The principalship: A reflective practice perspective* (4th ed.). Boston: Allyn & Bacon.

Seyfarth, J. T. (2002). *Human resources management for effective schools* (3rd ed.). Boston: Allyn & Bacon.

Sharp, W. (1989). *The role of the superintendent and school board in collective bargaining.* Paper presented at the annual meeting of the Midwestern Education Research Association, Chicago.

Shedd, J. B., & Bacharach, S. B. (1991). *Tangled hierarchies: Teachers as professionals and the management of schools.* San Francisco: Jossey-Bass.

Tyack, D., & Hansot, E. (1982). *Managers of virtue: Public school leadership in America, 1820–1980.* New York: Basic Books.

Tyack, D., James, T., & Benavot, A. (1987). *Law and the shaping of public education 1785–1954.* Madison: University of Wisconsin Press.

Weaver, H. R., & Landers, M. F. (2003). What attitudes do building administrators need to have toward special education. In H. R. Weaver, M. F. Landers, & E. A. Joseph (Eds.), *Administering special education: A practical guide for school leaders* (pp. 11–24). New York: Praeger.

Webb, L. D., & Norton, M. S. (2003). *Human resources administration: Personnel issues and needs in education* (4th ed.). Upper Saddle River, NJ: Merrill, Prentice Hall.

Wentling, T. L., & Piland, W. E. (1982). *Assessing student services. Local leader guide V* (2nd ed.). Springfield: Illinois State Board of Education.

Williams, M., & Macmillan, R. B. (2003). Litigation in special education between 1996–1998: The quest for equality. *Education & Law Journal, 12*(3), 293–317.

CHAPTER 11

Community Leadership

KEY FACETS OF THE CHAPTER

○ A superintendent's leadership role in school and community relations

○ Building and maintaining community support for public education

○ School district partnerships

○ A superintendent's personal community involvement

A superintendent's leadership role, professionally and politically, always has extended beyond a school district's organizational boundaries. In large measure, this is because the superintendent was generally viewed as public property and the superintendent's personal behavior was constantly scrutinized (Blumberg, 1985; Kowalski, 1995). Although this perception persists, community leadership expectations now have been intensified by the fact that the public also see superintendents as public resources. National studies (e.g., Glass, Björk, & Brunner, 2000) reveal that the amount of time superintendents spend away from their office and district schools is increasing. This trend is one of several that are making practice in this position and in the principalship progressively dissimilar.

This chapter focuses on three areas of superintendent community leadership. The first is district and community relationships. Superintendents play an essential role in determining how district personnel exchange information with various constituent publics, both by influencing organizational climate and by modeling desired behavior (Ledell, 1996). The second topic is community partnerships; these formal relationships have multiplied since the 1980s for both economic and political reasons (Kowalski, 2003a). Last, issues of personal involvement are explored. As public resources, superintendents are expected to play an active role in community life by serving on the boards of various civic groups, attending public functions, and frequently making public presentations (Lober, 1993).

DISTRICT AND COMMUNITY RELATIONS

Historically, states have exerted control over public education by promulgating laws and policies. District school boards and superintendents were given the role of regulators; that is, they were expected to ensure that state mandates were implemented (Kirst, 1994). Since the late 1980s, policymaking has tilted toward the local level, largely because of convictions that needed reform would not occur unless improvement initiatives were based on real student needs— needs that obviously are inconstant across and even within districts. As a result, districts and schools became the primary arenas for visioning and planning and school administrators were expected to function as change agents. This reform strategy has produced the seemingly contradictory expectation that administrators simultaneously preserve and improve society (Reyes, Wagstaff, & Fusarelli, 1999).

Emergent expectations of superintendents as reformers are framed by three responsibilities:

1. Informing the public about the intentions, processes, and anticipated outcomes of the district's reform agenda

2. Persuading the public to support the district's reform agenda

3. Ensuring that the values and purposes driving the school district are congruous with the values and beliefs in the larger community (Cohen, 1987)

As discussed at several previous points in the book, the superintendent's role as a communicator was redefined after America became an information-based society. Administrators are now expected to engage in honest, open, consistent, fair, and continuous two-way communication—with school board members, with employees, and with the community (Kowalski, 2004a). This communicative behavior is expected to produce credibility, confidence, goodwill, and social harmony (Seitel, 1992), conditions that enhance the success of school improvement efforts.

Public Education Purpose and the Community

Relationships between school districts and their various publics are framed by two realities:

- Despite considerable rhetoric suggesting the contrary, public schools remain one of the most democratic institutions in American society (Amundson, 1996).
- Contrary to what some believe, local school boards are neither powerless nor insignificant; their actions related to policy development and community support affect the district's productivity (Danzberger & Usdan, 1994; Kirst, 1994).

Together, these two facts comprise a political reality: major policy decisions promulgated at the district level are almost always influenced by pressure groups and community elites competing to advance their needs and wants (Tesconi, 1984). Consequently, political discourse grounded in community values and self-interests is a critical factor determining the extent to which school districts pursue reform and the nature of improvement initiatives (Kowalski, 2003b).

The history of public education reveals recurring cycles of attempted reforms throughout the past century exhibiting the fact that neither public dissatisfaction nor demands for change are new. Americans have always disagreed to some extent over the specific purposes for public schools (Spring, 1994) and this is why reform at the state level has been so difficult to achieve. Past reform eras, however, were often short-lived, highly centralized, and coercive. Commenting on past failures, Cuban (1988) concluded that such top-down approaches promoted simplistic solutions to complex problems nested in conflicting values. By ignoring these values, reform initiatives usually failed to change the culture of public education (Sarason, 1996) and once the pressure to change subsided, educators reverted to their standard practices (Fullan, 2001). Observing this proclivity, Clark and Astuto (1994) wrote, "No one can reform our schools for us. If there is to be authentic reform in American education, it must be a grassroots movement" (p. 520). Appropriately then, meaningful renewal requires educators to commit themselves to openly discussing the purposes of education first among themselves and then with the community at-large (Sarason, 1996).

Education policy has been, and continues to be, guided by several pervasive values, the most notable are *liberty, equality, adequacy, efficiency, fraternity,* and *economic development* (King, Swanson, & Sweetland, 2003). Tensions between liberty and equality—ethical values derived from the doctrine of natural rights—are especially important to school reform policy. While liberty pertains to the right to act without undue restriction, equality refers to the state of enjoying reasonably equal social, political, and economic rights (King et al., 2003). The simultaneous influence of these meta values remains visible in both law and policy. For example, court decisions in school finance litigation often reveal a determination to maintain equilibrium between the principles of liberty and equality (Burrup, Brimley, & Garfield, 1996). Alexander and Salmon (1995) noted the following in this regard:

> Equality and economic freedom are ultimately intermingled and highly interdependent. The role of the state in fostering care, protection, and equality as balanced against individual freedom and liberty forms the primary ground on which political philosophy is argued and tested at the polls, in the legislatures, and in the courts of this nation. (p. 134)

School finance litigation provides the quintessential example of value-driven conflict in public education. After more than 30 years of continuous litigation in nearly every state, a proper balance between liberty and equality continues to be contested (Whitney & Crampton, 1995).

Tensions between liberty and equality also are at the core of school reform disputes. The liberty-based concepts of school choice and vouchers are prime examples. Critics (e.g., Hawley, 1995; Miner, 1998) argue that these ideas lead to economic, religious, and racial segregation and therefore, they have a negative effect on equality. Proponents (e.g., Caire, 2002; Finn, 1986; Walthers, 1995) counter by arguing that students do better in schools that comply with family values and philosophy. Local community culture plays a pivotal role in determining the political acceptability of these reforms and thus, the extent to which they are considered. At a more practical level, the current reform era has brought to light four often competing objectives:

1. Promoting the intellectual attainment of students

2. Shaping good citizens in the interest of a better society

3. Preparing students for the workforce

4. Fostering lifelong learning skills (Armstrong, Henson, & Savage, 1989)

Although the strategy of pursuing reform at the local level is prudent professionally and politically, most school districts continue to become increasingly heterogeneous. Consequently, local reform also is problematic and almost always contentious—but to a lesser degree than is true at the national or state levels. District and school-based reform increases the likelihood that philosophical differences will be identified accurately and discussed rationally so that consensus for school improvement initiatives can be reached.

Keeping the Community Informed

In addition to facilitating inclusive philosophical discussions of public education purposes that lead to a vision, a superintendent's community leadership role includes informing the public of the strategies that will be deployed and outcomes that are expected. To do this, a superintendent must answer two questions:

- *What publics should receive this information?* Parents active in the schools, government officials, business executives, and school board members are good resources for answering this query.
- *What information needs to be communicated to these publics?* In answering this query, a superintendent needs to examine the extent to which the publics understand the concepts being pursued, the extent to which they accept the concepts philosophically and politically, and the extent to which resource allocations are necessary (Connor & Lake, 1994).

The National Institute on Educational Governance, Finance, Policymaking, and Management (1997) offers the following suggestions for disseminating public policy information:

- Information should be distributed in a timely manner.
- Information should be succinctly and clearly written; summaries are better than long reports.
- Information should be provided in a form that accommodates the intended audiences. Audiotapes, for example, may be preferred by busy individuals.
- Information should be objective, accurate, and fairly reported.

Unfortunately, school district officials have not always been prone to thinking, planning, executing, and evaluating services from viewpoints outside of their organizations (Topor, 1992). Many superintendents continue to be oriented toward internal reference groups (e.g., other administrators in the district, board members); consequently, they devote much less time to community-based interactions than their counterparts in private industry. Moving to continuous, two-way communication requires both an appropriate philosophy and an appropriate strategy to change traditional behaviors.

Most citizens expect to have substantial input and influence over educational decisions because they pay taxes to support schools. Moreover, citizens in a democracy learn to be political, prompting them to speak out when they believe they are excluded from important decisions. If their individual voices are ignored, they pursue leverage by forming coalitions (West, 1985). Even more noteworthy, disenfranchised citizens are prime targets for misinformation delivered by individuals and groups already opposing change (Ledell & Arnsparger, 1993). Despite administrators often being aware of these potential problems, stakeholders typically had little involvement in education reform (Patterson, 1993).

Building and Maintaining Community Support

School-reform expert Phillip Schlechty aptly observed that school restructuring efforts have created expectations that superintendents influence stakeholder decisions (Brandt, 1993). Not all practitioners, however, have had a positive attitude about this anticipation, especially those who define persuasion as arm twisting and gimmickry. In truth, persuasion is a relatively complex concept that should be understood at both its lowest and highest levels:

At its lowest level persuading may be identified as propaganda and attempts to distort or deceive. It is reporting good news but concealing bad and preaching by word and not by deed. At its highest level it is akin to educating in the most palatable manner in order to motivate people to act in their best interests. It is skillfully organizing a message to get a much needed point across. (West, 1985, p. 28)

The level of persuasion encouraged by Schlechty and other scholars pertains to the highest level; they envision influence as being consistent with a superintendent's moral and ethical standards. In many instances, efforts to influence the public simply entail the politically difficult task of telling the public the truth (Amundson, 1996).

Superintendents usually need direct assistance to gain necessary levels of community support. Some of it can come from other district employees and school board members, but more often than not, it also needs to come from community opinion leaders. The latter individuals "often serve as key sources of information about issues, and, in an informal sense, frame issues for discussion, debate, and action" (Ledell & Arnsparger, 1993, p. 9). Opinion leaders usually make themselves known. They attend school-related meetings; they exhibit an interest in education; they are good organizers who are respected by others; they are well-informed and ask relevant questions (Ledell & Arnsparger, 1993).

In summary, community leadership related to school improvement entails a process called *strategic marketing*. Applied to public education, it has been defined as planning, implementing, and controlling programs designed to establish voluntary exchanges of values and beliefs between school officials and targeted segments of the school district's population (Kotler & Fox, 1985). It includes obtaining accurate information (needs and values), developing relevant programs, and building public support for the programs. Each function requires community leadership on the part of the superintendent.

DISTRICT PARTNERSHIPS

The growth of school partnerships parallels public disfavor with education. Generally, partnerships are joint ventures involving two or more organizations working together to reach common goals. These relationships may or may not be defined by formal contracts and they can range from a company providing computers to an elementary school to a university and school district jointly operating a professional development school. Potential advantages of these ventures identified in the literature include capacity building and support for change (Crow, 1998), a proclivity to focus on real needs (Guthrie, 1996), reducing the fragmented delivery system of traditional public education (Crowson & Boyd, 1993), and support services to educators (Wang, Haertel, & Walberg, 1995).

Viewed as a promising technique for school improvement, the number of partnerships grew substantially in the mid-1980s; in 1983, only 17% of the nation's schools had such compacts, but by 1989 the figure had increased to 40% (Marenda, 1989). In 1990, the United States Department of Education estimated that the number of ventures involving schools and businesses exceeded 140,000 (Rigden, 1991). Economic, political, demographic, and philosophical factors were largely responsible for the growing popularity of partnerships; Table 11.1 explains these factors.

Table 11.1   Factors Associated With the Growing Popularity of School
Partnerships

Factor	Implication
Demographics	America is becoming a more diverse society and a growing number of students are living in poverty. These conditions increase the need and demand for services in public schools. Partnerships can support some of these services.
Economics	Many public school districts simultaneously face increased demands for services and dwindling resources. Hence partnership ventures are often forged as a means to overcome deficiencies in resources.
Social change	Consequences of educational failures have shifted from the individual to society. In an information age and global economy, there are fewer jobs for students without an adequate level of education.
Politics	Gaining taxpayer support for added resources and change initiatives is becoming increasingly difficult. Public skepticism about the quality of public education, a growing resistance to tax increases, and a declining percentage of taxpayers with children in the public schools contribute to an inadequate resources problem.
Philosophy	Many superintendents believe that authentic educational improvement is more probable when schools have a symbiotic relationship with constituent publics.

Defining Education Partnerships

Four terms are often used to describe relationships between school districts and other agencies and these terms often are used inappropriately with respect to levels of commitment and legal obligations. Defined accurately, these four terms are not synonymous but rather hierarchical, as depicted in Figure 11.1.

- *Networking* is the most basic type of association and it may be formal or informal. Networking often serves the sole purpose of facilitating communication (e.g., sharing information, statistics). Network members are freestanding participants, meaning that they retain complete organizational autonomy (Harris, 1993).

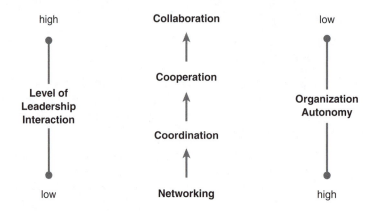

Figure 11.1   Levels of School District Linkage With Other Organizations and
Agencies

- *Coordination* almost always is defined by a formal agreement between
  or among the participants. The purpose is to coordinate organizational
  functions without executing them collectively. As an example, a school
  district and a community college agree to coordinate their adult education classes so that they are not directly competing with each other. The
  two organizations sacrifice little autonomy, continue to function as par-
  allel education providers, and maintain contact only in relation to the
  functions being coordinated (Loughran, 1982).
- *Cooperation* requires participants to relinquish some degree of autonomy
  in that the parties agree to joint services, typically with one party assuming a lead role. As an example, joint ventures among school districts in
  special education and vocational education fall into this category. One
  district is legally in charge as the designated local education agency and
  the member districts agree to support the operations (both fiscally and
  from a policy compliance standpoint).
- *Collaboration* requires the participants to commit to a common goal(s)
  and then sacrifice considerable autonomy in the pursuit of these objectives. Accordingly, administrators often have considerable contact with
  the partners. Collaborative arrangements are almost always formal in
  that they are based on written agreements. An example is a school district
  and a university jointly operating an experimental high school.

Although each of these concepts may be called partnerships, they clearly
are different with respect to autonomy, frequency of communication, and
administrator contact.

The most widely publicized public school partnerships have involved businesses. Foci for these ventures have spanned tutoring programs, field trips and special activities, donations (supplies, equipment), student jobs, summer jobs for teachers, loaned executives, and resource persons to speak to classes (American Association of School Administrators, 1988). The National Alliance of Business (1987) defined six levels of potential partnerships with districts and schools:

- *Level I—Policy.* These alliances are designed to shape new policy or modify existing policy by influencing state or national legislation.
- *Level II—Systematic educational improvement.* Groups work together to identify areas needing reform and make joint efforts over a long period of time to seek improvement in those areas.
- *Level III—Management assistance.* Business partners provide school administrators with management support and business expertise over a broad range of management areas.
- *Level IV—Training and development.* Business partners provide opportunities for educators to update skills and learn about labor markets, industrial/business operations, workplace needs, and career opportunities.
- *Level V—Classroom activities.* Business volunteers serve as guest instructors or entire classrooms visit business sites.
- *Level VI—Special services.* These are short-term projects, student-specific activities, or resource allocation to assist schools with a specific need or problem.

Determining the motives of business executives pursuing ventures with education may be difficult for superintendents. Intentions can range from a general commitment to improving community life and helping students to self-interest (e.g., improving the company's reputation or influencing curriculum to prepare potential employees). Wise (1981) noted that in the past, business executives exploring relationships with local schools tended to ask two basic questions: How can our business improve public schools? How can public schools respond more directly to the needs of our business?

School districts also establish formal relationships with other educational institutions, most notably other districts, colleges, and universities. With respect to ventures with higher education, the partnerships fall into one of the following four categories:

1. *Program assistance*—for example, advanced placement courses for high school students

2. *Programs and services for educators*—for example, staff development for teachers and administrators

3. *Curriculum and assessment projects*—for example, conducting program evaluation, assisting with the design of evaluation systems

4. *Sharing educational resources*—for example, consultants, sharing technology (Pitsch, 1991)

Other district partnerships are community based, such as associations with parents, volunteer groups, local government, churches, and other service providers (e.g., private hospitals or mental health clinics). In some instances, community-based partnerships involve multiple agencies such as churches, hospitals, and mental health agencies working with the district to provide services to troubled students, or the parks department and township trustees working with the district to provide recreation programs.

Partnerships also can be categorized according to their goals and intentions. In this vein, they are intended to enhance existing programs, provide new programs, or produce reform across one or more programs (Kowalski, 2003a). The first two categories involve extending current operations; the third category requires change. Reform-related partnerships reflect a mutual conviction that school improvement cannot be achieved without restructuring the district's organization, curriculum, or delivery systems (see Figure 11.2).

By intention
- Program enhancement (e.g., providing additional software for student computers)
- New programs (e.g., adding new courses on computer applications)
- School reform (e.g., changing the mathematics curriculum)

By possible partners
- Business or industry
- Community-government agencies or groups
- Other education agencies
- Parents or parent groups
- Private foundations

By type
- Adopt-a-school (nonreciprocal agreement where partner provides resources to a school)
- One-way, project driven (partner provides resources for a designated program)
- Limited, two-way (resources given to the school are greater than resources given by the school)
- Full, two-way (exchange of resources is equal or nearly so)

Figure 11.2   Categorization of School Partnerships

Critical Partnership Decisions

Arguably, many education partnerships have failed to live up to their potential—especially those developed in the 1980s and directed at school reform. During this period, a study of 133 schools in one of the nation's largest districts found that only 8 of 450 partnership projects with local businesses had actually produced instructional change (Miron & Wimpelberg, 1989). After 1983, many business elites presumed a cause-and-effect relationship between education and prosperity (Wynne, 1986), a judgment that prompted them to enter the school reform arena. Unfortunately, many of the partnership programs they developed or encouraged failed, either because they were based on questionable assumptions or because they were ill-conceived. Additionally, many of them were inadequately supported by material and human resources.

Avoiding collaboration's pitfalls requires superintendents to ask and answer essential questions before agreeing to move forward. Table 11.2 identifies the factors that underlie these questions and the range of answers. The following questions are perhaps the most important:

Table 11.2   Issues Associated With Forming School Partnerships

Factor	Range of Possibilities	Desired Condition
Compatibility of organizational cultures	Incompatible to compatible	Compatible cultures
Risk potential	Low to high	Low risk[1]
Needs focus	Organizational to individual	Balanced focus
Benefits received	One-sided to mutual	Mutual benefits
Communication	One-way to two-way	Continuous two-way
Goals	Rigid to flexible	Sufficiently flexible[2]
Organizational coupling	Loose to tight	Sufficiently tight[3]
Relationship duration	Short-term to long-term	Long-term relationship
Resource commitments	Minimal to substantial	Sufficiently substantial[4]

[1]Experience between and among partners is crucial for high-risk projects.
[2]Goals should be sufficiently flexible to adjust to changing conditions.
[3]Coupling should be sufficient to enhance cooperation and conflict management.
[4]Sufficient resources need to be committed to ensure that goals can be met.

- *To what extent do the school district and potential partners have compatible cultures?* Unless cultures are reasonably well-matched, excessive conflict is likely to deter goal attainment (MacDowell, 1989).
- *What degree of risk is involved?* Because partnerships can produce negative outcomes, superintendents are advised to build on previous successes; begin with a project that is likely to succeed (Page, 1987).
- *To what extent will the partnership focus on both organizational and individual needs?* Individuals often resist being pushed into projects that require more work and no opportunity for personal benefits.
- *Will both or all parties benefit?* When only one partner benefits, associations tend to be short-lived. (Page, 1987).
- *Are the goals sufficiently flexible?* Rigid long-term goals prevent periodic adjustments for unanticipated problems or outcomes (MacDowell, 1989).
- *To what extent must the partners sacrifice autonomy?* Each partner should know in advance if organizational autonomy will be reduced.
- *Do the partners share the same time frame expectations?* Most change in public education requires time and patience, yet many partners expect rapid results.
- *What will each partner be required to contribute in human and material resources?* Many ventures are understaffed and underfunded, causing conflict and eventually failure. Too often superintendents assume that they can integrate additional projects without budget increases.

Reasons for Failure and Success

Undoubtedly, there are many reasons why a partnership involving a school district can fail. The following obstacles, however, have been particularly prevalent.

- *Turf protection* refers to the tendency of organizational or divisional administrators to protect their legitimate authority. This form of conflict most often occurs in bureaucratic-like organizations where sharp distinctions in authority and responsibility are prescribed (Hoy & Miskel, 2005). Values and practices within an organization are often extended to partnerships. Consider the example of a district and community college that agreed to provide adult education jointly. Disputes over scheduling and instructor assignments increased as the project progressed. Eventually, the disputes led to officials in both organizations accusing each other of being uncooperative.

- *Insufficient planning* produces ambiguity that often attenuates good intentions. This problem usually results from superintendents being impetuous; that is, they are so anxious to commence the partnership that they give little forethought to the end products and the means for reaching them (Gardner, 1990). For example, a superintendent desirous of positive publicity immediately accepted the offer to forge a partnership with a computer company even though little discussion about the nature of the venture had occurred. Once established, the superintendent discovered that the company expected teachers to field test software—an assignment the teachers' union protested because additional compensation was not involved.

- *Inadequate resources* are a recurring problem because superintendents often concentrate entirely on potential gains and ignore necessary investments. An example of this problem was evident in a project between a school district and a local candy company. Both organizations shared a common goal of providing summer job opportunities for high school juniors and seniors. The district would benefit by providing relevant work experiences for students; the company would benefit by having trained seasonal workers. To become eligible, the students had to complete a four-week after-school program to learn how to operate certain equipment. The project quickly fell apart when the superintendent discovered that the necessary training had to be provided at the high school. Lacking sufficient space, equipment, and personnel to conduct the training, the superintendent had to rescind his commitment to the project.

- *Unresolved conflict* is almost always associated with the unwillingness of partners to address inevitable tensions. A drug-counseling project between a school district and local mental health agency experienced this problem. Conflict emerged when it became apparent that personnel in the cooperating organizations did not agree on appropriate therapies. Rather than resolving their differences, personnel in the schools and mental health agency worked around each other. Eventually, they concluded that the partnership could not succeed.

- *Unrealistic time parameters* also can destroy a partnership. This problem has been most noticeable in school-business ventures where executives are accustomed to seeing quick results. For example, a bank president agreed to provide $25,000 a year to fund a tutoring program for elementary school students in mathematics. When test scores failed to increase after just one year, he criticized school personnel for not using the money appropriately and discontinued funding.

Certain conditions also have been found to contribute to successful partnerships and their effect is usually synergistic (Kowalski, 2003a). The greater the number of conditions present, the greater their cumulative effect.

- *Partner recognition* is critical, especially for businesses and agencies that rely on public goodwill. Therefore, superintendents need to develop ways to ensure that positive publicity will credit the partners with helping public education.
- *Employee support* often determines whether projects meet their goal. In districts and schools, principals and teachers often assume much of the work associated with partnerships. If they do not endorse the program, they typically find ways to sabotage it—even when it has been planned meticulously.
- *Periodic progress reports* keep partners and district employees informed. Information voids can contribute to indifference, rumors, and even destructive actions. Three or four reports a year are considered a minimum.
- *Mutual benefits* prevent one-sided relationships. Although many arguments can be made for schools accepting handouts, mutually beneficial programs are far more likely to endure and prosper. A key to effective partnerships is establishment of an intersection of educational interests—a point at which partners are able to justify the commitments they make to each other (Wise, 1981).
- *Adequate resources* are essential. When quantity and quality of resources are congruous with the program's goals, a partnership's chances of succeeding increase markedly.
- *Policymakers are supportive and involved* allowing periodic adaptations to unforeseen problems or emerging needs.
- *Mission and objectives* statements provide vision and direction. When partners know where they want to go, they are better able to manage inevitable tensions and conflict.
- *Scope and complexity* increase incrementally. Like all relationships, partnerships require time to get stronger. Successful ventures usually start as simple projects and then get broader and more complex once participants become confident.
- *Trust* is arguably the most critical attribute of successful partnerships. Without it, linkages are likely to remain at the networking or coordination levels—and even then, mistrust breeds conflict.

Knowing what to avoid and what to include provide process knowledge for forging partnerships. With this information, superintendents are able to actually plan, develop, and deliver partnership programs. Bradshaw (2000) referred to this cycle as problem setting, direction setting, and structuring.

Commercialization and evidence of student outcomes are two caveats that superintendents should acknowledge. Over the past 10 to 15 years, many partnerships have been commercialized, raising important ethical questions. Contracts with media companies to broadcast news and commercials in schools and contracts with soft drink companies granting them exclusive sales rights are but two examples. In the former arrangement, districts typically receive free technology equipment; in the latter, they receive a fixed amount, a share of profits, or both. Faced with inadequate resources, school officials became more amenable to negotiating such agreements during the 1990s (Lewis, 1998). These iterations of partnerships depart from the spirit of having public schools work more closely with their communities. Once implemented, superintendents may find it extremely difficult to control corporate officials who want to influence school programs (Lickteig, 2003).

Critics of partnerships often have focused on the worth of these programs in relation to student learning. Faced with such challenges, administrators may find it extremely difficult to provide compelling positive evidence because it is extremely difficult to isolate outcomes directly attributable to collaboration—and it is especially difficult to determine the effects of partnerships on student outcomes (Cobb & Quaglia, 1994). Neither these potential problems nor the possible pitfalls discussed earlier should dissuade superintendents from pursuing collaborative agreements. Even so, they are valid reasons why superintendents should be cautious.

PERSONAL COMMUNITY INVOLVEMENT

As discussed in previous chapters, superintendents have to be both professional leaders and effective politicians (Björk & Keedy, 2001; Brunner, Grogan, & Björk, 2002; Kowalski, 1995). Moreover, they have been required to have a license to practice but denied even the basic trappings of true professions; instead, they are more often treated as political appointees (Kowalski, 2004b). Blumberg (1985) argued that the work of superintendents was characterized by three consequential conditions:

1. Superintendents lead institutions to which some of the most deeply held values in the American tradition are attached.

2. They assume their jobs as supposed experts, yet the application of their expertise depends on developing a supportive constituency among the school board, community, and professional staff.

3. In most school districts there are people who believe that they have expertise equal to or exceeding the knowledge of superintendents.

Unlike practitioners in more established professions, superintendents face the challenge of applying their knowledge base in a highly political context (Björk & Keedy, 2001; Kowalski, 1995).

The need to gain public acceptance and support explains why superintendents (and, more importantly, the districts they lead) should function as community leaders (Carnes, 1995; Goble, 1993). Membership in service clubs, service on city and county boards, and attendance at public functions serve several purposes. Most notably, they broaden a superintendent's understanding of prevailing needs, sentiments, and social conditions—information essential to forging visions and building support to achieve them. Community involvement also promotes two-way communication because it is a forum for both issuing and receiving information (Kowalski, 2004a). Such benefits are consequential because many community opinion leaders often are individuals not naturally connected to public education. Politically, superintendents profit when they reach out to these individuals and interact with them in community contexts (Alsbury, 2003).

The modern school district has multiple publics distinguished by demographic variables such as wealth, education, ethnicity, religion, age, and politics. Superintendents cannot communicate effectively with all of these groups unless they accurately identify and then interact with them (Thiemann & Ruscoe, 1985). Urban districts provide the quintessential example of the need for broad community interaction because school board members in these districts often see themselves as representing different constituencies. When a superintendent fails to communicate regularly and broadly, the superintendent risks jeopardizing personal relationships with the board members who conclude that their constituents are being ignored (Kowalski, 1995). As the country continues to become more diverse demographically, even rural district superintendents are discovering that they must interact with multiple publics. In addition, contact with various publics serves a multitude of purposes, including the following:

- Being able to get a better perspective of community needs and expectations
- Being able to establish an identity and working relationship with a broad base of citizens
- Being able to engage in two-way communication
- Being able to secure material and political support for reform initiatives

The necessity of community involvement also reflects the reality that the superintendent is the visible head of the school district. In this vein, much of what the superintendent does with adult nonemployees is symbolic and determines how the school's image, needs, and accomplishments are presented to the community (Sergiovanni, Burlingame, Coombs, & Thurston, 1992). Thus, access to community power structures and positive relationships with influential individuals comprising those structures often determine whether a superintendent can build essential political support for the district's initiatives.

Since the 1980s, the quest for school reform has elevated the importance of community leadership. Virtually any proposed change, no matter how well intentioned, is likely to be opposed by some segment of the population. In most instances, a superintendent cannot readily discern if opposition stems from misunderstandings, political or philosophical convictions, or simply an unwillingness to expand resources. In addition to diagnosing the causes of opposition, superintendents "have an obligation to protect the schools from being manipulated by special interest groups who seek to misinform the general public or advance a narrow agenda" (Ledell & Arnsparger, 1993, p. 35). Both problem identification and district protection are improbable for superintendents detached from and uninvolved in their political environments. Ledell and Arnsparger (1993) offered four suggestions to facilitate this aspect of community involvement: (a) periodically meet with a broad cross section of the community; (b) meet with reform opponents face-to-face; (c) remain focused on what the majority wants and expects; (d) get community members to visit schools. In addition, superintendents need to identify and penetrate informal communication networks that often are public opinion conduits (Kowalski, 2003b).

Engaging in political activity obviously is not risk free. Critics may charge, for example, that the superintendent is ignoring basic problems by spending too much time away from the office and schools. Interactions with community leaders also spawn possible ethical and legal concerns. Problems can emerge when practitioners fail to separate district interests from self-interests. Access to power elites can result in compromising situations that will test the integrity, honesty, and professionalism of even highly experienced administrators. Yet the need to scan the environment, to inform the public, and to gain essential economic and political support is too important to justify modern superintendents isolating themselves in the safety of their offices. Clearly, thousands of superintendents have proven that it is possible to be professional and politically effective. Doing so requires administrators to place the interests of the district above personal interests, to be honest and candid in communication, and to avoid illegal and unethical compromises that betray the community's trust.

FOR FURTHER REFLECTION

This chapter examined the community leadership role of superintendents. The responsibilities associated with function span school-community relations, district and school partnerships, and personal involvement in community activities. As you consider what you read in this chapter, answer the following questions:

1. What factors have contributed to the growing importance of school and community relations?

2. This chapter includes information about the multiple publics of school districts. What does the term "multiple publics" mean? Why is this term relevant to superintendents?

3. Education partnerships have increased in number significantly since 1980. What is the range of partnerships that have evolved?

4. What are the possible advantages of district partnerships for public education and for the partners?

5. What leadership responsibilities should a superintendent assume in relation to partnerships?

6. What problems are possible with regard to building and maintaining effective partnerships?

7. Why is it important for a superintendent to become personally involved in community-based activities?

8. In what ways does community involvement constitute a leadership activity for superintendents?

9. Superintendents are expected to be professional and political leaders. Would assuming these dual roles concern you? Why or why not?

10. What are some potential pitfalls of a superintendent engaging in political activities with community power elites?

Case Study

Bright City, home of Southeastern State University, is a community with just over 13,000 residents. The local district enrolls 2,600 students in 6 attendance centers. Over the years, the district and university have had a positive relationship focused largely on working together in the area of teacher education. The two primary examples are classroom observations and participation and student teaching. George Cartright, the superintendent of the Bright City School District, is a graduate of Southeastern and has been a member of the university's Alumni Board for the past six years.

Two years ago, after Dr. Sandra Walker was named president at Southeastern, the district's relationship with the university began to change. A former elementary school teacher and dean of education at another university, President Walker wanted to build a more comprehensive and formal relationship with the Bright City School District. Southeastern's education dean, Dr. Elizabeth O'Ryan, was initially reluctant to pursue change because she felt the current relationship was positive and mutually beneficial. President Walker, however, wanted to move beyond using the local schools as clinical sites; she wanted to forge a true partnership in which the two institutions would collaborate completely to operate two or three of the schools. The model she presented to Dean O'Ryan was based on the concept of professional development schools.

In her previous position as a dean of a large school of education, President Walker became convinced that education students were exposed to both good and bad teaching models under traditional observation, participation, and student teaching programs. She explained to Dr. O'Ryan that universities typically were not in a position to correct existing problems because they were at the mercy of the local districts. Thus, some students received positive experiences in schools, whereas others did not. In professional development schools, she contended, the two institutions would share authority and staff, enabling the education faculty to determine the types of teaching models their students would experience. She felt this change in authority was essential if Southeastern students were to avoid being socialized to negative teaching practices.

After having had three discussions on this topic, Dean O'Ryan concluded that President Walker was going to move in this direction with or without her. So she decided to support the idea. The president drafted an outline for the proposal, gave it to the dean, and told her to approach Superintendent Cartright with the idea. "If he is apprehensive or resistant, I'll get involved," she told the dean. "Otherwise, I would prefer that he and his colleagues view this as a School of Education initiative."

Dean O'Ryan met with the Mr. Cartright several days later. She outlined the idea and indicated that President Walker was enthusiastic about it but did not disclose that it actually was her idea. She then outlined basic elements for the agreement. The proposal was to have two schools involved—one elementary school and one secondary school. The two schools would each have advisory committees consisting of the principal, two teachers, and three Southeastern professors. The advisory committees would function much like school councils under site-based management. In addition, the university would assign one full-time and two part-time personnel to each school without cost to the district. All district professional staff assigned to the two schools would be eligible for a 50% tuition reduction for any graduate courses at Southeastern during the duration of the joint agreement. The two organizations also would sign a formal agreement for a period of three years that hopefully would be renewed as the project matured.

Superintendent Cartright reacted cautiously. "I'll have to discuss this with the school board but I see a great deal of opportunity here. As you probably know, not everyone thinks it's a good idea for us to be highly involved with the university."

Dean O'Ryan responded, "Southeastern has many resources and we should work together to ensure that the community's schools provide the very best education programs. I really see this as a win-win situation and I can't imagine why anyone would oppose it."

Despite her comments, Mr. Cartright was not convinced that the partnership would be embraced widely. After Dean O'Ryan left, he met with Peter Jones, the assistant superintendent, to share the proposal and to get his reaction.

"I see possible benefits and possible problems," the assistant told him. "What if the committee members can't get along? What if they have split votes on critical issues? As proposed, it could be three of us against three of them. And I'm not sure how the teachers' association is going to react to this idea. But on the other hand, not playing ball with them could create some major political problems."

The two men decided to present the idea to the school board privately so they could determine their reactions. They feared, however, that some, if not all, of the board members would be opposed to such a formal agreement. Their apprehensions stemmed from the following conditions:

- Prompted by teacher concerns, two board members recently complained that too many university students were being placed in the district.
- The board members in general were suspicious of professors. This suspicion was exacerbated by several recent letters written by professors and published in the local newspaper. The letters criticized the administration and school board for using "negative approaches" to student discipline.
- Two of the board members had been opposed by professors in the past election.
- Only one board member, Barbara White, a director of dormitory food services, is employed by the university. She has been one of the most passive board members and has not responded to criticisms voiced by her fellow board members.

The proposal to create a district-university partnership in conjunction with two professional development schools was presented individually to the board members prior to the public meeting. Superintendent Cartright explained that details of the proposal were included in the board member information packets and that the topic would be discussed at the next meeting. When they reached this agenda item during the meeting, Mrs. White immediately made a motion to approve the partnership concept. Brian Debow, a farmer and one of the board members who previously voiced concerns about the level of university involvement in the district, argued that the motion was out of order. He contended that the issue had been placed on the agenda simply for discussion purposes. He asked the board president to rule her motion to be out of order. Mrs. White countered that the partnership was an opportunity to pursue new ideas under the leadership of a new university president who had a great deal of interest in public schools. The board president asked Mr. Cartright to comment on the proposal. The superintendent said that although the concept had merit, he understood why some board members might be concerned. The board president then asked if it was the superintendent's intention for the board to merely discuss the idea or for the board to vote on the matter. He responded that the university officials wanted a decision as soon as possible but added that he did not want to stifle discussion. Shaking his head, the board president then said, "Okay, then we'll move forward. I find the motion to be in order. Is there a second?"

After a minute of silence, Mr. Debow seconded the motion and commented that he was doing so simply to move things along. The board president then invited additional discussion. Mrs. White commented that President Walker had called her several days ago and urged her to support the idea. Neither the superintendent nor assistant superintendent had any additional comments. Mr. Debow called for the question. The board then voted 4 to 1 to defeat the motion.

Local reporters were highly critical of the superintendent and school board the next day. The headline of the newspaper read: **School Officials Reject President Walker's Offer**. The front-page article described Superintendent Cartright as indecisive and charged that four of the board members never even gave the idea a fair hearing. Comments from principals and teachers verified that the proposal had been given to the school board even though it had never been discussed with them. The editorial also focused on the board's rejection. The editor encouraged the district's residents to voice their outrage over the board's decision which the editor described as "uninformed, myopic, and destructive." Feeling the sting of public criticism, each of the four board members telephoned Superintendent Cartright to let him know that he was to blame for the political fiasco.

Case Discussion Questions

1. Did the university president and dean contribute to the problem presented in this case? Why or why not?

2. What is your impression of the superintendent's leadership style? What evidence in the case contributes to your impression?

3. If you had been superintendent, how would you have reacted to the initial proposal from Dean O'Ryan?

4. Did the superintendent behave responsibly and professionally at the school board meeting? Why or why not?

5. Did the superintendent have a responsibility to respond to earlier criticisms of cooperation with the university (e.g., the comment about too many students being placed in the district and the letters criticizing discipline policies)? Why or why not?

6. In what ways did the two university administrators and the two district administrators violate principles underlying positive partnerships?

7. Are the board members justified in blaming the superintendent for creating a "political fiasco"? Why or why not?

8. At this point, what could be done to repair the damage resulting from the board's rejection of the partnership proposal?

REFERENCES

Alexander, K., & Salmon, R. G. (1995). *Public school finance.* Boston: Allyn & Bacon.

American Association of School Administrators (1988). *Challenges for school leaders.* Arlington, VA: Author.

Alsbury, T. (2003). Stop talking and do something: The changing role of superintendent involvement in school-community relations. *Journal of School Public Relations, 24*(1), 44–52.

Amundson, K. (1996). *Telling the truth about America's public schools.* Arlington, VA: American Association of School Administrators.

Armstrong, D. G., Henson, K. T., & Savage, T. V. (1997). *Teaching today: An introduction to education* (5th ed.). Upper Saddle River, NJ: Merrill/Prentice Hall.

Björk, L. G., & Keedy, J. (2001). Politics and the superintendency in the U.S.A.: Restructuring in-service education. *Journal of In-service Education, 27*(2), 275–302.

Blumberg, A. (1985). *The school superintendent: Living with conflict.* New York: Teachers College Press.

Bradshaw, L. K. (2000). The changing role of principals in school partnerships. *NASSP Bulletin, 84*(616), 86–96.

Brandt, R. (1993). On restructuring roles and relationships: A conversation with Phil Schlechty. *Educational Leadership, 51*(2), 8–11.

Brunner, C. C., Grogan, M., & Björk, L. (2002). Shifts in the discourse defining the superintendency: Historical and current foundations of the position. In J. Murphy (Ed.), *The educational leadership challenge: Redefining leadership for the 21st century* (pp. 211–238). Chicago: The University of Chicago Press.

Burrup, P. E., Brimley, V., & Garfield, R. R. (1996). *Financing education in a climate of change* (6th ed.). Boston: Allyn & Bacon.

Caire, K. M. (2002). The truth about vouchers. *Educational Leadership, 59*(7) 38–42.

Clark, D. L., & Astuto, T. A. (1994). Redirecting reform: Challenges to popular assumptions about teachers and students. *Phi Delta Kappan, 75*(7), 512–520.

Carnes, W. J. (1995). Unleashing the kraken: The perils of ignoring community values. *Educational Leadership, 53*(3), 84–86.

Cobb, C., & Quaglia, R. J. (1994). *Moving beyond school-business partnerships and creating relationships.* East Lansing, MI: National Center for Research on Teacher Learning. (ERIC Document Reproduction Service No. ED374545)

Cohen, P. M. (1987). *The public relations primer: Thinking and writing in context.* Upper Saddle River, NJ: Prentice Hall.

Connor, P. E., & Lake, L. K. (1994). *Managing organizational change* (2nd ed.). Westport, CT: Praeger.

Crow, G. M. (1998). Implications for leadership in collaborative schools. In D. G. Pouder (Ed.), *Restructuring schools for collaboration: Exploring issues for research and practice* (pp. 135–154). Albany: State University of New York Press.

Crowson, R. L., & Boyd, W. L. (1993). Coordinated services for children: Designing arks for storms and seas unknown. *American Journal of Education, 101,* 140–177.

Cuban, L. (1988). Why do some reforms persist? *Educational Administration Quarterly, 24*(3), 329–335.

Danzberger, J. P., & Usdan, M. D. (1994). Local education governance: Perspectives on problems and strategies for change. *Phi Delta Kappan, 75,* 366–401.

Finn, C. E. (1986). Educational choice: Theory, practice, and research. *Equity and Choice, 2*(3), 43–52.

Fullan, M. (2001). *Leading in a culture of change.* San Francisco: Jossey-Bass.

Gardner, A. L. (1990). *School partnerships: A handbook for school and community leaders.* East Lansing, MI: National Center for Research on Teacher Learning. (ERIC Document Reproduction Service No. ED331899)

Glass, T., Björk, L., & Brunner, C. (2000). *The 2000 study of the American school superintendency.* Arlington, VA: American Association of School Administrators.

Goble, N. (1993). School-community relations: New for the '90s. *The Education Digest, 59*(12), 45–48.

Guthrie, L. F. (1996). *How to coordinate services for students and families.* Alexandria, VA: Association for Supervision and Curriculum Development.

Harris, T. E. (1993). *Applied organizational communication: Perspectives, principles, and pragmatics.* Hillsdale, NJ: Lawrence Erlbaum.

Hawley, W. D. (1995). The false premises and false promises of the movement to privatize public education. *Teachers College Record, 96,* 735–742.

Hoy, W. K., & Miskel, C. G. (2005). *Educational administration: Theory, research, and practice* (7th ed.). Boston: Allyn and Bacon.

King, R. A., Swanson, A. D., & Sweetland, S. R. (2003). *School finance: Achieving high standards with equity and efficiency* (3rd ed.). Boston: Allyn & Bacon.

Kirst, M. W. (1994). A changing context means school board reform. *Phi Delta Kappan, 75,* 378–81.

Kotler, P., & Fox, K. (1985). *Strategic marketing for educational institutions.* Upper Saddle River, NJ: Prentice Hall.

Kowalski, T. J. (1995). *Keepers of the flame: Contemporary urban superintendents.* Thousand Oaks, CA: Corwin.

Kowalski, T. J. (2003a). *Contemporary school administration* (2nd ed.). Boston: Allyn & Bacon.

Kowalski, T. J. (2003b, April). *The superintendent as communicator.* Paper presented at the annual meeting of the American Educational Research Association, Chicago.

Kowalski, T. J. (2004a). School public relations: A new agenda. In T. J. Kowalski (Ed.), *Public relations in schools* (3rd ed., pp. 3–29). Upper Saddle River, NJ: Merrill, Prentice Hall.

Kowalski, T. J. (2004b). The ongoing war for the soul of school administration. In T. J. Lasley (Ed.), *Better leaders for America's schools: Perspectives on the Manifesto* (pp. 92–114). Columbia, MO: University Council for Educational Administration.

Ledell, M. A. (1996). Common ground: a way of life, not a checkoff item. *School Administrator, 53*(11), 8–11.

Ledell, M., & Arnsparger, A. (1993). *How to deal with community criticism of school change.* Alexandria, VA: Association for Supervision and Curriculum Development.

Lewis, P. (1998). Corporate sponsors help with financing. *Denver Business Journal, 50*(12), 6–7.

Lickteig, M. K. (2003). Brand-name schools: The deceptive lure of corporate-school partnerships. *The Educational Forum, 68*(1), 44–51.

Lober, I. M. (1993). *Promoting your school: A public relations handbook*. Lancaster, PA: Technomic.

Loughran, E. L. (1982). Networking, coordination, cooperation, and collaboration. *Community Education Journal, 9*(4), 28–30.

MacDowell, M. A. (1989). Partnerships: Getting a return on the investment. *Educational Leadership, 47*(2), 8–11.

Marenda, D. W. (1989). Partners in education: An old tradition renamed. *Educational Leadership, 47*(2), 4–7.

Miner, B. (1998). Why I don't vouch for vouchers. *Educational Leadership, 56*(2), 40–42.

Miron, L. F., & Wimpelberg, R. K. (1989). School-business partnerships and the reform of education. *Administrator's Notebook, 33*(9), 1–4.

National Alliance of Business (1987). *The fourth R: Workforce readiness*. Washington, DC: Author.

National Institute on Educational Governance, Finance, Policymaking, and Management (1997). *Meeting the information needs of educational policymakers*. Washington, DC: U.S. Government Printing Office.

Page, E. G. (1987). Partnerships: Making a difference over time? *Journal of Career Development, 13*(3), 43–49.

Patterson, H. (1993). Don't exclude the stakeholders. *School Administrator, 50*(2), 13–14.

Pitsch, M. (1991, September 11). School-college links seen as fundamental to education reform. *Education Week, 11*(2), 1, 12–13.

Reyes, P., Wagstaff, L., & Fusarelli, L. (1999). Delta forces: The changing fabric of American society and education. In J. Murphy & K. S. Louis (Eds.), *The handbook of research on educational administration* (2nd ed.; pp. 183–201). San Francisco: Jossey-Bass.

Rigden, D. W. (1991). *Business-school partnerships: A path to effective restructuring* (2nd ed.). New York: Council for Aid to Education.

Sarason, S. B. (1996). Revisiting "the culture of the school and the problem of change." New York: Teachers College Press.

Seitel, F. P. (1992). *The practice of public relations* (5th ed.). New York: Macmillan.

Sergiovanni, T. J., Burlingame, M., Coombs, F. S., & Thurston, P. W. (1992). *Educational governance and administration* (3rd ed.). Boston: Allyn & Bacon.

Spring, J. (1994). *The American school: 1642–1990* (3rd ed.). New York: Longman.

Tesconi, C. A. (1984). Additive reform and the retreat from purpose. *Educational Studies, 15*(1), 1–10.

Thiemann, F. C., & Ruscoe, G. C. (1985). Garnering stakeholders' support for educational excellence. *NASSP Bulletin, 69*(477), 41–44.

Topor, R. (1992). *No more navel gazing*. Mountain View, CA: Topor & Associates.

Walthers, K. (1995). Saying yes to vouchers: Perception, choice, and the educational response. *NASSP Bulletin, 79*(572), 52–61.

Wang, M. C., Haertel, G. D., & Walberg, H. J. (1995). The effectiveness of collaborative school-linked services. In L. C. Rigsby, M. C. Reynolds, & M. C. Wang (Eds.), *School-community connections: Exploring issues for research and practice* (pp. 283–310). San Francisco: Jossey-Bass.

West, P. T. (1985). *Educational public relations*. Beverly Hills, CA: Sage.

Whitney, T. N., & Crampton, F. E. (1995). State school finance litigation: A summary and analysis. *State Legislative Report, 20,* 1–16.

Wise, R. I. (1981). Schools, businesses, and educational needs: From cooperation to collaboration. *Education and Urban Society, 14*(1), 67–82.

Wynne, G. E. (1986). School-business partnerships: A shortcut to effectiveness. *NASSP Bulletin, 70*(491), 94–98.

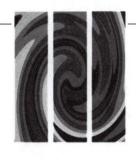

PART IV

*Contemporary and
Personal Perspectives*

CHAPTER 12

Contemporary Challenges

KEY FACETS OF THE CHAPTER

○ Heightened political action

○ Inadequate financial support for public education

○ Building mission and vision statements

○ Changing school district culture

○ Purported shortage of qualified superintendents

○ Underrepresentation of women and people of color

Being the chief executive officer of any organization is a difficult assignment and being a school superintendent is no exception. Social, political, economic, and legal problems penetrate the schoolhouse, and when they do, administrators are expected to deal with them. Reflecting on the superintendent's responsibility to manage tensions surrounding these problems, Cuban (1985) aptly noted that conflict had become the DNA of this position.

Perceived and actual difficulties identified by practitioners reflect a mix of personal and contextual variables (Blumberg, 1985; Kowalski, 1995). Individual characteristics such as personality, health, and stress tolerance, influence how administrators view their work (Hoy & Miskel, 2005), but perceptions also are shaped by factors such as the climate of the district, the nature of the local community, and available resources. Consequently, problems are not quantitatively or qualitatively uniform across districts. One superintendent's primary challenge may be settling a contract with a teacher's union, whereas another superintendent's primary challenge may be passing a tax referendum.

Challenges facing superintendents can be broadly categorized as social, institutional, and professional. This chapter does not provide an exhaustive list of concerns; instead, it demonstrates how emerging responsibilities influence practice by providing two examples of pervasive challenges in each of the three categories. Although institutional problems are commonly recognized, superintendents are less likely to reflect on the social and professional aspects of their practice.

SOCIAL CHALLENGES

Social challenges facing superintendents are exemplified by recurring problems such as poverty, violence, and changing family structures. These issues have been discussed previously in relation to other topics. Two socially driven issues are examined in greater depth here: heightened political activity and inadequate funding for public education. The former is produced by an intricate mix of demographic and philosophical variables that generate conflict as special interest groups pursue their agendas (Wirt & Kirst, 2001). The latter is produced by a combination of economic realities and attitudes about equality and efficiency in public education (King, Swanson, & Sweetland, 2003).

Heightened Political Action

Although many view education as a sacred trust that should be held above the political fray (Blumberg, 1985) and professionals regard political activities as antithetical to professional behavior (Kowalski, 1999), politics are integral to democratic traditions. Local schools, like all other public institutions, are affected by ongoing competition among interest groups seeking to advance their own interests by virtue of policies and resource decisions (Rowan & Miskel, 1999). Consequently, practice in the superintendency is never totally divorced from political realities (Wirt & Kirst, 2001), and as communities become more ethnically and racially diverse, the intensity of conflict and the intensity of political action escalate. As a result, superintendents must cope with diverse and often contradictory demands (Carter & Cunningham, 1997).

Scholars and practitioners agree that superintendents require political acuity and highly developed skills to work effectively with community and board power structures. Today, this need is magnified by conditions associated with the pursuit of district-level reforms. Unlike the 1980s when superintendents and other educators were cast largely as implementers of national and state policy (St. John & Clements, 2004), current practice sets new normative standards (Kowalski, 2001). More precisely, superintendents need to facilitate discussion in which all members of the district's various publics are encouraged to state and test their education values and beliefs (St. John & Clements, 2004). This communicative perspective of school improvement is most demanding in communities where divisiveness and political polarization have resulted in disunity and dissatisfaction.

Darling-Hammond (1988) astutely noted that there have been two very different streams of reform policy based on dissimilar ideas of teaching and learning. One led policymakers to conclude that schools needed improved regulations, and the other led them to conclude that schools needed better teaching. The latter perspective has nurtured school restructuring strategies. Today, reformers are divided by basic values. One side promotes a mix of excellence and efficiency; for example, they believe schools can be improved without additional resources simply by forcing them to compete (e.g., Chubb & Moe, 1990; Finn, 1991). The other side promotes a mix of excellence and equality; for example, they believe that more resources dedicated to equalizing educational opportunities across districts and schools are necessary (e.g., Darling-Hammond, 2000). This basic philosophical divide over school reform is exacerbated by demographic changes (St. John & Clements, 2004). Increasing levels of diversity, now found in most districts, present another important dimension to education politics for at least two reasons: the effects of philosophical polarization become more overt and contentious at the local level and political positions become even more fragmented as local issues are infused (Wirt & Kirst, 2001).

Analysts estimate that the population of the United States will increase from 281 million in 2000 to 394 million in 2050 and minority population is expected to account for 90% of this growth (U.S. Census Bureau, 1999). Given these population patterns, the percentage of students of color enrolled in public schools will steadily increase. Correspondingly, the percentage of children living in poverty also is expected to increase (Glass, 2004). The No Child Left Behind Act (NCLB) underscores the importance of redesigning schools to ensure that instructional approaches effectively meet already existing challenges presented by diverse student populations. However, the NCLB also demonstrates a problematic disjunction between political support for policy and economic support for implementing policy; the NCLB arguably may be the largest underfunded education mandate in history (Björk, Kowalski, & Young, in press).

Philosophical disputes get magnified by inadequate resources (Hanson, 2003; Wirt & Kirst, 2001). This partially explains why political activity is most intense in large urban districts where the population is typically very diverse and where the problem of insufficient funding is considered most critical (Kowalski, 1995). In a national study, 90% of large-district (i.e., with 25,000 or more students) superintendents reported that special interest groups had attempted to influence district policy and operations; this figure compares with 57% across all types of districts (Glass, Björk, & Brunner, 2000) In diverse population districts, multiple publics—usually divided culturally, economically, and philosophically— seek to protect their interests through political pressure. Examples of the resulting disputes have been most obvious in curriculum where topics such as multicultural education, bilingual education, and sex education have been fiercely contested; recently, some of the most intense battles have occurred over teaching the theory of evolution (Opfer, 2003).

Although political conflict stemming from education policy decisions certainly is not a novel issue, this byproduct now more directly affects superintendents (Kowalski, 2001). As noted earlier, the current policy environment has even changed from the 1980s when superintendents focused largely on implementing reforms rather than on developing them. Using an iteration of directed autonomy, most states have set broad guidelines, permitted local districts leeway to determine how they will meet these goals, and then held local district officials accountable for the outcomes (Weiler, 1990). This strategy has literally forced superintendents to concentrate both on how to implement policy (a traditional management role) and on what needs to be done (an emerging leadership role). This broader and more risk-laden assignment requires administrators to engage employees and the public in visioning and planning, making superintendents more directly affected by competing values, beliefs, and biases (Kowalski, 2001).

Inadequate Financial Support

The most recent national study of school superintendents (Glass et al., 2000) reported that 97% of all superintendents viewed finance issues as a factor inhibiting school effectiveness (p. 68). The sentiment expressed by these administrators also was articulated by board members; 35% said that finance issues constituted the most serious problem they faced (p. 66). For casual observers, financial resources may appear relatively unimportant to schooling, but to those who build, approve, and manage budgets, resources are paramount.

Table 12.1   School Finance Policy Concerns from a Values Perspective

Value	Finance Policy Concern
Adequacy	Most school districts lack sufficient resources to deliver necessary services and to implement best practices. Consequently, superintendents consistently cite a lack of financial resources as a primary problem (Glass et al., 2000).
Efficiency	Two different perspectives of the financial condition of public schools have been expressed by policymakers. One is predicated on the belief that outputs will not be increased appreciably without increased funding. The other is that outputs can be increased simply by forcing public schools to compete with each other and with private schools (Brimley & Garfield, 2005).
Liberty	Local control remains a widely supported value in public education. Efforts to shift the burden of school funding away from local tax revenues (primarily an ad valorem property tax) are often resisted on the premise that doing so would attenuate community control and increase state government control. Yet, the ability (i.e., taxable wealth) and willingness (i.e., tax effort) of school district residents to support public education is typically very uneven within a given state. Liberty, and thus local control, has been protected largely by political forces (King et al., 2003).
Equality	Reliance on district generated tax revenues has contributed to substantial differences in education spending among local districts in virtually all states. Litigation in more than 40 states has forced state legislatures to revamp funding policy to achieve greater equity. Yet, the courts have consistently ruled that some degree of inequality is necessary and acceptable to maintain liberty (Kowalski & Schmielau, 2001).

Several studies (e.g., Crampton & Whitney, 1996; Thompson, 1990) have shown that the 50 states have less-than-uniform laws and policies addressing public school financing. This is to be expected because public education is a state responsibility, and as such, relevant laws and policies are shaped by state constitutions. Funding formulas and revenue distributions, however, are also influenced by widely accepted values, most notably, by adequacy, liberty, equality, and efficiency. These values were discussed in detail in Chapter 7. Each value presents financial concerns as shown in Table 12.1.

Although concerns about adequacy are most apparent, tensions between liberty and equality also present a serious challenge to superintendents (King et al., 2003). On the one hand, administrators are expected to protect liberty by preventing excessive federal and state interventions that could erode local control. On the other hand, they have a legal and professional responsibility to ensure equal education opportunities for students. Consider the dilemma facing a superintendent in a low-wealth district. To protect liberty, the superintendent is expected to take the position that district residents have the right to control tax rates and spending; to protect equality, the superintendent is expected to take measures to ensure that the state meets its responsibility to fund education equally across districts. In many states, litigation filed on behalf of students in low-wealth districts has divided superintendents, pitting residents in low-wealth districts against those in high-wealth districts. Tensions between liberty and equality also can produce internal conflict for superintendents if they are torn between protecting the political interests of local taxpayers and acting ethically to protect the rights of all students.

The causes underlying inadequate funding are often difficult to diagnose because they are an intricate mix of philosophical, political, and economic issues. The consequences, though, are apparent. Scarce resources have required superintendents to make unpopular and painful decisions, such as closing schools, eliminating extracurricular activities and academic programs, increasing class sizes, reducing the district's workforce (including terminating teachers and administrators), and curtailing the acquisition of essential instructional equipment and materials. Even when they are able to sidestep these unpleasant decisions, they never escape the continuous conflict resulting from competition among special interest groups (Wirt & Kirst, 2001).

Although state litigation has required changes in funding formulas, directly or indirectly (King et al., 2003), the extent to which overall wealth and spending disparities have been diminished remains in question. Many superintendents, and especially those employed in low-wealth districts, face the dilemma of administering on an "uneven playing field"; that is, they are expected to match—or at least approximate—the outcomes of wealthier and less problem-ridden districts. For example, voters in low-wealth districts understandably resist tax increases when the proposed rates are higher than those in surrounding districts. Consequently, superintendents in low-wealth districts must devote an inordinate amount of time to educating the public and to building political support for necessary tax increases. District wealth also can influence superintendent vulnerability. For instance, taxpayers in low-wealth districts often recognize that critical needs are not being met but do not understand the underlying causes. Often it is easier to blame the superintendent for mismanaging resources than it is to recognize that schools are greatly underfunded.

Efforts to compensate for inadequate financing also involve risk. The following are examples of initiatives superintendents have pursued:

- *Local education foundations*—these are not-for-profit, tax-exempt community-based organizations functioning as third parties that generate revenues primarily from private gifts, businesses, and other foundations. According to the Iowa School Boards Association (2004), nearly half the districts in that state have helped to develop such an entity. Nationally, it is estimated that there are between 2,500 and 3,000 local education foundations facilitating the efforts of approximately 15% of all districts. Superintendents almost always are connected directly to these foundations, typically as a member of the governing board. The primary foci of community education foundations have been reform planning and implementation of reform initiatives.
- *Solicitation of goods, services, and money*—superintendents have pursued both direct and indirect donations. Most commonly, these donations have been tied to partnership programs and focused on special projects because they are not ongoing contributions (Addonizio, 2000).
- *Enterprise activities*—including activities such as leasing buildings or space within buildings (Addonizio, 2000). Many districts, for example, have started charging user fees to community groups who use schools during the evenings and vacation periods (Kowalski, 2002). One of the most popular and controversial efforts is contracting with companies for exclusive vending rights in schools. A growing number of districts have entered into agreements with major soft drink companies giving them exclusive distribution and advertising rights.

The long-term merits of alternative funding are yet to be determined. Some enterprise ideas, such as contracts with soft drink companies, already have been heavily criticized.

Finally, pressures stemming from inadequate funding have intensified markedly in the context of school reform. Often, new initiatives are not funded or only partially funded, resulting in local districts being asked to do more without a corresponding increase in resources.

INSTITUTIONAL CHALLENGES

Some of the major problems superintendents encounter are organizational in nature. Two involve institutional mission and vision. Mission pertains to the purposes of a school district; vision pertains to an image of what the district should like at some point in the future in meeting its mission. These two statements have often been confused or treated superficially and the consequences have been relatively minor. Today, however, the stakes are much higher because the statements are foundational to local improvement plans and because the statements should reflect community consensus.

Building Mission and Vision Statements

In the past, the mission of public school districts was taken for granted and visions essentially were ignored. The notion that the primary purpose of schools was to serve the nation by preparing numerate and literate citizens and workers by institutionalizing prevailing cultural norms, values, beliefs, and attitudes was an enduring theme of public schooling throughout the 19th and 20th centuries. The nation embraced three philosophical tenets that reflected a relationship between schools and society:

- *Reproduction*—the conservation and transmission of knowledge and culture (norms, values and beliefs), and traditions from one generation to the next.
- *Readjustment*—appropriately modifying pedagogy and curriculum in response to demographic, social, economic, and political changes experienced by society.
- *Reconstruction*—schools are viewed as agents of social change and are expected to anticipate and proactively position schools to continuously serve society well (Johnson, Collins, Dupuis, & Johnson, 1988).

During the formative years of American public education, the reproductive role dominated how people viewed education. As the needs of society and individuals in communities changed over time, the readjustment and reconstruction roles became increasingly prominent (Kowalski, 2003a). Although each role may be more important during particular eras than at other times, all remain highly relevant to the intrinsic function of schools in American society. The notion of reproduction (conservation, continuity and stability in society) inherently conflicts with the notion of reconstruction (proactive change). In other words, schools are expected to simultaneously ensure stability and change in society; hence, teachers, principals, and superintendents often believe that regardless of what they do, they are wrong.

Despite the fact that philosophical disputes over the purposes of education have not been resolved, the contemporary superintendent has been given the assignments of preparing an accurate mission statement and forging a relevant vision statement. A mission statement describes the overall purpose of the school district. Properly developed, it should describe the school district's reason for existing. Largely because states have imposed a mission on public schools, many superintendents have underestimated the power of a properly prepared district-specific statement (Coleman & Brockmeier, 1997). District mission statements serve multiple purposes, including informing the public and employees, cultivating unity of purpose, providing a frame of reference for strategic planning goals, and guiding difficult decisions (e.g., resource allocation decisions). Although states determine a common mission for their public school districts, school boards and superintendents must extend that basic mission to reflect commonly accepted purposes of the local community. As an example, not all school districts offer the same levels of extracurricular activities, adult education, and vocational education.

Effective mission statements are characterized by three attributes: (a) an explicit statement of purpose, (b) defining characteristics that distinguish the district from other districts, and (c) defining values that are shared by the publics comprising the district. Moreover, they should be clearly written, concise, widely accepted, continuously pursued, and periodically revised. The last two descriptors capture the reason why this task challenges superintendents. The process must be inclusive and ongoing.

In the realm of present reform strategies, the topics of visioning and strategic planning also have taken center stage (Scoolis, 1998). Visioning provides a mental image of what a district should look like in meeting its mission at some point in the future (Kowalski, 2003a). Experts suggest that district visions should be collective (i.e., the aggregate view of all district publics) and developed through consensus (Tomal, 1997). Many states now require school districts to develop a *visionary strategic plan* for school improvement.

The challenge of building a coherent and acceptable district vision requires both assessment and evaluation. The former is undeniably the easier task and involves identifying and predicting needs and community wants. The latter is far more difficult and subjective because it entails interpreting and prioritizing the identified needs and wants—that is, it is both rational and emotional. This difficult assignment is exemplified by current controversies surrounding alternative and vocational schools. While many educators and parents agree on the need to provide alternative education for many students not succeeding in the regular program, they typically disagree as to nature and purpose of alternative schooling (Gregory, 2001; Raywid, 1994). Similarly, needs assessments regularly produce evidence that vocational education is warranted, but uncertainty about the future and parental resistance often alter the extent to which these programs are developed and the nature of curriculum when they are offered (Lewis, 2000).

Unfortunately, a cursory inspection of district mission, vision, and strategic planning documents may reveal fundamental problems. In many instances, mission and vision have been confused (Rozycki, 2004); for example, mission is presented in the future tense and described as a vision. In addition, parents and employees may see no connections between mission and vision statements; accordingly, they pay little attention to either. In the midst of these negative conditions, underlying attitudes that change is unattainable are reinforced (Fullan, 2001). Both mission and vision are shaped by community and organizational cultures, which explains why the task is so difficult. Developing accurate and effective statements requires the superintendent to identify shared beliefs and to alter those beliefs if they obstruct school improvement.

Changing Organizational Culture

Beginning in the late 1970s (Finn, 1991), the current reform movement has evolved through several stages in which perceived problems, change strategies, and proposed solutions have been altered (Kowalski, 1998, 2003a). During much of the 1980s and 1990s, the superintendent's role in school improvement was largely overlooked (Berg & Barnett, 1998), primarily because change initiatives focused on intensifying elements of curriculum, instructional methods, or standards for teaching (Kowalski, 2003a). Today, superintendents are expected to assume a variety of roles when leading and managing school improvement efforts (Carter & Cunningham, 1997; Norton, Webb, Dlugosh, & Sybouts, 1996). As school boards focus more directly on developing improvement goals and strategies to achieve them (Glass, 2001), superintendents must decide when it is appropriate to lead, to manage, to facilitate, and to compromise (Kowalski, 2001). More challenging, they must make the decision while dealing with politics, the education of children, public disillusionment, incivility, and increased demands for community participation (Berg & Barnett, 1998).

Moving the reform policy arena to local communities has magnified the importance of community and institutional cultures. Noting this fact, analysts (e.g., Bauman, 1996; Sarason, 1996) have concluded that school systems will not improve unless the influence of prevalent change-resistant cultures is attenuated. As examples, educators in many schools still believe that they are more productive by virtue of working individually and in seclusion (Gideon, 2002) and that schools are more productive when they prevent community interventions (Blase & Anderson, 1995). Such beliefs are at the core of a school's culture—the shared fundamental values that inform employees how to address their work (Schein, 1996; Trimble, 1996) and how they should promote and accept change (Duke, 2004; Leithwood, Jantzi, & Fernandez, 1994). Schein (1992) argues that highly effective organizations have replaced change-resistant cultures with *learning cultures*—belief systems built "on the assumption that communication and information are central to organizational well-being and must therefore create a multi-channel communication system that allows everyone to connect to everyone else" (p. 370).

Unfortunately, many superintendents have reacted to reform demands rather than accepting the responsibility of being a change agent. Lacking a vision of the district's ideal future, their methods and goals often were unconnected (Haberman, 1994). Sarason (1996) concluded that administrators had not produced needed change because they understood neither organizational culture nor the processes necessary for changing it. Lacking this knowledge, they succumbed to convenience by attempting to replicate reforms instituted in other school districts (Kowalski, 2003a). Fullan (1999) noted that this alternative routinely failed because contextual variables, the district's capacity for change, and organizational culture were ignored.

Changing organizational culture is difficult because deeply embedded basic assumptions are often extremely difficult to identify (Firestone & Louis, 1999). For example, most teachers and principals may believe that a certain percentage of students are destined to fail, but they never articulate this conviction. A district's culture not only shapes perspectives on student learning, it also affects decision-making norms, attitudes toward problem solving (e.g., the value of research), and relationships (both among educators and between educators and others) (Joyce & Murphy, 1990). To change negative beliefs (i.e., convictions incongruous with the professional knowledge base and counterproductive to school improvement), a superintendent must first bring underlying values to the surface so they can be discussed, and then demonstrate why they are counterproductive (Fullan, 2001). These difficult assignments require a superintendent to be credible and trusted.

The nexus between school reform and organizational culture is demonstrated by a common occurrence with imposed change. Initially, employees who philosophically reject new ideas or procedures mask their feelings and engage in spiteful obedience. Once they sense that the pressure to change has subsided, they revert to their standard practices. This reversion also explains why staff development often is unsuccessful in relation to school reform; if underlying beliefs are not changed, educators usually return to the tried-and-true approaches to teaching and administering (Fullan, 1999).

Culture change is a formidable challenge for several reasons. First, engaging others in open and candid discussion of values and beliefs produces conflict and although conflict is now "seen as inevitable, endemic, and often legitimate"

(Owens, 2001, p. 308) by organizational theorists, educators traditionally have been socialized to avoid confrontations (Conforti, 1976). Second, culture change is very time-consuming. Experts (e.g., Fullan, 2001; Schein, 1992) believe that the process takes at least several years to accomplish. Third, instability in the superintendency often discourages practitioners from pursuing culture change. Not knowing how long they will remain in their current position, many practitioners have opted to pursue easier and more overt changes (e.g., remodeling schools, implementing a new mathematics curriculum, or reorganizing the administrative staff) (Kowalski, 1995).

PROFESSIONAL CHALLENGES

Some of the difficulties associated with superintendents are embedded in the education profession. Here we find both quantitative and qualitative issues related to recruiting and sustaining a sufficient supply of competent practitioners. From a qualitative standpoint, preparation and licensing have emerged as pivotal issues. The qualitative dimension has focused not only on the competence of superintendents, but also on the degree to which superintendents are representative of society and the profession. Frequently, practitioners pay less attention to challenges facing their profession because their consequences do not appear to affect the superintendents' practice. In truth, decisions made about the recruitment, preparation, and licensing of superintendents are likely to shape practice directly in the coming decade.

Adequate Supply of Qualified Superintendents

Since the early 1990s, claims of a critical shortage of school superintendents have been widely accepted. Two sources of evidence have often been used to bolster this claim: declining size of applicant pools and an increasing level of position instability. Data supporting declining applicant pools have been produced primarily by survey research conducted with superintendents (e.g., Cooper, Fusarelli, & Carella, 2000; Cunningham & Burdick, 1999), search consultants (e.g., Glass, 2001b; O'Connell, 2000; Rohn, 2001), state superintendents and association directors (e.g., Glass, 2001a), and school board members (e.g., Cox & Malone, 2001; Rohn, 2001). Such studies, however, have been based largely on respondent opinions and not on empirical data showing the actual levels of decline. Even so, smaller applicant pools do not amount to a critical occupational shortage (Kowalski, 2003b). Historically, the supply of licensed administrators has exceeded the number of positions available and this fact resulted in unusually large pools during the last half of the 20th century. For example, a study in the late 1970s (McCarthy, Kuh, & Zent, 1981) reported an oversupply of administrators in all areas except special education directors and federal program directors. A national study of search consultants conducted much more recently (Glass, 2001b) found the size of applicant pools for superintendencies to average approximately 30. The study's author concluded, "Applicant pools are not as small as depicted in media accounts" (p. 9).

The most common error made with respect to declaring an occupational shortage occurs when employers are displeased with a perceived deterioration in the caliber of applicants. This error is commonly found in situations where employers demand high quality but are unwilling to improve compensation or working conditions to attract the level of candidates they desire. In such situations, employers often proclaim that an occupational shortage forced them to settle for a person who does "not match their notion of the 'ideal'" (Veneri, 1999, p. 15). The perception of a shortage is tied to the fact that political—not economic—criteria have determined superintendent salaries in most districts. That is, school boards usually have set salary ceilings based on community standards and not market realities (Speer, 1996). When compared to their counterparts in private industry, superintendents are poorly compensated (Cunningham & Sperry, 2001). Although applicant pool reductions understandably bother board members who wish to retain their long-standing advantage in setting administrative salaries politically, they do not verify a shortage of superintendents.

With respect to the average tenure of superintendents, the conclusion that the position has become increasingly unstable is basically unwarranted. The actual length of time a superintendent spends in one position has remained amazingly stable over the past several decades, ranging from 6 years in 1971 (Knezevich, 1971) to 5.6 years in 1982 (Cunningham & Hentges, 1982), to 6.4 years in 1992 (Glass, 1992) and 6.7 years in 2000 (Glass et al., 2000). In addition, recent data reveal that superintendents are generally satisfied in their current positions (Glass et al., 2000) and are remaining in their careers, retiring later than during previous decades (Cooper et al., 2000). Although some districts have extreme difficulty finding and retaining highly qualified practitioners, others clearly do not. The nature of the community, the quality of the employing organization, resources, and the governing board are contextual variables that influence application rates and retention, not only in public education, but across all types of organizations and professions (Kowalski, 2003b).

The issue of supply has obvious connections to public policy regulating the practice of school administration. Consider just two examples: state pension policies and deregulation of school administration. Several states have enacted laws allowing superintendents to retire prematurely and to return to practice in the same state (in some instances even with the same employer) while drawing a full pension. The underlying rationale for this legislation has been a purported shortage of qualified practitioners advanced primarily by educators and their state and national organizations (Kowalski & Sweetland, 2002, in press). Using pension funds to manipulate the supply and demand of education, however, has a dark side. In Ohio, the rehiring of administrators and teachers has generated both professional and political concerns. From a professional perspective, concerns range from negative consequences on the state pension fund (e.g., the health insurance fund in the state retirement system is expected to be depleted unless current policy is amended) to producing disincentives for educators to become administrators (e.g., the number of vacancies in highly attractive jobs is diminished because practitioners in them are retiring and then being rehired). From a political perspective, concerns have ranged from board control over rehiring (e.g., a number of districts have already negotiated provisions with teacher unions over rehiring) to diminished taxpayer support for school systems (e.g., when taxpayers are informed of the total income of rehired superintendents, their reactions often are negative) (Kowalski & Sweetland, 2002).

The second example of misguided policy involves attempts to deregulate school administration. Recently, for example, a national document, *Better Leaders for America's Schools: A Manifesto* (Broad Foundation & Thomas B. Fordham Institute, 2003), has advocated eliminating superintendent licensing, or at least making licensing voluntary. Advocates argue that there are countless retired military officers and corporate executives willing to become superintendents if they are spared the indignity of having to complete professional preparation and passing licensing examinations. If the floodgates are opened to these individuals, society can solve the purported shortage problem rather easily. These arguments, preposterous to most experienced administrators, are beginning to take their toll. Of the 41 states that still require preparation and licensing for superintendents, 22 (54%) allow waivers or emergency certificates to be issued and 15 (37%) allow or sanction alternative routes to licensure (i.e., other than university-based study) (Feistritzer, 2003).

Every present and future superintendent needs to take a position on the profession's future. Decisions on this matter are complicated by self-interests (e.g., perpetuating the myth of a shortage for personal reasons) and political pressures (e.g., agreeing with political elites who seek to deregulate public education). Three alternative futures are possible: the profession can be deregulated, allowing virtually anyone with a college degree and clean criminal background to occupy this pivotal position; the profession can survive the current attacks and emerge intact; the profession can reform itself, thus responding to legitimate criticisms that have deterred the profession's stature and practitioner efficacy (Kowalski, 2004).

In Chapter 2, practice in the superintendency was analyzed by examining five cogent role characterizations. Policy decisions about preparing and licensing superintendents in the future should be framed by such data and not by emotional or purely political arguments. Table 12.2 summarizes the knowledge and skills required for each of these roles. Although two sets of standards (those developed by the American Association of School Administrators [AASA] and those developed by the Interstate School Leaders Licensure Consortium [ISLLC]) have largely captured the knowledge, skills, and dispositions required for practice (see Table 12.3), such criteria have not discouraged antiprofessionists from continuing their crusade to deregulate the practice of school administration (Kowalski, 2004).

Table 12.2   Knowledge and Skills Associated With Superintendent Role Conceptualizations

Role	Pertinent Knowledge and Skills
Teacher-scholar	Pedagogy; educational psychology; curriculum; instructional supervision; staff development; educational philosophy
Manager	Law; personnel administration; finance/budgeting; facility development/maintenance; collective bargaining/contract maintenance; public relations
Democratic leader	Community relations; collaborative decision making; politics
Applied social scientist	Quantitative and qualitative research; behavioral sciences
Communicator	Verbal communication; written communication; listening; public speaking; media relations
Multirole*	Motivation; organizational theory; organizational change and development; leadership theory; ethical/moral administration; technology and its applications; diversity/multiculturalism; human relations

*This category includes knowledge and skills pertinent to all or nearly all roles.

Table 12.3 Interface of Knowledge and Skills and the AASA and ISLLC Standards

Role and Pertinent Knowledge/Skills	AASA Standard	ISLLC Standard
Teacher-scholar		
Pedagogy	6	2
Educational psychology	6	2
Curriculum	5	2
Instructional supervision	6	2, 5
Staff development	6, 7	2
Educational philosophy/history	2	5
Manager		
School law	2, 4, 7	3, 6
Personnel administration	7	3
Finance/budgeting	4	3
Facility development/maintenance	4	3
Collective bargaining/contract maintenance	4, 7	3, 5
Public relations	3, 4	3, 6
Democratic leader		
Community relations	3	1, 4, 6
Collaborative decision making	1, 2	1, 4
Politics	1, 2, 8	1, 6
Governance	2	6
Applied social scientist		
Quantitative and qualitative research	4, 5	1
Behavioral sciences	1, 8	4, 6
Measurement and evaluation	5, 6	2
Communicator		
Verbal communication	3	1, 4, 6
Written communication	3	1, 4, 6
Media relations	3, 8	6
Listening	3	1, 6
Public speaking	3	1, 6
*Multirole**		
Motivation	5, 6, 7	2
Organizational theory	1, 2, 7	1, 2, 5
Organizational change and development	1	1, 4, 6
Leadership theory	1	1, 2, 5
Ethical/moral administration	8	5
Technology and its applications	3, 4, 6	2, 3
Diversity/multiculturalism	1, 3, 8	1, 2, 4
Conflict management	1, 2	1, 4, 6

*This category includes knowledge and skills pertinent to all or nearly all roles.

Underrepresentation in the Superintendency

Although democratic societies have championed egalitarian practices for more than a century and have emancipated women and people of color in society, White males continue to hold the vast majority of executive positions in public and private organizations. In fact, the superintendency may be the most male-dominated profession in the United States (Glass et al., 2000). Since 1900, the percentage of women in the superintendency has varied considerably. For example in 1910, 8.9% of school superintendents were female; this increased to 11% by 1930. Rates then began a steady decline to 9% in 1950, before precipitously declining to 1.3% in 1971 and hitting an historic low of 1.2% in 1982 (Blount, 1998). In 1992, however, the number of women superintendents rose to 6.6% and climbed to 13.2% in 2000—the highest level achieved since 1900. Women made the greatest gains in suburban/urban districts serving between 3,000 and 24,999 students; representation in these districts increased nearly threefold, moving from 5% in 1992 to 14.1% in 2000. Equally noteworthy, however, 68% of these female superintendents were employed in districts with fewer than 2,999 students and 71% were employed in their first superintendency (Glass et al., 2000).

Figures for female superintendents are disturbing in light of the education profession's demographics. For example, women comprise 65% of teachers, 43% of principals (Shakeshaft, 1999), 57% of central office administrators, and 33% of the assistant and associate superintendents (Hodgkinson & Montenegro, 1999, pp. 113–115), but less than 15% of superintendents. Although women have made progress at all levels of school administration since 1990, their inroads have been most limited with respect to the high school principalship and superintendency (Hodgkinson & Montenegro, 1999).

The career paths of male and female superintendents differ. Women are likely to have been elementary teachers, district instructional coordinators, assistant superintendents, and high school teachers, whereas men are more likely to have been high school principals (51% for men and only 18.5% for women) (Brunner, 2000). Unfortunately, central office staff positions often do not provide opportunities for women to gain experience in finance, administration, and community relations, areas viewed by 80% of superintendents as essential to their success (Glass et al., 2000). Research (e.g., Anderson, 2000; Kowalski & Stouder, 1999) reveals that family support and positive self-image are often identified as critical factors by women who have become superintendents.

Although most information on the representation of racial and ethnic minorities in the superintendency tends to focus on African Americans, studies of Hispanics in school administration (Ortiz, 1998; Quilantan, 2002) and findings from national studies have expanded the understanding of the diversity. Early historical reports on African Americans in the superintendency from 1930 to 1950 suggest their representation was sparse and was concentrated in predominantly southern states where districts served African American populations exclusively or primarily (Collier, 1987). The tendency of different racial backgrounds serving in areas where persons of the same race live in significant numbers is supported by the American Association of School Administrator's report, *Women and Racial Minority Representation in School Administration* (Montenegro, 1993).

Although the representation of people of color in the superintendency remains shamefully small, it has increased since 1980. For example, in 1980, 2.1% of those serving in the position were in this demographic group (Cunningham & Hentges, 1982). Representation increased to 3.9% in 1992, however, nearly half (46%) of these superintendents served in urban districts with more than 50,000 students (Glass, 1992). The most recent national study, disaggregated data on racial and ethnic groups, reported that slightly over 5% of superintendents were people of color: 2.2% African American, 1.4% Hispanic, 0.8% Native American, 0.2% Asian American, and 0.5% Other. The modal placements of superintendents of color are large/urban or small town/rural districts (Glass et al., 2000).

Although the percentage of superintendents classified as racial and ethnic minorities increased by 31% between 1990 and 1999 (Glass et al., 2000), many practitioners in this demographic group are concerned that the rate may plateau or decline if their presence in preparation programs declines (Björk, 1996). Increasing the number of minority candidates for the superintendency becomes more likely if there are more minority teachers, principals, and central office staff (Hodgkinson & Montenegro, 1999). Increasing representation, however, has been affected by competition from other professions; during the 1980s, doors to more lucrative professions were opened to women and people of color (Glass et al., 2000; Björk, Keedy, & Gurley, 2003).

In school administration, career patterns of persons of color are essentially unique. Although nearly 80% of White superintendents began their careers as assistant principals or principals, only 65% of persons of color have the same experience; they more frequently begin their careers at the central office level. For example, 22% of minority superintendents began their administrative careers as a director or coordinator, whereas only 13.3% of their White counterparts did so (Glass et al., 2000; Björk et al., 2003).

Issues of underrepresentation are intertwined with other professional issues, such as reforming preparation and licensing (Kowalski & Brunner, 2005). For example, deregulation, discussed previously, has been touted as an alternative for increasing minority representation. Superintendents can exert considerable influence in promoting women and people of color; women who become superintendents often point to collegial support as a critical factor (Keller, 1999). Such support is provided by superintendents when they serve as mentors or sponsors and when they initiate recruitment and employment activities designed to increase the number of women and people of color in administrative positions. For the majority of White, male practitioners, the issue of underrepresentation may appear irrelevant, but in truth, the manner in which this challenge is addressed will have far reaching consequences for the profession. This point is especially important in light of the fact that men and women in the superintendency appear dissimilar in many ways, ranging from dominant political preferences to career paths to perceptions of career barriers (Glass et al., 2000).

FOR FURTHER REFLECTION

This chapter examined selected examples of contemporary challenges facing superintendents and demonstrated how social, institutional, and professional conditions can affect the future. As you contemplate your administrative career, you should consider your dispositions toward these and other contemporary issues. In addition, you should ask yourself if you are willing to play an active role in addressing these common problems.

As you consider what you read in this chapter, answer the following questions:

1. What factors have contributed to heightened political activity in public education?

2. Why is heightened political activity a challenge for superintendents?

3. In what ways do the conflicting values of liberty and equality affect issues of adequate financing for public education?

4. What political and professional challenges are created for superintendents as a result of inadequate financing?

5. What are the differences between a district's mission and its vision?

6. What is a school district culture?

7. Why is culture change essential to school reform? Why is it so difficult to accomplish?

8. Because a purported shortage of superintendents works to the political advantage of practitioners, why should they be challenged by this claim?

9. Do you agree that retirement policy and attempts to deregulate administrator licensing are tied to the purported shortage of practitioners? Why or why not?

10. The percentage of female superintendents has increased markedly since the 1970s. Why do many still claim that women are underrepresented in the position?

11. From a professional perspective, why should all superintendents be concerned about the underrepresentation of people of color in this position?

Case Study

Dr. Rachel Watson became superintendent of Washington Heights School District (WHSD) two years ago. She is an experienced educator, having served as a teacher for 16 years and an elementary school principal for 8 years. She came to Washington Heights from a neighboring district, so she was quite aware of the problems she would face. The school system serves a small community on the fringe of a large metropolitan area. Developed after World War II, the community consists of modest homes developed by a steel company to provide inexpensive housing for its employees. Over the past two decades, the small suburb has lost 15% of its population and the average family income has declined by 13%.

Ever since the school district was created, superintendents have faced financial problems stemming from a low property tax base. The steel mill that built more than 50% of the houses was located in the adjacent city district and did not generate tax revenue for the WHSD directly. In addition, there has never been more than a handful of businesses paying property tax in the district and consequently; approximately 90% of the revenue from this tax comes from residential property—much of it small, single-family dwellings that are more than 50 years old.

Dr. Watson's financial woes are exacerbated by the needs of her students. Nearly 75% qualified for free and reduced lunches; between 15% and 20% have been classified as special needs students; the dropout rate is the fifth highest in the state; only 11% of last year's high school graduating class entered college; 43% of the district's students scored below the acceptable standard on last year's state proficiency tests.

The district's five school buildings are in poor condition and referenda to support facility improvement have failed five times in the past nine years. After the last failed referendum, a political action group, spearheaded by several local ministers, began waging a campaign to merge WHSD with the adjacent city school system. The group's leaders argue that the merger would raise the assessed valuation per pupil and help resolve facility problems. The city school system has lost 30% of its enrollment since 1970 and several school buildings in reasonably good condition stand empty. The merger initiative received little attention until the school board and superintendent in the city school system announced they would agree to the merger.

State law governing school district mergers requires (a) that all involved school boards approve the merger; (b) that a plan for distributing school board membership in the new district is approved by the state board of education; and (c) that a plan stipulating the status of all personnel in the affected districts is approved by the state board of education. The proposed merger has divided the Washington Heights community, including the WHSD employees and school board. The teachers' union endorses the merger, largely because it assumes its members would benefit from being placed on the city system's salary schedule, which is approximately 7% higher than their present salary schedule. The district's 12 administrators oppose the merger, fearing that many of them will be demoted to lower administrative positions or returned to the classroom. Among the five board members, two support the merger, two oppose it, and one remains undecided. The undecided board member happens to be Dr. Watson's most avid supporter and she has told the other board members that she will not take a position on the merger until the superintendent presents a formal recommendation.

As the merger debate intensifies, both board factions are pressuring the superintendent to side with them. They also want her to persuade the remaining board member to do likewise. Dr. Watson has told the board members that she is conducting research on the proposed merger and will prepare a recommendation when she finishes her study. She outlined a number of matters that needed scrutiny and estimated that she might not be ready to make a recommendation for at least six months. The four board members who already have decided how they will vote found her timeline to be unacceptable. They were told by the school attorney that actually implementing the merger could take 12 to 16 months after it is officially approved by the two school boards and the state. Consequently, a motion was made to require the superintendent to make a recommendation within 45 days; the motion passed by a margin of four to one.

Case Study Questions

1. If you were Dr. Watson, what factors would you weigh in formulating a recommendation on the merger?

2. What arguments could the superintendent make against the proposed merger?

3. What arguments could she make in favor of the proposed merger?

4. In what ways do inadequate finances contribute to the problem facing Dr. Watson?

5. Could the state have taken action to avoid the financial problems of the WHSD? If so, what are those actions?

6. One alternative for deciding this matter would be a referendum; that is, the voters in the district, rather than the school board, could make the decision. Would this be a good idea? Why or why not?

7. Both factions want Dr. Watson to influence the undecided board member. Should a superintendent engage in persuasion? If so, under what conditions?

REFERENCES

Addonizio, M. F. (2000). Private funds for public schools. *Clearing House, 74*(2), 70–74.

Anderson, D. M. (2000). Strategies used by women superintendents in overcoming occupational barriers. *Planning and Changing, 31*(1/2), 21–34.

Bauman, P. C. (1996). *Governing education: Public sector reform or privatization.* Boston: Allyn and Bacon.

Berg, J. H., & Barnett, B. G. (1998, April). *The school district superintendent: Attention must be paid.* Paper presented at the annual meeting of the American Educational Research Association, San Diego, CA.

Björk, L. G. (1996). Educational reform in changing contexts of families and communities: Leading school-interagency collaboration. In K. Lane & M. Richardson (Eds.), *The school safety handbook: Taking action for student and staff protection* (pp. 253–275). Lancaster, PA: Technomic.

Björk, L., Keedy, J., & Gurley, D. K. (2003). Career paths of superintendents: Results from the study of the American superintendency. *Journal of School Leadership, 13*(4), 406–442.

Björk, L., Kowalski, T., & Young, M. (in press). National education reform reports: Implications for professional preparation and development. In L. Björk & T. Kowalski (Eds.), *The contemporary superintendent: Preparation, practice and development.* Thousand Oaks, CA: Corwin.

Blase, J., & Anderson, G. (1995). *The micropolitics of educational leadership: From control to empowerment.* New York: Teachers College Press.

Blount, J. M. (1998). *Destined to rule the schools: Women and the superintendency, 1873–1995.* Albany: State University of New York Press.

Blumberg, A. (1985). *The school superintendent: Living with conflict.* New York: Teachers College Press.

Brimley, V., & Garfield, R. R. (2005). *Financing education in a climate of change* (9th ed.). Boston: Allyn and Bacon.

Broad Foundation & Thomas B. Fordham Institute (2003). *Better leaders for America's schools: A manifesto.* Los Angeles: Authors.

Brunner, C. C. (2000). Female superintendents. In T. E. Glass, L. Björk, & C. C. Brunner (Eds.), *The study of the American school superintendency 2000: A look at the superintendent of education in the new millennium* (pp. 77–125). Arlington, VA: American Association of School Administrators.

Carter, G. R., & Cunningham, W. G. (1997), *The American superintendent: Leading in an age of pressure.* San Francisco: Jossey-Bass.

Chubb, J. E., & Moe, T. (1990). *Politics, markets and America's schools.* Washington, DC: The Brookings Institute.

Coleman, D. G., & Brockmeier, J. (1997). A mission possible: Relevant mission statements. *School Administrator, 54*(5), 36–37.

Collier, V. (1987). *Identification of skills perceived by Texas superintendents as necessary for successful job performance.* Unpublished doctoral dissertation, University of Texas, Austin.

Conforti, J. M. (1976). The socialization of teachers: A case study. *Theory Into Practice, 15*(5), 352–359.

Cooper, B. S., Fusarelli, L. D., & Carella, V. A. (2000). *Career crisis in the superintendency? The results of a national survey.* Arlington VA: American Association of School Administrators.

Cox, E. P., & Malone, B. G. (2001). Making the right choice. *American School Board Journal, 188*(7), 40–41.

Crampton, F., & Whitney, T. (1996). *The search for equity in school funding.* NCSL Education Partners Project. Denver, CO: National Conference of State Legislatures.

Cuban, L. (1985). Conflict and leadership in the superintendency. *Phi Delta Kappan, 67*(1), 28–30.

Cunningham, L. L., & Hentges, J. T. (1982). *The American School Superintendency.* Arlington, VA: American Association of School Administration.

Cunningham, W. G., & Burdick, G. R. (1999). Empty offices. *American School Board Journal, 186*(12), 25–26, 27–30.

Cunningham, W. G., & Sperry, J. B. (2001). Where's the beef in administrator pay? *School Administrator, 58*(2), 32–36.

Darling-Hammond, L. (1988). The futures of teaching. *Educational Leadership, 16*(3), 4–10.

Duke, D. (2004). *The challenge of educational change.* Boston: Allyn & Bacon.

Feistritzer, E. (2003). *Certification of public-school administrators.* Washington, DC: The National Center for Education Information.

Finn, C. E. (1991). *We must take charge.* New York: The Free Press.

Firestone, W. A., & Louis, K. S. (1999). Schools as cultures. In J. Murphy and K. S. Louis (Eds.), *Handbook of research on educational administration* (2nd ed., pp. 297–322). San Francisco: Jossey-Bass.

Fullan, M. (1999). *Change forces: The sequel.* Philadelphia: Falmer.

Fullan, M. (2001). *Leading in a culture of change.* San Francisco: Jossey-Bass.

Gideon, B. H. (2002). Structuring schools for teacher collaboration. *Education Digest, 68*(2), 30–34.

Glass, T. E. (1992). *The study of the American school superintendency: America's education leaders in a time of reform.* Arlington, VA: American Association of School Administrators.

Glass, T. E. (2001*).* *Superintendent leaders look at the superintendency, school boards and reform.* Denver, CO: Education Commission of the States,

Glass, T. E. (2001a). *State education leaders view the superintendent applicant crisis.* Denver, CO: Education Commission of the States.

Glass, T. E. (2001b). *The superintendent crisis: A review by search consultants.* Denver, CO: Education Commission of the States.

Glass, T. E. (2004). Changes in schools and society. In T. J. Kowalski (Ed.), *Public relations in schools* (2nd ed., pp. 30–46). Upper Saddle River, NJ: Merrill, Prentice Hall.

Glass, T. E., Björk, L., & Brunner, C. C. (2000). *The study of the American superintendency 2000: A look at the superintendent of education in the new millennium.* Arlington, VA: American Association of School Administrators.

Gregory, T. (2001). Fear of success? Ten ways alternative schools pull their punches. *Phi Delta Kappan, 82*(8), 577–581.

Haberman, M. (1994). The top 10 fantasies of school reformers. *Phi Delta Kappan, 75*(9), 689–692.

Hanson, E. M. (2003). *Educational administration and organizational behavior* (5th ed.). Boston: Allyn and Bacon.

Hodgkinson, H. L. (1991). Reform versus reality. *Phi Delta Kappan, 73*(1), 8–16.

Hodgkinson, H., & Montenegro, X. (1999). *The U.S. school superintendent: The invisible CEO*. Washington, DC: Institute for Educational Leadership.

Hoy, W. K., & Miskel, C. G. (2005). *Educational administration: Theory, research, and practice* (7th ed.). New York: McGraw-Hill.

Iowa School Boards Association (2004). *School foundations on the rise*. Retrieved on September 27, 2004 at http://www.ia-sb.org/finance/foundations.asp

Johnson, J. A., Collins, H. W., Dupuis, V. L., & Johnson, J. H. (1988). *Introduction to the foundations of American education* (7th ed.). Boston: Allyn & Bacon.

Joyce, B., & Murphy, C. (1990). Epilogue: The curious complexities of cultural change. In B. Joyce (Ed.), *Changing school culture through staff development* (pp. 243–250). Alexandria, VA: Association for Supervision and Curriculum Development.

Keller, B. (1999, November 10). Women superintendents credit support from colleagues. *Education Week, 19*(11) 25.

King, R. A., Swanson, A. D., & Sweetland, S. R. (2003). *School finance: Achieving high standards with equity and efficiency* (3rd ed.). Boston: Allyn & Bacon.

Knezevich, S. J. (1971). *The American school superintendent: An AASA research study*. Arlington, VA: American Association of School Administrators.

Kowalski, T. J. (1995). *Keepers of the flame: Contemporary urban superintendents*. Thousand Oaks, CA: Corwin.

Kowalski, T. J. (1998). The role of communication in providing leadership for school reform. *Mid-Western Educational Researcher, 11*(1), 32–40.

Kowalski, T. (1999). *The school superintendency: Theory, practice, and cases*. Upper Saddle River, NJ: Merrill-Prentice Hall.

Kowalski, T. J. (2001). The future of local school governance: Implications for board members and superintendents. In C. Brunner & L. Björk (Eds.), *The new superintendency* (pp. 183–201). Oxford, UK: JAI, Elsevier Science.

Kowalski, T. J. (2002). *Planning and managing school facilities* (2nd ed.). Westport, CT: Bergin & Garvey.

Kowalski, T. J. (2003a). *Contemporary school administration: An introduction*. Boston: Allyn & Bacon.

Kowalski, T. J. (2003b). Superintendent shortage: The wrong problem and wrong solutions. *Journal of School Leadership. 13,* 288–303.

Kowalski, T. J. (2004). The ongoing war for the soul of school administration. In T. J. Lasley (Ed.), *Better leaders for America's schools: Perspectives on the manifesto* (pp. 92–114). Columbia, MO: University Council for Educational Administration.

Kowalski, T. J., & Brunner, C. C. (2005). The school superintendent: Roles, challenges, and issues. In F. English (Ed.), *The Sage handbook of educational leadership* (pp. 142–167). Thousand Oaks, CA: Sage.

Kowalski, T. J., & Schmielau, R. E. (2001). Potential for states to provide equality in funding school construction. *Equity and Excellence in Education, 34*(2), 54–61.

Kowalski, T. J., & Stouder, J. G. (1999). Female experiences related to becoming a superintendent. *Contemporary Education, 70*(4), 32–40.

Kowalski, T. J., & Sweetland, S. R. (2002). Unrestricted reemployment of retired administrators: Effective policy or cause for concern? In G. Perreault (Ed.), *The changing world of school administration* (pp. 312–324). Lanham, MD: Scarecrow Education.

Kowalski, T. J., & Sweetland, S. R. (in press). Retire-rehire policy in state pension programs for school administrators. *Planning and Changing*.

Leithwood, K., Jantzi, D., & Fernandez, A. (1994). Transformational leadership and teachers' commitment to change. In J. Murphy & K. S. Louis (Eds.), *Reshaping the principalship* (pp. 77–98). Thousand Oaks, CA: Corwin.

Lewis, M. V. (2000). Vocational education and the dilemma of education. *Journal of Vocational Education Research, 25*(4), 575–584.

McCarthy, M., Kuh, G., & Zent, A. (1981). *Investigation of supply and demand of school administrators in six states between 1975–76 and 1979–80*. East Lansing, MI: National Center for Research on Teacher Learning. (ERIC Document Reproduction Service No. ED014280)

Montenegro, X. (1993). *Women and racial minority representation in school administration*. Arlington, VA: American Association of School Administrators.

Norton, M. S., Webb, L. D., Dlugosh, L. L., & Sybouts, W. (1996). *The school superintendency: New responsibilities, new leadership*. Boston: Allyn and Bacon.

O'Connell, R. W. (2000). *A longitudinal study of applicants for the superintendency*. East Lansing, MI: National Center for Research on Teacher Learning. (ERIC Document Reproduction Service No. ED452590)

Opfer, V. D. (2003, November). *Personalization of interest groups and the resulting policy nonsense: The Cobb County school board's evolution debate*. Paper presented at the annual meeting of the University Council for Educational Administration, Pittsburgh.

Ortiz, F. I. (1998, April). *Who controls succession in the superintendency? A minority perspective*. Paper presented at the Annual meeting of the American Educational Research Association: San Diego.

Owens, R. G. (2001). *Organizational behavior in education* (6th ed.). Boston: Allyn and Bacon.

Quilantan, M. C. (2002). *Mexican-American women: Unique superintendents in Texas*. Unpublished doctoral dissertation, University of Texas-Pan American.

Raywid, M. (1994). Alternative schools: The state of the art. *Educational Leadership, 52*(1), 26–31.

Rohn, C. (2001, August). *Superintendent shortage. Perception or reality?* Paper presented at the annual meeting of the National Council of Professors of Educational Administration, Houston.

Rowan, B., & Miskel, C. G. (1999). Institutional theory and the study of educational organizations. In J. Murphy & K. S. Louis (Eds.), *Handbook of research on educational administration* (2nd ed., pp. 359–384). San Francisco: Jossey-Bass.

Rozycki, E. G. (2004). Mission and vision in education. *Educational Horizons, 82*(2), 94–98.

Sarason, S. B. (1996). *Revisiting the culture of the school and the problem of change.* New York: Teachers College Press.

Schein, E. H. (1992). *Organizational culture and leadership* (2nd ed.). San Francisco: Jossey-Bass.

Schein, E. H. (1996). Culture: The missing concept in organization studies. *Administrative Science Quarterly, 41*(2), 229–240.

Scoolis, J. (1998). What is vision and how do you get one? *Thrust for Educational Leadership, 28*(2), 20–21.

Shakeshaft, C. (1999). The struggle to create a more gender-inclusive profession. In J. Murphy & K. S. Louis (Eds.) *Handbook of research on educational administration.* Englewood Cliffs, NJ: Prentice-Hall.

St. John, E., & Clemens, M. M. (2004). Public opinions and political contexts. In T. J. Kowalski (Ed.), *Public relations in schools* (3rd ed.) (pp. 47–67). Upper Saddle River, NJ: Merrill, Prentice Hall.

Speer, T. L. (1996). The color of money. *Executive Educator, 18*(7), 17–20.

Tomal, D. R. (1997). Collaborative process intervention: An alternative approach for school improvement. *American Secondary Education, 26,* 17–20.

Thompson, D. C. (1990). *Methods of financing educational facilities in the United States.* Report to Special Committee on School Finance, Kansas Statehouse. East Lansing, MI: National Center for Research on Teacher Learning. (ERIC Document Reproduction Service No. ED327916)

Trimble, K. (1996). Building a learning community. *Equity and Excellence in Education, 29*(1), 37–40.

U.S. Census Bureau (1999). *Dynamic diversity: Projected changes in U.S. race and ethnic composition.* Washington, DC: Author.

Veneri, C. M. (1999, March). Can occupational labor shortages be identified using available data? *Monthly Labor Review,* 15–21.

Weiler, H. N. (1990). Comparative perspectives on educational decentralization: An exercise in contradiction? *Educational Evaluation and Policy Analysis, 12*(4) 433–448.

Wirt, F. M., & Kirst, M. W. (2001). *The political dynamics of American education* (2nd ed.). Berkely, CA: McCutchan.

CHAPTER 13

Personal Practice Management

KEY FACETS OF THE CHAPTER

○ Time requirements

○ Nature of the work

○ Rewards and frustrations expressed by superintendents

○ Time management

○ Stress management

○ Decision management

○ Communication management

Nearly two decades ago, Crowson (1987) wrote, ". . . the superintendency is a position strangely awash in contradictions and anomalies and, frankly, a distinct puzzle to those who seek to make a bit of conceptual sense out of this intriguing job" (pp. 49–50). Since then, considerable efforts have been made to expand the literature. Even so, the work lives of superintendents remain an ambiguous topic for many, partly because critical variables affecting practice, such as the size, wealth, and political nature of districts, are not constant.

This chapter profiles superintendent work lives and reviews the commitments that superintendents often must make to their practice. With regard to understanding what superintendents do, four subtopics are explored: time demands, the nature of work, common rewards and frustrations, and future demands. Changes in the nature of the position are examined in the context of stress and personal growth.

SUPERINTENDENT WORK LIVES

While most educators readily understand that superintendency differs from the principalship and other administrative positions, the quantity and quality of the dissimilarities are often indistinct. Arguably, the work lives of superintendents changed substantially in the last half of the 20th century (Blumberg, 1985; Kowalski, 1995) and unlike most other administrators, they now spend much of their time outside of their offices and outside of schools interacting with adult nonemployees. As a result, most employees do not observe what superintendents do when they physically step outside the district's organizational boundaries (i.e., outside the district's offices and schools). This aspect of practice alone, makes the work life of a superintendent subject to speculation, rumors, and misinterpretations.

Time Requirements

A first step toward gaining insight into the nature of this position is to examine time demands. How much time a superintendent spends in practice daily probably varies substantially, both because of the district and because of the individual being studied. In general, however, many superintendents devote more than 65 hours per week to their jobs, which includes attendance at functions such as banquets, athletic events, and community meetings—many of which occur during evening hours and on weekends. Studies of large-district superintendents (e.g., Kowalski, 1995) found that the average workweek is approximately 75 hours. One veteran superintendent noted, "Twelve-hour workdays are the rule, and we often are expected to be at our best during board of education meetings, after we already have put in a full day" (Domenech, 1996, p. 41). No doubt some superintendents spend less time at work, but it is rare to find a practitioner who admits to working less than 60 hours per week.

Superintendents commonly spend two to three evenings per week on job-related activities. In large school districts, a superintendent may even meet with the school board as often as two or three times a week, and other meetings or special events frequently are scheduled on weekends. With so many potential

activities outside the normal workday, superintendents often must plan carefully to find time for personal and family activities. Thus it is not surprising
that studies of first-year superintendents (e.g., Pavan, 1995) identify time management as an important issue. Even highly experienced practitioners often
find it difficult to do everything expected of them. When asked to describe
a typical workday, a superintendent of a major city school system shared the
following schedule:

5:00 to 5:15 a.m.:	Arrived at the office, drank a cup of coffee and read the morning paper
5:15 to 5:45 a.m.:	Read my mail from the previous day and did paperwork
5:45 to 6:45 a.m.:	Finished writing a speech for a breakfast meeting that day
7:15 to 9:00 a.m.:	Attended a breakfast meeting and delivered the speech
9:00 to 9:30 a.m.:	Drove across town to attend a chamber of commerce board meeting
9:45 to 10:30 a.m.:	Attended the chamber meeting
10:30 to 10:45 a.m.:	Returned to my office
10:45 to 12:00 p.m.:	Met with the secondary principals
12:00 to 1:45 p.m.:	Met with several staff members individually; returned 12 phone calls
1:45 to 2:00 p.m.:	Drove to the teachers' union offices
2:00 to 4:15 p.m.:	Met with board of directors of the teachers' union (not a pleasant meeting)
4:15 to 4:30 p.m.:	Held postmortem of meeting with union officials with two staff members who attended the meeting with me
4:30 to 4:45 p.m.:	Drove back to my office
4:45 to 6:15 p.m.:	Returned approximately 15 more telephone calls and met with several staff members
6:15 p.m.:	Left the office and went home

6:30 to 7:30 p.m.:	Had a drink and ate dinner with my wife
7:30 to 8:30 p.m.:	Prepared speech to be delivered to administrators and supervisors the next day
8:30 to 9:30 p.m.:	Returned several more phone calls, read the paper, watched the news on TV
10:15 p.m.:	I collapsed!

For superintendents in small districts, the time commitments are often equal—or even greater—because they usually do not have surrogates who can represent them and the district at athletic events, special school programs, and meetings taking place during evening hours or on weekends.

Although the superintendency is demanding, it provides a privilege uncommon to other district professional educators—superintendents have greater autonomy to determine their daily schedules. They are held accountable, however, for their time management decisions. In this vein, superintendents, more so than principals and teachers, are treated as true professionals. Not all superintendents believe that they have this independence: some contend that neglecting any demand for their time has negative effects. Thus they try to cope with unrealistic time demands by simply working harder and faster—a precarious decision that often results in errors, fatigue, and even serious illness. Other superintendents find the need to make choices about personal priorities and schedules that are discomforting; they would prefer to be in a more structured position. These individuals may find it impossible to avoid job dissatisfaction because the position demands decisiveness and risk taking.

Work Requirements

Descriptions of administrative work are usually discussed in two frames: social context and role expectations. The former focuses on the degree to which administrators interact with others. Depictions in this frame examine a superintendent's practice in relation to meetings and encounters with parents, employees, board members, and so on (Frase & Hetzel, 1990; Walton, 1973). The latter focuses on duties and responsibilities of the position (Kowalski, 2003). The discussion of the five primary role conceptualizations of the position presented in Chapter 2 is a prime example.

From a social perspective, the superintendent's job is highly symbolic (Sergiovanni, Burlingame, Coombs, & Thurston, 1999) because this office holder is more readily identified with the school district than is any other individual. Thus the superintendent's internal and external interactions are assessed and evaluated almost continuously. Whether delivering a speech to a service club, giving testimony before a legislative committee, or engaging in conversations with parents, the superintendent formally and symbolically is representing the district's philosophy and programs (Sergiovanni et al., 1999). After studying work behaviors in the late 1970s, Morris (1979) characterized school administration as taking place in a highly verbal environment and concluded that the overall use of verbal information was different in school districts than in other types of organizations. Since then, expectations for superintendents to be highly effective communicators have been magnified and we now have a deeper understanding of why verbal and nonverbal behaviors are equally important (Kowalski & Keedy, 2004). While dealing with demands for change, for example, patrons and employees have been keenly observant of superintendent behavior and they often give greater credence to overt behavior than to words (Slater, 1994).

How do superintendents characterize the nature of their work? One study of urban superintendents yielded a portrait describing practice as being hectic, demanding, exciting, highly interactive, high status, and rewarding (Kowalski, 1995). Nationally, approximately 33% of all superintendents believe that the status of their position is actually increasing, whereas slightly less than 20% believe it is decreasing (Glass, Björk, & Brunner, 2000). These differences are probably explained by differing personal experiences rather than by insights about the position in general.

Superintendents indirectly describe their practice by identifying board expectations. In this regard, management and instructional leadership emerge as the two most common expectations; just 3% indicated that their primary expectation was to be a reform leader (Glass et al., 2000). Over the next several years, these figures are likely to shift somewhat if the current strategy of school-based reform is sustained.

Despite intense emphasis on leadership, data reveal that management remains an essential part of superintendent's practice, especially in small districts where support staff are not available to assume managerial responsibilities. Consequently, leadership expectations have not displaced or reduced management expectations, they merely have enlarged the overall expectations of the position (Kowalski & Brunner, 2005).

Rewards and Frustrations

What do superintendents see as the most rewarding and frustrating parts of their jobs? Expectedly, opinions on this matter are less than uniform, but certain factors recur when work is discussed. Commenting on life in the superintendency, one highly experienced superintendent wrote:

> Nobody ever said public life was devoid of frustrations—or that every member of the general public, all staff, each board of education member, every parent, all town officials, all students, and every other person and groups of persons with whom school leadership is in professional contact will always be intelligent, insightful, open, empathetic, tolerant, emotionally secure, flexible, well motivated, or any other way you'd prefer them to be. (Cattanach, 1996, p. 337)

This superintendent reminds us that even the most competent practitioners experience some frustration in this top-level position. Even so, levels of job dissatisfaction appear to have been grossly exaggerated. For example, when asked to identify the level of self-fulfillment in their position, only 6% of a national sample of superintendents said it was "none" or "little" (Glass et al., 2000). Perhaps even more noteworthy, findings pointing to relatively high rates of job satisfaction also have been documented in studies involving all types of school administrators (e.g., Boothe, Bradley, & Flick, 1994).

A single intrinsic motivator—a deep commitment to help others—may partly explain job satisfaction among superintendents. When asked what they like about their jobs, superintendents often identify aspects such as developing new programs and empowering others to be more effective (e.g., Wallace, 1992). A study of Canadian superintendents revealed that satisfaction with work was most associated with (a) the work itself, (b) positive feedback about performance, (c) problem solving, and (d) seeing a project successfully implemented (Holdaway & Genge, 1995). The fruits of a superintendent's labors, unlike those of a teacher, are often highly visible and discernible in a relatively brief period of time. For example, a sense of accomplishment may come from a newly developed strategic plan or a newly constructed school building. And even though superintendents often say they experience personal satisfaction from helping students, teachers, and principals, their actual influence on district academic achievement has not been well documented (Hart & Ogawa, 1987).

Some superintendents also identify legitimate power and prestige as rewarding elements (Kowalski, 1995). By virtue of their positions, they can be change agents and, accordingly, they can create ideas and opportunities that influence the "bigger picture" in a school district. Commenting on his career, one superintendent noted that he entered the position to test his hypothesis that he could be a true instructional leader (Wallace, 1992). A study of aspiring administrators found that the most powerful motivator for becoming a superintendent was the opportunity to exercise power and organizational control (Daresh & Playko, 1992). In a context of school reform, the superintendent's leadership and managerial involvement in curriculum and instruction has become central to effective schooling (Björk, 1993; Bredeson, 1996; Petersen & Barnett, 2003).

Extrinsic rewards also are influential for many practitioners. For instance, superintendents receive notoriety because of considerable media exposure, and because in many communities, their salaries place them in a relatively high income bracket. In some instances, the salary gap between the superintendent and the next-highest-paid district administrator is substantial—for example, $35,000 or more. In addition, superintendents routinely receive more lucrative fringe benefit packages than do other district employees.

Personalities and job-related factors also contribute to frustrations. As examples, a superintendent may be pessimistic by nature or a superintendent may be dissatisfied because he sees himself trapped in a small rural district. One study of urban superintendents identified the following frustrations:

- A general lack of fiscal resources
- The political nature of the position
- Unrealistic workloads
- An inability to get things done quickly
- Apathetic students and staff
- School board meddling in administration
- Elitism and racism (Kowalski, 1995)

Two of these issues—inadequate funding and politics—are frustrations that recur among superintendents in virtually all types of districts.

Concerns about funding have both adequacy and equity dimensions. That is, some superintendents are frustrated by a lack of adequate fiscal resources for their districts while others are frustrated by what they consider to be an inequitable distribution of resources among districts. The latter concern has been most visible in litigation in which low-wealth districts have challenged state school finance formulas (King, Swanson, & Sweetland, 2003). Approximately every 10 years, the American Association of School Administrators conducts national opinion studies of superintendents; in the most recent one (Glass et al., 2000), 36% of the respondents identified financial issues as the greatest problem facing local districts. A Canadian study conducted during the mid-1990s reported a very similar finding; inadequate funding was found to be the greatest concern and inequity of funding was found to be the second greatest concern among superintendents in that country (Webber, 1995).

Politics has long been a troublesome issue for school administrators. However, the nature of political issues and the context in which these tensions occur vary across school districts. In large urban settings, for example, competition for scarce resources among units of local government frequently produces overt hostility that prompts mayors to try to control superintendent and school board actions (Kowalski, 1995). Being at odds with local political leaders is typically disadvantageous, disconcerting and counterproductive for the school officials. These unpleasant situations, however, are not unique to large cities. Administrators in all types of districts may experience politically induced frustrations, from both external (e.g., state department of education mandates that are underfunded) and internal (e.g., factionalism among board members or members of the district's administrative team) variables (Shelton, Beach, & Chissom, 1989). Tensions inherent in the interface of professionalism and democracy may cause administrators to become dissatisfied with the political elements of their work (Hoyle, Björk, Collier, & Glass, 2005; Kowalski, 2004).

Superintendents in rural districts often face frustrations relatively unique to their work environments, such as low salaries, the inability to escape managerial duties because of a lack of support personnel, and the difficulty of providing a sufficiently comprehensive educational program (Grady & Bryant, 1991). Practitioner frustrations among this group also may stem from the fact that they are usually less-well prepared academically for practice than their peers in other types of districts; for example, a study of rural Oklahoma superintendents found that only 14% had doctorates (well below the average for all superintendents which is approximately 50%) and even more noteworthy, the highest graduate degrees held by half of them were in areas other than school administration (Garn, 2003).

Talking about their greatest frustrations, superintendents often refer to conflict nested in the competing interests of the organization, its employees, and students (Kowalski, 1995). Conditions during a teachers' union strike provide an example. Administrators may find themselves in the middle, empathizing with teachers on the one hand and with the school board, community, and students on the other hand. Virtually every problem making its way to the superintendent's desk affects the community, the school district, students, and employees; unfortunately, the interests of these parties are often discordant.

Many superintendents also express frustration with the unrealistic expectation that they act unilaterally to reform a school district. They are bothered because they know that top-down, dictatorial approaches to change simply do not work well in public education (Murphy, 1991). Many newer practitioners have been socialized to believe that shared leadership and collaborative change process are more effective (Hoyle et al., 2005); consequently, they experience considerable conflict when they find themselves working with board members who believe that reform should be mandated by authoritarian superintendents (Kowalski, 2003).

COPING STRATEGIES

Time Management

Time management is essential for superintendents because contextual variables that produce demands on them (e.g., organizational size and available resources) rarely can be transfigured. The process controlling your time has three phases:

1. Studying how you spend your time by keeping a log or diary

2. Evaluating how you allocate your time in light of priorities and emerging issues

3. Planning and building a time schedule for your future work (Rees, 1986).

The following are some of the more specific techniques that contribute to the process:

- Establishing priorities for your time
- Being brief in your communication
- Clustering tasks into time blocks (e.g., allocating five hours per week for school visits)
- Setting deadlines and remaining focused so that issues or problems do not linger
- Delegating selected activities to others
- Learning to say no
- Scheduling quiet time for yourself
- Learning to plan your time (Hartley, 1990)

Another useful tactic is to avoid individuals who repeatedly demand and then waste your time. Armenta and Darwin (1998) described them as disorganized, indifferent to managing their own time, and poor listeners. In addition, they rarely make appointments, equate the quality of communication with the quantity of communication, and try to dominate conversations. While avoiding these persons totally is impractical, setting boundaries for interacting with them is not. When they initiate contact, indicate how much time you are willing to spend with them or indicate that they must set an appointment, again allowing you to determine the length of the interaction.

At the same time that the quantity of information managed by superintendents has increased substantially, the number of support staff who assist them with answering phones, preparing letters, and keeping personal calendars has declined by 30% (Johnson, 2003). The reason is quite clear: technology has changed the manner in which organization executives communicate and manage their time. Recognizing the realities of organizational administration in an information age, many practitioners are directly taking responsibility managing their calendar, correspondence, and time.

Stress Management

The superintendency historically has been portrayed as a high-stress job (Sharp & Walter, 1995); however, this perception is both accurate and wrong. Noting that there have been many persisting misconceptions, most authors addressing this issue (e.g., Gmelch, 1996; Milstein, 1992; Wiggins, 1988) conclude that the superintendency is not by its nature an excessively stressful position. Perhaps it is more accurate to generalize that it is a demanding position, a depiction pointing out the importance of mental and physical stamina (Domenech, 1996). Studies frequently reveal that superintendents disagree about the stressfulness of their work; a recent national study, for example, found that half stated that they had experienced little or moderate stress, whereas the other half stated that they had experienced considerable or very great stress (Glass et al., 2000). These opposing opinions are largely explained by personal experiences influenced collectively by individual stress tolerance differences, variability in the context of work, and variability in coping strategies (methods individuals use to deal with stress) (Kowalski, 2003).

Despite differences in how practitioners view and deal with job-related tensions, all superintendents should treat stress management as an essential tool (Quick, Nelson, & Quick, 1990). The reasons are rather apparent. First, certain stress-producing functions, such as making important decisions and adjudicating conflict, remain pervasive in administrative work (Ramsey, 1996); conflict is so prevalent that Cuban (1988) referred to it as the DNA of the superintendency. Second, stress tolerance and work context are subject to change; as a result, your ability to apply coping techniques and the effectiveness of the techniques become somewhat inconstant (Kowalski, 2003). As an example, a superintendent who moves to an urban district may find the politics associated with the position to be much more stressful than that previously experienced (Goldstein, 1992).

Most of us recognize that work can be a primary contributor to poor health but we are less likely to know that social, biological, and psychological forces combine to determine our level of health. Illnesses such as heart problems, strokes, and cancer, for example, are now routinely linked to unhealthy lifestyles and stress (Wood & Wood, 1996). For this reason, many health professionals use a biopsychosocial paradigm to study how lifestyle contributes to illness. Within the social component, negative influences include loneliness, feelings of exploitation, and violence; in the biological component, negative influences include a lack of physical activity, poor diet, or existing disease or injury; in the psychological component, negative influences include depression, stress, and poor coping skills (Green & Shellenberger, 1990). When a number of these negative conditions exist simultaneously, they place us at greater risk of serious health problems.

Stress in humans has been defined as a nonspecific response of the body to a demand (Selye, 1976). Any demand, whether associated with family life, occupation, or societal conditions, affects us. Yet, not all of us are affected in the same way. The severity of stress is partly determined by the specific demand and partly by the individual (Coleman, 1960). This explains why a specific demand may have a dramatically different effect on two individuals in the same position. Problems associated with adjusting to stressors in our work are commonly identified as *frustrations* (the thwarting of a motive), *conflict* (contradictory goals or means that vie with each other), and *pressure* (perceived demands) (Coleman, 1960). For example, superintendents are frustrated by not having sufficient resources or by not being able to reach their goals; they experience conflict by having to choose between two important programs because both cannot be funded; they experience pressure by not being able to devote sufficient time to family obligations.

Multiple factors determine the severity of stressors, including duration (the extent to which the stressor perseveres), the importance of the need not being met, self-efficacy (self-confidence), personal competence to deal with stress, unfamiliarity (the degree to which the person understands and has previously experienced this type of stressor), suddenness (the unexpected emergence of a stressor), and the individual's tolerance (Coleman, 1960). In addition, stress levels are affected by the number of stressors present at any given time, with those that are unpredictable and uncontrollable tending to be more stressful than others (Wood & Wood, 1996).

The stress cycle has four stages: (a) stressors (issues that generate stress); (b) perceptions (how you appraise the stressor); (c) responses (how you react to the stressor); and (d) consequences (that is, the intensity and long-range negative effects you experience) (Gmelch & Parkay, 1995). Put another way, you experience a potentially stressful event, your mind or body evaluates the stressor as being threatening or benign, you select coping mechanisms, and you experience a stress reaction (Lazarus & Folkman, 1984). Clearly the degree of stress you experience is related to your perception of the adjustment demands you face. If your perception is reasonably accurate, and if you have the personal resources to respond appropriately, the stressor is unlikely to harm you.

Under severe pressure, superintendents may experience problems such as a loss of energy, a loss of concentration, anxiety, or exhaustion. When reasoning is hampered, administrators may behave uncharacteristically and do things they later regret. When stress is uncontrolled, it usually reduces your body's resistance, producing greater risk of exposure to physical illness.

Burnout is a popular term used to connote a condition resulting in a significant decline in productivity caused by excessive stress. The problem is characterized by four circumstances: some degree of physical and emotional exhaustion; socially dysfunctional behavior (e.g., isolating oneself from others at work); psychological impairment (e.g., developing negative feelings about oneself); organizational inefficiency (e.g., not doing one's work) (Cedoline, 1982). The symptoms often include the development of negative emotions (e.g., frustration, depression), the emergence of interpersonal problems (e.g., moodiness, emotional withdrawal, excessive irritability), the development of health problems (either emotional or physical), a decline in work performance, and the development of feelings of meaninglessness (e.g., feeling that work is pointless) (Potter, 1993). As these symptoms indicate, burnout is a serious condition. Some writers, however, have used the term rather loosely to describe less severe effects of working in stressful situations.

What types of adjustment demands are most common in administrative work? Although conflict is pervasive in districts and schools (Hanson, 2003), many of the stressors identified by practitioners actually fall into the category of frustrations. Table 13.1 illustrates this by examining the common stressors identified by Cedoline (1982) and Gmelch (1996) with respect to possible implications and types of adjustment demands. In certain districts, for instance, superintendents are especially troubled by confrontational school boards (conflict) and dissatisfied constituents (pressure) (Goldstein, 1992). Another adjustment demand that faces many new superintendents relates to role change. In particular, individuals who move directly from a principalship to the superintendency often find the necessary adjustments to be greater than anticipated. While much of the day is still consumed meeting with people, the new superintendent finds that the nature of the problems and the types of people change. Also, many who enter the superintendency are individuals who set high personal goals. A study in one state, for instance, found that self-induced pressures were a primary stressor (Eastman & Mirochnik, 1991).

Table 13.1   Selected Stressors Commonly Identified by Administrators

Stressor	Possible Implications	Adjustment Demand
Lack of sufficient resources	Inability to perform at desired level	Frustration
Lack of support from public/superiors	Lowered aspiration, apathy, substitute goals	Frustration
Excessively high self-expectations	Feelings of inadequacy; working too hard	Pressure
Work overload/excessive paperwork	Ignoring responsibilities, work errors	Frustration
Collective bargaining	Divided loyalties, indecision, anxiety	Conflict
Lack of clear direction	Role ambiguity, confusion	Conflict/frustration
Evaluating others	Excessive tension, disputes over outcomes	Conflict
Gaining public approval/support	Compromising values/ethics	Pressure/conflict
Making controversial decisions	Tensions from competing demands	Conflict

Adjustment demands to stress can be constructive (*eustress*) or destructive (*distress*) (Saville & Kavina, 1982). For example, conflict can lead a superintendent to become more highly involved in an issue, an experience that may produce a positive outcome for the school district and enhance the superintendent's self-confidence. Stressors often raise awareness and draw the individual's attention to important matters. "Stress becomes a problem when it ceases to be a healthy stimulus, but instead creates a burden the individual cannot handle without harmful effects" (Cedoline, 1982, p. 2).

Studies of occupational stress have identified four types of distress as especially prevalent:

1. *Time distress* (e.g., feeling that you are overwhelmed by deadlines and that you simply cannot get everything done on time)

2. *Anticipatory distress* (e.g., being anxious about your work, dreading the next catastrophe)

3. *Situational distress* (e.g., feeling threatened because you constantly face situations that you cannot control)

4. *Encounter distress* (e.g., having to face people you consider unpleasant or unpredictable) (Albrecht, 1979)

Contrary to a popular belief, stress awareness cannot prevent circumstances that contribute to distress. You can learn, however, to manage situations in which these circumstances arise. For example, you determine your perceptions of and attitudes toward stress; moreover, you select the coping techniques (Gmelch, 1996). Thus, the ultimate effects of stress on you are determined by a combination of your health, your knowledge of stress, and your ability to engage in positive stress management. Negative responses, such as overeating or abusing alcohol, become problems when superintendents have not established a repertoire of effective responses "equally balanced in the social, physical, intellectual, entertainment, managerial, personal, and attitudinal categories" (Gmelch & Parkay, 1995, p. 61).

In summary, stress can become a debilitating condition in any administrative position when (a) you do not really know yourself, (b) you do not understand stress, (c) you are indifferent to dealing with stress, and (d) you select negative coping mechanisms (see Table 13.2). By applying stress-management techniques appropriately, you are more likely to evaluate stressors accurately, a consequential advantage because your perception of a stressor is more critical than the stressor itself (Lazarus & Folkman, 1984).

Decision Management

A superintendent's practice revolves around daily decisions that range in significance, difficulty, and process. In recent decades, an increasing percentage of decisions have moved from being made by individual administrators to being made by groups. Group decisions require collaboration and are subject to team dysfunctions (Lencioni, 2002); however, like individual decisions, they are managed more effectively when decision makers recognize the promises and pitfalls provided in normative and descriptive decision-making models.

The difference between the concepts of decision and of decision making is distinct. The former is defined as all judgments that influence a course of action; the latter pertains to both a decision and the acts that were necessary to operationalize it (Griffiths, 1959). By comparison, problem solving entails a series of related decisions (Tallman & Gray, 1990). Most authorities "consider decision making to be the essence of the administrative process" (Sharman, 1984, p. 13).

Table 13.2   Examples of Problems Related to Coping With Stress

Problem	Example
Not knowing yourself	Inability to identify personal stress tolerance
Not understanding stress	Not being able to diagnose and predict possible effects
Indifference toward managing stress	Ignoring stress or believing that problems will resolve themselves
Misperceptions about stressors	Blaming others for personal problems or stress-related symptoms (e.g., nervousness or high blood pressure)
Inappropriate coping techniques	Resorting to unhealthy outlets (e.g., overeating, abusing alcohol)

The practice of applied decision making in education has been heavily influenced both by John Dewey's scientific method and by principles of scientific management emphasizing rationality and efficiency (Giesecke, 1993). Rationality refers to "a set of skills or aptitudes we use to see if we can get from here to there—to find courses of action that will lead to the accomplishment of goals" (Simon, 1993, p. 393).

In reality, there is no single rational model of decision making; rather, there are numerous related models representing a rational perspective (Zey, 1992). Griffiths (1959) concluded that most rational models had these recurring elements:

- Recognizing, defining, and limiting the problem
- Analyzing and evaluating the problem
- Establishing criteria or standards by which a solution will be evaluated or judged as acceptable and adequate
- Collecting data
- Formulating and selecting the preferred solution and testing them in advance
- Putting the preferred solution into effect

Figure 13.1 illustrates the linearity of an eight-step rational model.

Rational models have been popular because they are expected to provide rules for a potentially disorderly process; a precise process of deductive problem solving; and predictability, order, technical competence, impersonality, and rationality (Tanner & Williams, 1981). Their popularity diminished during the 1950s and 1960s as leading theorists challenged their underlying

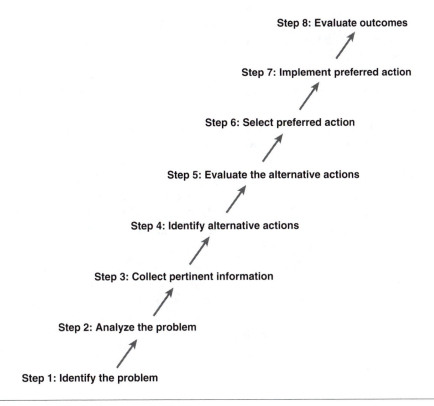

Step 8: Evaluate outcomes

Step 7: Implement preferred action

Step 6: Select preferred action

Step 5: Evaluate the alternative actions

Step 4: Identify alternative actions

Step 3: Collect pertinent information

Step 2: Analyze the problem

Step 1: Identify the problem

Figure 13.1   An Eight-Step Decision-making Model

assumptions. Simon (1970), for example, argued that for administrators to make completely rational and objective decisions, they would have to view all decision alternatives in panoramic fashion, consider all consequences that would follow each choice, assign values to each alternative, and select the best alternative from the set. Superintendents often recognize that in their world of work, ambiguity and uncertainty make it virtually impossible for them to meet these standards. As an example, problems and needs do not emerge, nor are they resolved consistently in an orderly, linear manner. In this vein, Owens (1995) wrote, "decision making is usually an iterative, ongoing process whereby the results of one decision provide new information on which to base yet another decision" (p. 175). Rational paradigms often fail to give adequate consideration to the political dynamics of the "informal" organization and the fact that district decisions are made in the context of mixed motives, ambiguities, and limited information—characteristics of social systems that attenuate the potential of rational paradigms (Chance & Chance, 2002).

As the deficiencies of rational models became known, new hybrid or *bounded* models emerged, and although they had various labels, they shared the goal of addressing the questionable assumptions about choices and outcomes found in traditional rational models. More specifically, they modified earlier models without eliminating linearity (i.e., a sequential framework). Simon (1976), for example, divided decision making into four phases: an intelligence activity (involving identifying problems), a design activity (consisting of identifying possible courses of action), a choice activity (involving deciding on a course of action), and a review activity (the evaluation of outcomes). In bounded models, the idea of *satisficing* plays a central role. It has been defined as an individual's or organization's tendency to select something less than ideal (Hellreigel & Slocum, 1996). Simon (1976) noted that rather than continuously seeking ideal decisions as prescribed in rational models, administrators tended to select alternatives that were reasonably likely to produce acceptable results. Bounded models also differ from the traditional rational models in that decision making is not seen as a value-free enterprise; instead, administrator biases are recognized (Hellreigel & Slocum, 1996). In summary, bounded models prescribe an orderly approach without ignoring the effects of uncertainty, values, competing interests, and biases.

Other models, both normative and descriptive, also enlighten practice. The following is a brief summary of three of them.

- *The Garbage Can Model*—This descriptive paradigm reveals that organizational decisions frequently are not made rationally or linearly. A district or school is portrayed as a garbage can that contains problems, solutions, and participants. The purpose of the imagery is to describe choice opportunities (Cohen, March, & Olsen, 1972). These opportunities are events that focus attention and create opportunities for change (Hanson, 1996). In schools, this might be a principal's dismissal or a serious accident on school property. Decisions reflect the fact that a particular solution and a particular problem floating in the can find a sponsor. The sponsor then decides to expend extensive time and energy to promote a preferred solution to the problem. The sponsor "may prevail because other participants sponsoring other problems and solutions reduce their participation or drop out from involvement altogether" (Hanson, 1996, p. 144). As a result, decisions made in this manner are typically inconsistent and poorly defined (Schmid, Dodd & Tropman, 1987).

- *Political Model*—Because school districts operate in political environments and because they are political organizations (Sergiovanni & Carver, 1980), decisions often reflect the influence of competing forces and external interventions (individuals, groups, or agencies outside of the district's organizational boundaries). In the political model, the focus is on bargaining between opposing factions; decisions are negotiated based on the amount of power possessed by opponents. The goals of the school district are often displaced by the goals of the competing interest groups (Estler, 1988). Common characteristics of the political model include an interdependency of decision participants that prevent unilateral decisions in certain areas, a dispersal of power, coalition building, bargaining, and compromise (Giesecke, 1993). In simple terms, decisions are based on individual or group interests rather than on a rational choice framed by organizational objectives.

- *Moral-Ethical Model*—Simon (1976) noted that decisions should entail both factual propositions and ethical standards in that they select one future state of affairs in preference to another. Ethical leadership is very much grounded in values. Values provide a superintendent with a structured rationale that guides decision making (Hitt, 1990). Starratt (1991) developed one of the most widely used models in school administration based on three dimensions: critique, justice, and caring. His work is predicated on the notion that human factors, expressly moral in nature and previously neglected, need to be infused into the decision-making processes of a learning community. A more direct ethical model, offered by Blanchard and Peale (1988), focuses on three decision-related issues: legality (Will the decision violate either civil law or company policy?); balance (Is the decision fair to all concerned?); conscience (How would the administrator feel about himself or herself if the decision was widely publicized?). Ethical models often are viewed as being incongruous with political models because fairness and compassion replace power and compromise.

Decision-making behavior also is affected by personal action theories representing a confluence of theoretical constructs and personal values and beliefs. There are two types of action theories: *espoused theories* (those that influence what we think and believe) and *in-use theories* (those that influence what we really do). The former exist at the conscious level and are more often altered as a person gains exposure to new knowledge and experiences; the latter often exist at the unconscious level and are usually highly resistant to change (Argyris & Schön, 1974). Espoused theories in school administration are influenced by professional study and reinforced by professional standards. Theories-in-action, by contrast, are learned from experiencing life—both inside and outside of the school (Osterman & Kottkamp, 1993).

Schön (1983, 1990) described three intermediate zones of practice—uncertainty (e.g., problems do not always occur to superintendents as well-informed structures), uniqueness (e.g., superintendents often encounter problems that are not discussed in text books), and value conflict (e.g., when solving problems superintendents must often choose between positions supported by conflicting values)—which demonstrate that the complexity and ambiguity of practice in all professions requires more than technical knowledge. He noted that decisions may be problematic in several of these ways simultaneously. For example, a first-year superintendent may have to decide which programs to cut for necessary budget reductions. Having never made such a decision previously, the superintendent is uncertain of the ramifications of this decision and at the same time, groups are lobbying the superintendent to accept their favored decision.

The art of reflective practice places theoretical knowledge in perspective and illuminates the value of experience. Schön (1990) differentiated between "knowing-in-action" and "reflecting-in-action." The former is embedded in the socially and institutionally structured context shared by those who enter school administration. The latter represents a type of artistry that becomes important when problems and challenges are unique and less than rational. Superintendents, like other professionals, develop an implicit repertoire of techniques and strategies for making decisions. Using action theories, they form mental images of likely outcomes. When decisions produce expected results, there is little need to give further thought to the situation (in fact, positive experiences serve to verify convictions already embedded in the administrator's tacit knowledge). Occasionally, however, surprises may trigger both reflection in-action and reflection-on-action, causing the superintendent to think about unanticipated consequences as they are occurring and after the consequences are known (Kowalski, 2003). Without reflecting, administrators do not come to understand how their behavior may be driven by implicit compliance with organizational cultural norms and their own work habits (Osterman & Kottkamp, 1993).

The theory of experiential learning defined by Kolb (1984) is a cyclical process with four distinctive stages: experience, observation and reflection, abstract reconceptualization, and experimentation. In this context, experience provides a basis for learning; but experience alone does not guarantee learning. Learning is accomplished when the practitioner uses the four stages of experiential learning to provide a nexus between theory and the real world of practice. As a model for professional growth, reflective practice focuses on both a continuous restructuring of the professional knowledge base and the improvement of personal performance. This is accomplished by infusing uncertain, unique, and value-laden experiences into personal theories of action. When this is achieved, decisions can be analyzed in a framework of contextual variables that involve emotions, competing interests, and behavioral regularities common to schools and school districts.

Communication Management

As discussed at several points earlier in the book, being an effective communicator has become a pervasive role expectation for superintendents. Studies examining highly effective superintendents (e.g., Morgan & Petersen, 2002; Stipetic, 1994) exhibit how their communicative behavior can influence school culture, teacher behavior, and even student outcomes. Studies also show that successful practice is dependent on a superintendent's knowledge of communication and the processes the superintendent uses to deploy that knowledge (Kowalski, in press; Kowalski & Keedy, 2004).

The challenge of managing interpersonal communication is framed by the following capacities:

- *Ability to encode and decode messages effectively.* A superintendent's spoken and written communiqués usually become public record and are used as evidence in formal and informal performance evaluations (Lehr, 2001). Consequently, practitioners need to develop their skills in relation to constructing and interpreting communication.
- *Ability to construct appropriate communication channels.* When formal communication channels (those created and sanctioned by district administrators) are ineffective, informal channels bypass them. Because informal communication often breeds rumors and misinformation, a superintendent needs to develop inclusive channels that meet the needs of organizational members (Wentz, 1998).
- *Ability to listen.* Listening has three dimensions—what is heard, what is understood, and what is remembered (Spaulding & O'Hair, 2004). People judge others on the basis of these criteria. Superintendents who routinely demonstrate good listening skills are usually perceived as respectful, interested, and concerned (Burbules, 1993).
- *Ability to be credible.* Administrators earn credibility when they do what they say they will do. Others judge them on the basis of what is said and what is done; credibility is established when the two are consonant (Kouzes & Posner, 1993). Credibility has been especially important in areas such as teacher empowerment (Johnson, 1998) and community involvement in school improvement (Sherman, 1999).

- *Ability to master nonverbal communication.* Nonverbal communication is often symbolic and occurs at the unconscious level. According to Argyle (1988), this skill is a way of expressing emotions (e.g., excitement, disappointment), an avenue for conveying interpersonal attitudes (e.g., sincerity, openness), an avenue for presenting one's personality to others (e.g., aggressive, introverted), and an extension of verbal communication (e.g., reinforcing words, substituting gestures for words).
- *Ability to communicate in context.* Contextual variables may interfere with communication and contribute to misinterpretations, even to the extent that a message is completely distorted (Hoy & Miskel, 2005). Thus, superintendents need to understand how factors such as prejudice, ethnic diversity, gender differences, and organizational structure can influence communication.
- *Ability to work with and through all types of media.* The modern superintendent is expected to exchange information using both print and broadcast media. This requires an understanding of journalism, the will to develop positive relationships with reporters, an understanding of how to deal with negative news, the capacity to get the school district's messages before the public, and the competence to manage crisis situations (Kowalski, 2004).
- *Ability to acquire and use appropriate communication technologies.* The nexus between technology and effective communication is widely recognized. Superintendents must be aware of the availability of these technologies and they must have the knowledge necessary to deploy them (Rowicki, 1999).
- *Ability to resolve conflict through communication.* Although communication may occur without conflict, "conflict cannot occur without some type of communication" (Harris, 1993, p. 396). As schools adopt more open climates and as governance becomes more democratic, the quantity of conflict increases. An administrator's communicative behaviors may both contribute to conflict and become a vehicle for resolving it (e.g., building cooperation). Consequently, practitioners must know the dynamics of conflict and they must be able to communicate appropriately to manage it (Spaulding & O'Hair, 2004).
- *Ability to connect organizational culture and communication to organizational behavior.* Behavior in schools is frequently unpredictable and bewildering. Because communication is observable, it provides a window for understanding the deepest levels of institutional culture and for determining how basic assumptions and beliefs shape behavior. To do this, however, administrators must understand the relationship between culture and communication (Kowalski, 2004).

FOR FURTHER REFLECTION

This chapter examined two issues important to superintendents: the nature of a superintendent's practice and management strategies related to coping with the demands made by the position. As you consider what you read in this chapter, answer the following questions:

1. What differences have you observed between the work lives of principals and superintendents? Do these differences conform with the content of this chapter?

2. What do superintendents commonly see as occupational rewards? How do you assess these possible rewards from a personal perspective?

3. What is the difference between quantity and quality concerns for adequate financing of public education?

4. What is time management? Why is the process essential for superintendents?

5. How has technology affected the need for time management?

6. Based on your personal strengths and weaknesses, which aspects of the superintendency do you consider to have the most potential for stress?

7. Why do superintendents not view job-related stress uniformly?

8. How can decision-making models assist superintendents?

9. Under what circumstances can stress be positive?

10. Why is it important for superintendents to manage communication?

Case Study

Albert Davidson is the oldest of six children and the first member of his immediate family to graduate from high school and college. He was an above-average student and a gifted athlete. After graduating from high school, he attended a state university on a football scholarship; his goal was to be a social studies teacher and football coach. After completing his bachelor's degree he was awarded a National Collegiate Athletic Association scholarship and attended graduate school, earning a master's degree in history. He began teaching two months later at the age of 24.

After teaching and coaching football at a large-city high school for five years, Albert was persuaded by his principal to seek a principal's license. He did so by completing seven courses at a local university. Shortly thereafter, he accepted a position as an assistant principal in the school where he had been teaching. Although he missed teaching and coaching, he found administrative work to be equally rewarding, even though much of his time was spent dealing with discipline issues.

After three years, Albert faced another career decision. A professor he had met while completing requirements for the principal's license encouraged him to pursue a doctoral degree. Although he had just recently married, he decided that going back to school full-time was an advantageous decision. After two years, he was nearing completion of his Ph.D. and began applying for jobs, primarily high school principal positions. He also applied for the superintendency in Colburn, a small-town district where he had attended school and where his parents still resided. Thinking he would not be competitive for a superintendency, he described his application to his wife as a "long shot."

The Colburn School District enrolled approximately 2,100 students and most of the board members knew Albert. To his surprise, he was invited to interview for the position and he was even more shocked when it was offered to him. At the same time, he had been offered a principalship at a large high school in an urban area. His Ph.D. adviser recommended that he accept the principalship because of his limited experience. Albert, however, was extremely flattered by the opportunity to return to Colburn; he accepted the superintendency.

At the time they moved to Colburn, Albert's wife, Jackie, was pregnant and she decided to leave the teaching profession—at least temporarily. While Albert readily readjusted to Colburn, Jackie, who grew up in a large city, did not. She thought the adjustment would be easier since nearly half of Colburn's population were African Americans. The first few months were hectic because Albert was finishing his dissertation and adjusting to his new job. He left home early and returned late almost every day and on Friday nights, he and Jackie usually attended a district athletic event.

By the start of the second semester, Albert completed his Ph.D. and Jackie gave birth to a baby boy. Yet Albert was not spending more time away from work. Jackie thought that he was becoming irritable and he often refused to discuss his job. She tried to persuade him to spend more time with her and the baby.

As summer approached, Jackie decided to express her feelings about living in Colburn. Although Albert had been spending slightly more time at home recently, she still found it difficult to adjust to the community. One evening, during dinner, she told him, "I'd feel a lot better if I knew we were not going to stay here forever. In a couple of years, I want to return to teaching and I don't want to do it here. Working in the same district where you are superintendent is not a good idea and to do otherwise would require driving at least 30 miles. Most of all, I don't think it is a good idea to raise our son here. He would have more opportunities in a larger city."

Albert assured Jackie that he did not plan on staying in Colburn. "But I made a commitment to these people. I signed a three-year contract and I told them that if things worked out, I'd probably stay for at least five years. The board members have been very good to me and I'm learning a great deal. After four more years, I can apply for a better position."

Albert was the first African American to serve as Colburn's superintendent. He wanted to do well and to make his parents proud of him. Besides, leaving after just one or two years might reduce the chances that his successor would be an African American. Jackie pleaded with him to compromise. She asked that they try to relocate after he finished his third year. Albert agreed to consider that plan.

At the beginning of his second year as superintendent, Albert experienced his first major dispute with several school board members. The conflict involved disciplinary action taken against a football player. Albert supported the high school principal's decision to remove the student from the team after he had gotten in a fight at school. Two board members and the football coach were quoted in the paper as saying the penalty was excessive and not in the best interest of the school. The board president attempted to intervene but Albert refused to reduce the penalty. At the next board meeting, the board members voted 3 to 2 to reinstate the football player after he served a five-day suspension.

Two weeks later, one of the elementary schools was destroyed by a fire that fortunately occurred while the building was not occupied. Albert had to find temporary classroom space for nearly 200 students, he had to deal with insurance adjusters, and he had to start plans to replace the school. All of these tasks placed more demands on his already heavy work schedule.

Albert began having trouble sleeping and lost 15 pounds over the next few weeks. He was no longer keeping his commitment to spend time with his family and Jackie was becoming increasingly dissatisfied with remaining in Colburn.

Albert had succeeded at virtually everything before becoming a superintendent; frustration had not been common. For the first time in his life, he questioned whether he could handle all the pressure he was experiencing. He began having doubts about being a superintendent and doubts about remaining in Colburn.

Case Discussion Questions

1. Evaluate Albert's decision to choose the superintendent position over the principal position. Would you have done the same? Why or why not?

2. To what extent is the location of Albert's job contributing to the pressures he is experiencing?

3. What factors appear to be generating stress for Albert? Is the quantity and quality of these factors an issue? Why or why not?

4. What are some coping strategies Albert could use to deal with stress?

5. Do you believe that Albert needs to make a decision about his career alone or in conjunction with his wife? Defend your response.

6. If you were Albert's good friend, what would you advise him to do?

REFERENCES

Albrecht, K. (1979). *Stress and the manager.* Upper Saddle River, NJ: Prentice Hall.

Armenta, T. D., & Darwin, E. V. (1988). Coping with time-robbers. *Principal, 78*(1), 64.

Argyle, M. (1988). *Bodily communication* (2nd ed.). London: Methuen.

Argyris, C., & Schön, D. A. (1974). *Theory in practice: Increasing professional effectiveness.* San Francisco: Jossey-Bass.

Björk, L. (1993). Effective schools—effective superintendents: The emerging instructional leadership role. *Journal of School Leadership, 3*(3), 246–259.

Blanchard, K. H., & Peale, N. V. (1988). *The power of ethical management.* New York: William Morrow.

Blumberg, A. (1985). *The school superintendent: Living with conflict.* New York: Teachers College Press.

Boothe, J. W., Bradley, L. H., & Flick, T. M. (1994). This working life. *Executive Educator, 16*(2), 39–42.

Bredeson, P. (1996). Superintendent roles in curriculum development and instructional leadership: Instructional visionaries, collaborators, supporters, and delegators. *Journal of School Leadership, 6*(3), 243–264.

Burbules, N. C. (1993). *Dialogue in teaching: Theory and practice.* New York: Teachers College Press.

Cattanach, D. L. (1996). *The school leader in action: Discovering the golden mean.* Lancaster, PA: Technomic.

Cedoline, A. J. (1982). *Job burnout in public education: Symptoms, causes, and survival skills.* New York: Teachers College Press.

Chance, P. L., & Chance, E. W. (2002). *Introduction to educational leadership and organizational behavior.* Larchmont, NY: Eye on Education.

Cohen, M. D., March, J. G., & Olsen, J. P. (1972). A garbage can model of organizational choice. *Administrative Science Quarterly, 7*(1), 1–25.

Coleman, J. C. (1960). *Personality dynamics and effective behavior.* Chicago: Scott, Foresman.

Crowson, R. L. (1987). The local school district superintendency: A puzzling role. *Educational Administration Quarterly, 23*(3), 49–69.

Cuban, L. (1988). Conflict and leadership in the superintendency. *Phi Delta Kappan, 67*(1), 28–30.

Daresh, J. C., & Playko, M. A. (1992). *Aspiring administrators' perceptions of the superintendency as a viable career choice.* East Lansing, MI: National Center for Research on Teacher Learning. (ERIC Document Reproduction Service No. ED346564)

Domenech, D. A. (1996). Surviving the ultimate stress. *School Administrator, 53*(3), 40–41.

Eastman, M., & Mirochnik, D. A. (1991). *Stressed for success: A study of stress and the superintendency.* East Lansing, MI: National Center for Research on Teacher Learning. (ERIC Document Reproduction Service No. ED336854)

Estler, S. (1988). Decision-making. In N. Boyan (Ed.), *Handbook of research in educational administration* (pp. 305–319). New York: Longman.

Frase, L., & Hetzel, R. (1990). *School management by wandering around*. Lancaster, PA: Technomic.

Garn, G. (2003). A closer look at rural superintendents. *Rural Educator, 25*(1), 3–9.

Giesecke, J. (1993). Recognizing multiple decision-making models: A guide for managers. *College & Research Libraries, 54*(2), 103–114.

Glass, T., Björk, L., & Brunner, C. (2000). *The 2000 study of the American school superintendency*. Arlington, VA: American Association of School Administrators.

Gmelch, W. H. (1996). Breaking out of the superintendent stress trap. *School Administrator, 53*(3), 32–33.

Gmelch, W. H., & Parkay, F. W. (1995). Changing roles and occupational stress in the teaching profession. In M. O'Hair & S. Odell (Eds.), *Educating teachers for leadership and change: Teacher education yearbook III* (pp. 46–65). Thousand Oaks, CA: Corwin.

Goldstein, A. (1992). Stress in the superintendency: School leaders confront the daunting pressures of the job. *School Administrator, 49*(9), 8–13, 15–17.

Grady, M. L., & Bryant, M. T. (1991). A study of frequent superintendent turnover in a rural school district: The constituents' perspective. *Journal of Rural and Small Schools, 4*(3), 10–13.

Green, J., & Shellenberger, R. (1990). *The dynamics of health and wellness: A biopsychosocial approach*. Forth Worth, TX: Holt, Rinehart & Winston.

Griffiths, D. E. (1959). *Administrative theory*. New York: Appleton-Century-Crofts.

Hanson, E. M. (1996). *Educational administration and organizational behavior* (4th ed.). Boston: Allyn & Bacon.

Hanson, E. M. (2003). *Educational administration and organizational behavior* (5th ed.). Boston: Allyn & Bacon.

Harris, T. E. (1993). *Applied organizational communication: Perspectives, principles, and pragmatics:* Hillsdale, NJ: Lawrence Erlbaum Associates.

Hart, A. W., & Ogawa, R. T. (1987). The influence of superintendents on the academic achievement of school districts. *Journal of Educational Administration, 25*(1), 72–84.

Hartley, H. J. (1990). Make time to manage your time more effectively. *Executive Educator, 12*(8), 19–21.

Hellreigel, D., & Slocum, J. W. (1996). *Management* (7th ed.) Cincinnati, OH: South-Western College.

Hitt, W. D. (1990). *Ethics and leadership: Putting theory into practice*. Columbus, OH: Battelle.

Holdaway, E. A., & Genge, A. (1995). How effective superintendents understand their own work. In K. Leithwood (Ed.), *Effective school district leadership* (pp. 13–32). Albany: State University of New York Press.

Hoy, W. A., & Miskel, C. G. (2005). *Educational administration: Theory, research, and practice* (7th ed.). Boston: McGraw-Hill.

Hoyle, J., Björk, L, Collier, V., & Glass, T. (2005). *The superintendent as CEO: Standards-based performance*. Thousand Oaks, CA: Corwin.

Johnson, D. (2003). Personal productivity in your own hands. *School Administrator, 60*(11), 8.

Johnson, S. M. (1998). Telling all sides of the truth. *Educational Leadership, 55*(7), 12–16.

King, R. A., Swanson, A. D., & Sweetland, S. R. (2003). *School finance: Achieving high standards with equity and efficiency* (3rd ed.). Boston: Allyn & Bacon.

Kolb, D. A. (1984). *Experiential learning: Experience as the source of learning and development.* Englewood Cliffs, NJ: Prentice-Hall.

Kouzes, J. M., & Posner, B. Z. (1993). *Credibility: How leaders gain and lose it, why people demand it.* San Francisco: Jossey-Bass.

Kowalski, T. J. (1995). *Keepers of the flame: Contemporary urban superintendents.* Thousand Oaks, CA: Corwin.

Kowalski, T. J. (2003). *Contemporary school administration* (2nd ed.). Boston: Allyn & Bacon.

Kowalski, T. J. (2004). School public relations: A new agenda. In T. J. Kowalski (Ed.), *Public relations in schools* (3rd ed., pp. 3–29). Upper Saddle River, NJ: Merrill, Prentice Hall.

Kowalski, T. J. (in press). Evolution of the superintendent as communicator. *Journal of Communication Education.*

Kowalski, T. J., & Brunner, C. C. (2005). The school superintendent: Roles, challenges, and issues. In F. English (Ed.), *The Sage handbook of educational leadership* (pp. 142–167). Thousand Oaks, CA: Sage.

Kowalski, T. J., & Keedy, J. (2004, April). *Superintendent as communicator in an information age: Providing and assessing essential skills.* Paper presented at the annual meeting of the American Educational Research Association, San Diego.

Lazarus, R. S., & Folkman, S. (1984). *Stress, appraisal, and coping.* New York: Springer.

Lehr, A. E. (2001). Why school administrators should be model writers. *Phi Delta Kappan, 82,* 762–764.

Lencioni, P. (2002). *The five dysfunctions of a team.* San Francisco: Jossey-Bass.

Milstein, M. M. (1992). The overstated case of administrator stress. *School Administrator, 49*(9), 12–13.

Morgan, C. L., & Petersen, G. J. (2002). The role of the district superintendent in leading academically successful school districts. In B. S. Cooper & L. D. Fusarelli (Eds.), *The promises and perils facing today's school superintendent* (pp. 175–196). Lanham, MD: Scarecrow Education.

Morris, J. R. (1979). Job(s) of the superintendency. *Educational Research Quarterly, 4*(4), 11–24.

Murphy, J. T. (1991). Superintendents as saviors: From the Terminator to Pogo. *Phi Delta Kappan, 72*(7), 507–513.

Osterman, K. F., & Kottkamp, R. B. (1993). *Reflective practice for educators: Improving schooling through professional development.* Newbury Park, CA: Corwin.

Owens, R. G. (1995). *Organizational behavior in education* (5th ed.). Boston: Allyn & Bacon.

Pavan, B. N. (1995). *First year district superintendents: Women reflect on contradictions between education and politics.* East Lansing, MI: National Center for Research on Teacher Learning. (ERIC Document Reproduction Service No. ED389077)

Petersen, G., & Barnett, B. (2003, April). *The superintendent as instructional leader: History, evolution, and future of the role.* Paper presented at the annual meeting of the American Educational Research Association, Chicago.

Potter, B. (1993). *Beating job burnout: How to transform work pressure into productivity.* Berkeley, CA: Ronin.

Quick, J. C., Nelson, D. L., & Quick, J. D. (1990). *Stress and challenge at the top: The paradox of the successful executive.* New York: John Wiley & Sons.

Ramsey, K. (1996). Back to the trenches. *School Administrator, 53*(3), 22–28.

Rees, R. (1986). SOS: A time management framework. *Education Canada, 26*(2), 8–15.

Rowicki, M. A. (1999). *Communication skills for educational administrators.* East Lansing, MI: National Center for Research on Teacher Learning. (ERIC Document Reproduction Service No. ED432830)

Saville, A., & Kavina, G. (1982). Use stress to improve your job performance. *Executive Educator, 4*(4), 18–19.

Selye, H. (1976). *The stress of life.* New York: McGraw-Hill.

Schmid, H., Dodd, P., & Tropman, J. E. (1987). Board decision making in human service organizations. *Human Systems Management, 7*(2), 155–161.

Schön, D. A. (1983). *The reflective practitioner.* New York: Basic Books.

Schön, D. A. (1990). *Educating the reflective practitioner.* San Francisco: Jossey-Bass.

Sergiovanni, T. J., Burlingame, M., Coombs, F., & Thurston, P. W. (1999). *Educational governance and administration* (4th ed.). Boston: Allyn & Bacon.

Sergiovanni, T. J., & Carver, F. D. (1980). *The new school executive: A theory of administration* (2nd ed.). New York: Harper & Row.

Sharman, C. S. (1984). *Decision making in educational settings.* (Phi Delta Kappa Fastback No. 211). Bloomington, IN: Phi Delta Kappa Educational Foundation.

Sharp, W. L., & Walter, J. K. (1995). *The health of the school superintendency.* East Lansing, MI: National Center for Research on Teacher Learning. (ERIC Document Reproduction Service No. ED389067)

Shelton, B. S., Beach, R., & Chissom, B. S. (1989). Perceived political factors related to superintendents' administration of school districts. *Educational Research Quarterly, 13*(2), 11–17.

Sherman, L. (1999). The superintendent who listens. *Northwest Education, 5*(2), 12–19.

Simon, H. A. (1970). *The new science of management decisions.* New York: Harper & Row.

Simon, H. A. (1976). *Administrative behavior.* New York: The Free Press.

Simon, H. A. (1993). Decision making: Rational, nonrational, and irrational. *Educational Administration Quarterly, 29,* 392–411.

Slater, R. O. (1994). Symbolic educational leadership and democracy in America. *Educational Administration Quarterly, 30*(1), 97–101.

Spaulding, A. M., & O'Hair, M. J. (2004). Public relations in a communication context: Listening, nonverbal, and conflict-resolution skills. In T. J. Kowalski (Ed.), *Public relations in schools* (3rd ed., pp. 96–122). Upper Saddle River, NJ: Merrill, Prentice Hall.

Starratt, R. J. (1991). Building an ethical school: A theory for practice in educational administration. *Educational Administration Quarterly, 27*(2), 185–202.

Stipetic, J. D. (1994). Can school superintendents make a difference? A review of the literature on the superintendent as instructional leader. *Planning & Changing, 25,* 19–27.

Tallman, I., & Gray, L. N. (1990). Choices, decisions and problem solving. In W. R. School & J. Staw (Eds.), *Annual review of sociology* (Vol. 16, pp. 405–433). Palo Alto, CA: Annual reviews.

Tanner, C. K., & Williams, E. J. (1981). *Educational planning and decision making: A view through the organizational process.* Lexington, MA: D. C. Heath.

Wallace, R. C. (1992, April). *On exiting the superintendency: An autobiographical perspective.* Paper presented at the annual meeting of the American Educational Research Association, San Francisco.

Walton, H. F. (1973). *The man in the principal's office: An ethnography.* New York: Holt, Rinehart & Winston.

Webber, C. F. (1995). *A Profile of the school superintendency: Issues and perceptions.* East Lansing, MI: National Center for Research on Teacher Learning. (ERIC Document Reproduction Service No. ED383111)

Wentz, P. J. (1998). Successful communications for school leaders. *NASSP Bulletin, 82*(601), 112–115.

Wiggins, T. (1988). Stress and administrative role in educational organizations. *Journal of Educational Research, 82*(2), 120–125.

Wood, S. E., & Wood, E. G. (1996). *The world of psychology* (2nd ed.). Boston: Allyn & Bacon.

Zey, M. (1992). *Decision making: Alternatives to rational choice models.* Newbury Park, CA: Sage.

CHAPTER 14

Becoming a Superintendent

KEY FACETS OF THE CHAPTER

- ○ Superintendent selection process

- ○ Search consultants

- ○ Personal career planning

- ○ Special career planning challenges for women and persons of color

- ○ Pursuing a superintendency

- ○ Negotiating an employment contract

Administrators become superintendents in different ways. Some say that the job was a lifelong goal for which they planned meticulously; others claim that they never sought the position but were essentially pushed into it by school board members. Regardless of how they got to the top, most superintendents admit to a common deficiency: they were not prepared sufficiently to deal with unique aspects of superintendent selection and employment (Hess, 1989). The novel experiences to which they refer include having to go through an extensive selection process that begins with an evaluation of written materials and extends to multiple interviews—often with school boards, selection committees, and even the general public. They also include intense media scrutiny and having to negotiate an individual multiyear employment contract— experiences that they did not have as teachers or as principals.

This chapter explores four issues concerning preparing administrators to pursue the superintendency. The first is the superintendent selection process;

special attention is given to the options school boards have for meeting what is arguably their most important responsibility. The second is career planning. This process is explained and its advantages are identified. The third is advice relative to applying for the position. Positive and negative behaviors are discussed. The last topic, the employment contract, is analyzed in relation to its development and potential content.

SUPERINTENDENT SELECTION PROCESS

Selecting a superintendent is almost certainly the most important task a school board must perform (Hord & Estes, 1993), yet it is neither a routine assignment nor one for which most members possess knowledge and experience. Thus it is not surprising that school boards have been less than uniform in conducting the superintendent search. In the worst case, board members simply surge forward not knowing what they want to accomplish. In these cases, the search process is typically disorganized, highly political, and often unsuccessful. Such faulty employment searches contribute to leadership instability—a problem that is detrimental to both the employer and employee. At the other end of the spectrum we find school boards that take the time to envision their ideal goal and then develop a plan for reaching it. These boards often spend more time planning the search process than they do executing it. Clearly, school boards that use a measured approach are more likely to find a competent and compatible superintendent than are school boards that use a thoughtless approach (Jernigan, 1997).

Planning the Search Process

Superintendent searches should begin with a vision—the board's (and possibly the community's) shared image of an ideal chief executive officer. Once this characterization has been constructed, the board can develop a plan for conducting the search. This process is framed by six essential queries:

1. *Who will have procedural control of the search process?* Procedural control refers to structuring and managing the search process. Basically, boards have three options in relation to this question: they can assume complete control; they can share control with a consultant or a selection committee; they can delegate control to a consultant or selection committee.

If the first alternative is pursued, board members must decide if the control will be exercised by a single board member (e.g., the board president), a board committee, or the entire board.

2. *Is the ideal superintendent most likely to be found as a result of a national, regional, or restricted search process?* The scope and cost of a search typically reflects the board's intent with regard to finding a superintendent. National searches are costly and time-consuming and boards are not likely to pursue them unless they are committed to finding a specific type of leader who may not be readily available locally.

3. *What types of recruitment activities are necessary to find the ideal superintendent?* Superintendent applicants can be pursued in various ways, ranging from meeting basic legal requirements (e.g., posting the vacancy with district employees) to developing elaborate recruitment and application packets.

4. *What characteristics define the ideal candidate?* No search should begin without agreement among the board members regarding desired and required qualifications. Yet many boards have given little or no thought to this query before commencing a search. In the absence of agreed upon criteria, each member will assess and evaluate applicants on the basis of the member's own values and biases—an outcome that often leads to divided votes on the appointment of a new superintendent.

5. *What timelines need to be established?* Searches vary markedly in time parameters. Some are done within four or five weeks, whereas others stretch out over an entire year.

6. *Who will participate in the search process?* Searches conducted solely by the board members are becoming increasingly rare because both district employees and taxpayers are demanding a voice in this decision.

As a potential applicant, you can discern a great deal about the school board, the district, and the position by looking carefully at how these questions have been answered. Each provides insights regarding the board's image of an ideal applicant and the board's intent to attract a competitive applicant pool. As an example, a school board engaging in a perfunctory search (e.g., they are determined to promote an internal candidate but need to meet the legal requirements of having a search) is unlikely to relinquish any control, conduct a national search, develop costly recruitment materials, set broad timelines, or establish an inclusive search process.

Trend Toward Consultants

Historically, school boards, except for a handful of the very largest districts, conducted superintendent searches independently. This practice was supported by three prevailing conditions:

1. Applicant pools were generally very large, even in small districts. Consequently, board members were confident that they could find a highly qualified practitioner without having to recruit broadly.

2. Board members feared that taxpayers would criticize them if they used consultants, largely because of the cost involved.

3. Board members feared that consultants would control the search process, thus minimizing their discretion (Kowalski, 2003b).

Since the early 1980s, however, the trend has been to use professional search consultants. The most recent national study of superintendents (Glass, Björk, & Brunner, 2000) reported that only about half of all searches were managed directly by school boards. The others were managed by search firms, state school board associations, or other consultants (e.g., professors). The reasons for retaining management services vary among and even within states but in general, they are associated with a reversal in the size of applicant pools, greater community scrutiny of board performance in superintendent selection, and the increased potential for legal and political problems (Kowalski, 2003b). The size and social status of school districts appear to be important issues with respect to using search consultants; a study in Ohio (Johnson & Howley, 2001) found that board presidents in larger and more urban districts express a preference for retaining consultants, whereas board presidents in smaller and more rural districts do not. Search consultants may assist school boards in the following functions:

- Reaching consensus on selection criteria
- Developing a master plan for the search
- Preparing promotional materials, including vacancy announcements and brochures
- Making personal contacts with practitioners who would be highly desirable applicants
- Responding to applicant inquiries and questions
- Communicating with potential applicants
- Assessing and screening applicants

- Validating applicant credentials and references
- Conducting or assisting with initial interviews
- Negotiating an employment contract
- Adjudicating disputes between applicants and the school district

More generally, these duties are discussed in three broad categories: helping to secure candidates, helping to screen candidates, and helping to employ the right candidate.

School boards that decide to use a consultant have four options.

1. *Retaining a private consultant*—Private consultants are either individuals or firms engaged entirely or primarily in superintendent searches. During the early 1990s, for example, two of the nation's largest executive recruiting firms—Korn/Ferry International and Heidrick and Struggles—entered this segment of the market (Meet the Power Brokers, 1994). However, most full-time search consultants are former superintendents and former school administration professors. Major advantages of this option are consultant experience and access to national applicants (i.e., these firms typically have established a national or regional catalog of highly qualified applicants). The major disadvantage is cost. This option is almost always the most expensive; for a school district of approximately 20,000 students, the search could cost up to $80,000. Cost often reflects the complexity and size of a school district, as well as the consultant's established record (Zakariya, 1987).

2. *Retaining a school administration professor*—School administration professors serving as search consultants differ from private consultants in that they typically are providing this service on a part-time basis. Consequently, they are likely to conduct fewer searches annually and often have less time to devote to the process. However, they present two common advantages: cost (they typically charge less than full-time consultants) and the ability to attract in-state applicants (professors typically know many potential local applicants). Conversely, they may not be as effective as private consultants in producing a national applicant pool and objectivity is more likely to be a concern (i.e., some may view professors as being biased toward their former students).

3. *Retaining a state association*—In many states, school board and superintendent associations provide consultant services to local boards. During the 1990s, 39 state school board associations offered search consultant services (Meet the Power Brokers, 1994).The primary advantages

of this option typically are local knowledge (the consultants are from the same state and they understand pertinent issues such as state laws, the district's history, prevailing contract features, and available local candidates) and cost (the cost is typically much lower compared to private consultants and professors). This option may have the same disadvantages as those mentioned for professors—namely, a restricted ability to attract a national applicant pool and concerns about objectivity.

4. *Retaining university placement bureau officials*—Universities preparing administrators commonly maintain placement bureaus designed to assist alumni with employment. In some states (e.g., Indiana and Michigan), officials from these bureaus have made their services available to local districts to search for new superintendents. The advantages include cost (typically the consultants, placement bureau employees, are simply reimbursed for their expenses) and access to in-state applicants. The disadvantages are concerns about not being able to attract out-of-state applicants and objectivity. Litigation on this issue in Michigan during the 1980s raised serious conflict-of-interest questions. For example, can placement officials represent both sides in an employment process (i.e., represent applicants who are alumni of their institutions at the same time they are representing the interests of the employing school boards)?

The trend toward using search consultants has been incremental (Boring, 2003); and school boards often have used lower-cost options before moving to higher-cost options. Generalizations about using consultants are precarious because the quality of services provided and the outcomes have been less than consistent. Nevertheless, applicants can surmise that applicant pools in districts conducting national searches and using search consultants will be larger and more competitive than those in other districts.

Selection Criteria

Searches are often influenced by board member perceptions of the departing superintendent. If the board members admire and respect this individual, they are likely to emphasize the departing superintendent's positive characteristics in setting selection criteria. However, if the previous superintendent was dismissed or had a negative relationship with board members, boards are likely to identify selection criteria that emphasize the strengths they believe will compensate for the previous superintendent's weaknesses (Johnson, 1996). In fact, levels of satisfaction with the previous superintendent often influence the entire search process. For example, board members dissatisfied with the departing superintendent may adopt procedures that make it virtually impossible to employ an applicant who was a member of the departing superintendent's administrative team (e.g., by emphasizing that candidates with experience as superintendent in other districts will be given preference).

Unfortunately, only a limited number of studies have examined the reasons why school boards select superintendents. One such study conducted in Missouri found that the self-presentation skills of candidates, their backgrounds as confirmed by references, and their interests in student achievement and district educational effectiveness were the three most influential factors (Anderson & Lavid, 1985). Reviewing research in this area, Miklos (1988) identified the following attributes as potential influences: character, judgment, personality, physical and mental health, intelligence, sense of humor, open-mindedness, voice, and cultural background. School boards, however, do not always emphasize criteria favored by the profession. A study by Ramirez and Guzman (2003) found that boards were more prone to emphasize transactional characteristics than transformational characteristics. Advanced degrees, especially earned doctorates, are another factor that may carry considerable weight in certain districts (Hord & Estes, 1993). The extent to which any of these attributes may affect board decisions is especially unpredictable in those situations in which the board has not specified selection criteria.

Confidentiality and Inclusiveness

Superintendent searches also are defined by conditions of confidentiality and inclusiveness. The former pertains to whether the school board will publicly disclose the names of applicants; the latter pertains to the extent to which district employees and other community members are involved in the search process. Open door or "sunshine" laws in many states (e.g., Florida) practically prevent school boards from withholding applicant identification. Even so, the issue of confidentiality continues to be debated and remains a point of disagreement even among search consultants (Kenney, 2003). Advocates for conducting confidential searches (e.g., Chopra, 1989) argue that applicant disclosure policies dissuade many highly qualified candidates, such as sitting superintendents who do not want their current employer to know that they are exploring other options, from applying. In this age of information, no applicant should assume confidentiality, even if it is promised. Often school boards are unable to prevent the media from identifying applicants, especially if the final stages of the search process have been reached.

Inclusion is promoted philosophically on the grounds that public schools belong to the people and thus they should have a voice in naming the organization's top executive (Boring, 2003). Some authors (e.g., Pesce, 2003), nevertheless, continue to claim that including too many people can be inefficient and divisive. Moreover, critics of inclusive searches point out that because selecting a superintendent is the board's most critical responsibility, it should not be delegated or even shared. School board members, however, face growing demands to be inclusive (Lowery, Harris, & Marshall, 2002). As a result, many have tried to reach a compromise. For example, they have formed search committees—an option that provides broad participation but sidesteps the perceived problems of having large numbers of individuals directly involved. Another compromise has been to conduct open forums prior to shaping the search process, an approach allowing district employees and community members to have input in areas such as selection criteria but not a direct role in evaluating and selecting candidates.

Although confidentiality and exclusivity have become less common, school boards still vary considerably in their attempts to apply these conditions. Drawing conclusions about motives, however, can be precarious: some boards attempt to keep applicant names confidential to attract applicants who might not otherwise apply; other boards do so as a way to maintain complete control over the selection process. Likewise, some boards conduct inclusive searches because they are committed to democratic decision making; other boards do so because they fear the political power of employee unions and community pressure groups.

CAREER PLANNING

Although it is true that some individuals become superintendents purely by accident, many others reach this position because of careful planning, skillful positioning, and hard work. In essence they tailored their educational experiences and professional education toward a single career goal—the superintendency. More importantly, they took the time to reflect systematically on their personal and professional growth, and they interfaced this knowledge with their career goals. Career planning is an individual activity and a continuous process that helps you determine what you want to do with your life and to map a strategy for reaching your goals (Steele & Morgan, 1991).

Failing to Plan

Unfortunately, many aspiring administrators are not very organized when it comes to thinking about their future. They forgo career planning because they conclude that the costs (time, energy) outweigh the potential benefit (the career plan produces a significant advantage). So instead of opting for an organized approach, they come to believe that being in the right place at the right time will allow them to grab the brass ring. Figler (1979) described three categories of behavior associated with this mindset; they are presented here with adaptations to aspiring superintendents:

- *The Divine Calling*—These individuals argue that they were preordained to become superintendents and they recognized this fact early in life. Thus, others will honor their commitment and allow them to fulfill their destiny.
- *Hang Loose*—These individuals claim that you cannot plan what will happen in life; fate will largely determine whether they reach the superintendency.
- *Grocery Store Mentality*—These individuals believe that career decisions are like grocery shopping: You buy a product off the shelf depending on the circumstances at the time you are shopping. If a superintendency is available and if the timing is right, then a decision may be made to move in that direction.

Aspiring superintendents in all three categories share a common characteristic: they are willing to let others dictate a career agenda.

Indifference toward career planning has been particularly noticeable among professional educators as evidenced by the fact that many teachers study school administration but never obtain a license to practice administration, or they never apply for administrative jobs. When questioned about her motives for studying school administration, one teacher commented, "Right now I have no intent of becoming an administrator but I figured that getting my master's degree in this area might open some doors to me later in my career." The attitude reflected in this comment is arguably problematic for the following reason.

> Mismatches of individual abilities, needs, and aspirations on the one hand and job opportunities or requirements on the other, do occur in educational administration. When careers in education typically span periods of more than thirty years, it is tragic to discover how few give attention to or understand the rudiments of career planning. (Orlosky, McCleary, Shapiro, & Webb, 1984, p. 22)

Apathy toward career planning among professional educators is especially disconcerting in light of the fact that highly successful executives in all fields have been found to be individuals who take responsibility for developing and managing their personal plans (Graen, 1989).

Advantages

One advantage of career planning is that it causes you to gain a better understanding of personal strengths and weaknesses. Introspection is a powerful tool for understanding ourselves and our dispositions toward work. One could have a very good grasp of school administration theory without having an objective picture of personal interests and abilities. Self-assessment entails looking objectively at a range of conditions such as personality, academic preparation, professional experience, personal interests, physical and mental health, special skills and abilities, and leadership capabilities. Accurate information in these areas allows the person to correctly answer questions such as the following: "Do I have the skill and stamina to be effective in this position?" "Will I be happy doing this job?" "Am I really ready to assume so much responsibility?"

Career planning encourages an interface of personal life and work life. So, in addition to having an understanding of yourself, you have a more complete understanding of the profession. You are better able to weigh the differences between being a principal and being a superintendent; you are better able to anticipate and cope with obstacles that may interfere with your journey toward the top job. Everyday experiences are analyzed in the context of short-term and long-term goals. Most noteworthy, individual career planning allows you to pursue your intentions systematically and logically—an asset particularly cogent to the superintendency (Craig & Hardy, 1996).

There are many potential benefits associated with career planning; Table 14.1 lists the more commonly cited ones. It is unlikely that you will be able to take charge of your professional future unless you know yourself, know what is required to become a superintendent, know the potential pitfalls, and integrate this information into an ongoing plan.

Individual Plan Elements

Too often aspiring administrators mistakenly believe that there is one best path to the superintendency and when they encounter barriers, they may completely relinquish their goal. In truth, people reach the superintendency in different ways. Gender, ethnicity, age, academic degrees, and geographic location are variables that often determine what constitutes an ideal approach. This is why career plans should be constructed individually.

An individual career plan can take many forms. More effective approaches, however, are characterized by four qualities:

Table 14.1   Positive Attributes of Personal Career Planning

Attribute	Implications
Understanding needs and wants	The individual seeks linkages between personal life and work life.
Understanding opportunities	Planning requires information about the superintendency, state laws, employment processes, and so forth.
Mentoring, sponsorship, and networking	The value of having support mechanisms becomes more apparent.
Examining motives	The individual considers intrinsic and extrinsic motivations and gains a better understanding of why the superintendency is a career goal.
Examining potential barriers	The individual considers possible obstacles to reaching the superintendency.
Framing difficult career decisions	Answering questions such as "Should I get a doctorate?" become easier in the context of a career plan.
Assessing performance periodically	Career plans require periodic assessment; the individual becomes aware of personal and professional growth.
Preventing complacency	The goal of reaching the superintendency reminds the individual of what is to be accomplished.
Understanding individuality	Over time, the individual becomes aware of personal differences with respect to other educators who aspire to be superintendents.
Preparing for uncertainty	Many aspects of career are unexpected; career planning lessens the trauma and facilitates appropriate responses.

- *Continuity*—The process is continuous rather than finite.
- *Flexibility*—The process is adjusted periodically without losing overall value.
- *Veracity*—The process is erected on a foundation of honest and objective information.
- *Influence*—The process actually produces behavioral differences. (Kowalski, 2003a)

Although plans should be individualized, they should have common components woven into them. Figure 14.1 illustrates these common components. The first is a *vision of life*. Here you address issues such as income, prestige, family life, and security. Essentially, you mentally answer the question, "What do I want out of life?" *Assessment of self* entails knowing your strengths and weaknesses—information that can come from several sources, ranging from reflection to assessment data generated via an established process (e.g., from an administrative assessment center). *Career needs statements* identify gaps between what you are deriving from work and what you need to derive to achieve your goals. Career needs are like quality of life needs but they are framed in the context of work and profession. They might include needs related to status, social interactions, and professional challenges. *Long-term goals* are self-explanatory; however, you may have multiple goals that specify what you hope to accomplish at various stages of your career. For instance, obtaining a large-district superintendency may be your ultimate goal and obtaining your first superintendency is an intermediate goal. Goals are of limited value unless they are accompanied by *strategies for goal attainment*. These are contingencies for achieving your objectives and they include short-term goals allowing you to judge whether your progress is satisfactory. Finally, all plans should include an *evaluation* component that is both summative and formative. Summative data lets you know if you are making satisfactory progress; formative data lets you know whether you need to change your strategies or short-term objectives.

Special Challenges for Women and Persons of Color

The process of career planning is especially crucial for those who do not have social or political advantages for reaching the superintendency. White males, for example, have often benefited from being sponsored by the "good ole boys" network (Hord & Estes, 1993) and they still constitute the vast majority of school superintendents (according to Glass et al. [2000], 87% of superintendents in 2000 were males and 95% were White). Although every aspiring superintendent faces career barriers, women and minorities usually encounter unique and more complex obstacles. These impediments are commonly classified as internal and external. In the former category are issues such as socialization, personality, aspiration level, personal beliefs, attitudes, motivation, and self-image. The latter category includes environmental circumstances such as stereotyping, discrimination, and family responsibilities (Leonard & Papalewis, 1987; Shakeshaft, 1981). Many key decision makers in

Figure 14.1   Elements of a Personal Career Plan

superintendent selection are prone to concentrate on individual qualities, while ignoring or not understanding external barriers faced by women and minorities (Chase & Bell, 1994). In this vein, Shakeshaft (1989) observed that qualifications and competence do not eradicate sexism and racism in society. Studies of female superintendents (e.g., Brunner, 1996; Grogan, 1996; Kowalski & Stouder, 1999) reveal that they often differ in their perceptions of career barriers and they use different approaches for dealing with them.

Other factors also point to the unique experiences of minorities and women. For example, studies (e.g., Mertz & McNeely, 1988) have found that women and minorities reach the superintendency via various career paths. In fact, women often have exhibited a greater range of strategies than have males in seeking the superintendency (Pavan, 1988, 1995). Moreover, minority and female candidates have been expected to be better educated and more experienced than other applicants, pointing to the need for them to earn advanced degrees and to gain experience in a wide variety of settings (Jackson & Shakeshaft, 2003; Valverde & Brown, 1988). Studying the experiences of women and persons of color, Tallerico (2000a) concluded that routine practices used by search consultants often combine with school administration's professional norms and dominant ideological and sociocultural values to constitute an advantage for nonminority males.

Collectively, the prevalence of career barriers, various strategies for dealing with them, alternative routes to the superintendency, higher expectations related to qualifications, and common search procedures demonstrate why engaging in career planning during the early stages of professional practice is especially important for women and minorities (Dopp & Sloan, 1986). Career plans can be especially helpful in relation to considering mentoring, sponsorship, and networking. Mentors provide encouragement, help build confidence, and demonstrate friendship, mutual trust, and advice related to career development (Pence, 1989); sponsors help create professional opportunities that help overcome social and political barriers (Kowalski, 2003a); networks are formal or informal connections to individuals who may provide information or direct assistance in career development (Funk, 1986). Even though mentoring and sponsorship have been widely advocated in the literature (e.g., Edson, 1988), and despite the fact that 77% of male superintendents and 83% of female superintendents report having had a mentor (Glass et al., 2000), several studies have found that female administrators (e.g., Angulo, 1995; Sharratt & Derrington, 1993) and minority administrators (Moody, 1983, 1984) seeking to become superintendents often are at a disadvantage because they lack this support (Tallerico, 2000b). Likewise, women often have had difficulty gaining access to influential networks that historically have been male dominated (Funk, 1986).

APPLICATION PROCESS

A veteran superintendent (Negroni, 1992) observed, ". . . landing that first superintendency takes special job-search and interviewing skills, and effectively launching it requires some clear-headed strategies" (p. 21). Unfortunately as noted earlier, many who seek the position have not been adequately prepared to do so. Individuals hampered by limited insights or misconceptions often fail to get the job or, even worse, they end up in a position that offers them little opportunity for success. Learning the "ins and outs" of applying for the position should occur during professional preparation because more than 80% of superintendents report that they started applying just one to three years after receiving the necessary license (Glass et al., 2000).

Before Applying

Applying for a superintendent vacancy is never inconsequential. On a personal level, you have to spend time, energy, and possibly money (e.g., costs for transcripts or other documents) to comply with the employer's requirements. More importantly, your application creates obligations for the employer and for the persons you list as references. Continuously applying for jobs that are out of reach or applying for positions and then exhibiting ambivalence (e.g., withdrawing your application) is ill-advised. Eventually, an applicant can develop a negative reputation among school board members, search consultants, and potential references. This problem is avoided by answering fundamental questions before submitting an application:

- *Am I ready?* Even after completing the academic work required for a license, some administrators are not confident that they have enough experience to be a superintendent. Readiness is an individual matter; some practitioners believe they are ready after only two or three years in a lower-level administrative position, whereas others believe that they have to spend 10 or more years in a variety of school and district positions.
- *Do I have sufficient information about the job?* Applying for a position you know little or nothing about is foolish. All too often school boards use boilerplate announcements rather than providing specific and candid information. Thus, vacancy announcements alone provide only part of the information you need. In addition, you should try to determine if the board has a preference for inside or outside candidates. In the past, most boards have favored outside candidates, but this trend is changing in many districts as board members seek leadership continuity as a way to improve district performance (Mathews, 2002).
- *Are there personal or family considerations that prevent me from accepting the position?* On occasion, individuals apply for positions without having discussed the issue at the family level. Subsequently, they may discover that a spouse or children are adamantly opposed to relocating.
- *Will being an applicant affect my current position?* In some instances, employers may react negatively after discovering that you are seeking a new position. Having a positive relationship with your immediate supervisor and making your career plans known to your supervisor is one way to avoid this trap.
- *Do I have sufficient information about the search and selection processes?* Before submitting an application, you should know the search parameters. For example, you should know precisely what application materials are required, how many references to list, and the timelines for the various stages (e.g., application deadline, interviewing period, and date of anticipated decision).
- *Do my personal strengths match the school district's needs?* More often than not, issues of the day influence selection decisions made by school board members (Johnson, 1996). Knowing that your strengths match the district's needs places you in an advantageous position.

- *Will I accept the position if it is offered?* This may be the most important question. Applying for a superintendency when you are not really interested in the position borders on unethical behavior. You are wasting your time, the employer's time, and the goodwill of mentors and sponsors.

Dispelling doubts prior to making application requires a bit of research, especially if the position is in an unfamiliar school district. For example, you need information about the community served by the district; the district's prevailing strengths, needs, and problems; and the recent history of relationships between the school board and superintendent (Sternberg, 2002). Fortunately, data gathering is easier today than ever before because of the Internet and immediate access to information from state agencies and organizations. Deciding to become an applicant is easier when you can interface employer and personal data. A study of first-year superintendents (Johnson, 1996) identified the following key issues that often guide selection decisions:

- How a candidate makes the members of the search committee feel about themselves
- The sufficiency of a candidate's intelligence, knowledge, and experience
- A candidate's personal appearance and communication skills
- A candidate's human relations skills
- A candidate's other personal attributes (e.g., health, toughness, stamina, courage, and compassion).

In summary, before you decide to apply you should know yourself and know the prevailing conditions in the employing district. Only by connecting these pieces of information are you able to make an informed choice.

Applying

The importance of preparing your application materials properly should be obvious. Unless you are known to the person or persons conducting the initial screening (i.e., the review of written application materials), you will be judged on the basis of how you describe your qualifications. A curriculum vita and letter of application provide first impressions; they are indicators of your organizational abilities and written communication skills (Cummings, 1994). Skilled screeners usually detect boilerplate application letters and overstated resumes. The best policy is to personalize your letter, stress your enthusiasm for the position, and, at all costs, avoid errors.

The curriculum vita should be concise, yet provide the necessary information about your education and professional experiences. Most of all, it should be accurate and neat. When a reviewer finds misstatements in your documents, it can totally destroy credibility and even jeopardize your professional standing. Likewise, the appearance of your curriculum vitae is important; even a coffee stain may be sufficient to create a negative impression. Most screeners differentiate between quantity and quality; therefore, filling your curriculum vitae with insignificant information to make it longer can do more harm than good. Persons seeking a first superintendency should be prepared to demonstrate why and how their personal experiences and educational background are sufficient qualifications (Negroni, 1992).

References also are important. As a rule of thumb, your best choice is to select individuals connected in some fashion to the superintendency. They are apt to have the most credibility when it comes to attesting to your qualifications. The most common references are former professors, practicing superintendents, present supervisors, and school board members. The following guidelines are useful in relation to professional references:

- Never list someone as a reference unless you have the person's permission.
- By not listing your current supervisor as a reference, you are apt to create suspicion. If there are reasons why you do not list your current supervisor, it may be advantageous to communicate those reasons in your application materials.
- Listing only character references, such as ministers, elected officials, or family members is certain to raise suspicions.
- Provide accurate information for contacting your references (telephone numbers, addresses).
- If possible, select references known to the employers or references who are widely known in the profession.
- If you are instructed to submit letters of reference, ask your references to write original letters; generic letters that begin "To Whom It May Concern" may do more harm than good.

After Applying

As part of the screening process, your references may be contacted. If this action is not stipulated in the vacancy notice, assume that it will be done. If the employing school board has ensured applicant confidentiality, you should expect that they will seek your permission before contacting references—but as stated previously, never assume that efforts to maintain confidentiality will be successful.

In situations involving search consultants, preliminary interviews may be conducted with as many as 10 to 15 applicants. These sessions may occur via telephone or face-to-face. Several search firms, for instance, routinely conduct initial interviews at airport hotels, allowing candidates to fly in and out in the same day. Preliminary interviews usually are held because the consultant does not know the candidate. Other purposes may include clarifying or extending application information, evaluating verbal communication skills, assessing personal characteristics (e.g., sense of humor, appearance); assessing commitment to pursuing the position, and discussing the applicant's specific problems or needs.

Interviews with school board members or search committees often occur in two stages. The first round of interviews involves a select number of semifinalists, maybe as many as seven or eight applicants. Later, the applicant pool is narrowed to two or three finalists who are invited to have a second interview. Although this two-stage interview process is the norm, some boards conduct only one interview and others may conduct three or more.

Being selected as a semifinalist means that you have some qualities that are attractive to the employing officials. Interviews serve the purpose of validating and personalizing those qualities. Personal appearance, poise, confidence, personality, and communication skills are sure to be scrutinized. So when preparing for an interview, follow these guidelines:

- *Look and act like a professional.* Although community standards obviously vary, board members uniformly recognize that a superintendent is their official representative. Dress, mannerisms, and social skills are closely observed (Pigford, 1995).
- *Arrive on time.* Being late for an interview can be interpreted in many ways—all detrimental to the candidate (Davis & Brown, 1992). If possible, arrive for your interview 10 or 15 minutes before the scheduled time.
- *Be informed about the school district and the community.* Most school board members are impressed by candidates who have taken the time to learn about them, the school district, and the community prior to the interview. Comments and questions should reflect your interests in studying relevant educational and administrative issues (Cummings, 1994; Dagavarian & Holt, 1995).
- *Exhibit your communication skills.* Interviewer perceptions are influenced by both verbal and nonverbal behaviors. Maintain eye contact when speaking or listening; avoid using jargon that may not be understood. Provide concise answers to questions, and do not attempt to dominate the discussion (Davis & Brown, 1992).

- *Be prepared to ask questions.* Almost always, candidates are given an opportunity to ask questions. Not asking questions or asking perfunctory questions may detract from your overall performance (Steele & Morgan, 1991). The best questions are genuine, reflecting a need or desire to obtain certain information.

- *Show respect for the interviewers.* As an interviewee, you are a guest and proper respect should be given to the school board members or other interviewers. Be courteous and polite at all times (Pigford, 1995).

- *Think before you answer questions.* Talking before you think is a bad idea. Messages you want to convey and the impression you want to leave should be carefully crafted. Your answers should be "long enough to cover the subject, but short enough to hold interest" (Cummings, 1994, p. 35).

- *Follow directions.* Skilled interviewers are likely to observe if you follow instructions (Davis & Brown, 1992). By trying to set your own rules, you may come across as a controlling individual who does not work well with others.

- *Be prepared to discuss strengths.* During an interview, you are likely to be asked to identify your strengths and weaknesses. While discussing special talents and accomplishments is advantageous, some veteran superintendents (e.g., Cattanach, 1996) recommend that you avoid listing shortcomings because doing so can be self-defeating. Rather than refusing to answer the question, you can gracefully sidestep it by suggesting that others can respond more objectively.

- *Seek to determine if the board's philosophy is compatible with your philosophy.* The interview should be a two-way communication experience. It is possibly the only time prior to employment that the candidate can assess the compatibility of values and beliefs.

- *Evaluate the school board's performance.* The interview also is an opportunity to evaluate your interviewers. You probably do not want to work with school board members who consistently disagree and fight with each other, who are close-minded, and who are indifferent to distinctions between policymaking and policy implementation (Freund, 1987).

Regardless of the final outcome of your interviews, you should seek performance feedback so that you can benefit from the experience. This often is easier to do when a search consultant is involved (Underwood, 1994).

If you become a finalist, expect the school board to scrutinize your current job performance. In many instances, board members will visit your place of work and talk with individuals with whom you come in contact. As soon as you learn that you have been selected as a finalist, you should identify the conditions under which you will accept or reject the position if it is offered to you.

NEGOTIATING AN EMPLOYMENT CONTRACT

Standardized contracts are the norm for teachers and most administrators, but not for superintendents. Individually designed and negotiated agreements between a school board and superintendent take many different forms and reflect substantial variance with regard to scope. Even in states where superintendents are required to sign a teacher's contract, the documents are typically extended by an addendum setting special employment conditions. Initial contracts for superintendents are almost always multiyear agreements; in many states, they are required by law to span several years. Customarily, a superintendent's contract will include provisions for performance evaluation, renewal, and dismissal.

Process

Negotiating an employment contract with a school board can be intimidating, especially if the process is conducted by the school attorney. This is not a time for you to be timid (Freeman, 1985) because the initial agreement affects all future contracts (O'Hara, 1994). It not only sets a base salary and fringe benefits that frame future compensation packages, it determines the conditions under which your employment will or will not be renewed. Recognizing the magnitude of initial employment agreements, some superintendents actually have retained agents (e.g., an attorney or consultant) to negotiate on their behalf. The perceived advantages include the expertise of the agent and removal of the superintendent from a situation in which stating demands face-to-face heightens the possibility of creating adversarial relationships between you and the board members. Possible disadvantages of retaining an agent include cost and negative board-community reactions. A modified approach involves having an agent as a behind-the-scene advisor; that is, your agent drafts a proposed contract and counteroffers but you actually negotiate the employment contract. There is no standard rule to follow about having an agent; each situation is unique and requires analysis. Keeping in mind that setting the initial employment contract is usually a first stage in shaping superintendent-board member relationships (O'Hara, 1994), considerable attention should be given to the school board's attitude toward having to deal with an agent. In making a decision relative to retaining an agent, never lose sight of the fact that expert legal counsel is as important for you as it is for the school board (Heller, 1991).

If you decide to negotiate your employment contract directly, avoid three relatively common mistakes. First, do not accept what is offered impetuously. Study the provisions to ensure that they are sufficiently comprehensive, fair, reasonable, and flexible. Second, do not ignore warning signs predicated on the hope that you will receive a more favorable contract in the future, either because the board will become more familiar with you or because membership on the board will change. Third, do not negotiate without doing your homework. When you are unaware of what provisions may be and are included in other superintendent contracts, you enter negotiations at a distinct disadvantage (O'Hara, 1994). Contacting the state superintendent association is one method for obtaining this information.

Content

As noted earlier, some states specify the nature of the superintendent's employment contract either entirely or partially. A good starting point to studying what should be in the contract is to obtain information about superintendent employment contracts from neighboring school districts and from state-level sources (Clark, 1983). A national study of superintendents revealed that relatively few changes occurred in their employment contracts during the 1990s; however, two provisions, mandatory evaluation and contract revision clauses, were becoming more common (Reeves, 2001). Table 14.2 lists possible clauses that can be negotiated. Obviously, provisions must be in compliance with state laws; consequently, differences among states require that the legality of each provision be established. Often this is done by the school attorney. State statutes usually address contract length, tenure, dismissal provisions, licensing requirements, and general responsibilities. Several states also have statutory ceilings on compensation and list of permissible fringe benefits.

The scope of *fringe benefits* provided to superintendents varies substantially. At one end of the spectrum, districts only provide the same benefits received by all other professional employees. At the other end of the spectrum, the benefits are totally different, broader, and more lucrative than those provided to other employees. Figure 14.2 shows some of the more prevalent fringe benefits found in superintendent employment contracts. Fringe benefits should be considered in relation to salary and state retirement programs. Collectively, these three factors comprise the total compensation package. Most new superintendents overlook the importance of state pension programs because they focus largely on salary and fringe benefits. Some states with relatively high mean salaries have relatively poor retirement systems and vice versa (Kowalski & Sweetland, 2002, in press).

School boards are expected to engage in *performance evaluation* to determine a superintendent's competence and job performance (Genck &

Table 14.2   Possible Provisions in a Superintendent's Contract

Provision or Clause	Purpose
Term	Identifies the beginning and ending dates of the contract.
Licensure	Identifies the required license that must be held by the superintendent for the contract to be valid.
Renewal	Specifies the terms under which the contract may be or must be renewed. Some multiyear contracts contain provisions for automatic renewal each year. For example, a contract is automatically renewed unless the board takes specific action to do otherwise by a specified date. This type of provision is often called a "rollover clause" or "evergreen clause."
Salary	Establishes actual amount of compensation and method of payment; does not include fringe benefits.
Responsibilities	Details the specific responsibilities of the superintendency in that school district.
Employment termination	Specifies the conditions under which employment may be terminated. In some instances, school boards insist that contract language specify how either party may terminate employment.
Termination compensation	Specifies whether a superintendent is entitled to special compensation if terminated. Such provisions often provide severance pay, and more lucrative arrangements are often called "golden parachutes."
Professional growth	Identifies expectations and support for professional growth, e.g., attending workshops, national conferences.
Outside activities	Specifies conditions under which a superintendent may assume responsibilities not directly related to employment with the school district, e.g., working as a consultant, teaching a university class, serving on a board of directors.
Fringe benefits	Identifies benefits in addition to base salary. Both vacation days and provisions for reimbursing the superintendent for job-related expenses are typically included in this clause.
Personal protection	Relates to issues of protection in areas of professional and civil liability. Comprehensive liability coverage does not include errors-and-omissions; therefore, such protection is advisable in the employment contract (Clark, 1983).
Retirement	Specifies conditions pertaining to the superintendent retiring, e.g., amount of notice that must be given. Many superintendents have retirement provisions that exceed those granted to other district employees. This matter may be addressed in a retirement clause or under fringe benefits.
Performance evaluation	Identifies the process for formally evaluating the superintendent and time lines for completing this responsibility.
Savings	Protects the contract from being invalidated if one clause or provision is found to be in violation of federal or state law.

Indirect compensation

- Annuities, tax shelters
- Expense allowances
- Automobile (restricted or unrestricted use)
- Payment of professional membership dues
- Relocation costs (moving expenses for a new superintendent)
- Retirement pick-up (having the employer pay the superintendent's portion)

Insurance

- Disability
- Health
- Liability
- Life

Leaves

- Professional (e.g., sabbatical, consulting days)
- Number of paid vacation days

Figure 14.2   Areas Where Superintendent Fringe Benefits Might Exceed Those Provided to Other Employees

Klingenberg, 1991; Stufflebeam & Millman, 1995). Studies examining this issue (e.g., Edington & Enger, 1992; Kowalski & Koryl, 1997), however, usually reveal that a considerable percentage of school boards either neglected this duty entirely or addressed it only informally. Formal performance evaluation requires a plan (Candoli, Cullen, & Stufflebeam, 1994); thus you should inquire if the school board has such a plan, if they have used it in the past, and if they intend to use it in the future. Ideally, the plan should contain both summative and formative provisions. The most opportune time to discuss performance evaluation is when you are forging an employment contract (Redfern, 1980). You should pay special attention to the following issues: frequency of evaluations; proposed instrumentation; nexus between your job description and performance evaluation; the purpose and philosophy of conducting performance evaluations; evaluator(s) identity; procedural policy; and nexus between evaluation outcomes and contract renewal (Kowalski, 1998). Beyond the primary goals of determining whether a superintendent should be retained and of providing assistance for the superintendent to grow professionally, a well-structured plan fortifies the division of roles and responsibilities between superintendents and board members (McCurdy, 1992).

FOR FURTHER REFLECTION

This chapter addressed four topics cogent to entering practice as a school district superintendent. They are the superintendent selection process, career planning, applying for the position, and forging the employment contract. As you think about the content of this chapter, answer the following questions:

1. How are superintendent searches conducted in your state? Is there a prevalent pattern in your region of the state?

2. What are the possible advantages and disadvantages of retaining a consultant for a superintendent search?

3. What options do school boards have in relation to retaining search consultants? What are the advantages and disadvantages of each option?

4. What is individual career planning? Why is it deemed beneficial to educators who seek to become superintendents?

5. Why is career planning especially essential for women and people of color?

6. Why are mentoring, sponsorship, and networking relevant to pursuing the superintendency?

7. What questions should you ask and answer before deciding to apply for a superintendent vacancy?

8. Is it a good idea to apply for a superintendent position even though you are ambivalent about the position? Why or why not?

9. What factors should you consider in selecting references to support your application?

10. What is the difference between a professional reference and a character reference?

11. Is it a good idea to put every one of your experiences in a curriculum vitae? Why or why not?

Case Study

Although it was Saturday evening, Lucy Harrison was sitting in her office sifting through three days of telephone messages and mail. She had been out of town to attend a second interview for a superintendent position in another state. Despite her efforts to concentrate on the material before her, her thoughts kept reverting to the major decision she had to make within five days.

Lucy grew up in Georgia, the second of 11 children in her family. Her outstanding accomplishments as a high school student were rewarded with an academic scholarship to a private college in a neighboring state. There she earned a bachelor's degree in elementary education, graduating with honors. Her parents, neither of whom had graduated from high school, were understandably proud. After college, Lucy became a second grade teacher in one of the large school districts in the Atlanta metropolitan area.

Lucy loved teaching and her enthusiasm was obvious to her principal, fellow teachers, and parents. Her students came from a variety of social, economic, and ethnic backgrounds, but she felt very comfortable working with all of them. While teaching second grade, Lucy married Marcus Harrison, a young lawyer she had known in college. During the next four years; she gave birth to their first child and managed to complete her master's degree attending evening and summer classes.

The idea of becoming a principal had never occurred to her until her principal, Mr. Barnes, suggested the idea. He was impressed with the leadership she had exhibited as a teacher, especially on curriculum projects involving other teachers. He convinced her to take several postmaster degree courses necessary for her principal's license.

Lucy's opportunity to be a principal arrived unexpectedly. Mr. Barnes was forced to retire in the middle of the school year because of health problems and he lobbied to have Lucy become his replacement. At first, the assistant superintendent for elementary education was apprehensive about taking his advice; there were at least a dozen assistant principals who could be transferred into the job. But after receiving a letter of support for her that was signed by every school employee, he decided to follow Mr. Barnes' recommendation.

At age 32 she found herself as an interim principal of a relatively large elementary school. She had been told that her performance would determine whether she would be appointed to the position permanently and the following May, that is exactly what occurred. During the next eight years, her husband became a full partner in his law firm, she gave birth to a second child, and she completed an Ed.D. program. Professionally, being principal proved to be more rewarding than she first thought. Her energetic and collaborative leadership style earned her a reputation as one of the district's most effective principals.

Lucy's next career advancement also was unplanned. The assistant superintendent for elementary education announced his retirement and a group of her fellow elementary school principals nominated her for the position. Somewhat reluctantly, she agreed to become a candidate and eventually was appointed to the position.

Now five years later, she had to face another career decision. Her superintendent had recommended her to a national search consultant, indicating that she was an excellent prospect for superintendency. When the consultant contacted her, Lucy was very flattered and agreed to send her curriculum vitae to the consultant. Several weeks later, he asked her if she would become an applicant for a superintendent vacancy in southeastern Ohio. Lucy discussed the issue with her husband and they decided that although relocating was probably not feasible, she might be able to learn some valuable lessons from this opportunity.

Lucy was selected as one of seven semifinalists for the position. When she attended the initial interview, she immediately was impressed with the community and the school board. The district enrolled approximately 5,000 students and nearly 75% of last year's high school graduates entered four-year colleges. Her interview with the board was enlightening but she returned to the Atlanta area believing that she would not become a finalist. She was wrong.

Approximately two weeks after her initial interview, the search consultant called and informed her she was a finalist. Moreover, he hinted that she was the leading finalist. The board wanted Lucy to attend a second interview the following week. Without thinking, she immediately said that she would. That evening when she shared the information with her husband, he urged her to withdraw from the search process. He pointed out that the first interview was arguably a learning experience for her but that there was nothing to be gained from a second interview since accepting the position if it were offered was improbable. Lucy thought about her husband's advice and decided not to follow it. Instead, she agreed to attend the second interview. Her strategy was to ask for a compensation package that the board would reject. That way, she could gracefully end her candidacy. The ploy, however, backfired. Rather than being put off by her requests, the board was impressed with her aggressive posture on compensation. They offered her the position.

Now as she sat in her office, Lucy faced what she considered to be a "no win" decision. If she accepted the position, the effects on her marriage could be negative. Her husband already made it clear that he had no intention of leaving his law firm. If she declined the offer, especially after all her demands were met, she could jeopardize her standing with this and other search consultants.

Case Discussion Questions

1. To what extent has Lucy's career shaped the predicament she is now experiencing?

2. If you were Lucy, what would you have done when you were first contacted by the search consultant?

3. Did Lucy's husband give her good advice about the first interview? Why or why not?

4. Lucy attended the second interview with a strategy of making demands that the board members would undoubtedly reject. What are the advantages and disadvantages of this strategy?

5. Based on the information provided in the case, do you believe that Lucy followed the advice presented in the chapter about becoming a superintendent applicant? Why or why not?

6. What options does Lucy now have? What are the advantages and disadvantages of these options?

7. What factors might cause an administrator to pursue a position without an intention to accept it if it were offered?

8. How might Lucy's decisions been different if she had developed a personal career plan?

REFERENCES

Anderson, R. E., & Lavid, J. S. (1985). Factors school boards use when selecting a superintendent. *Spectrum, 3*(3), 21–24.

Angulo, M. E. (1995). *Women superintendents of Illinois.* East Lansing, MI: National Center for Research on Teacher Learning. (ERIC Document Reproduction Service No. ED381855)

Boring, M. R. (2003). *Superintendent search.* Olympia, WA: Washington State School Directors' Association.

Brunner, C. C. (1996, March). *Developing women leaders: The art of "stalking" the superintendency.* Paper presented at the Annual Meeting of the American Association of School Administrators, San Diego, California.

Candoli, C., Cullen, K., & Stufflebeam, D. (1994). *Superintendent performance evaluation: Current practice and directions for improvement.* East Lansing, MI: National Center for Research on Teacher Learning. (ERIC Document Reproduction Service No. ED376584)

Cattanach, D. L. (1996). *The school leader in action: Discovering the golden mean.* Lancaster, PA: Technomic.

Chase, S. E., & Bell, C. S. (1994). How search consultants talk about female superintendents. *School Administrator, 51*(2), 36–38, 40, 42.

Chopra, R. K. (1989). In superintendent searches, discretion is the better part of valor. *American School Board Journal, 176*(1), 37.

Clark, J. F. (1983). Drafting the superintendent's contract. *American School Board Journal, 170*(5), 29–31.

Craig, R. M., & Hardy, J. T. (1996). Should I be a superintendent? A feminine perspective. *American Secondary Education, 25*(10), 17–22.

Cummings, J. R. (1994). Becoming the successful candidate. *School Administrator, 51*(2), 28–30, 35.

Dagavarian, D. A., & Holt, L. (1995). How to interview with a search committee. *Executive Educator,17*(10), 39–40.

Davis, B. I., & Brown, G. (1992). Your interview image. *Executive Educator, 14*(6), 22–23.

Dopp, B. K., & Sloan, C. A. (1986). Career development and succession of women to the superintendency. *Clearing House, 60*(3), 120–126.

Edington, J. M., & Enger, J. M. (1992, November). *An analysis of the evaluation processes used by Arkansas school boards to evaluate superintendents.* Paper presented at the Annual Meeting of the Mid-South Educational Research Association, Knoxville, Tennessee.

Edson, S. K. (1988). *Pushing the limits: The female administrative aspirant.* Albany: State University of New York Press.

Figler, H. E. (1979). *PATH: A career workbook for liberal arts students.* Cranston, RI: Carroll.

Freeman, R. R. (1985). Don't be timid: Negotiate a decent superintendent contract. *Executive Educator, 7*(11), 14–15.

Freund, S. A. (1987). Looking at superintendent candidates? They're checking you out, too. *American School Board Journal, 173*(1), 37.

Funk, C. (1986, May). *The female executive in school administration: Profiles, pluses, and problems.* Paper presented at the Annual Conference on Women and Work, Arlington, Texas.

Genck, F. H., & Klingenberg, A. J. (1991). *Effective schools through effective management* (Rev. ed.). Springfield: Illinois Association of School Boards.

Glass, T., Björk, L., & Brunner, C. (2000). *The 2000 study of the American school superintendency.* Arlington, VA: American Association of School Administrators.

Graen, G. B. (1989). *Unwritten rules for your career.* New York: John Wiley & Sons.

Grogan, M. (1996). *Voices of women aspiring to the superintendency.* Albany: State University of New York Press.

Heller, R. W. (1991). Negotiating for retirement. *American School Board Journal, 178*(8), 18–22.

Hess, F. (1989). Job seekers say you have a lot to learn about superintendent searches. *American School Board Journal, 176*(5), 39.

Hord, S. M., & Estes, N. (1993). Superintendent selection and success. In D. Carter, T. Glass, & S. Hord (Eds.), *Selecting, preparing, and developing the school district superintendent* (pp. 71–84). Washington, DC: Falmer.

Jackson, J., & Shakeshaft, C. (2003, April). *The pool of African American candidates for the superintendency.* Paper presented at the Annual Meeting of the American Educational Research Association, Chicago, Illinois.

Jernigan, S. (1997). Dangerous expectations: Why a superintendent search often breeds discontent and unsatisfying results. *School Administrator, 54*(2), 8–11.

Johnson, S. M. (1996). *Leading to change: The challenge of the new superintendency.* San Francisco: Jossey-Bass.

Johnson, S., & Howley, A. (2001). Superintendent selection: Variation based on district size and rurality. *Rural Educator, 23*(2), 21–26.

Kenney, L. C. (2003). Confidential searches. *School Administrator, 60*(6), 6–12.

Kowalski, T. J. (1998). Critiquing the CEO. *American School Board Journal, 185*(2), 43–44.

Kowalski, T. J. (2003a). *Contemporary school administration: An introduction* (2nd ed.). Boston: Allyn & Bacon.

Kowalski, T. J. (2003b). Superintendent shortage: The wrong problem and wrong solutions. *Journal of School Leadership, 13,* 288–303.

Kowalski, T. J., & Koryl, M. (1997). The status of performance evaluations for Indiana school superintendents. *Indiana School Boards Journal, 43*(2), 30–33.

Kowalski, T. J., & Stouder, J. G. (1999). Female experiences related to becoming a superintendent. *Contemporary Education, 70*(4), 32–40.

Kowalski, T. J., & Sweetland, S. (2002). Unrestricted reemployment of retired administrators: Effective policy or cause for concern? In G. Perreault (Ed.), *The changing world of school administration: The 10th annual yearbook of the National Council of Professors of Educational Administration* (pp. 312–324). Lanham, MD: Scarecrow.

Kowalski, T. J., & Sweetland, S. R. (in press). Retire-rehire policy in state pension programs for school administrators. *Planning and Changing.*

Leonard, P. Y., & Papalewis, R. (1987). The under-representation of women and minorities in educational administration: Patterns, issues, and recommendations. *Journal of Educational Equity and Leadership, 7*(3), 188–207.

Lowery, S., Harris, S., & Marshall, R. (2002). Hiring a superintendent: Public relations challenge. *Journal of School Public Relations, 23*(1), 70–79.

Mathews, J. (2002). Succession: Insiders vs. outsiders. *School Administrator, 59*(5), 16–26.

McCurdy, J. (1992). *Building better board and administrator relations.* Arlington, VA: American Association of School Administrators.

Meet the power brokers (1994). *School Administrator, 51*(2), 20–23.

Mertz, N. T., & McNeely, S. R. (1988). *Career path of school superintendents.* East Lansing, MI: National Center for Research on Teacher Learning. (ERIC Document Reproduction Service No. ED305716)

Miklos, E. (1988). Administrator selection, career patterns, succession, and socialization. In N. Boyan (Ed.), *Handbook of research on educational administration* (pp. 53–76). New York: Longman.

Moody, C. D. (1983). On becoming a superintendent: Contest or sponsored mobility? *The Journal of Negro Education, 52,* 383–397.

Moody, C. D. (1984). Sponsored mobility and black superintendent candidates. *Education Digest, 49*(3), 40–43.

Negroni, P. J. (1992). Landing the big one. *Executive Educator, 14*(12), 21–23.

O'Hara, D. G. (1994). The superintendent's first contract. *School Administrator, 51*(7), 19–21.

Orlosky, D. E., McCleary, L. E., Shapiro, A., & Webb, L. D. (1984). *Educational administration today.* Columbus, OH: Charles E. Merrrill.

Pavan, B. N. (1988). *Job search strategies utilized by certified aspiring and incumbent female and male public school administrators.* East Lansing, MI: National Center for Research on Teacher Learning. (ERIC Document Reproduction Service No. ED302879)

Pavan, B. N. (1995). *First year district superintendents: Women reflect on contradictions between education and politics.* East Lansing, MI: National Center for Research on Teacher Learning. (ERIC Document Reproduction Service No. ED389077)

Pence, L. J. (1989). *Formal and informal mentorships for aspiring and practicing administrators.* Unpublished Ph.D. dissertation, University of Oregon, Eugene.

Pesce, M. A. (2003). Too many cooks. *American School Board Journal, 190*(3), 28–29.

Pigford, A. B. (1995). The interview: What candidates for administrative positions should know and do. *NASSP Bulletin, 79*(569), 54–58.

Ramirez, A., & Guzman, N. (2003). The superintendent search: An analysis of ISLCC Standards compared to school board developed selection criteria. *Education Leadership Review, 4*(2), 34–37.

Redfern, G. B. (1980). *Evaluating the superintendent.* Arlington, VA: American Association of School Administrators.

Reeves, K. (2001). Tying the contract knot. *School Administrator, 58*(2), 22–30.

Shakeshaft, C. (1981). Women in educational administration: A descriptive analysis of dissertation research and paradigm for future research. In P. Schmuck, W. Charters, & R. Carlson (Eds.), *Educational policy and management of sex differentials* (pp. 403–416). Berkeley, CA: McCutchan.

Shakeshaft, C. (1989). *Women in educational administration* (updated ed.). Newbury Park, CA: Sage.

Sharratt, G., & Derrington, M. L. (1993). *Female superintendents: Attributes that attract and barriers that discourage their successful applications.* East Lansing, MI: National Center for Research on Teacher Learning. (ERIC Document Reproduction Service No. ED362941)

Steele, J. E., & Morgan, M. S. (1991). *Career planning and development.* Lincolnwood, IL: VGM Career Horizons.

Sternberg, R. E. (2002). The new job: Tailored fit or misfit? *School Administrator, 59*(5), 6–14.

Stufflebeam, D. L., & Millman, J. A. (1995). Proposed model for superintendent evaluation. *Journal of Personnel Evaluation in Education, 9*(4), 383–410.

Tallerico, M. (2000a). Gaining access to the superintendency: Headhunting, gender, and color. *Educational Administration Quarterly, 36*(1), 18–43.

Tallerico, M. (2000b). Why don't they apply? Encouraging women and minorities to seek administrative positions. *American School Board Journal, 187*(11), 56–58.

Underwood, K. (1994). The search consultant's obligations. *School Administrator, 51*(2), 24–25, 27.

Valverde, L. A., & Brown, F. (1988). Influences on leadership development among racial and ethnic minorities. In N. Boyan (Ed.), *Handbook of research on educational administration* (pp. 143–157). New York: Longman.

Zakariya, S. B. (1987). What you get (and what you pay) when you hire a superintendent search service. *American School Board Journal, 174*(11), 35, 37–38.

Author Index

Subject Index

About the Author

Theodore J. Kowalski, Ph.D., is a former public school teacher, principal, associate superintendent, and superintendent. He has taught at Purdue University and served as professor and director of doctoral programs in educational administration at Saint Louis University. From 1981 to 2000, he was employed at Ball State University, where he was dean of the Teachers College. In 2000, he became the Kuntz Family Chair in Educational Administration, an endowed professorship at the University of Dayton.

Professor Kowalski is the author of more than 160 professional publications, including 17 books. He is the editor of the *Journal of School Public Relations,* serves on the editorial boards of two other professional journals, and was editor of the *2001 Yearbook of the National Council of Professors of Educational Administration.* He has extensive experience as a planning consultant, speaker, and workshop facilitator. In addition to the superintendency, his primary research interests include organizational behavior, school public relations, and decision theory.